Teaching English in Middle and Secondary Schools

Rhoda J. Maxwell
Mary Jordan Meiser

University of Wisconsin–Eau Claire

Macmillan Publishing Company
New York

Editor: Robert B. Miller
Production Supervisor: Betsy Keefer
Production Manager: Linda Greenberg
Cover Designer: Proof Positive/Farrowlyne Associates, Inc.
Cover Art: Hans Hofmann, SANCTUM SANCTORUM, 1962, University
Art Museum, University of California at Berkeley, gift of the artist.
Illustrations: Precision Graphics

This book was set in Aster by Carlisle Communications, Ltd. and printed and bound by R.R.
Donnelly & Sons Company. The cover was printed by New England Book Components, Inc.

Copyright © 1993 by Macmillan Publishing Company,
a division of Macmillan, Inc.

Printed in the United States of America

Macmillan Publishing Company
866 Third Avenue, New York, New York 10022

Macmillan Publishing Company is part of the Maxwell Communication Group of Companies.

Library of Congress Cataloging-in-Publication Data
Maxwell, Rhoda J.
    Teaching English in middle and secondary schools / Rhoda J.
Maxwell, Mary Jordan Meiser.
        p.   cm.
    Includes bibliographical references and index.
    ISBN 0-02-377960-8
    1. English language—Study and teaching (Secondary)—United
States.   2. Language arts (Secondary)—United States.   I. Meiser,
Mary Jordan.   II. Title.
LB1631.M393   1993
428'.0071'273—dc20   92-27515
                                              CIP

Acknowledgments
Exhibits 2.1–2.5 (pp. 39–43) were excerpted with permission from the Wisconsin Department of
    Public Instruction, 125 South Webster Street, Madison, WI 53702.
Exhibit 2.2 (p. 40) was adapted from R. R. Allen and R. McKerron, *The Properties of Publication
    Communication.* Copyright 1981 by Kendall/Hunt Publishing Company. Used with permission.
Excerpts in chapter 7 by Rei Noguchi, *Grammar and Teaching Writing,* Urbana: National Council of
    Teachers of English, 1991, are used by permission.
Pg. 220: "Goldfish" by Andrew Carrigan. From *Poetry: Voices, Language Forms* by Stephen Dunning
    et al. Copyright © 1970 by Scholastic Magazines, Inc. Reprinted by permission of Scholastic Inc.
Excerpts in chapter 11 by Timothy Shanahan and Lester Knight, "Guidelines for Judging and
    Selecting Language Arts Textbooks: A Modest Proposal," *NCTE Concepts Paper No. 1,* Urbana:
    National Council of Teachers of English, 1991, are used by permission.

Printing: 2   3   4   5   6   7   Year: 3   4   5   6   7   8   9

We dedicate this book to our children

Bill and Becky—R.J.M.
Mark and Susan—M.J.M.

Preface

Teaching is a difficult task; no one instructor or text can offer all of the answers to the complex questions facing teachers as they take over the responsibility of their classrooms. Teaching can seem like a balancing act as teachers try to incorporate all the facets of teaching English. At the same time they must plan for students who seem to have little in common with each other or with the teacher's own experiences. This book is not a panacea; rather we offer a comprehensive view of teaching that takes into account the great variety of backgrounds, abilities, and interests of secondary students, so that both novice teachers and their students have viable opportunities for success.

In developing this book we used a holistic, integrated approach to teaching English, including group activities throughout to provide listening and speaking opportunities in literature, composition, and language. We do not stress one curricular component of English over another, but do emphasize the relatedness of all the parts: literature and reading, composing and writing, speaking and sharing, listening and responding, acting and creating, and language and meaning. We separate strands of English teaching, but only as a way of exploring each area in some depth. Recognizing the importance of an integrated approach, we make connections among the strands in all of the chapters. For example, although oral language is a separate chapter, it also appears in chapters on literature, composition, and improving writing skills. Also, because our society continues to debate issues of basic skills, we devote a chapter to grammar as well as relating it to material in other chapters. We believe that teachers who understand the nature of language learning and the acquisition of skills can successfully integrate grammar throughout English curriculum. This type of integration appears in all the chapters.

Research studies form the basis of teaching. We stress the practical application of theoretical ideas, basing our teaching suggestions on research and effective classroom practice. The balance between theory and practice asks that teachers understand *why* they select the activities and materials they do. We also ask readers to examine their assumptions and beliefs about teaching in light of the diverse learners in secondary classrooms, realizing that their own experiences may be different from those of their students. Such connections between teaching and learning guided the writing of this book; teaching means helping students learn, not teaching a body of knowledge per se without first considering the experiences and personalities of the students.

Because of the pluralistic nature of our society, we devote sections in both the language and literature chapters to help prepare new teachers for the realities of their future classrooms. Chapter 9, "The Nature of Language," and Chapter 10, "Varieties of American English," cover language acquisition theory and practical ways of implementing theory into practice. In Chapter 3, "Teaching Literature," and Chapter 4, "Selecting Literature," we include literature by and about minorities and women. Multicultural literature selections provide resources for experienced teachers as well as for those beginning their careers.

The organization of this book is somewhat flexible. The order in which the chapters are taught can vary depending on the structure of the methods course. Instructors may wish to use Chapter 11, "Understanding Curriculum and Instruction," early in the course to examine the place of English teaching in the larger context of a total curriculum. Chapter 9, "The Nature of Language," and Chapter 10, "Varieties of American English," may come before the chapters on literature and composition. The book is designed to adapt to an individual instructor's syllabus.

We could not have written this book without the help of our students: those in secondary schools who unwittingly were a major part of our learning process; our undergraduate students who help us to understand the fears and uncertainties of becoming a teacher; our graduate students who as experienced teachers keep us aware of the realities of the classroom. All of these students are our teachers and we are grateful for the opportunities to learn from them.

In particular, we thank our friends who read our drafts with care and patience, offering suggestions, guidance, and encouragement: Laura Apfelbeck, John Fortier, Donna Hitchens, Craig Hitchens, Nik Lightfoot, and Becky Olien.

We would like to thank the following reviewers: John Bushman, University of Kansas; John Conner, University of Iowa; Margaret Early, University of Florida; James Marshall, University of Iowa; Arlene Mitchell, University of Cincinnati; Ruie Pritchard, North Carolina State University; Linda Shadiow, Northern Arizona University; and Wayne Slater, University of Maryland.

R.J.M
M.J.M

Contents

▼ 3
Teaching Literature   48

▼ 4
Selecting Literature   74

▼ 5
Teaching Composition   105

▼   6
Evaluating Composition   139

▼   7
Improving Writing Skills: Usage, Syntax, Mechanics   156

▼ 8
Understanding Grammar   184

▼   13
Developing Thematic Units   298

C H A P T E R 1

Teaching and Learning English Language Arts

CHAPTER HIGHLIGHTS

* A brief history of English education.
* A professional knowledge base.
* Characteristics of learners and teachers.

> Perhaps most important, interdisciplinary, inquiry-centered learning often includes something which has been ignored in a great many recent reform reports: the **joy** of learning. By "joy" I do not mean the "fun of easy gratification and quick laughs," but the genuine joy of mastery, the pleasure of gaining control. The same intellectual joy can be found in the mastery of language and learning. . . . (30)
>
> —*Stephen Tchudi*

▼
THE JOY OF LEARNING

Stephen Tchudi's observation that most recent educational reform reports ignore "the joy of learning" reflects a national loss. In the 1990s, American society itself appears less resilient, less optimistic, and less intellectually curious. It is no surprise, then, that American students fail to grasp what Tchudi, a prominent English educator, believes is the heart of teaching and learning—the intellectual joy of discovery and mastery. Given the complexity of educating young people and the multiple roles and expectations placed on schools and teachers, it is perhaps understandable that the joy in learning is infrequent in many schools. Sara Lawrence Lightfoot, professor of education at Harvard University, believes that "when you're worried about discipline, or preoccupied with completing a prescribed curriculum in a particular amount of time, you lose the sense of joy and possibility—the sense of play" (157). Like Tchudi, Lightfoot is concerned about the nature of learning and of teaching. In her book *The Good High School*, she describes the end of a class where a teacher shouts, "The struggle—I love it! I love it!" (cited in Moyers 157). In this classroom, the joy of discovery and mastery is present and teacher and students engage in a process that not only involves struggle, but also joy.

▼
CREATING A LEARNING ENVIRONMENT

Teaching and learning are indeed hard work. For the teacher, the creation of the learning environment—the struggle to structure inquiry in ways that capture young learners—is a primary concern. For the student, maintaining commitment to the discipline of learning is the struggle. No matter how well we teach, learning does belong to the student. As English language arts teachers, we can structure, facilitate, and nurture learning, but we can neither impose nor control it. Janet Emig, English educator and past president of the National Council of Teachers of English, describes learning as leading a "marvelously independent life of its own," a useful perspective for teachers. "Marvelously independent" captures the essence of learning, for it suggests that students follow diverse, individual paths of learning, measuring time and demonstrating growth uniquely, ultimately coming to know in their own way. Nonetheless, the English language arts classroom can and should be a powerful catalyst to learning, a place where the intellectual joy of learning and mastery is evident to even the most reluctant learner.

How we view and subsequently structure our classroom and our teaching of English language arts affects the learning and outlook of every student entrusted to us. A teacher who believes that English is a subject to be taught, mastered, and tested structures learning differently from one who believes that English is a process through which students seek to understand themselves, others, and their world. These latter teachers believe, as Lightfoot does, that learning must be playful, that ideas turned upside down and sideways move students toward important conclusions.

Where do such diverse views of teaching come from? In some cases they come from tradition and teaching as one has been taught; in others, from courses and programs that have integrated new learning in the English language arts and related fields of study. A contemporary view of teaching English draws on a rich tradition but at the same time reflects current research and effective classroom practice. In the past decade, we have benefited from extensive research conducted in elementary, secondary, and college classrooms; we have learned the value of ethnographic as well as experimental designs, and we have gained a multidimensional picture of how students learn. Sometimes this research showed us that our methods and materials were a poor match with how students learn or how the language arts function as processes. At other times, research validated time-honored approaches and materials. In all cases, we were learning more about the processes of teaching and learning in the English language arts, adding substantially to our knowledge. For a perspective on just how this process has worked for more than 100 years, we need to explore very briefly the historical context of our profession.

▼
HISTORY OF ENGLISH EDUCATION

An historical background of English education provides a context for our present-day teaching of English language arts. Theoretical concepts first found voice in the 1800s, and despite may changes the perceptions of early educators still shape the teaching of English language arts. The period between 1890 and 1920 is particularly interesting as the time when the teaching of English came into its own. Prior to 1890, much discussion concerned the qualifications of English as a school subject. Educators questioned whether the content of English was rigorous and academic enough to be worthy of study. However, the Committee of Ten, formed by the National Education Association in 1892, unified the teaching of English. In a landmark recommendation, the Committee suggested that English be studied five hours a week for four years of high school. Students were expected to understand the expressed thoughts of others, be able to express their own, and cultivate a taste for reading.

English acquired prestige as a school subject because of college entrance exams. Harvard, quickly followed by other eastern colleges, published a list of required reading for prospective students. These lists and entrance exams dictated the content of English taught in high school for all students, whether they were college bound or not (Maxwell 2). Secondary teachers had little influence on their schools' curricula. Students' characteristics, such as developmental levels, interests, prior knowledge, and needs, were not taken into consideration. The curriculum was developed apart from students' lives.

G. STANLEY HALL

A new emphasis and direction, coupled with a tremendous growth in secondary schools, made this a time of enthusiastic study and debate. Pedagogical theory was reshaped by the new science of psychology. A pivotal figure in this movement was G. Stanley Hall. In the early 1900s, Hall espoused a scientific approach for studying education, but his work was child-centered and had little to do with research. Hall was influential in the development of the child study movement, and his work focused education back onto the child. Although many of his teachings are outdated, especially his views of heredity, Hall established child study as a science at Johns Hopkins University and attracted scholars like Arnold Gesell.

Hall's natural education theory supported a free, spontaneous environment for students. Language was to be used and enjoyed and was not to become a formal study. Hall believed that language was not properly coordinated with other studies and was taught too much as an isolated subject. Grammar, he believed, was emphasized far too much in the schools at the expense of vocabulary and reading. Language should be taught as a vehicle of thought and not constrained by grammar. Teaching grammar, Hall argued, often resulted in students becoming self-conscious and fearful of speaking or writing "because of the criticism of word or letter to which he is subjected" (Partridge 242). Today, discussions on the appropriate way to teach grammar are as heated and unresolved as they were in the 1800s.

EDWARD L. THORNDIKE

The scientific approach to the study of education was described largely in psychological terms. Edward L. Thorndike was the man most responsible for the shape of educational psychology throughout the 1920s and 1930s, and his views influenced educational psychology textbooks until the middle of the 20th century. Thorndike believed that a complete science of psychology would explain every facet of everyone's intellect, character, and behavior. Failure to understand was not the failure of psychology, but lack of a sufficiently detailed study of the changes that occurred. He believed strongly in the power of the psychological approach and wrote that through reliance on such a science "we shall become masters of our own souls" (175). Thorndike's work was based on response-stimuli experiments in animal studies, which he transferred to theories of human learning. His studies produced tables of numbers, which lead to an emphasis on testing and classifying students by ability. One present-day outcome is the use of ability tracking in the schools.

JOHN DEWEY

John Dewey, a student of G. Stanley Hall at Johns Hopkins, also believed in a scientific approach to education, but his perspective was very different from Thorndike's. Dewey conceived of the scientific approach as a means of understanding a body of knowledge. He was a seminal thinker in the relationship of subject matter to learning and developed a theory directly related to classroom activities. Whereas Thorndike believed that tasks should be broken down to the smallest segments, Dewey wrote that we have trouble remembering what we learn in school because we learn things in isolation. He believed that we are motivated to learn by a present need or curiosity. Unless goals are set by students themselves, little learning occurs. In traditional schools, goals were set by the teacher, a practice Dewey sought to change. He was thus an early advocate of the student-centered classroom.

The static form of instruction that was used in schools at the time—assign, study, recite—seemed illogical to Dewey. He believed that learning is a dynamic process that occurs when one wants to solve a problem. In the laboratory schools that Dewey developed, students designed curriculum together and shared activities. Following the guidelines of the scientific method, students thought of problems or projects, set up plans, and tested them out for satisfactory completion of the project.

In the past, learning was imposed on students and meant memorizing textbooks. Decisions about learning were traditionally made by administrators and teachers, with no input from students. Students had only a passive role in school, and the curriculum and lessons were intended to prepare them for some remote future. Although a major concern in becoming a mature, responsible adult is accepting responsibility for one's own actions, this concept was ignored in schools. In contrast, Dewey wanted a close relationship between actual experience and education. Learning *through* experience became the basis for the new education. Experience education has been characterized as an "anything goes" approach, but this is a misrepresentation of Dewey's model. He actually wanted students to have more control and responsibility in their own education.

Although Dewey believed that all genuine education comes through experience, he did not mean that all experience is equally educative. Each experience has to be connected with further experience, not simply pieced together haphazardly in a series of hands-on lessons. Teachers are an important part of the process because students have to be taught the significance of what they see, hear, and touch. Guidance from teachers remains an important aspect of the classroom. Dewey's progressive education was not a planless improvisation, but a developed philosophy.

DORA V. SMITH

Like Dewey's philosophy, much of what we think of as current appeared in the literature during the 1930s. For example, Dora V. Smith, in an address to the National Council of Teachers of English in 1936, urged teachers to keep in mind the needs and interests of their students. She enforced the idea that English teachers "should know where we are going, and be able to justify our course" (qtd. in Monseau 99). This advice is important today as we teach a more diverse and multicultural group of students than ever before.

Like Dewey, Smith emphasized active learning through experience in language, literature, and writing. In particular, she said, "We must get out of the clutches of Latin grammar and become students of our own language to see how it works" (72). She was one of the first to give adolescent literature serious professional attention and instituted the first course in adolescent literature at the University of Minnesota, the first such course at any university (78). With regard to teaching grammar, she believed that usage cannot be looked upon as right or wrong but is "rather a matter of acceptable and unacceptable in particular times and in particular circumstances" (73). In light of the writings of Smith and others like her, many practices in present-day classrooms seem dreadfully out of date.

The gap between what we know and what we do is a serious problem that must be addressed. Numerous studies point out that, in spite of what they learn in classes and through experience, new teachers tend to teach the way they were taught. In most cases, that means turning one's back on both knowledge and common sense. New teachers, in fact all teachers, must look first at their students' needs, then explore ways to best meet those needs, rather than go into a classroom armed with a lesson plan conceived apart from the context of the students' lives.

▼ _____

A PROFESSIONAL KNOWLEDGE BASE

Knowledge in our field continues to grow, mainly because teachers continue to ask questions about teaching and learning in English language arts:

- What do we know about listening and speaking? About reading and literature? About writing? About language?
- What environment stimulates and nurtures the processes of oral and written language?
- Which strategies help us teach each of these areas more effectively? Help students learn more effectively?
- What do we know about how students learn? How do we account for diversity? What role does culture play? What role does gender play? How does socioeconomic status affect learning?
- What do we know about students as developing adolescents? How does this knowledge affect our lessons and activities?
- How do we measure student learning appropriately?

These are important questions for us, not only as professional teachers in the English language arts, but also as part of a learning community that includes other teachers, administrators, and parents/caregivers.

ADDRESSING THE QUESTIONS

Throughout this text we address the above questions, providing answers to some and speculating about others. Although we have based the text on current research and effective classroom practice, we cannot hope to have all the answers. Consequently, this text should not be viewed as a "cookbook" for teaching. We do provide many examples of activities that classroom teachers have developed and found successful, but they are just that—examples. Teachers grow in knowledge and develop individual approaches to planning and implementing lessons. Further, teachers are as diverse as their students; what works well for one may not work at all for another. Most experienced teachers recognize the individuality of their teaching, which has led to a belief that there is no single method of teaching and no "correct" way to teach. Although we need many teaching methods and strategies, there is nonetheless a "correct" way: one that is congruent with the way adolescents learn and the way the language arts themselves function. As English language arts teachers, we cannot ignore knowledge of these basic human processes. We begin, then, with a brief explanation of the language arts from this perspective.

▼ ───

CHARACTERIZING THE ENGLISH LANGUAGE ARTS
INTERACTIVE PROCESSES

When we speak of the language arts as interactive processes, we characterize them from two perspectives: the process through which they interact with one another and the process through which we interact with them to construct meaning. Listening, speaking, reading, and writing interact and influence one another and thus contribute to a growing competency in each area. Our classrooms therefore need to be places where students actively and consistently engage in all the language arts. *Interactive* also means an active process through which we both bring meaning to and extract meaning from an oral or written text. Classrooms where students learn to make sense of themselves and their world undoubtedly have teachers who believe that students construct meaning rather than have it given to them.

AN INTEGRATED CURRICULUM

Because the language arts influence and strengthen one another, students need lessons with consciously balanced listening, speaking, reading, and writing activities. Teachers may emphasize one area in a given unit or lesson, but students should be actively engaged in all of them. In a literature unit, for example, reading is a primary activity, but in a balanced, integrated curriculum students would be involved in varied and purposeful activities that ask them to write, speak, and listen as well. Integrating the language arts fosters student development in each of them and makes learning more interesting. A curriculum that puts students through four weeks of reading literature, followed by two weeks of writing essays, followed by one week of giving speeches is both boring and ineffectual.

PURPOSEFUL COMMUNICATION

Whether we listen, speak, read, or write, we are engaged in communication. We are concerned with understanding ourselves and others and with expressing ourselves well enough to be understood. In every communicative act, we have purpose and audience and context; consequently, if we want students to learn, we need to keep all three in mind. Through them, we acknowledge that motivation comes from purpose and meaning, from students who have something to say and teachers who want to listen.

COGNITIVE PROCESSES

The use of language demands that we engage in an ongoing cognitive process. Because the language arts have traditionally been viewed as a subject to be taught, we have sometimes forgotten that they are, first and foremost, active processes. Speaking and listening have been more readily perceived in this way than have reading and writing, but the emphasis on reader response theory and writing processes reminds us that all the language arts depend upon cognitive processes.

What does this mean in the classroom? First, students need a structure that provides for and stimulates active participation. Second, students need time and experience to achieve competency in each of the language arts. Third, teachers must realize that language processes occur holistically. In speaking, listening, reading, or writing, we use various skills at the same time, but we reach competency and proficiency in different skills at different times. As teachers, our choices of methods and materials are dictated by the knowledge that sustained experience is critical to student learning. Our tolerance for error expands with awareness that cognitive overload can and does occur, that the complexity of a task may cause a student to falter badly, and that even our best students have lapses in performance.

A DEVELOPMENTAL PHENOMENON

When we listen, speak, read, or write, we are limited by our level of maturation—physically, cognitively, and linguistically. Some tasks are too difficult for us when they are introduced; some are too easy. Despite similarity of chronological age, students within a classroom vary in maturation and thus in their ability to deal with certain assignments. They may also vary considerably across the language arts, performing well in one area but not in another. Similarly, students may vary considerably from task to task within a particular area and may appear to get "worse" rather than better. In terms of development, however, these students are demonstrating normal behavior. This perspective reminds us that our lessons must address varying levels of development within one classroom and that we must maintain a realistic view of performance standards.

▼
THE LEARNERS

Teaching and learning are reflections of one another. Teachers and students must interact in order to create the best conditions for both. How individual teachers structure their classroom for this interaction is critically important and depends upon many factors, ranging from resources to personalities, and from personal knowledge to school policy. Among the many factors that influence teachers' decisions about how and what to teach, the makeup of the students is a major one. "Makeup" covers a wide range of considerations: age, gender, race, ethnicity, socioeconomic status, and language proficiency, to name but a few. At the same time, we can make some broad distinctions about learners, the first of which is the difference between middle school and high school students.

WHAT IS A MIDDLE SCHOOLER?

The term *middle schooler* generally refers to students in grades 6 through 8, regardless of their placement in a K–8 traditional elementary building, middle school, or junior high school. Nancie Atwell's text for English language arts teachers, *In the Middle*, helps to define these students as young adolescents in transition from elementary to secondary schooling and suggests pedagogy appropriate to the developmental changes characteristic of this age group.

Although the language arts involve basic processes that remain similar regardless of age (e.g., a 12 year old and 18 year old work through the same writing processes), differences in maturation are critical. We cannot expect the same level of knowledge, skill, or performance from a middle schooler as from a high school junior. Nor can we expect the same attention and concentration levels. Adolescents aged 12 to 14 are very different from their high school counterparts, and developing activities for this age group is not just a matter of making them less sophisticated.

The National Association of Secondary School Principals (NASSP) published a statement describing students "in the middle." "We know that at no other period in the life cycle does such a variance exist in the rate of individual development" (n. pag.). These differences are apparent in their intellectual, emotional, social, and physical development. According to NASSP (n. pag.), these changes may lead them to be:

- Impulsive in actions and impatient with restrictions.
- Preoccupied with popularity and self-conscious about appearance.
- Deeply influenced by mass media and responsive to fads.
- Plagued by mood swings and subject to forgetfulness and boredom.
- Assertive in independence and moved by competitive situations.

- Charged with energy, confused by self-doubt, and fearful of failure.
- Embarrassed by social customs and veneered with "wisecracks."

Working with young adolescents can be difficult for teachers but also extremely rewarding. Middle school students do challenge authority, but they also rely on their teachers for guidance and support. Providing opportunities for choice within structure is important when working with middle schoolers. Despite individual differences, they have in common an overwhelming sense of fairness. They expect people to be fair with them, and they react strongly when they believe they have been treated unfairly. To work well with this age, teachers need to explain the reasons behind their expectations for behavior and social interactions. They must also be willing to listen to the students and to provide a supportive environment, which is not always easy to do.

Middle school educator John Arnold argues that although some structural changes in schools, such as interdisciplinary teams, block schedules, and advisor/advisee systems, can be helpful, the most important way to help middle schoolers is to "positively affect the day to day interactions in the classrooms" (1). In other words, the responsibility rests with individual teachers. Teachers need to keep in mind that young adolescents are trying to make sense of themselves and their world. Experiences that focus on the real world benefit their learning: articles from current newspapers and magazines, interviews with a variety of people, and trips to real world locations, for example. Arnold explains that we must be aware of the young adolescent's limited capacity for abstraction, so more hands-on activities are better. "This necessitates having a rich variety of materials in classrooms for students to manipulate so they can build, measure, compare, contrast, and create" (3). Students also need opportunities to discuss, argue, plan, and reflect. Taking into account the traits of young adolescents helps middle level teachers provide a learning environment conducive to students' optimal intellectual and social growth.

▼ ───

LEARNING STYLES

Rita Dunn, Jeffrey S. Beaudry, and Angela Klavas tell us that everyone has a learning style that is a "biologically and developmentally imposed set of personal characteristics that make the same teaching method effective for some and ineffective for others" (50). Learning styles affect how we respond to an environment, how we remember information, and how we learn. Dunn et al. report that research demonstrates that the opportunity to work in an environment that supports our style enables us to learn more and retain it longer (51–52). Characteristics of learning style include responses to the amount of noise, illumination, temperature, and seating arrangements. Some people work better in the morning, others at night. Some learn best by listening; others by reading, note-taking, seeing, or some combinations of approaches (50). Students who cannot sit still might be driven by a learning style that requires movement. Students who ask detailed questions about writing formats are not necessarily dependent, but rather may have a learning style that prefers explicit, detailed directions (Jensen and DiTiberio 173). As George Jensen, a researcher in the area of personality and teaching, points out, data force us to look for individual differences and not expect everyone to be the same.

With more than 100 students to teach every day, teachers cannot feasibly identify each one's learning style. What is important is awareness that every class has a mixture of styles, some or all of which differ from the teacher's, and that teachers tend to use the style that works best for them. Teachers need to discover their own teaching style through a reliable identification instrument so that they become aware of their own preferences. With this knowledge, they can be more conscious about choosing various methods for presenting materials or creating learning environments. It is vital that teachers vary their methods and presentations to accommodate more students more of the time.

▼

TEACHING ALL STUDENTS

Teachers are responsible for teaching, to the best of their ability, every student in their classroom. More special needs students (e.g., emotionally disturbed, mentally disabled, limited English proficiency) are mainstreamed today than in the past, so that many students who were formerly taught in self-contained, special classes now spend at least part of the day in a regular English language arts class. Resource teachers may be present in the class or may meet with regular classroom teachers outside of class to assist them in working with these students. Mainstreaming has many benefits for all students because they learn to work and socialize with others of varying capabilities. Such knowledge does a great deal to dispel fears about differences among us.

GROUP WORK

Planning activities appropriate for a wide range of abilities and interests is a basic strategy for addressing diverse student needs. Group work is especially beneficial because listening and speaking are natural outcomes when students come together in small groups. Students too shy to speak up in class find it easier to express themselves, and all students feel a stronger sense of belonging. Teachers benefit, too, especially when large class size is a problem, because each group can work on a task and report the results orally or in one written report.

Group work accommodates students of all abilities. Therefore, groups should include a variety of levels, not only so that the lower-ability student can be helped by the more able, but because every student has something to offer. Students who have difficulty writing may excel verbally; those who never hand in work could be among the most creative. And students who have trouble understanding tasks or materials receive help from others. A spirit of cooperation is essential in accomplishing the business of the world, and groups help prepare students for life outside the classroom.

READING LEVELS AND INTERESTS

Choosing an appropriate range of reading material is an important teaching strategy. Too often, all students are assigned the same material whether they can read it or not. The results are disastrous. Depending upon school policy, students are either passed along to the next grade regardless of what they accomplish, or they repeatedly fail until they reach the age when schooling is not mandatory. Often the lack of appropriate material is not a school budget problem but the failure of teachers to insist that all students have a right to learn.

Along with caring about reading level, teachers need to care about student interests. Classrooms should be filled with reading material of many kinds—newspapers, magazines, popular books, pamphlets—and on many subjects. We need to be mindful that our objective is to promote an enjoyment of reading, not to bend minds to adult tastes. When we think of reading material for our classroom, we need to remember that we are selecting for adolescents, many of whom have reading preferences very different from our own.

CLASSROOM CLIMATE

Many factors contribute to the environment in a classroom. Some are physical and static, such as temperature, lighting, wall color, room size, and furnishings. Some less static influences include the number of extraneous interruptions, (e.g., intercom announcements), student absences, and the number of teachers who use the room.

Teachers can do much to create an environment conducive to learning. Placement of student desks makes a profound difference in how students view a classroom. A circle makes the back row disappear, establishing equality in the class and facilitating discussion. When students can see one another, discussion takes on the attributes of conversation and becomes more spontaneous and natural. Not all students like the circle arrangement, especially those who sleep in the back row, but eventually the arrangement creates a sense of community. Equally important is the placement of the teacher's desk. A big desk in front of the class acts as both a physical and an emotional barrier, a statement of who's boss. A desk in front is actually awkward when teachers are writing on the board or using an overhead projector; it creates a barricade at the very time when we are most concerned with student attentiveness and response. Because language arts activities advocate teacher participation and movement among students, the desk isn't used during class time. Placing it at the back of the room makes sense.

Another way of establishing a sense of community is to display student work. Rooms decorated only with posters of writing skills or great authors are seldom interesting to students. Posters that have nothing to do with teaching English, but are amusing and colorful, are appropriate, but student work should always be included. The more such work is displayed, the more the room seems like it belongs to the students. "Work" can be articles, cartoons, and drawings brought by students as well as assigned work. We can ask students to plan some of the bulletin boards, creating original work or finding materials appropriate for upcoming areas of study. Such student involvement can bring out hidden skills. The student who doesn't read well may have artistic talent. The student who doesn't say much may be a planning and organizational genius.

EMOTIONAL CONCERNS

The teacher's behavior is a critical element of classroom climate. Contrary to a popular myth, teachers should smile, even new teachers trying to create a sense of authority. In fact, a smile does much to dispel the appearance of nervousness because a person who is confident smiles and appears at ease while talking. Authority has far more to do with respect than with a stern face. If a teacher respects his or her students and makes that respect obvious by listening to them and taking their ideas and heartfelt thoughts seriously, the environment will be conducive to a shared sense of community, the kind of place where learning can happen.

▼

THE REALITY OF STUDENTS' LIVES

We cannot ignore the situations and conditions of students' lives: The student whose parent has just died, the student whose girlfriend has just dropped him, the student who just failed her chemistry exam, the student whose parents have just separated, the student who works nights to help support the family, the student who gets up at 4:00 A.M. to do farm work, the student whose parent suffers from cancer, or the student who has total responsibility for younger siblings. Every class is certain to have students for whom daily life brings increasing difficulty, responsibility, uncertainty, or pain. Given this reality, teachers must be both understanding and flexible. A head on the desk or turned toward a window does not necessarily indicate disrespect or disinterest in class, but only that, for the time being, a larger and more compelling concern is present.

Students' lives have become increasingly more troubled, reflecting a society with a widening gap between the "have's" and "have not's" and with uncertain values, questionable ethics, and periodic violence. We need, then, to maintain awareness of the student whose parent has been jailed for dealing drugs, whose sister has been picked up for shoplifting, whose brother has been injured or killed in a gang fight, whose alcoholic parent is abusive on a daily basis, whose household has a six persons per room occupancy, or whose life revolves in a cycle of poverty and deprivation. For such students, just getting to school is a major accomplishment.

Keeping such a perspective is not easy, but it is the only fair one to have. Further, students' experiences must have a bearing on how we teach and what we expect from them. For example, we cannot expect students with neither the physical space nor emotional environment to complete homework assignments. We must be aware, as high school teacher Candy Carter points out, that few students today, regardless of socioeconomic class, have not "been confronted with opportunities to use drugs or drink to excess" (26). Many have done so and continue to do so. Parental interest may be lacking altogether or may have simply deteriorated into despair.

Our idealism as teachers may be sorely tried by circumstances beyond our control. We cannot continue to teach students as if they have no life outside of our classrooms. In reality, their lives can be frightening, exhausting, and overwhelming. Carter argues that "students often come to school with so much unfinished business from home that it takes a real master to bring art and life together" (27). Teachers cannot solve students' problems, but with understanding, empathy, and patience, classrooms can at least be places where they find refuge for a time. And perhaps, through responding to literature, writing journals, and listening to and talking with peers, students can begin to find answers to their questions and perhaps make sense of their lives.

▼ ───

WHAT CAN TEACHERS DO?

Fifteen years ago, Dwight Burton and his colleagues asked students what they needed. They responded that "they needed some hope, some feeling that mankind will not merely survive but that it deserves to survive" (17). These are sobering words and are as likely to arise from the students of the 1990s. What does this mean for our classrooms? It means mainly that we must provide both a model of personal integrity and opportunities for students to explore their beliefs and values. Through literature, classroom drama, and writing, for example, students can safely explore themselves and their world, find people to admire, and see beyond the limits of their present situation. Students also need a classroom environment that encourages and respects the range of human emotions. In his study of American schools, John Goodlad tells us:

> Data . . . suggest to me a picture of rather well-intentioned teachers going about their business somewhat detached from and not quite connecting with the 'other lives' of their students. What their students see as primary concerns in their daily lives, teachers view as dissonance in conducting school and classroom business. (80)

Goodlad goes on to note that "classes at all levels tend not to be marked with exuberance, joy, laughter, abrasiveness, praise . . . but by emotional neutrality" (112) and "whether we looked at how teachers related to students or how students related to teachers, the overwhelming impression was one of affective neutrality—a relationship neither abrasive nor joyous" (111). We can think of no worse environment for students or for ourselves. To prevent it, we need to take a serious look at students' needs and interests as we choose materials and plan lessons.

PRACTICAL MEASURES

Burton and his colleagues suggest that, in learning about our students, we forget about school records such as IQ and grades from the previous year. Instead, we should take an inventory in the first week of classes: What television shows do they regularly watch? What magazines do they read? What hobbies interest them? What sports do they participate in or watch as avid fans? What music do they listen to? What musical instruments do they play? What choral events do they participate in? Do they have jobs? What responsibilities do they have at home? What topics most interest them? What school subjects are they most interested in? Of all the people they know, whose advice is most important and why? (25). We can also tailor the inventory to the community and the school, including important events or simply awareness of the environment.

We need to inventory ourselves as well. Recognizing our match or mismatch with any group of students is important in lesson planning. Once we have gathered some information, we can refer to it as we plan. We can develop units around student interests, cultivate diversity in our choices of reading materials and non-print media, and direct individual students to books, magazines, and movies. In class discussions, we can draw upon individual interests and expertise. Then, when students talk, we need to listen. When they write in their journals, we need to respond. Few things are as powerful as genuine response and interest in what someone has to say.

▼

WHAT QUALITIES DOES A TEACHER NEED?
REALISM

Although teaching assignments and conditions vary considerably, successful teachers share certain characteristics. As we have already noted, successful teachers know something about students, both from what research tells them and from what students themselves say. Successful teachers also know things about themselves. For example, our upbringing, culture, and social class do influence us. Many English teachers come from middle class backgrounds that may conflict with those of some students. Further, we aren't facing a classroom full of prospective English teachers for whom English is easy and pleasurable.

Being knowledgeable and realistic about ourselves and our students is an important base for teaching.

OPENNESS

Being honest with both ourselves and the students is an important characteristic. If we don't know something, we should say so. We can tell students that we'll look it up, or we can do it together. We can also share some experiences with students, not divulging sensitive or highly personal incidents, but certainly recounting experiences that meant something to us. We also need to do what we expect the students to do: read, write, and share. A certain hypocrisy is involved when English teachers require students to read and to write, but fail to do so themselves.

POSITIVE EXPECTATIONS

We need to see students as individuals, not as the fifth-hour class or the slow group. Developing or strengthening the attitude that every student has a right to learn is an essential part of teaching. Believing that every student brings to the classroom knowledge that enriches others in the learning community is equally essential. Similarly, effective teachers believe that their students *can* learn. These attitudes foster both individual growth and class cohesiveness. If students feel good about themselves, they are more likely to participate.

RESPONSIVENESS

Our attitude is always the baseline for what happens. The time we spend initially getting to know the students and allowing them to know one another and us is time well spent. Similarly, being honest, genuine, and responsive sets the tone for productive work. We are not advocating being "the friend" and throwing discipline and structure aside. Students need us to take charge, to orchestrate, to lead; neither we nor they can function in an environment that lacks structure and planning. At the same time, we can do this in a manner that incorporates students rather than dominates them.

FLEXIBILITY

Planning well is part of teaching well. However, plans are carried out among individuals who hear, respond, and think in unique ways. Every classroom experience is full of surprises, and while teachers need carefully thought-out plans, they also need to be ready to change those plans on a moment's notice. We cannot remove the equivocal nature of teaching, nor would we want to when we consider that our focus in teaching is people, not subject matter.

▼

DRAWING CONCLUSIONS

In 1986, Richard Lloyd-Jones, then president of the National Council of Teachers of English, outlined qualifications for future teachers of English language arts. In addition to many of those we have mentioned, Lloyd-Jones lists insatiable curiosity and a strong will to discover and try out new ideas (3). It is not enough, however, just to try out new ideas; we must reflect upon them. The habit of reflection, of thoughtful analysis of what we do and observe in our classrooms, is a critical part of teaching well. Mitch Cox, a high school teacher, describes the connections among planning, teaching, and reflection.

> Planning is the prewriting stage where attention must be given to the connections among the teacher/writer, students/audience, and the needs and goals of the two. It is also recursive, involving revision not only after an initial delivery of a lesson but also during the act of teaching itself. In fact, planning for the present always requires looking back to the previous year and being ready to adjust ideas to past experience. (33)

Looking back requires a written response to the teaching activities: How one feels about the day, what could have gone better, and what went right, too. Given this, teachers' most valuable tool in assessing their teaching is a reflective journal. Jotting down impressions at the end of each day provides time for contemplation. With a journal, patterns of problems and successes are easier to see and to understand. Too often, students are blamed for the failure of plans or activities that didn't work. When we transfer blame for poor results to students, we close the door to considering how and what we ourselves might change to achieve better results. To be effective teachers, we must continue to be learners as well.

DISCUSSION QUESTIONS

1.   "We *can* talk," said the Tiger-lily:
      "When there's anybody worth talking to."

   Alice in Wonderland was astounded by the talking flowers, and perhaps even more by their discriminating attitude. Unfortunately, the Tiger-lily sounds remarkably like some senior high school students. Why shouldn't *you* be surprised if a number of students feel just like the Tiger-lily? More importantly, what can you do about it?

2. In *A Place Called School*, a national study of the American high school, John Goodlad tells us that teachers and students are often disconnected: "What their students viewed as primary concerns in their daily lives, teachers viewed as dissonance . . . not quite connecting with them as problems in the lives of their students" (80). Reflect on your middle and senior high school experience in English language arts classes. Is Goodlad's observation valid?

Goodlad also reports that American schools lack emotion: the "overwhelming impression was one of affective neutrality" (111). Again reflect on your experience and evaluate the validity of this statement.

What can English language arts teachers do to diminish a sense of isolation or alienation within the classroom?

3. James Moffett and Betty Jane Wagner, two prominent English educators, note:

> Too often, teachers do not know why they are doing what they do, and an alarming number admit that they don't believe in what they are doing. (3)

This is a serious charge. Discuss its implications. Why would teachers admit they don't believe in what they are doing? What does this suggest to you about the importance of research in the English language arts? Make a two-column list about what you *do* believe and what you *do not* believe about teaching and learning.

SUGGESTED ACTIVITIES

1. Create a student survey that you could use during your early days of teaching to get to know your students better. Choose a community you know well, perhaps your own, in order to include items about related events or the environment outside of the school. Try your survey out on some friends or classmates. Be sure to take the survey yourself. When you have the responses back, reflect on what you have learned.

2. The English language arts *are* processes, not static knowledge. Consider listening, speaking, reading, and writing from the perspective of active, ongoing processes; then discuss what differences this perception makes when placed against your knowledge of the classroom. What, for example, do you recall of your own experience in middle or senior high school classes? Were your lessons and activities based on assumptions of processes?

3. Keep a reflective journal for a week. Choose one of your classes as the subject of your journal and reflect on your responses to it and your learning. You'll have to keep a double-entry journal in order to do this: one side for the class activities, tasks, and so forth and the other for your responses to each specific activity or task. At the end of the week, read your journal and reflect on the process overall. What have you learned about yourself relative to this one class?

REFERENCES

Arnold, John. "A Responsive Curriculum for Emerging Adolescents." *Middle School Journal* May 1985: 1–6.

Burton, Dwight L., et al. *Teaching English Today*. Boston: Houghton, 1975.

Carroll, Lewis. *Alice in Wonderland and Through the Looking Glass*. San Rafael: Classic Publishing, 1970.

Carter, Candy. "Are Teenagers Different?" *What is English?*. Comp. Peter Elbow. New York: MLA; Urbana: National Council of Teachers of English, 1990. 24–27.

Cox, Mitch. "Bards and Beatles: Connecting Spontaneity to Structure in Lesson Plans." *English Journal* Mar. 1991: 33–41.

Dunn, Rita, Jeffrey S. Beaudry, and Angela Klavas. "Survey of Research on Learning Styles." *Educational Leadership* Mar. 1989: 50–58.

Emig, Janet. Exploring Theories of Learning for Teaching Writing. Conference on Teaching Composition to Undergraduates. Clearwater Beach, 5 Jan. 1992.

Goodlad, John. *A Place Called School*. New York: McGraw-Hill, 1989.

Jensen, George. Applying Personality Theory to the Classroom. Conference on Teaching Composition to Undergraduates. Clearwater Beach, 5 Jan. 1992.

Jensen, George, and John T. DiTiberio. *Personality and the Teaching of Composition*. Norwood: Ablex, 1989.

Lightfoot, Sara Lawrence. In *The World of Ideas: Conversations with Bill Moyers*. Ed. Betty Sue Flowers, pp. 156–166. New York: Doubleday, 1989.

Lloyd-Jones, Richard. "What English Teachers Need to Know—and to Be." News Release. Urbana: National Council of Teachers of English, 1986. N. pag.

Maxwell, Rhoda J. "The New Scientific Education, 1890–1920." Unpublished paper. 1982.

Meiser , Mary. "Teaching Kids, Not English." Afterwords in *Wisconsin Dialogue*. Eau Claire: University of Wisconsin, Spring 1989.

Moffet, James, and Betty Jane Wagner. *Student-Centered English Language Arts K–13: A Handbook for Teachers*. Boston: Houghton, 1976.

Monseau, Virginia R. "Dora V. Smith: A Legacy for the Future." *Missing Chapters*. Eds. Jeanne Marcum Gerlach and Virginia R. Monseau. Urbana: National Council of Teachers of English, 1991.

Murphy Jr., Richard J. "Learning to Teach." National Association of Secondary School Principals. *English Education* 23(1991): 178–187.

"On the Threshold of Adolescence." Reston: National Association of Secondary School Principals, 1983.

Partridge, G. E. *Genetic Philosophy of Education*. New York: Sturgis and Walton, 1912.

Tchudi, Stephen. "Invisible Thinking and the Hypertext." *English Journal* Jan. 1988: 22–30.

Thorndike, Edward L. *The Fundamentals of Learning*. New York: Columbia Teachers College, 1932.

CHAPTER 2

Oral Language: The Neglected Language Arts

CHAPTER HIGHLIGHTS

- Listening and speaking: Basic principles and curricular goals.
- Classroom talk: Teachers, students, and cultural differences.
- Oral language activities for adolescents.
- Evaluating oral language.

> Schools are language saturated institutions. They are places where books are thumbed, summarized, and 'revised'; notes are dictated, made, kept, and learned; essays are prepared; examination questions are composed and the attendant judgments made. Teachers explain, lecture, question, exhort, reprimand. Pupils listen, reply, make observations, call out, mutter, whisper and make jokes. Small knots gather over books, lathes, easels, or do nothing in classrooms, laboratories, workshops, craftrooms, corridors and toilets to chatter, discuss, argue, plan, plot and teach one another.
>
> —*Douglas Barnes*

▼

SOME BASIC PRINCIPLES

As Barnes reminds us, oral language is the most pervasive environment of our schools. Not only do we seldom perceive it in this way, but we also tend to forget that oral language is an important instructional area in the English language arts. At the secondary level, responsibility for oral language has most often been relegated to *the* speech course or fragmented into isolated units. John Fortier, a high school English and speech teacher, reflects on a possible reason for this:

> A number of factors have combined to prevent oral language instruction from achieving the gains that writing instruction has. We sometimes perceive speaking, unlike writing, as a competence which develops independently without instruction. After all, students come to school talking, but few are able to write. (2)

An additional factor may lie in the traditional preparation of secondary teachers, in which written language has been the focus for methods courses. As one of our English education majors put it, "I know it was sort of a shock to some of the methods students to think about teaching speaking and listening skills because they didn't really consider that 'English' " (Lightfoot). Quite often, secondary English textbooks reinforce the notion of the primacy of written expression, generally of two varieties: literature and composition/grammar. Fortunately, a renewed emphasis on an integrated and balanced English language arts program has also brought more resources for teaching oral language.

Before looking specifically at listening and speaking, we need to focus on some very basic oral language principles. Fortier (adapted 3–5) summarizes these:

a. Not all students share the same level of competency in oral language; in fact, some students enter school impoverished by a lack of verbal interaction in the home environment. The implication for teachers is clear: Students do need to talk in school, not "idle chatter but focused discussion."

b. Similar to other language skills, the acquisition of oral language skills is developmental. We should not expect students to progress at the same rate or demonstrate the same ability, regardless of similar chronological age.

c. Students need varied and purposeful experience in oral communication, just as they do with written communication. This means shifts from familiar audiences and contexts to more distant ones, as well as opportunities to share feelings, entertain, give information, and persuade. Each of these purposes has its own problem relative to audience and setting; therefore, students would learn to solve diverse communication problems. Our responsibility is to create these contexts, everything from role playing to group activities, from conferencing to public speaking before an entire class.

d. We should not break speaking into subskills, nor should we isolate speaking from the other language arts. Oral language activities integrated with reading and writing, a planned part of every unit and daily classroom interaction, enhance student competency.

e. Because speaking is not totally oral, students need to learn about body language, eye contact, gesture, and so forth. Being aware of how listeners are responding is a critical skill. Similarly, students need to be sensitive to how culturally bound these areas are. For example, in mainstream American culture, eye contact is expected to be direct, indicating honesty and self-confidence. In other cultures, such directness would be considered ill-mannered.

Oral language skills, as Fortier points out, do not simply develop on their own, nor do students gain proficiency in oral language without a carefully designed curriculum. Student interaction and response—authentic communication—are vital to sustained development of important communicative functions. Teachers who create a classroom environment focused on the learner draw upon a natural adolescent inclination to communicate. At the same time, these teachers are well aware of the variance in oral language competencies and provide appropriate structure to foster growth and versatility in listening and speaking.

▼
LISTENING: NOT THE SAME AS HEARING

Listening is both the most used and the least understood of all communication arts.

—Wisconsin Department of Public
Instruction 1986, 67

Considering the percentage of school time during which students are expected to be quiet and listen, we might assume they develop into good listeners. This is far from true, however. Many misconceptions exist about listening, the first being that listening cannot be taught. Listening can and should be taught, not through talking about listening skills but rather through engaging students in authentic communication events. A second misconception is that listening and hearing are the same thing. Given the continual bombardment of "noise" in modern life, we can hardly blame students for tuning out. Nevertheless, as teachers we have the responsibility of teaching students the difference.

Another misconception that causes no end of trouble is the statement "you're not listening" being used to mean "you don't agree with me; therefore you're not listening." Parents and teachers often chastise students for not listening when they actually mean that the students rejected what they heard. The implication for the classroom is a serious one, for it touches on the integrity of speaking and listening as a shared experience. Sometimes we also fail to differentiate among the varying purposes of listening. There is considerable difference between listening critically and listening aesthetically, for example.

MAJOR CURRICULAR GOALS AND CLASSROOM BARRIERS

Once we are aware of general curricular goals in listening, we can structure lessons to include them. On a basic level, students should be able to recognize the speaker's purpose, as well as their own in listening—whether to gain information, to analyze, or to appreciate aesthetically. Students must also be aware of both verbal and nonverbal cues that contribute to their understanding of a verbal text. Their own role in providing feedback in both of these forms is similarly critical.

The skill of giving *effective* feedback is a learned one. Students usually think of feedback only when they solicit it. It is not surprising then that the notion of learning to respond more effectively is a new one. Without conscious attention to strategies which provide specific and helpful feedback, students are likely to ignore a vital aspect of communicating well.

Teachers must be aware of barriers to effective listening. Unfamiliarity with the vocabulary, syntax, or content may be one cause; dialect and native language differences may be another, but *any* student may face barriers. A much more difficult situation arises when students simply tune out lessons that involve complex content. Some students choose not to listen to ideas or explanations that demand full attention. Others may stop listening when they don't agree; usually they are framing their rebuttal or preparing some sort of response before the speaker has completed his or her message. Because adolescents are sensitive to situations in which *their* words are ignored, some straight but sensitive talk about being fair might help.

Structuring classroom activities so that students are encouraged or compelled to listen is an important part of teaching listening skills. Although high-interest lessons build in attentiveness, we still need consciously to incorporate activities that develop good listening skills. Teaching purposeful listening involves two major activities: Listening to recognize the organization of spoken discourse and listening to follow spoken directions. The former is particularly important because students comprehend much better when they recognize "the plan." For example, students who recognize cause and effect or comparison and contrast as the organizing principle grasp the content far more efficiently. We enhance this ability by giving students a plan for what they will hear: an overview and an explanation of new or difficult words or concepts.

Listening to oral directions is, of course, a basic part of most classes. However, we tend to repeat directions so often that students know they can catch whatever they need at "point future." Without making an issue of it, we can help students by not being so generous with repetition. For students who comprehend more slowly, we do need to make adjustments, but this can usually be done on an individual basis as needed.

LISTENING AS PROCESS

Ideally, listening is part of student activities that involve the other language arts. The following listening skills (adapted from Devine) are among the most important in curricular planning. Students should be able to:

- Remember significant details accurately, as well as simple sequences of words and ideas.
- Follow oral directions accurately.
- Paraphrase an oral message accurately.
- Follow a sequence in plot development, character development, and a speaker's argument.
- Understand both literal and connotative meanings.
- Understand meaning derived from a spoken context.
- Listen for implications of significant detail.
- Listen for implications of main ideas.
- Distinguish between old and new material.
- Distinguish between relevant and irrelevant material.
- Predict outcomes.
- Draw conclusions.
- Identify and summarize main ideas.
- Relate the speaker's ideas and information to their own life.

Teachers can align listening skills with a variety of instructional methods and materials as they plan lessons. Oral readings, informal drama, media presentations, and even some forms of evaluation require listening well and providing either oral or written evidence of comprehension. These basic listening skills are never completely mastered, but rather are continually improved upon as students mature and gain experience. Without sustained, focused experience at every curricular level, however, most students remain "hearers" rather than listeners.

Students also need to develop critical listening skills. Because these skills are most associated with argument and persuasion, some curriculum guides list them as part of a unit dealing with media. However, students need sustained experience. The following list, adapted from Sara Lundsteen, professor of education at North Texas State University, notes the most important skills for students:

- Using criteria, distinguish "fact from fancy."
- Judge the validity and adequacy of main ideas, arguments, and hypotheses.
- Distinguish well-supported statements from opinion and judgment.
- Evaluate the use of fallacies (e.g., self-contradiction, false analogy, failure to present all choices).

- Recognize emotional appeals and loaded words.
- Detect and evaluate speaker bias.
- Evaluate qualifications or credentials of speaker.
- Recognize basic propaganda devices.

These skills are, of course, linked with critical thinking. Thus, in devising ways for students to practice listening, teachers are also devising ways to promote higher-order thinking skills. Although many of the critical listening skills appear to be cognitively advanced, when appropriately woven into lessons, they are not beyond even young adolescents. For example, a 12 year old with a vested interest in an argument can be a very critical listener. Similarly, young adolescents who associate critical listening with people and events that matter to them and with getting on in the "real world" soon appreciate the value of becoming a better listener. Making that bridge to the "real world," however, depends upon English language arts teachers. An awareness of critical listening skills is only the first step; finding ways to make students not only aware but actively involved in them requires sustained teacher thought, time, and energy.

▼

SPEAKING: MORE THAN JUST TALK

Speaking is a process, not a series of episodes, units, or courses.

—*Wisconsin Department of Public*
Instruction 1986, 90

Speaking has most often been perceived as "something the speech teacher takes care of," rather than as one of the major strands of the English language arts curriculum. Consequently, in many school districts curriculum for speaking translates into a single speech course. This essentially isolates speaking from conscious attention in the development of daily lessons and units in English classrooms. However, speaking is essential in all language arts classes, not only for its own sake but also because it influences the development of other language arts competencies.

MAJOR CURRICULAR GOALS

As a curricular area, speaking parallels writing in important ways. Like writing, speaking must be purposeful, serving an authentic communicative need geared to audience and context. Moreover, in both media students need to experience the range of communicative functions. The Speech Communication Association's National Project on Speech Communication Competencies marked the origin of the functional communication approach to curriculum development (see Allen and Brown 1976; Wood 1977; Allen, Brown and Yatvin,

1986). They delineate the **five communicative functions** in this way (adapted from Wisconsin Department of Public Instruction 1986, 90−91):

- *Expressing feelings.* This pertains to communication acts that either express or respond to feelings, as well as attitudes.
- *Ritualizing.* This type of discourse is formulaic and culturally determined; it allows people to take part in social interactions and to maintain social relationships.
- *Imagining.* In this type of discourse, people place themselves in imaginary situations. Although we typically think of this discourse as fantasy or story-telling, it also includes communicative acts critical to academic discourse: theorizing, speculating, and dramatizing.
- *Informing.* Informative discourse is, of course, central to schooling. We need to provide information or to seek it. Often, then, we are stating, questioning, explaining, justifying, answering, and demonstrating.
- *Controlling.* This is persuasive discourse, in which people are trying to control behavior through effective use of language. This function is also central to schooling, in which every speech act from permitting to rejecting, from justifying to arguing, and from persuading to bargaining is commonplace.

The major goals of the speaking curriculum are centered on these five communicative functions. The first goal, of course, is that students learn to speak effectively in all five functions. This does not mean that teachers should develop units around them; rather, the goal should be an integrated language arts curriculum in which all four language arts are present in daily lessons. For example, students may be reading novels as part of a thematic unit. Although we would expect and plan for discussion, we would also consciously build in questions and activities that focus more specifically on one or more of the speech functions. Asking students to speculate on plot, imagine future character development, or justify a character's action are different speech functions. Asking students to choose a scene for dramatizing or to write and then perform a scene using characters from the novel draws once more upon different language competencies. If we keep the competencies in mind when we plan unit activities, we can be reasonably sure that our speaking curriculum is balanced.

As we plan classroom activities, we also need to consider different levels of audience, everything from pairs to small groups to full class. Students need varied experience to develop speaking competencies and awareness of audience. Some students may be comfortable in pairs but not in front of a full class; others may feel inadequate in group work. Without consistent experience in all types of speaking situations, they might not develop a level of comfort which will serve them well as adults. Another related goal is competency and comfort among diverse racial and ethnic groups. Teachers fortunate enough to have a diverse student population find that cultural differences in speaking and listening can be easily identified and discussed. Lacking such diversity, we have to find ways to increase student awareness of the cultural base of language. All languages express the five communicative functions, but how they do so is a matter of culture.

It might be argued that if students are engaging in these various functions through conversation alone, there is no need to place them in the curriculum. The problem is that student talk *is* culture-bound and, equally important, is not the talk of academic discourse. Moreover, students do not necessarily extend or evaluate talk, ask good questions, or consider the significance of a message. They are not quick to determine the presence or absence of evidence or to evaluate the line of reasoning. Nor are they necessarily aware of language strategies, such as argumentation and persuasion, much less able to evaluate strategies for social acceptability and civic responsibility. These are critical competencies in a modern society, especially one founded on democratic principles. We also have an important role in teaching students the responsibility inherent in freedom of speech. Although it is one of America's most cherished values, it can be abused. Students need to understand the difference between the right to express an opinion and the "non-right" to verbally abuse, defame, or denigrate another human being.

▼
INFORMAL CLASSROOM DRAMA

Informal classroom drama, also referred to as creative or improvised drama, is different from theatre in that "students invent and enact dramatic situations for themselves" (Wisconsin Department of Public Instruction 1990, 107). This activity is a teaching strategy used to enhance various academic and social skills, including improvement of all language skills, analytic thinking, problem solving, and sustained concentration. Betty Jane Wagner points out that "improvisational drama, perhaps more obviously than other oral language activities, ties directly into both literary and nonverbal knowing" (196). Students involved in classroom drama also strengthen their self-concept and their ability to work cooperatively (Wisconsin Department of Public Instruction 1986, 108). Because students are both the "inventors and actors," the role of the teacher is one of facilitator.

Informal classroom drama offers a safe place to learn and practice new skills. It also offers a bonus—a way for growing adolescents to cope with the rapid changes in their emotions and bodies. Anyone who has taught middle school can attest to the "worms in a tin can" phenomenon: The students appear to wiggle all day long. Some senior high school students demonstrate a similar tendency. Kids need movement, and informal drama can provide it. The social aspects are similarly important. Role-playing allows students to try out various personas, observe them in other students, and generally gain some insight. Older students also have an opportunity to recognize the complexity of choice and the gravity of consequences in a controlled environment. Cognitively, informal drama provides a means of taking abstract ideas and making them comprehensible through concrete expression. "Justice," for example, sounds good, but what does it really mean? And is it as simple and clear as the dictionary definition? Through drama, students enact the meaning and thus deal with it concretely (Wisconsin Department of Public Instruction 1990, 92). Wagner suggests using informal drama in various ways: as a whole class activity of simultaneous pantomime action as teacher or student reads the text aloud; as a planned dramatization (not reading from script), with two groups of student volunteers to act it out, followed by class discussion comparing the two versions; as a dramatized scene that was *not* part of a story just read but would fit contextually. Wagner believes that "drama in the classroom entails unremitting pressure to develop listening and conversational skill" (197–98). Moreover, students "grow in their capacity to send and receive increasingly complex and mature verbal messages effectively, independently, creatively, and symbolically" (210). Additionally, most students enjoy it, which is why, believes Wagner, its educational importance is often underestimated.

▼ ───

TEACHER TALK, STUDENT TALK

> The most obvious characteristic of classroom talk is that there is so much of it. (10)
>
> *—V. J. Edwards and A. D. Furlong*

Edwards and Furlong, although referring to British secondary classrooms, characterize our mainstream classrooms as well, "The theme is simply 'everybody listen.' For much of the time in classrooms, there is a *single* verbal encounter in which whatever is being said demands the attention of all" (11).

All of us recognize the truth in this, although more recently the use of peer response groups and cooperative learning groups has involved more voices in genuine dialogue. However, the perception still exists in many schools that a quiet classroom is a good classroom, that the appropriate role of the teacher is to speak and of the student to listen. This tradition may be linked to more than just respect for authority and for the teacher as the source of knowledge. Unfortunately, as Edwards and Furlong point out, teachers are judged by their ability "to keep [the class's] collective attention on the matter at hand" (12); that is, discipline is very much a part of classroom talk. Because increased student interaction brings with it the threat of loss of control, some teachers prefer to control most of the talk. Edwards and Furlong put it this way: "Teachers usually tell pupils when to talk, what to talk about, when to stop talking, and how well they talked" (14). Or, as Michael Stubbs, another British researcher, noted, "there is a sense in which, in our culture, teaching *is* talking" (12). Research supports this view. In a famous study of classrooms, Flanders learned that in the traditional "chalk and talk" classrooms, teachers talk about 70% of the time (cited in Stubbs 12).

A more contemporary classroom improves upon this ratio. Students are involved in far more talk, both structured by the teacher and more informally. The teacher's role shifts from "dispenser of information" to "facilitator of learning." The curriculum also shifts from teacher-centered to student-centered, as the teacher plans activities in which work is no longer an individual, silent affair. Students interact with one another, in pairs or small groups, to share or pool information, provide feedback, develop material together, and so forth. A truly integrated language arts curriculum, one in which listening, speaking, reading, and writing are part of nearly every lesson, demands student interaction. Although teachers structure such interaction through tasks and stipulation of whether or not students should work in pairs or small groups, for example, teachers thereafter function as consultants. Most teachers "drift" around the room, spot-checking the work underway and relinquishing their traditional role as sole provider and controller of information.

Does this suggest that teachers never lecture or lead discussions? Of course not! In fact, it is critical that we do so, modeling processes and questions that students need to internalize. The issue is one of ratio and balance between teacher talk and student talk. A related concern is that of classroom arrangements that facilitate more student interaction. Straight, orderly rows of desks seldom encourage interaction and genuine exchange. The flexibility to move into circles, pairs, or small groups is an important consideration of classroom space. Similarly, a corner where students can curl up with a book or access a quiet space for quiet work is equally important.

▼ ──

IMPROVING DISCUSSION QUESTIONS

Jane Schaffer candidly appraises her skill as a novice teacher:

> In my earlier days, I remember asking such inane questions as, 'What about the river in *Huckleberry Finn*?' and then becoming irritated when students did not respond. I figured they had not done their homework or were not really trying hard enough. I look at this question now and understand several problems with it. (40)

Consider this basic principle for classroom discussion: Students need to care about the questions. They do not care about questions that are simply a "test" of whether or not they read the assignment, nor do such questions advance their thinking or oral language skills. Too often, questions at the end of textbook selections are useless, mainly because they are minitests of the worst sort: a factual, look in the text and get the answer word for word type of question. Such questions are not only mindless but boring. Mainstream students are accustomed to such questions, but non-mainstream students may be baffled by why teachers want them to answer something they already know. As

Shirley Brice Heath's *Way With Words* illustrated, many cultures don't ask those kinds of questions. We need to figure out what kind of questions will interest students, as well as make sense to them.

Most students respond to questions that relate the material to their own lives. The idea is not to infringe upon their privacy, but rather to link the themes or ideas to adolescence or young adulthood, to contemporary situations. Students also respond to interpretative questions for which they know there is no right or wrong answer when they know that their genuine response counts. At the same time, we can train them to support their responses through reference to the text. This is a critical skill, one most lacking in American students, according to National Assessment of Educational Progress reports in the past decade. An excellent way to make students better respondents to interpretative questions is to train them to write the questions themselves. Schaffer suggests requiring students to address topics they really want to discuss and asking for three questions per student. The teacher then chooses several for discussion, dictates them to the class, and allows students time to think about their responses (40). Allowing time for reflection is another critical feature of good discussions. We often tend to avoid silence and call on the first student to respond, thus cutting off thinking time and recognizing the same students too frequently.

Planned closure is an important feature of good discussion. All of us have experienced classes in which discussion was suddenly cut off in midstream because the class had run out of time. Because we cannot truly recreate the discussion later, it is better to plan for closure. Stopping 5 or 10 minutes before the end of the hour and asking students to summarize, either orally or on paper, is one method. Another is asking them to comment on what they learned during that discussion with specific and well-focused comments. Students might also write one question that had not been answered in the discussion (Schaffer 41). All of these activities require good listening skills. For this reason, we cannot initially expect very complete or very good responses, but they improve with experience and the knowledge that our request is genuine. If we return to Jane Schaffer's question about *Huck Finn*, at this point, we can probably detect her reasons for calling it "inane." Just what *is* wrong with it?

▼ ——————————————————————————————

USING STUDENTS AS TEACHERS

We sometimes underestimate the instructional role our students can play. When this happens, we deny them the opportunity both to hone their conversational skills and to provide leadership, which also enhances their self-esteem. We are not suggesting just "turning them loose," especially if they are working with younger students. Student teachers need some guidelines, both for their own security and for the well-being of the one being tutored. The time initially spent on guidelines and keeping an eye on them, however, yields real benefits for all concerned.

ACROSS GRADE LEVELS

Many middle school students are capable of assisting elementary students with their assignments. Their explanations may be the very ones that bridge the knowledge gap. Similarly, senior high students may be excellent teachers of middle school or elementary students. Students may be chosen for their knowledge and skills in any discipline, not just the English language arts. Students with limited English proficiency especially need opportunities for "school talk."

PEER TUTORING

Within the English language arts class, peers are valuable resources. They can read to one another, ask questions to check comprehension, act as audience and respondent in writing, and teach usage and mechanics.

SMALL GROUP WORK

Within a group, formally or informally, kids can and do teach other kids. Projects that involve cooperation, dialogue, and give and take are important components of a unit. Speaking and listening skills are continually exercised when students must rely on one another to complete the tasks.

▼

TALK AND CULTURAL DIFFERENCES

Differences between students' home language and the school language can be a critical factor in student achievement. As Courtney Cazden, professor of education at Harvard, reminds us: "Ways of talking that seem so natural to one group are experienced as culturally strange to another" (67). School language is, in some ways, strange to all students. It is especially strange to students outside the mainstream culture. We need to be aware of this reality, observe our students, and find ways to facilitate their adaptation to this new culture, the mainstream classroom. Lisa Delpit, a researcher in language and literacy, notes: "All students deserve the right both to develop the linguistic skills they bring to the classroom and to add others to their repertoire" (264). Linguistic skills include not only syntax and grammar but also discourse style and language use. How we ask questions, give directions, listen, and interpret are culturally bound. Understanding new ways of using language will continue to be part of the American classroom for student and teacher alike, as projections for the year 2000 indicate that the minority school-age population will increase to 42% (cited in Duenas Gonzales 16).

▼ ————————————————————————————————————

ORAL LANGUAGE ACTIVITIES FOR ADOLESCENTS

The following activities, developed by experienced teachers and published in professional journals, are intended to serve as stimuli for thinking and discussion. They're not recipes for instant success. Although working out units and lessons is a highly personal affair, reading about them and listening to teachers talk about what has worked well in their classes are important parts of professional growth.

INTERDISCIPLINARY

One of the best ways to ensure that oral language activities are purposeful is to integrate them with content area material. Students both learn the material more thoroughly and practice speaking and listening skills in a focused but varied environment. Nora Elegreet-DeSalvo and Ronald Levitsky developed an interdisciplinary unit for middle school students which could be adapted for any grade level. Working with material from American history, they chose immigration as the unit theme. Students were assigned to fictitious immigrant families who came to America between 1845 and 1915; they chose appropriate surnames and first names and personal roles within the family, the only stipulation being that three generations be represented.

Using factual knowledge about immigrants of representative ethnic groups, students developed their roles. They listened to authentic music and then wrote their own songs of farewell. By watching films, they gained a sensitivity to a historical period, feelings, and so forth. They then chose situations faced by immigrants (e.g., going to a store) and wrote scripts dramatizing the experience. These dramatic sketches were presented to the class. The central question that guided the unit was "What is an American?" Students then moved on to consider new immigrants in America and discussed the issues facing these immigrants and the country.

INTEGRATED LANGUAGE ARTS
Literature

Literary interviews offer students at every curricular level experience in written and oral language. In a model suggested by Terry Johnson and Daphne Louis, students take on the role of a literary character. They are then interviewed by a partner and later by the entire class. Although the first questions are based on story information, additional questions can relate to events not in the actual story but plausible given the plot and characters. In planning, both partners develop the questions to be asked, but they do not rehearse the responses. As Johnson and Louis note, "the keys to success are well thought-out questions and an interviewee who is able to enter into their chosen character" (134). Students need some instruction on interviewing skills. A good way to bring this into the classroom is through use of radio or television interviews, enabling students to formulate criteria through observation and experience.

Some variations on the literary interview are the "mystery guest," the panel interview, and the "stop-action" interview. The mystery guest is someone who wanders into the classroom and is questioned by a co-conspirator at first and then by the class. The panel interview involves several characters from a story. Or one could be inventive and collect characters from different stories who might have some very interesting things to say to one another! The stop-action interview occurs during dramatization of a story. At pre-arranged points, the actors freeze. One of them is "unfrozen" by the interviewer, who poses questions regarding the current situation, other characters, or future plans. The use of this variation, caution Johnson and Louis, should be both infrequent and brief (136). Although written for elementary teachers, Johnson and Louis's text, *Literacy Through Literature,* offers creative activities and ideas for middle level and secondary teachers as well. Making appropriate adaptations from elementary to secondary material, or vice versa, is a vital teacher skill in the English language arts, one well worth developing.

Mary Ellen MacArthur suggests poetry presentations in place of the more traditional written "favorite author" paper. In doing so, she helped students make connections between literature and the arts; at the same time, she provided a context for visual and oral interpretation, as well as for performance. She asked her senior high school students to choose a poem from those studied in American literature and incorporate visual, dramatic, and musical elements, or any combination of the arts, into an oral presentation. Her students responded with slides, videos, computer graphics, cartoons, photos, music, and a variety of props (69–71). This assignment has potential for any grade level and any type of poetry; it also provides students from diverse cultures with a means to explore and present their literary heritage.

Verbal Folklore and American Dialects

Verbal folklore is yet another way for students to present their heritage. Folk speech and naming, proverbs, riddles and other verbal puzzles, and rhymes are one aspect; folk poetry, myths, legends, folk tales, and folk songs are another. Verbal folklore, which includes drama, dances, and games, allows students of all cultures to present their culture and practice oral skills at the same time (Duenas Gonzales 23). All cultures have an oral tradition, but not all have maintained its primacy.

Some students may not be well-versed in their own folklore and may have to do some library work before making an oral presentation.

Oral language activities that promote an understanding of American dialects arise out of literature and the performing arts. Jesse Colquit suggests that teachers begin by reading aloud, introducing students to literature, poetry, music, and drama that reflect dialect differences. Colquit (71–75) recommends the following resources for this purpose:

1. *The Split Cherry Tree* by Jesse Stuart for showing students the beauty of mountain dialect and the diversity of dialect within a single family. Students could role play or do dramatic readings of various passages.
2. James Russell Lowell's "The Courtin'" compared with Robert Frost's "Mending Walls" to illustrate the Northeast dialect of a century ago and today.
3. "Friendly Persuasion" by Jessamyn West, a collection of short stories written in the Quaker dialect.
4. "The Heifer Hide" in *The Jake Tales*, Richard Chase's collection of Appalachian mountain folktales.
5. *Huckleberry Finn*.
6. Ballads and country music for western and southern dialects.
7. For contrasting Black dialect of the 19th and 20th centuries, Paul Lawrence Dunbar's "In the Morning" and Langston Hughes' "The Ballad of the Landlord." Hughes' poetry provides contrasting voices in Black dialect and standard American English.

A school librarian can assist in finding other representative titles for illustrating American dialects.

Storytelling

Storytelling is another oral language activity that works well with students of any age. Lynda Williams, a high school teacher, believes that too many teachers have been afraid to experiment with storytelling, perhaps fearing that the students will think it babyish. In her experience, however, high school students loved listening to stories; what's more, it changed some of their attitudes toward reading, as well as provided good listening practice (36). For this activity, students must come prepared to listen and suspend belief; the teacher must also clue students into listening, perhaps for certain words or concepts, especially if they will be asked to analyze the piece later. The teacher reads first, a selection of only approximately 10 minutes: Simon's death in *Lord of the Flies* or Catherine's death in *Wuthering Heights*. In this way, the teacher models reading performance, which differs from acting. Williams notes that some students may not want to read aloud at first, and that the teacher shouldn't worry about it. What is important is the balance between good oral reading models and experience. Other activities include the use of mystery stories as a way of helping students to make predictions, asking them "whodunit?" or reading a short story to the class and then asking the students to read it individually and note the differences between the oral and silent readings (37).

Using Television

"Students are hungry for serious dialogue about what they see on television," notes Barbra Morris (40). She has therefore devised some activities to turn students from couch potatoes into informed critics. To teach students to be keen listeners and critics, she asks them to keep individual written logs of a program's content. They are to write down as much as they can of what they see and hear, keeping as thorough a record as possible. Although students initially are frustrated, the end results "yield rich first hand evidence" for class discussion of the elements of various programs. They are able to discriminate features of programs and make text analyses, leading them to rediscover what familiar programs actually contain. In Morris' experience, as students listen to one another, they soon "realize superficial, unsubstantiated, or unspecific generalizations are a waste of class time" (36).

VCRs give teachers another method of developing activities to enhance both listening skills and critical thinking. They can tape a variety of programs—the *MacNeil/Lehrer News Hour,* a local newscast, weekend cartoons, a sitcom, a sports event, or a musical event—and then design preview and/or postview questions to elicit thoughtful and critical responses. Programs can be divided into various categories (e.g., sports, news, comedy, drama) and given to pairs or small groups of students, with instructions to design questions or prepare oral summaries for exchange with other pairs or groups. Before giving students these tasks, however, teachers should work through one with the class to model the process.

TRANSFORMING THE TALK SHOW

Most students have seen various talk shows, such as *The Oprah Winfry Show,* and understand the format quite well: prepared questions, ad lib questions, give and take. This format can be easily adapted for use with literature.

Using Slides

Using slides, believes Jack Cameron, promotes visual literacy and focused, genuine discussion. He encourages teachers to create their own collection of slides for the following classroom activities: random reaction to literal or implied information conveyed by the slide (e.g., time of day, clues to season); multisensory reaction to nonvisual details suggested by the picture (e.g., if standing by the photographer, what sounds, smells, textures, and so forth would one experience?); interpretation of the picture in metaphorical terms; interpretation of the picture in terms of the human condition (e.g., who are these people, what is their relationship, and so forth). Cameron notes that students talk freely about issues, "express what has usually gone unexpressed," and, through talk, "make sense of their experience" (14–19). These activities could easily be adapted for writing as well. Students of all ages could develop descriptive sketches, poetry, dramatic monologue, or dialogue for specific slides.

Using Film

Portions of popular films can be used to develop and foster critical viewing and listening skills. Richard Fehlman urges teachers to choose film segments for their complexity and insight—in other words, an artistic text. These could be used in connection with literary texts. By using only segments, teachers can avoid potential problems with censorship; to avoid legal problems, says Fehlman, be certain to "footnote" the segment you are using, just as you would a literary text.

One way to approach this activity is thematically. Self-awareness, for example, is a popular literary and film theme. Fehlman notes the opening scene in *Rocky* as one place to examine this concept, leading to a discussion of the difference between confidence and conceit. Child-parent relationships provide another common and high-interest theme: in *Tender Mercies,* the scenes between Mac and his daughter; in *Ordinary People,* the scenes between Conrad and his mother; in *Cat on a Hot Tin Roof,* the basement scene between Big Daddy and Brick, where attention to the physical setting is critical to understanding the relationship. Adaptations of book to film are another way of using film segments. Fehlman suggests using segments that are similar rather than dissimilar. *To Kill a Mockingbird* offers two: Atticus' summation to the jury and Bob Ewell's attack on the children (84–87). For younger students, *Sounder* provides an interesting view of literary text and film adaptation.

Drama Activities

Johnson and Louis make an important distinction between drama and theatre: "Drama encompasses every person in the room; there is no stage and no audience. Theatre, on the other hand, involves actors and a passive audience" (162). They also advise avoiding any type of "star" system and an emphasis on performance. Drama and mime can be used in connection with a story, with students acting out the events. Alternatively, teachers can introduce students to some of the dramatic situations that arise from the narrative before they read the story themselves. This requires breaking the story into a series of dramatic scenarios to which the students respond. Partner and group work are appropriate here. After students have read the story, they can dramatize actual scenes.

Readers' theatre is a class activity in which students sit in a group and read their parts directly from a script, as though it were a radio production. Neither movement nor memorization of lines is required. Although the activity works well with prepared scripts, Johnson and Louis believe that students are engaged more fully if they begin with a narrative and transform it into a play themselves (166). Teachers prepare students for this activity through modeling the process: Take part of a story and create a play script; ask the class to examine both and note the changes; then take a second part of the story and have the class work on transforming it. Finally, students take another part of the story, work on it in pairs, and eventually exchange their work with another pair of students. Students are expected to provide constructive criticism. After this experience, students could work with a story of their own choosing, either alone or in pairs. Johnson and Louis recommend that teachers go over criteria for story selection first to ensure that students choose a story with ample conversation and several characters (166).

Mask Making, Pantomime, and Improvisation

Although it was written for the elementary level, Bette Bosma's book on using folk literature is a rich resource for teachers of all grade levels. Bosma points out that students "become less inhibited doing pantomime and improvisation when using masks" (56). It isn't that masks hide the student, but rather that the mask facilitates the student's releasing self into the character. Students may use children's stories or turn to Native American or African folklore, in which masks play a significant role. Bosma suggests consulting *Who's in Rabbit's House?* by Verna Aardema, in which Leo and Diane Dillon's illustrations "depict the story as being performed by masked players" (57). Bosma also recommends *Masks, Face Coverings, and Headgear* by Norman Laliberte and A. Mogelon as a resource. After exploring various types of folklore (e.g., myth, fable, legend, fairy tale, folk tale), students could write their own and then create the masks for pantomime or oral presentation.

Puppets

Bosma believes that the "sharply drawn characters of fairy tales and animal tales make wonderful puppets. From the simplest paper bag puppet to the most elaborate papier-maché model, storybook characters can be easily identified by accentuating particular features" (59). For students who have had no experience with puppets, regardless of age, this might be the best way to start. Writing conversation for the puppets, adding background music, and supplying other props can all be handled by the students themselves, with very little teacher guidance. Puppets could be used for various literary pieces, everything from dramatic poetry to *The Canterbury Tales*. Older students could prepare a production for presentation to younger students, either within a school setting or within the community, such as a hospital. It is important to remember that *no* student is too old or too sophisticated for puppetry. Our national love affair with *Sesame Street* and the Muppets should be evidence enough that puppets are for everyone.

▼ _____

EVALUATING ORAL LANGUAGE ACTIVITIES

Teachers are sometimes puzzled about how to evaluate oral language activities. However, when we consider the similarities between oral and written expression delineated earlier in this chapter, we see the potential for evaluation of oral work. Written work can be evaluated through holistic and analytic measures, based on criteria for what is important in a particular piece. Oral activities may be evaluated in the same way. If an oral activity involves too many people for fair judgment of individual work, we always have the option of not assigning a grade. Another option when a number of students are performing simultaneously is to assign less weight to that grade. It is important to remember that we don't grade all the writing students do; we don't need to grade all their oral activities either. Evaluation—letting students know how they are doing—is important, but we shouldn't confuse it with grading, a numerical blip in time. Because peer evaluation is an important means of teaching criteria, critical listening, and judgment, the examples provided here could be used by peers or teacher. The examples were designed by Wisconsin teachers for *Classroom Activities in Listening and Speaking,* a 1991 publication of the Wisconsin Department of Public Instruction.

Although these particular examples focus on performance, the process of developing oral presentations might also be evaluated. Like criteria developed for evaluating the processes of a written text, criteria for development of an oral text may provide students with a more comprehensive view of the process itself. Understanding effective process strategies, along with subsequent opportunities to apply them, benefits students in many ways. Teachers benefit as well because they have a more complete picture of the learning process of individual students.

EXAMPLES USING SCALES
Evaluating Storytelling

Exhibits 2.1 and 2.2 demonstrate two different ways of assigning numerical value. In either case, it is assumed that students are thoroughly familiar with the criteria. Note that the forms allow for peer evaluation.

EXHIBIT 2.1 STORYTELLING EVALUATION FORM—MIDDLE SCHOOL[1]

Storyteller: _____

Story title: _____

Date: _____

1. Vocal delivery

   a. Volume   _____ (10)

   b. Articulation and pronunciation   _____ (10)

   c. Pitch   _____ (10)

   d. Rate   _____ (10)

   e. Quality   _____ (10)

2. Physical delivery

   a. Posture and movement   _____ (10)

   b. Facial expression   _____ (10)

   c. Gestures   _____ (10)

   d. Eye contact   _____ (10)

3. Creativity, story structure, etc.   _____ (10)

                              TOTAL   _____ (100)

4. Comments:

Evaluator: _____

[1]   Wisconsin Department of Public Instruction 1991, 43.

EXHIBIT 2.2 STORYTELLING EVALUATION FORM—HIGH SCHOOL[1]

Student: _____

Evaluator: _____

Date: _____

Scale: 1 = weak 2 = fair 3 = average 4 = good 5 = excellent

Delivery evaluation		*Circle one*		
Stance and movement	1	2	3	4	5
Facial expression	1	2	3	4	5
Gestures	1	2	3	4	5
Eye contact	1	2	3	4	5
Rate	1	2	3	4	5
Pitch	1	2	3	4	5
Quality	1	2	3	4	5
Pronunciation	1	2	3	4	5
Articulation	1	2	3	4	5
General impression	1	2	3	4	5

[1]   Adapted from Allen and McKerrow 191; cited in Wisconsin Department of Public Instruction 1991, 145.

Evaluating Exposition

Just as with written expression, criteria change along with the purpose of the activity. Differences between performance expectations for high school and middle level students also show in the criteria and the scale (Exhibits 2.3 and 2.4).

EXHIBIT 2.3 EVALUATION FORM FOR EXPOSITIONS—HIGH SCHOOL[1]

Speaker: _____

Evaluator: _____

Date: _____

Scale: 5 = excellent   4 = good   3 = average
         2 = needs minor attention   1 = needs major attention

Introduction   *Circle one*

| Showed recognition of speaker's place in the symposium | 5 | 4 | 3 | 2 | 1 |

Served several introductory functions   5   4   3   2   1

Name them: _____

_____

Body

Organized speech in clear pattern   5   4   3   2   1

Name of pattern: _____

Used a variety of verbal supporting materials   5   4   3   2   1

Name them: _____

_____

Presented information clearly   5   4   3   2   1

Made information interesting   5   4   3   2   1

Conclusion

Used a variety of concluding devices   5   4   3   2   1

Name them: _____

_____

Closed on a strong note   5   4   3   2   1

Delivery

Used effective vocal delivery   5   4   3   2   1

Used effective physical delivery   5   4   3   2   1

Comments:

[1]   Wisconsin Department of Public Instruction 1991, 234.

EXHIBIT 2.4 EVALUATION FORM FOR EXPLANATIONS—MIDDLE SCHOOL[1]

Student: _____

Evaluator: _____

Date: _____

	Circle yes or no

Introduction

Partitioned speech into sections   Yes   No

Body

Organized speech in a clear pattern   Yes   No

Name of pattern: _____

Used variety of expository materials   Yes   No

Name them: _____

_____

Made information interesting   Yes   No

Example: _____

Conclusion

Summarized main points   Yes   No

Delivery

Used effective oral delivery   Yes   No
  (varied rate, pitch, force, quality)

Used effective nonverbal delivery   Yes   No
  (eye contact, facial expression, gestures,
  bodily movements)

Comments:

[1]   Wisconsin Department of Public Instruction, 1991, 101.

Evaluating Ritualistic Communication in High School

Ritualistic communication is so "everyday" that we often forget about it. Every time we greet people or pick up the phone, we are involved in it. Although we do not evaluate students on many everyday uses of this communication, we can evaluate them on some rather important skills, such as interviewing. Exhibit 2.5 could easily be part of unit activities.

EXHIBIT 2.5 RADIO INTERVIEW EVALUATION FORM[1]

Evaluator: _____

Date: _____

Directions: Put the name of the student interviewer and interviewee in the blanks below and rate them on the following by circling the appropriate number.

Scale: 5 = always   4 = often   3 = sometimes   2 = seldom
        1 = never

Interviewer: _____

Had interesting introduction	5	4	3	2	1
Asked open-ended questions	5	4	3	2	1
Asked one question at a time	5	4	3	2	1
Wasn't tied to written notes	5	4	3	2	1
Listened to interview, asked follow-up questions, and/or restated answers that weren't clear	5	4	3	2	1
Had creative and interesting conclusion	5	4	3	2	1
Overall radio show was creative and interesting	5	4	3	2	1

Interviewee: _____

Gave complete answers to questions	5	4	3	2	1
Spoke clearly and loudly enough	5	4	3	2	1
Kept a cheerful, pleasant attitude	5	4	3	2	1
Kept a poised body position	5	4	3	2	1
Had good eye contact with interviewer and/or audience	5	4	3	2	1

Name two things you learned about interviewee's topic area:

[1]   Wisconsin Department of Public Instruction, 1991, 186.

DISCUSSION QUESTIONS

1. Consider this piece of writing by an Apache child:

    > Have you ever hurt about baskets?
    > I have, seeing my grandmother weaving
    >   for a long time.
    > Have you ever hurt about work?
    > I have, because my father works too hard
    >   and he tells how he works.
    > Have you ever been hurt about cattle?
    > I have, because my grandfather has been working
    >   on the cattle for a long time.
    > Have you ever hurt about school?
    > I have, because I learned a lot of words
    >   from school.
    > And they are not my words. (qtd. in Cazden 67)

    Speculate on this child's school experience and its connection with oral language. If this child were entering your 8th-grade classroom in the next academic year, what would you do to prepare?

2. Believing that students do need to talk and work with one another, you arrange your classroom and structure their activities differently from your colleagues. How would you prepare your students for purposeful work in this seemingly less structured setting? What would you say to a building principal who questions your methods?

3. Reflect on your own middle/junior high school and senior high school classes: Who talked? How often? For what reasons? Have American schools changed since Flander's 1970 study that documented "teacher talk" as 70% of all talking in the classroom?

SUGGESTED ACTIVITIES

1. Formal speaking activities aside, few English textbooks have devoted much attention to speaking and listening activities. Using texts from the same grade level, review their handling of listening and speaking as major strands in English. Then examine their literature texts. Have the authors included a variety of oral language activities? Does any one of the major speech functions appear to dominate?

2. Choose a piece of young adult fiction and develop oral language activities for your students. Consider both the interactive roles (e.g., pairs, small groups) and activities based on the literature itself. Review the five communicative functions before you begin work on this project.

3. Learn more about informal classroom drama. Then, with some of your classmates, invent and enact a scene.

4. Using a video that would interest teens, develop activities to enhance student listening skills. Be sure to learn more about specific listening skills first. Lundsteen and Galvin are good sources.

5. Work in pairs to consult several resource texts for integrated oral language activities at either the middle school or senior high school level. Choose several activities to present to your classmates, justifying your choices with reference to specific oral language skills that students need to develop or enhance.

6. Bette Bosma's *Fairy Tales, Fables, Legends and Myths: Using Folk Literature in Your Classroom* is a rich resource for creative drama. Although it is primarily a resource for elementary classrooms, its potential for adaptation is worth pursuing. Explore this resource with reference to mask-making, storytelling, reader's theatre, and puppets. Choose one activity and prepare to carry it out with your classmates.

RESOURCES FOR TEACHING ORAL LANGUAGE
General Texts in Listening and Speaking

Chistianbury, Leila, and Patricia P. Kelly. *Questioning: A Path to Critical Thinking.* Urbana: National Council of Teachers of English, 1983.

Devine, Thomas G. *Listening Skills Schoolwide.* Urbana: National Council of Teachers of English, 1982.

Dudley-Marling, Curtis, and Dennis Searle. *When Students Have Time to Talk . . . Creating Contexts for Learning.* Portsmouth: Heinemann, 1991.

Galvin, Kathleen. *Listening by Doing.* Lincolnwood: National Textbook, 1984.

Hynds, Susan, and Donald L. Rubin, eds. *Perspectives on Talk and Learning.* Urbana: National Council of Teachers of English, 1990.

Lundsteen, Sara W. *Listening.* Urbana: National Council of Teachers of English, 1979.

Moffett, James, and Betty Jane Wagner. *Student-Centered Language Arts Curriculum K–13: A Handbook for Teachers.* 4th ed. Boston: Houghton, 1991.

Phalen, Patricia, ed. *Talking to Learn: Classroom Practices in Teaching English.* Vol. 24. Urbana: National Council of Teachers of English, 1989.

Wisconsin Department of Public Instruction. *Classroom Activities in Listening and Speaking.* Madison: Wisconsin Department of Public Instruction, 1991.

Working with Drama

Haseman, Brad, and John O'Toole. *Dramawise.* Portsmouth: Heinemann, 1989.

Kelly, Patricia P., and Warren Self, eds. *Drama in the English Classroom.* Urbana: National Council of Teachers of English, 1989.

O'Neill, Cecily, and Alan Lambert. *Drama Structures: A Practical Handbook for Teachers.* Portsmouth: Heinemann, 1982.

Swartz, Larry. *Dramathemes.* Portsmouth: Heinemann, 1988.

Tarlington, Carole, and Patrick Verriore. *Role Drama: A Teacher's Handbook*. Portsmouth: Heinemann, 1991.

Wisconsin Department of Public Instruction. *Guide to Curriculum Planning in Classroom Drama and Theatre*. Madison: Wisconsin Department of Public Instruction, 1990.

Plays and Other Dramatizations for Adolescents

Barlow, Judith, ed. *Plays by American Women 1900–1930*. New York: Applause, 1985.

Gallo, Don, ed. *Center Stage*. New York: Harper, 1990.

Kohl, Herbert. *Making Theater: Developing Plays with Young People*. Urbana: National Council of Teachers of English, 1988.

Porter, Sue. *Action Packed: 30 Ideas for Drama*. Portsmouth: Heinemann, 1989.

———. *Play It Again: Suggestions for Drama*. Portsmouth: Heinemann, 1989.

Scher, Anna, and Charles Verrall. *Another 100+ Ideas for Drama*. Portsmouth: Heinemann, 1987.

Swortzell, Lowell, ed. *All the World's a Stage*. New York: Delacorte, 1972.

Watts, Irene N. *Just a Minute: Ten Short Plays & Activities for Your Classroom*. Portsmouth: Heinemann, 1991.

Collaborative Work

Golub, Jeff, et al. *Focus on Collaborative Learning*. Urbana: National Council of Teachers of English, 1988.

Hill, Susan, and Tim Hill. *The Collaborative Classroom: A Guide to Co-operative Learning*. Portsmouth: Heinemann, 1990.

Reid, JoAnne, Peter Forrestal, and Jonathan Cook. *Small Group Learning in the Classroom*. Portsmouth: Heinemann, 1990.

Rubin, Donald L., and William M. Dodd. *Talking into Writing*. Urbana: National Council of Teachers of English, 1987.

REFERENCES

Allen, R. R., and Kenneth L. Brown. *Developing Communication Competence in Children*. Skokie: National Textbook, 1976.

Allen, R. R., Kenneth L. Brown, and Joanne Yatvin. *Learning Language Through Communication: A Functional Perspective*. Belmont: Wadsworth, 1986.

Barnes, Douglas. *From Communication to Curriculum*. Harmondsworth, Eng.: Penguin, 1976.

Bosma, Bette. *Fairy Tales, Fables, Legends, and Myths: Using Folk Literature in Your Classroom*. New York: Teachers College Press, 1987.

Cameron, Jack. "Promoting Talk Through 35mm Slides." *English Journal* Sept. 1980: 14–19.

Cazden, Courtney B. *Classroom Discourse*. Portsmouth: Heinemann, 1988.

Colquit, Jesse. "Oral Language Activities for Promoting an Understanding and Appreciation of Dialect Differences." *English Journal* Oct. 1989: 71–75.

Delpit, Lisa D. "Language Diversity and Learning." *Perspectives on Talk and Learning*. Eds. Susan Hynds and Donald Rubin. Urbana: National Council of Teachers of English, 1990. 247–266.

Devine, Thomas. *Listening Skills Schoolwide: Activities and Programs*. Urbana: National Council of Teachers of English, 1982.

Duenas Gonzales, Roseann. "Teaching Mexican American Students to Write: Capitalizing on Culture." *English Journal* Oct. 1982: 20–24.

Edwards, A. D., and V. J. Furlong. *The Language of Teaching: Meaning in Classroom Interaction*. London: Heinemann, 1978.

Elegreet-DeSalvo, Nora, and Ronald Levitsky. "We Left Our Homeland. A Sad, Sad Day: An Interdisciplinary Approach." *English Journal* Oct. 1989: 62–65.

Fehlman, Richard H. "Quoting Films in English Class." *English Journal* Sept. 1987: 84–87.

Fortier, John. "What To Do Until the Doctor Comes: Speech in the English Language Arts Classroom." *Wisconsin English Journal* Jan. 1987: 2–6.

Galvin, Kathleen. *Listening By Doing*. Lincolnwood: National Textbook, 1984.

Heath, Shirley Brice. *Ways With Words: Language, Life, and Work in Communities and Classrooms*. Cambridge: Cambridge UP, 1983.

Johnson, Terry D., and Daphne R. Louis. *Literacy Through Literature*. Portsmouth: Heinemann, 1985.

Laliberte, Norman, and A. Mogelon. *Masks, Face Coverings, and Headgear*. New York: Van Nostrand Reinhold, 1973.

Lundsteen, Sara W. *Listening*. Urbana: National Council of Teachers of English, 1979.

MacArthur, Mary Ellen R. "Poetry's Presentations: That's Entertainment." *English Journal* Apr. 1989: 69–71.

Moffett, James, and Betty Jane Wagner. *Student-Centered Language Arts and Reading K–13: A Handbook for Teachers*. 2nd ed. Boston: Houghton, 1976.

Morris, Barbra S. "The Television Generation: Couch Potatoes or Informed Critics?" *English Journal* Dec. 1989: 35–41.

Schaffer, Jane C. "Improving Discussion Questions: Is Anyone Out There Listening?" *English Journal* Apr. 1989: 40–42.

Stubbs, Michael. *Language, Schools and Classrooms*. London: Methuen, 1972.

Wagner, Betty Jane. "Dramatic Improvisation in the Classroom." *Perspectives on Talk and Learning*. Eds. Susan Hynds and Donald Rubin. Urbana: National Council of Teachers of English, 1990. 195–212.

Williams, Lynda. "Storytelling, Oral Literature or . . . Any Other Name Would Sound So Sweet." *English Journal* Nov. 1982: 36–37.

Wisconsin Department of Public Instruction. *Guide to Curriculum Planning in the English Language Arts*. Madison: Wisconsin Department of Public Instruction, 1986.

———. *Classroom Activities in Speaking and Listening*. Madison: Wisconsin Department of Public Instruction, 1991.

———. *A Guide to Curriculum Planning in Classroom Drama and Theatre*. Madison: Wisconsin Department of Public Instruction, 1990.

Wood, Barbara S., ed. *The Development of Functional Communication Competencies: Pre-K–Grade Six and Grades Seven–Twelve*. 2 vols. Urbana: ERIC Clearinghouse on Reading and Communication Skills, 1977.

CHAPTER 3

Teaching Literature

CHAPTER HIGHLIGHTS
- Background of literature study.
- Response theory.
- Prereading activities.
- Student responses.
- Comprehension.
- Reading activities.
- Vocabulary study.
- Sharing books.
- Evaluating students.

In some measure all of us make up the play as we read it. We have to, in order for it to exist as a literary work at all. (17)

—*Bruce Miller*

▼

READING LITERATURE

The teaching of literature in secondary schools has undergone a dramatic change in the past 10 years. Emphasis has shifted from the text to interactions between text and reader; that is, what the reader brings to the reading is as important as the words in the text. The text provides many possibilities for interpretation. Bruce Miller describes reading as a subjective experience because readers bring their own experiences and knowledge to their understanding of a text (19–20). The research behind the reader response approach, which is based on the interaction between reader and text, has been going on for years, but not until recently has it made an impact in the secondary schools. Although the selection of literature—that is, what literature we choose to have students read—is of concern, teachers acknowledge that the most carefully selected literature does not benefit students if they do not read it. Students also benefit little if they read the selections with no interest or understanding. For students to become lifelong readers, a goal in every curriculum we've seen, they must see reading as an enjoyable activity. As we think of how to help students become lifelong readers, we have two major concerns as educators: How to teach literature and what literature to teach. This chapter looks at the methods of teaching literature and the following chapter deals with literature selection.

▼

BACKGROUND OF LITERATURE STUDY

A brief review of literary analyses can help provide a perspective for teaching literature in secondary schools. Historical criticism—that is, studying literature in the context of the period in which it was written—is a method of learning about literature that has been used since the 1900s. The works are studied in relation to others written during the same period and also compared with those written during other periods. By the 1930s, social criticism, literature studied through its reflection of society, became an important way of gaining insights into the works. The work of both Sigmund Freud and Carl Jung also had a strong impact on the way we examine literature. In these traditional approaches, the work itself is of secondary importance.

New Criticism, begun after World War II, became the dominant system by the 1950s and remains an important influence. New Criticism is concerned only with the work itself and not with the author, period, or social influence. Structuralism and deconstructuralism are based on the same premises—that the meaning and understanding are found in the text itself and that information about the author or social and historical influences have no bearing on the study of literature. It is not within the scope or intent of this text to discuss the various literary critical approaches. Such studies are more appropriate for college literature classes. However, future English teachers do need to consider how these various critical approaches influence and inform the teaching of literature to secondary students.

Literary study in middle and high schools has two major focuses. The first is to help students develop an appreciation and enjoyment of literature. In elementary school, students become familiar with a wide variety of literature and have many opportunities to appreciate different styles, backgrounds, story lines, and genres. Generally speaking, the emphasis is on a subjective analysis. In the higher grades, students are introduced to the use of formal analysis, and literature becomes the *study* of literature. Too often, students receive the impression that what they think and feel about literature no longer counts. In *A Handbook of Critical Approaches to Literature,* the authors explain that they do not see a dilemma between teaching literature by subjective versus formal analysis. Rather, they believe that the "intelligent application of several interpretive techniques can enhance the study of literature" (Guerin et al. 7). However, formal analysis often takes precedence over subjective, creating a rift between the student and the text. In addition, formal analysis can become mired in detail when inappropriately taught to secondary students.

Studying literature too often meant finding hidden meanings in the text. Students assumed that there was "one meaning" and that through careful reading and studying, all readers should arrive at the same understanding of the text, regardless of their own past experiences and knowledge. Most of us have had the experience of coming to an understanding of a text, only to be told that we were mistaken. What the story or poem really meant—the right meaning—was what an authority claimed. A reader's perception, experience, and personality had little to do with the meaning. Such theory established a hierarchy of readers with the renowned critic at the top and the inexperienced student at the bottom. Pedagogy based on this view divides readers into two groups—those who know the right answers and those who don't. For those in the latter group, and there are many, reading is not an enjoyable activity, and so they avoid reading. This approach allows no room for a variety of interpretations, even when readers can back up their interpretations with examples from the text. The experiences and knowledge students bring with them when they read don't count in this kind of literature study; what does count is learning one particular interpretation. If students listen carefully in class, they can even "ace" the exam without reading the text! When there is no personal connection between the text and the reader, students don't have to understand or apply what they read. Reading in this way is a passive activity. With such an arrangement, how can we convince students that reading is a pleasurable activity, one to be enjoyed lifelong? And how can we help students learn formal analysis if they do not first see connections between themselves and the literature?

▼

READER RESPONSE THEORY

The reader response theory is an approach to literature study that stresses the relationship between text and reader. Briefly, students respond to the text after careful reading and develop an understanding of the literature from their own and others' responses. Several scholars and researchers help us understand why the response theory makes sense in the English language arts classroom.

Wolfgang Iser has written extensively about the role of the reader in interpretation. He describes a literary work as having two poles: artistic and aesthetic. The artistic comes from the author in the creation of a work of art and the aesthetic from the reader in response to the art. The meaning of the text is the result of the interaction between the two poles. A meaning is not an absolute value, but a dynamic happening (21). If the meaning is dynamic, it can change from reader to reader or even with multiple readings by the same person. A reader might have a somewhat different interpretation when reading a text for a second time or after learning what the text means to other readers. Iser dismisses the attempts to discover a single hidden meaning in a text as a phase of interpretation that belongs to the past. He believes that we have moved beyond the New Criticism, which focused entirely on the text itself, to a belief that each reader brings to a text a uniqueness that shapes the interpretation. Iser quotes Susan Sontag, "to understand is to interpret"; the understanding comes from the reader, not from any outside source except the text itself (6).

Louise Rosenblatt is the person most responsible for advancing the theory of reader response. More than 50 years ago, Rosenblatt studied the way her students responded to literature, and from her research she developed the transactional approach to teaching literature. Her philosophy parallels Iser's; she believes, "The reader counts for at least as much as the book or poem itself" (vi). The interaction between reader and text creates meaning. The reading becomes a "transaction": The text provides words and ideas; the reader provides the personal response to the words and ideas; and the relationship between the two creates meaning. Teachers of English language arts teach specific human beings with individual hearts and minds "to discover the pleasures and satisfactions of literature." The teacher's job is to help create a relationship between the individual book or play and the individual student (33).

Rosenblatt believes that the human experience presented by literature is the primary reason for reading (7). We read through the lens of our own understanding. The reader "brings to the work personality traits, memories of past events, present needs and preoccupations, a particular mood of the moment . . ." (30–31).

Robert E. Probst, an educator whose work focuses on implementing response theory in the classroom, explains that readers sometimes find that they need to rethink initial conceptions and revise their notions about the text (31). Students must first feel free to deal with their own reactions to the text. Then the teacher creates opportunities for students to share their reactions by asking questions and comparing their reactions with each other in small groups. Creating an atmosphere of security in which students are comfortable with each other is essential (33). Through sharing, students examine their responses and come to a deeper understanding of the text. Rosenblatt believes firmly that readers do not stop with their initial responses, but that those responses lead them to reflection and analysis (75). She does not encourage the "uncritical acceptance of texts" (Probst 35). Teachers must help students assume responsibility for their own understanding of what they read.

▼ _____

IMPLEMENTING THE RESPONSE THEORY
USING FACTUAL INFORMATION

If the connections between reader and text are the most important things to stress in teaching literature, and we believe they are, what do we do with all those literary facts and interpretations we learned in high school and college? Remember learning all about Shakespeare and the Globe theater before reading one of the plays? Rosenblatt describes facts about the author, literary traditions, history of the age, and so forth; as "merely secondary and peripheral," and stresses that such facts are "even distracting or worthless unless it is very clearly seen that they are secondary" (33). We have found that knowing the background information is useful when teaching literature, not as lecture material but as supplemental material that comes up naturally in a discussion or in response to a student's question. Admittedly, keeping all those wonderful bits of knowledge to oneself is difficult, but telling students too much sets up the dichotomy of the teacher as the holder of truth and students as those who know little or nothing. Such an arrangement encourages passive learning. We all remember information better when we either discover it ourselves or acquire it when we actively wonder about it. No matter how wonderful our lecture, if students are not interested, it is wasted effort. Our task, then, is to provide ways to generate interest and to convince students that what they know and feel counts in the English language arts classroom.

WRITING RESPONSES

Students using a reader response method respond in writing as they read. They can write about what the story makes them think about, about a particular word or phrase, or about a feeling evoked by the piece. In short, they can write about anything the text makes them think of, although they may at first have trouble understanding what it is they are "supposed" to write. Students who are not accustomed to responding to literature initially need quite a bit of guidance. Many find it hard to believe that what they think counts, and they try to discover what the teacher wants them to put down. Getting students to trust themselves takes patience on the part of the teacher. The best way to counteract their lack of faith in their own ideas is to comment positively on the little they do write and encourage them to write more by asking questions that draw them out. Little by little, they learn to believe they do have something of significance to say.

In the beginning, questions might provide the structure they need to get started.

1. What characters remind you of someone you know? In what ways do they make you think of the person or people you know?

2. What experiences in the text make you think of ones you have had?

3. What objects make you think of things you have had or places you know about?

4. Perhaps movies or television shows come to mind as you read. Describe the connections. (The connections might be the action or characters or setting.)

5. If you were one of the characters, in what ways would you have reacted similarly or differently?

6. Describe how you feel at the end of the story (or chapter). In what ways does the story seem plausible? If you were the author, what might you want to write differently?

It is important to avoid questions with yes or no answers as much as possible. We want the students to think about what they are reading, to make connections with the text. Yes or no answers are too simplistic, and students either don't see or ignore the "explain your answer" instruction added on.

It is best to keep the list of questions short and ask students to respond to all of them if possible. Too many questions just overwhelm them, whether they are senior high students or middle schoolers. On the other hand, asking them to write whatever comes to mind might be equally difficult. They need some guidance, especially when responding is new to them. As they become more comfortable with this approach, they write more. Some readers go off on a tangent following a thought or feeling the text evoked; they may write pages without referring directly to the text. Others follow the text in detail, commenting on a phrase or idea. Both responses are acceptable, as are all the responses that fall between these two.

What is not acceptable is a lack of a response or something so trite that it is a non-response; for example, "This story is stupid." Talking to the student individually is most helpful. Go over the reading together, asking questions: Is this a part you didn't care for? What did you think about this? How about when the character did this? Often, students worry that their response is what is "stupid" and cover up their feeling of inadequacy by giving flip comments. When people are told repeatedly that their answers are wrong, they need a lot of courage to put themselves on the line again. We have to rebuild trust so that students are willing to commit themselves to expressing an opinion.

For a poem or story short enough to be read in a day, students write responses for the entire work. For longer pieces, the responses are broken up by chapters or whatever students can be expected to read in a day, including class and homework time, because the responses will be used in class.

USING RESPONSES

The responses the students write are an integral part of literature study and may be incorporated into class activities in several ways. Using a variety of approaches is best, partly to keep students interested, but also to achieve different results.

1. *Use responses to improve/spark discussions.* Even if students do nothing with the responses other than write them, their discussion will improve. When students write about literature, they can't help but think more deeply about it. An experience a teacher had illustrates this point. She stepped in for a teacher who had to leave unexpectedly in midday. The class had been assigned to read "Neighbor Rosicky" by Willa Cather. Although their teacher did not use reader response, she asked them to write about the main character for 10 minutes before they discussed the story. Some of the students looked unsure of what was expected, but she suggested they describe the kind of person Rosicky was and whom he reminded them of. After 10 minutes, she asked them to share what they had written, or at least a part of it. They started out slowly, but soon they had a very lively discussion going. They talked to each other as much as to the teacher, and more than one said, "Well, I didn't write this down, but what she (or he) just said made me think of. . . ." Granted "Neighbor Rosicky" is an easy story to respond to, but, on the other hand, the students and the teacher didn't know each other and that always makes discussion difficult. The only difference between the class getting involved or not was the act of writing responses. It allowed students, reluctant to participate, to think through their responses before taking the risk of sharing publicly.

2. *Use responses as a written dialogue among students.* Students write their responses and then form groups of four or five, and each one reads what he or she has written. The teacher tells the students that they can add to their responses after hearing what the others have to say. They do not have to come to a consensus; each individual's responses are respected. Students challenge each other, however, and ask why someone responded in a particular way. When students explain their responses, they have to start with the place in the text that made them think of the event or feeling they recounted. For example, a student might say, "When he walks away from his father and doesn't look back, it made me think of. . . ." or "it made me feel like. . . ." They don't defend their responses, but rather they explain what part of the reading prompted it.

This way of sharing responses accomplishes three things: (1) Students must read with attention; (2) they learn how others think and read; and (3) they find out what others in the class are writing. The latter gives students confidence in their own work. Those who are unsure of themselves discover that their responses are as valid and interesting as anyone else's. Response writing does not depend on academic ability, provided that students are assigned reading they can handle. In the following chapter, we describe ways to accommodate different reading levels in the same class.

Having students write and share responses is an excellent way to keep the students on task for reading. When they meet in groups to share and someone contributes nothing, other students complain. Even students who have not read the assignment often join in the conversation. Although it is obvious they are not prepared, listening to the others talk and adding comments of their own helps them understand the literature at least partially. Sharing responses in groups is far superior to a pop quiz to see if students have done the reading. The quiz method, although widely used, only affirms those who did the reading and lowers the self-esteem of those who did not. Exceptions occur, but most of the time the same students read or do not read the assignments. There is nothing motivating about failing yet another test. One might think a student would read to avoid the embarrassment of failing, but that's not how it works for students who have trouble succeeding in school. They either act out, disrupting the class, or withdraw. Every person should be given opportunities to succeed in school, and setting it up so that the same kids fail repeatedly is truly unfair.

3. *Use responses to create a dialogue between individual students and the teacher.* The responses are handed in, and the teacher writes comments about the responses. These comments are not evaluations, but rather thoughts that occurred when reading what the student wrote. The role of the teacher is similar to that of the students in a peer group, not a voice of authority who declares whether the student is right or wrong. The support provided by the teacher is valuable to students and gives them the sense that what they write is interesting and important. On the other hand, negative evaluations or comments damage the relationship between teacher and student. No one participates easily or works well in a threatening environment.

Students' written responses also provide the teacher with a sense of how well the students understand and enjoy the literature selections. A student's question, "How come we never get to read a happy ending?" made one teacher realize the need to read something a little more lighthearted for a change. Even if they don't comment directly, it is not difficult to tell if they are interested in what they read. Also, the dialogue provides an opportunity to encourage students to respond more fully to the text. Questions can help students expand on what they wrote. For example:

- "I would like to hear more about when you. . . ."
- "Your comment about Maya made me think of how I felt when. . . ."

- "What happened after (whatever is appropriate)?"
- "I can really understand how you felt. Have your feelings changed at all now?"

Any comment that supports and encourages is appropriate. Teachers get to know students better and students get to know teachers better as both share their thoughts and feelings about literature.

4. *Use responses as a source of discussion questions for the whole class.* As teachers read the students' responses, they keep notes on issues that are raised and disagreements that students have on motivations of characters, the plot movement, and so forth. It is amazing how different students' reactions can be, and these differences are springboards for discussion. The teacher acts as a moderator, keeping the discussion focused on the text and perhaps playing devil's advocate if students seem too willing to accept an idea. The teacher is not the last word on who is right or wrong. Encouraging a variety of interpretations helps students think for themselves.

5. *Encourage students to use responses when they write papers based on the literature.* As students look through their responses, they can find patterns or themes that suggest writing topics. Going back to the text for a second reading adds detail and substance to the points they want to make. Because the focus for their papers comes from their own responses, their interest is high and they have a personal stake in writing a convincing paper. The bonus for a teacher is that these papers are much more interesting to read than those in which the topic is not student-selected.

The uses of responses are not mutually exclusive; they can be used in any combination. In fact, it is a good idea to vary activities based on responses. We all become tired of the same routine after a while, and the benefits decrease. The point of reader response is that students' thoughts and feelings about what they read are validated in their study of literature.

▼
COMPREHENSION

Recent research studies have focused on how to implement reader response in secondary classrooms. The most difficult part for teachers, as they change over to this approach, is to give up their study guides. Teachers fear that they won't know whether the students are comprehending the material if they are not required to answer specific teacher-made questions.

Frank Smith, in *Comprehension and Learning,* describes comprehension as "making sense of information" (10). Students comprehend what teachers want them to know when the new information meshes with what they already know. If the new knowledge is completely foreign to their previous experience, it is very difficult for them to comprehend. The better we can integrate new information with prior knowledge, the easier it is not only to learn in the first place but also to remember (71). When a teacher asks a student, "Don't you see what the author is trying to say?" he or she probably is asking, "Why can't you locate the same kind of information that I do?" (107). Actually, both questions are based on the assumption of predetermined meanings that students are supposed to discover, without taking into account their individual responses. When teachers, through reader response, help students connect the text with their own experiences, comprehension is an easier goal to attain. The new information students discover is, right from the beginning, related to their prior knowledge.

The concern about discarding study guides is a legitimate one for teachers. We want students to know certain information about the text. However, there is a much better way to arrive at the same goal—better because it is not just busy work for a student but comes from discussing the work with others in the class. First, teachers are surprised at the amount of information that comes up without teacher intervention in discussions based on the students' responses. The students' wide-ranging interests and knowledge touch on most of the points found in a teacher-prepared study guide. A teacher who takes notes on students discussions knows what is covered and what is not. For example, if the text is *No Promises in the Wind* by Irene Hunt and the setting of the Depression never comes up, a teacher might ask during the discussion, "Does it make a difference when the novel took place?" There is no right or wrong answer to this; the father's behavior might be the same today if he were out of work. The story focuses more on father-son relationships than on the Depression, but some students and teachers believe the novel is basically a way to learn about the 1930s. Who is to say what is the correct reading? But through such a discussion it becomes clear that the setting is the Depression Era, and students remember that much longer when the information comes from people arguing whether the setting makes a difference to the reading of the novel than from filling in a blank on a worksheet answering, "What is the setting of the novel?" Teacher-posed questions should rarely have one factual answer, but rather should be couched in "What do you think?" terms. Knowledge arrived at through discussion fits Frank Smith's definition of comprehension.

▼
―――――――――――――――――――――――――――――

FORMAL ANALYSES

We have emphasized reader response theory because we strongly believe that this approach achieves the desired results with secondary students. Furthermore, without connections between reader and text, further analysis has limited effect. However, this is not to say that no other critical analysis is appropriate. A variety of approaches can be used, depending on the developmental stages of our students and on the literature being read. A combination of critical analyses works best. Reader response itself requires close reading of a text when students search for the connections between their responses and the text itself. Close reading is also the mainstay of New Criticism. A reader's responses should lead to interpretation of the text.

Simmons and Deluzain, in *Teaching Literature in Middle and Secondary Grades,* emphasize that older students need to move beyond only an appreciation of literature to understanding of implied meanings, structure, and form. However, teachers must be careful not to emphasize information about the text over the text itself. Often the best approach is a matter of degree. We mentioned earlier that extensive information about Shakespeare's time is not appropriate for study before reading the play itself, but ignoring the historical implications of a plot during the process of reading is not appropriate either.

Some historical or biographical information about the life and times of the author or a major fictional character helps the reader to understand what is happening. For example, Dickens' *Tale of Two Cities* requires background information while students are in the process of reading, but the information must be kept in perspective: One wouldn't read the book in order to learn about the French Revolution. The social implications of an author's intentions help students understand Steinbeck's *Grapes of Wrath* or Stowe's *Uncle Tom's Cabin.*

Archetypal approaches help students understand the use of motifs, themes, and stereotypes throughout literature. If English teachers follow the advice of Edward Corbett to use external factors only insofar as they help in understanding the works and draw on approaches that best fit the particular text, students are not overwhelmed by the study of literature (Guerin 297). The important point is that we are teaching students, not books.

▼ _____

PREREADING ACTIVITIES

Generating interest may involve discussing some of the themes in a story or novel before the students read it. Contrary to what many students believe, there are many themes in a literary work, especially in the longer pieces. For example, *To Kill a Mockingbird* has several strong themes: a father's relationship with his children, growing up, prejudice against blacks, and fear of people different from ourselves. The themes a teacher decides to focus on depend on the age and literary experience of the students. Whatever theme we choose for the focus of study, several resources can provide ideas for generating interest as a prereading activity. *Literature—News That Stays News* is an example of such a resource, and the examples that follow are student suggestions from this text.

a. *Lord of the Flies.* Students do impromptu writing on "What I would do if I were leader of a group stranded on an island." The following day students share and discuss what they wrote. The teacher encourages the students to compare their own ideas with those in the novel they are about to read (Jane Beem 3–6).

b. "Young Goodman Brown." Students close their eyes and imagine they are in the world's most peaceful setting. They write down as many details as possible, using all of their senses. Then they are to imagine the most terrifying place and describe it in writing. The responses are grouped on a chart and discussed. The discussion helps students to see the similarities in their images, and this helps them to understand the images in Hawthorne's story (Evelyn Farbman 38–41).

c. *Romeo and Juliet.* The work is introduced with a brainstorming session in which the teacher asks students questions like "What makes people fall in love?" and "What makes people fight?" Responses are encouraged, and the session ends with questions that lead into the actual reading. For example, "Do people ever decide whom they are going to love or how much they are going to fall in love?" Students keep their notes and refer to them as they read (Jim Christ 66–69).

d. The following activity is from *Structuring Reading Activities for English Classes:* "The Great All-American Cross Country Motorcycle Run" is designed for the "Prologue" to *Canterbury Tales* (11). Before students begin reading the "Prologue," the teacher describes an imaginary present-day trek on motorcycles and then hands out pictures of interesting people who want to participate in the trek. Pictures from *National Geographic* work well. Tape them on brightly colored cardboard, and give one picture to each group of students. Group members write an application letter for their participant. Each letter is read to the class, and students discuss what kinds of problems the travelers might have on the trip, how they could entertain themselves, and which travelers would get along with others and which would not.

   The scenario can be something like this: They are going to Colorado to see, for one last time, a beautiful river that will soon be destroyed by a dam project. One student group (Kimberly Paap, Jennifer Ulesick, Colleen Ahern) wrote:

> Dear Sirs:
>
> Momma Mia! When I heard about the trip I knew this is what my late wife, Maria, would have wanted me to do. Being the owner of Anthony's Fish Market, I am aware of the importance of the wildlife of the river and would truly appreciate one last look at this environment.
>
> I would definitely enjoy spending time with a group of people. I have a large group of friends in the old neighborhood and am known as "the entertainer." I acquired this nick-name from my talent as an accordion player and group comedian.
>
> I still have my motorcycle from the old country, the one Maria and I rode around the country on when we were first married. This would be like a second honeymoon for me and my late Maria—although a little less romantic.
>
> Sincerely,
> Anthony "Tony" Rossel

e. The teacher may ask the students before they begin reading *All Together Now*, "What are the characteristics of a good friend?" The responses are listed on the board as the class brainstorms what friendship means. Then students write about the most unusual friendship they have had. Students share these and discuss the responsibilities of friendship. This theme is only one of several in the novel. The prereading activity becomes a springboard for later discussions.

In general, prereading activities generate interest in reading the text, rather than provide factual information as "background." That's not to say that some of the activities wouldn't be related to background, particularly a historical period. However, the discussions are always student-centered and are not lectures. The teacher phrases questions to increase student participation and makes references to earlier discussions to strengthen the connections between readers and their responses.

▼ _____

READING ACTIVITIES

Assignments related to the text and given throughout the time students are engaged in reading add interest and understanding. Some activities come from the responses the students write, whereas others are not directly related to responses. However, the responses always help students with assignments related to the text because of the closer connections they have with characters, motivations, and outcomes. Activities that link the text with the reader's understanding help to heighten interest.

Activities from *All Together Now* provide an example of connections between text and experience. The main character is 12-year-old Casey, who is spending the summer with her grandparents. Her father is fighting in the Korean War and her mother is working at two jobs, leaving little time to spend with her daughter. The story focuses on Casey's relationships throughout the summer.

1. After reading the description of Hazard in chapter 2, describe in your response journal your impression of him. Whom does he remind you of?

2. Casey allows Dwayne to assume that she is a boy. What is her motivation? Describe a time when you told a lie for similar reasons. Assume you were caught in the lie. Write a persuasive letter explaining your reasons for telling the lie and why you should be excused from blame.

3. In chapter 8, Dwayne gives Casey a gift that means a lot to her. Why is it so significant? Write about a gift you received that was special and explain why it meant so much to you.

4. Pansy and Hazard's honeymoon was not a happy experience. What values and expectations did each have that got in the way of their happiness?

5.   In chapter 11 Marge blows up at Dwayne. What words and images are used to describe Dwayne's feelings? Write about a personal experience when you felt much the same as Dwayne did.

6.   Describe your impression of Gwen when you first meet her in chapter 6. Trace the development of her character throughout the novel, taking notes as you read. Reread your notes and describe how your impression of her changed, using passages from the text to explain.

7.   Casey is angry because Dwayne has to spend the night in jail, and she feels that the adults have let her down. Describe a time when you felt that parents or friends let you down. Could the situation have turned out differently? Describe a time when you felt that you let someone down.

8.   Point of view is a strong influence on our opinions of others. Write a description of yourself or someone you know very well; then write how someone else might view that person.

9.   By the end of the novel, Casey has learned much about responsibility and love. Describe the changes she has gone through and the results of those changes, using passages that illustrate significant learning experiences for Casey (Maxwell 7–8).

Teachers can create many different activities for their students. The following illustrations show the possible variety and scope:

1.   Kurt Lothe, a high school student, wrote an article describing the activity his English teacher, Mr. Mead, had the class do for *Crime and Punishment*. He suggested that they turn the story into a musical rather than write the usual paper. The students organized committees and over the next few days worked on dialogue, created scenes, and wrote lyrics. They rewrote some of the scenes to add humor to the story. Showtime was in two weeks. Kurt explains, "What began as an alternative to another paper turned into one of the most memorable things I have done in my high school career. Not only does a musical like this provide an escape from the daily routine of the classroom, but it allows one to explore a character's feelings and emotions that reading alone cannot accomplish" (76–77).

2.   Vicki L. Olson describes several activities for *The Cay*, by Theodore Taylor. As students began reading, she had them write predictions to help get them involved in the book. Then students listed three or four things that could happen to Philip and his family now that the Germans had attacked Aruba and brought war to the Caribbean. Students wrote predictions on the chances of Philip and his mother making it to Miami. Then students meet in groups to share their predictions and the reasons behind them, later sharing with the large group.

Having students write predictions can be used at any grade level and for just about any reading. It is a way of connecting with the text. There is not a right or wrong answer but students have to defend their ideas by explaining the evidence on which they built the prediction.

3. Don Gallo suggests a classroom activity useful with a variety of stories and novels. Choose a key character from the text. Choose one major problem that character has. Write a letter that your character might write about that problem to Dear Abby. When the writing is finished, place all the letters in a pile. Each student selects a letter and writes a response to the problem as Abby might answer. This works well with a serious novel like *Sophie's Choice* or *Death of a Salesman,* but also with a humorous story like "The Secret Life of Walter Mitty."

4. Assignments can build toward an activity that is to be completed after the literature is read. Karen Cooke, an English education student, devised assignments for "Neighbor Rosicky" by Willa Cather that created the background for such an activity.

    a. Before assigning "Neighbor Rosicky," read the poem "Choices" by Nikki Giovanni. Have students write a response to the poem in their journals. They can explain what the poem meant to them or what it made them think of while they were listening.

    b. In their journal, students write a poem about either their best friend or someone they value highly. They are encouraged to share their poems with the rest of the class or in small groups.

    c. In their journals students write what they feel the word *neighbor* means. They discuss their responses in small groups.

    d. After reading "Neighbor Rosicky," students write a short paper about why they think Cather titled the story "Neighbor Rosicky" instead of "Mr. Rosicky." Why was he considered a neighbor? (This is not to be evaluated as a formal paper.)

    e. Backed up with examples from the story, the students write what they think was of most value to Rosicky.

    f. The teacher divides the class into groups. The groups are the directors and producers for a film based on "Neighbor Rosicky." They use film and TV stars to cast their roles. Then they write a brief description of each character and give the reasons for their casting selections.

    g. The final assignment is writing a biography of Rosicky, using facts and inferences gleaned from the reading.

Teaching units that use many kinds of literature are discussed in the chapter on developing units. Here we provide one example of teaching a literature selection using an approach that incorporates reader response. The activities tap experiences and knowledge the students have and connect them with the text. *Romeo and Juliet* could become the basis for a unit that includes other literature selections. Barbara Dressler, a high school English teacher, wrote the following three-week unit for teaching *Romeo and Juliet:* Students read the play aloud during class time. Frequent stops are made to clarify any questions that arise from the language and vocabulary differences. Then students listen to audio tapes of parts of certain acts to become familiar with the Shakespearean language style. After reading each act, a videotape of parts or all of that act is shown. Following the videotape viewing, students work in small groups to outline the act. Writing activities follow this group work.

SMALL GROUP WORK

Students are divided into groups according to their choice of a minor character in the play (Paris, Tybalt, Mercutio, Lord and Lady Capulet, Friar Laurence, the Nurse, and so on). The groups discuss the traits of the character and how he or she influences the course of the play. Groups then report to the entire class.

WRITING ASSIGNMENTS GIVEN TO STUDENTS
Act One

1. As Juliet, write a letter to a friend telling how you met and fell in love with Romeo.
2. As Romeo, write a letter to a friend telling about your new love and explaining why you've forgotten Rosaline.
3. As Benvolio, write an explanation of how and why you want to help your lovesick friend, Romeo.
4. As an attendant of the Prince, write a description of the street fight.

Act Two

1. Write a description of Friar Laurence. Tell why Romeo turns to him for help.
2. Write Tybalt's letter to Romeo.
3. Write a description of scene 4 through the eyes of Peter.

Act Three

1. Imagine Juliet has asked you for advice. Write her a letter telling her what you think she should do at this time.
2. As the Prince, dictate a letter to your secretary explaining your banishment of Romeo.
3. Write a speech for Lord Capulet to give at Juliet's wedding.

Act Four

1. Write what Lady Capulet would say if she discovered that Juliet was planning to take the potion.

2. Write what Lord Capulet would say if he discovered that Juliet was planning to take the potion.

3. Write a letter from Friar Laurence to Romeo.

Act Five

1. As the page, tell what happened between Paris and Romeo.

2. Write a persuasive speech Friar Laurence could use to try to convince Juliet to leave the tomb with him.

3. As Friar Laurence, explain your involvement in this affair to your superior.

After reading and discussing the entire play, students select from the following assignments:

1. Using the play's prologue as a model, write an original epilogue for *Romeo and Juliet*.

2. As Romeo or Juliet, write a diary entry for each of the five days of the play.

3. As Juliet, write two letters to an advice columnist. As the columnist, write a letter in reply to each of them.

4. Rewrite the ending of the play as it would have been if Friar John had not been quarantined but was able to deliver the message to Romeo.

5. Write a front page news article that could appear in the newspaper the day after Romeo and Juliet were found dead.

There are many assignments a teacher can use for any literature. The important thing to remember is that the assignments occur throughout the reading; in longer works this is essential. The activities should be designed for individual work, small groups, and the entire class. Discussion is vital to provide students with opportunities to interact and discover what others are thinking and writing.

▼

TEACHING POETRY

Activities for poetry follow the same guidelines as those described for short stories and novels. Students' reactions are often a feeling of "I don't get it" when reading poetry, as if there is a hidden meaning. Student responses are as valid with poetry as with other types of literature, and the same general guidelines are appropriate. Poetry is meant to be heard. When teachers share a poem with students, it is important to read the poem aloud as they follow along with a printed copy. The teacher asks them to allow their minds to react to the words, letting thoughts flow freely, and not to think about what the poem "means."

Students then write down responses without talking to anyone else. A teacher may want to provide suggestions if students have difficulty responding.

- What images do I see as I hear the poem?
- What do the words remind me of?
- What feelings have I had that are similar to the ones expressed in the poem?

Students compare their responses and discuss the similarities and differences. Poetry, more than prose, elicits widely different comments. The classic example in Rosenblatt's work elicited two opposing views when students reacted to Theodore Roethke's "Papa's Waltz." One group believed the poem represents a joyful romp of a father with his son, whereas others saw it as the father's abusive behavior, probably caused by alcohol. The differences arise out of the different background experiences of the students. Also, many young women believe the father is dancing with a daughter, and images of themselves as small children come back strongly. Both views are correct, and students can point to specific examples in the poem to back up their interpretations.

One of the problems with teaching poetry is that students often have had little experience with poetry since elementary grades. Moreover, it is usually taught in a separate unit pulled out of the regular context of literature. If students become more familiar with a wide variety of poetry, responding to it becomes easier. Poetry is best taught throughout all thematic units, and regardless of the day's activity, one should try to read a poem to the students every day, not to "study" it, but to enjoy it.

▼
VOCABULARY STUDY IN READING

Vocabulary study has several purposes, and how we teach vocabulary depends on the specific purpose. Teaching reading vocabulary does not require pronunciation or spelling. Spelling has nothing to do with speaking and listening and very little with reading. Pronunciation is important only when speaking, and further, we know the meanings of many words that we neither speak nor write.

Vocabulary study in reading has two purposes: to learn the meanings so the present text can be understood and to increase reading vocabulary so that meanings in future texts will be understood. It is important to realize that none of us needs to know the meaning of every word to comprehend what we read. Without thinking about it, we skip over many words when we read, inferring the meaning from the context. To stop and look up each word slows a reader down so much that he or she loses interest. Occasionally, readers might write down words they don't know, but they keep right on reading and look them up later. The reason for doing this is a love of words, not a need to understand the story better.

Words are never to be taken out of context, either for learning or for testing. We know how important context is in figuring out meaning, and it goes against all common sense to give students a list of words to learn and ask them to look the words up in a dictionary and use each in a sentence. To illustrate, a teacher assigned a list of words from a short story by Poe, and a very competent student looked up the word *dank*. Learning that it meant moist, she wrote, "My, these brownies are dank." When the teacher explained the connotation to her, she thought it so funny that she shared it with the rest of the class. After that, every time they ate brownies someone would say, "Mmmmmm, good—so dank." Although that turned out to be a shared joke, the teacher learned that students must have context to understand connotations and she never gave them words in isolation again.

Another experience involved a student who struggled with reading. While taking a vocabulary test he commented that the teacher forgot to include the meaning of a particular word. The test was one in which students were to match words to appropriate meanings. As she looked at the paper the teacher could see the meaning he was supposed to choose; of course, she wrote the test and knew all the answers. She asked him what he thought the word meant, and in his own words he gave a very reasonable definition. The teacher told him that she had forgotten to include that meaning and wrote it on his paper. Many students could generalize the meaning supplied for the test and come up with the "right" answer, but she was penalizing the ones who could not. Yet, these students did know what the word meant. The tests were more "guess what meaning the teacher has in mind" than tests of vocabulary knowledge.

Because words must remain in context, one way to identify those the teacher has chosen for study is to give the line and page number of each word. Another method is to reprint the sentence or part of the sentence on a handout. For example: "He usually agreed with her in earlier years, sometimes grudgingly, but without *rancor*" (from *No Promises in the Wind*). The directions ask students to write what *rancor* means in the context. To help them use context, they first write what they think the word means, and if they are unsure or just want to check, they look it up in a dictionary. The students meet in groups to go over the meanings, and this is usually where the dictionaries are used to solve arguments.

If a teacher wants to test students on reading vocabulary, the same sentences appear in the test as were on the handout, perhaps in different order. In their own words, students write the meaning as used in that sentence. Spelling should not be evaluated, nor do students need to write complete sentences because that is not what is being tested. Rather, teachers look for accurate meanings of the words in the context in which they appeared in the text. Grading time is minimal, guessing doesn't help students, and the test is true to the principle that context provides clues for word meanings.

Many times words in the text are esoteric or specialized, such as foreign phrases or words that are not commonly used, and students need not remember them beyond the passage they are reading. For these words, a teacher can simply tell the students the meaning.

▼

SHARING BOOKS

This section might be called Book Reports except that we are strongly opposed to them, at least as they are generally used. Having students fill out a book report form or follow a particular format wastes the teacher's and the students' time. When asked why they require the reports, teachers usually respond, "So I will know if the students are reading." Ironically, book reports won't provide that information. It is too easy to write a report without actually reading the book, which makes it difficult to know who reads and who doesn't. And book reports are boring. Teachers try to make them more interesting by providing options to the standard report, but generally the options, although more fun to do, can also be done without reading. There is no way teachers can be sure students actually read the books except by asking, and the students are surprisingly honest.

Sharing books, however, is a vital part of a literature class. Most of us like to read; after all, teaching English is our chosen field. When we read something we especially enjoy, we try to think of someone who would also like it. Friends and family pass books around, usually with the comment, "You have to read this! You'll love it." We can replicate that enthusiasm in the classroom if we provide the opportunities.

Students pay attention to what other students read, which can be frustrating for a teacher who spends a lot of time suggesting books to a student who ignores the advice and chooses a book a classmate casually recommends. The solution is to structure time so that students can share, and this can be done in various ways.

The most informal, and often the most successful way, is setting aside part of a period to talk about books. Students know ahead of time when this will be, but they do not have to prepare anything. Not everyone has to talk about a book, although everyone is encouraged to do so. Some share information about a magazine article they read, which is fine. The requirement is that it must be reading material rather than a TV show. The teacher, too, shares reading of interest to the students. The discussions are casual, and students stay seated when sharing. Students show high interest in the discussions; questions and conversations are common.

One time in a book-sharing session, one of the students walked out of the room. A few minutes later he reappeared with a book under his arm. When the teacher asked where he had gone, he explained that he had gone to check out the book one of his classmates was talking about. He said, "If I waited until class was over, I was afraid someone else would get it before me." Such eagerness to read is precisely the objective of book sharing.

A more structured way to create book-sharing time is for students to form groups based on the type of book they read. After students select the book they want to read, they jot down the type (e.g., biography, mystery, adventure), and the teacher forms the groups, so that the mystery buffs talk about mysteries together, the biography readers talk together, and so on. Readers with a strong liking for one type of book enjoy talking to others who share their reading tastes. This is especially true of science fiction fans, but everyone likes to share a common interest. The students meet in groups after they read the books. This grouping is appropriate only once in a while because, of course, we want to increase the variety of books students read as well as give them a chance to talk about their favorites, but interest groups are very popular with students and they increase reading enjoyment.

As a spin-off on the interest grouping, each group can create a skit involving characters from the books each student read. Students perform the skits for the class live, although it is a good idea to videotape them and have them available on Parent's Night. We've had talk shows with characters across historical times and from different fields; in one Joan of Arc and Einstein held a discussion about responsibility in making the world a better place. Another time students dressed in gym clothes dribbled and passed a basketball around while discussing feats of the various sports figures they had read about. Admittedly, students could do these activities without reading the whole book, but the activities provide opportunities for informal dramatics and are based on literature and so are well worth the class time.

Another way to share books is to keep a card file in the room with student-written summaries and other information about books they have read. They include their name so others can ask more about the book if they care to. Many of the students use this source instead of browsing in the library when looking for a book to read. This also provides a way for shy students, who may be reluctant to speak in class, to share their reading.

At the end of the year, all the students write a paragraph about a book they would highly recommend for others to read over the summer. Every student goes home for the summer with a copy of all the book descriptions. A middle-school student (D. Stevens) wrote:

> *Lord of the Flies* by William Golding
> When they land the boys are overjoyed to have no grownups. But soon work has to be done: the fire kept burning, the huts built, the hunting done. There is Piggy. He is fat and very grownup. He knows how to do things but the crowd rejects him. He gets killed by a rolling rock that cracks his skull open. Ralph is the "leader" because he blew the conch first. On the other hand, Jack, though he doesn't know at first, is bloodthirsty!

To increase reading enjoyment and move toward the goal of creating life-long readers, reading and talking about books must become an integral part of the class. Groups work well because they focus the activity, but talking about books needs to be a common, almost daily, activity. Teachers can encourage this by talking about books they themselves read. At first, students may seem surprised that teachers know about, let alone read, romance novels, Stephen King, or any contemporary popular authors. The same is true about magazine articles. When teachers first share articles from *Road Rider* or *Rolling Stone,* they may be met with a few looks of disbelief, but students do begin to talk more freely about what they read. Book sharing increases enjoyment in reading and makes the goal of helping students become lifelong readers more attainable.

▼
EVALUATING STUDENTS

Using reader response for literature study invalidates true/flase, multiple choice, and even short-answer tests. This does not mean that we cannot evaluate students' knowledge and understanding of literature, but it does mean we must make sure we truly test their knowledge and not force them to guess what the teacher is thinking.

In "Testing Literature: The Current State of Affairs," Alan C. Purves summarizes a longer report of a study funded by the U.S. Department of Education. Tests published for secondary school students are, for the most part, multiple-choice questions that focus on comprehension at a relatively low level of understanding. The questions are based on the meaning of specific parts or the main idea of a passage. The questions test literature as if it were the same as articles in encyclopedias or research papers. Little attention is paid to artistic characteristics of literature such as language, structure, and point of view. Purves' report is a strong deterrent to purchased tests and encourages teachers to create their own method of evaluation.

We can achieve this in several ways. First, not all assignments should be graded. For instance, response writing is checked only for the effort the student made in reading and responding. The same is true for journal writing, even if the assignments are fairly specific. Length is not an accurate measure of the effort, but the involvement of a reader with the text is clear to a teacher.

Discussion is another important area of literature study. However, keeping track of who answers questions in class is a very tricky business and an unreliable way to assess interest and involvement. Some teachers believe that noting when students respond to a question motivates discussion, and on occasion that may indeed be the case. The danger is that only the high-achieving students will care about the discussion grade. Also, some shy students find it very difficult to talk in class, and it would be wrong to penalize them. Responses and discussions are crucial to active class participation, but they are informal activities that do not need to be evaluated with a grade.

Many of the reading activities that teachers assign can be graded on a more formal basis, but a teacher should be very clear about the purpose of the assignment and grade accordingly. For instance, if the activity is to write down characteristics that will help readers to understand character's motives, the evaluation should focus on whether the student described the characteristics. Teachers too often grade all activities alike, even though the purposes are quite different. They may count spelling, punctuation, and grammar, for example, even though the assignment was to discuss viewpoint. The levels of writing described in the chapter on evaluating composition clarify the connection between purpose and evaluation.

Over the span of time that students are reading a text, the teacher may use questions as a way of helping with understanding. Students often answer questions as homework assignments, then discuss their answers and hand them in the following day. Questions, of course, depend on the literature, but as a guide, one might use questions something like these:

- What factors influenced the actions of the characters?
- How did relationships between people influence actions?
- Why do you approve or disapprove of a character's action?
- Why would they behave the way they do?
- In what ways are their actions realistic or unrealistic?

Answers vary, but a teacher can tell if a student has read the material and is answering in a way that is true to the text. Because these are more formal than responses, they are graded more formally. A point system works well, such as five points for each question; the total score rather than a letter grade goes on the paper. Using points more clearly specifies acceptable and unacceptable answers for each question rather than assigning a grade for the work as a whole.

A more formal evaluation is the essay exam. New teachers are tempted to use a test someone else wrote, either another teacher or a publishing company. However, students do not always understand the questions even if they did understand the novel. The exams do not necessarily test what was covered in class; if a teacher plans to use the exam and be fair to the students, he or she must teach test material, whether it seems appropriate or not. Ready-made tests cannot reflect the dynamics of the classroom discussions and learning. Short-answer, true/false, and matching questions all test lower-level comprehension, and that is not what we want to test. We want to see if students grasp connections between ideas, make inferences about motivations and outcomes, analyze points of view, and judge a work on its effectiveness; in other words, we want to test higher-order thinking.

Teachers often express two objections to essay exams. First, some have the notion that the evaluation of essay answers is not objective. On a multiple choice or true/false question, the answer is either right or wrong; the teacher needs only to count up the number of correct answers and convert that number to a grade: 80 percent right is a B, 90 percent an A. Something about numbers makes us believe we are being objective and therefore fair. However, the test itself is subjective and unfair, even though one can count correct responses. It is very difficult, if not impossible, to write multiple choice, true/false, and matching questions that are not misleading. Short-answer questions test recall, the lowest level of critical thinking. When teachers or unknown test makers create a test, they make decisions about what is important for students to remember and learn. That's where the subjectivity comes in. By giving students more latitude in explaining what they know and understand, we give them a more objective test.

The second objection is that an essay exam takes longer to grade than an op-scan sheet or short-answer test. The extra time is not excessive, however. As teachers read the answers, they have a clear idea of what they are looking for, even though it may be expressed in a variety of ways. It is best to evaluate one question at a time on all the students' exams. That way teachers get a good idea of how the responses compare in development of ideas, detail, and examples. They should shuffle the papers before reading the next question to balance the influences of preceding paper answers. Several studies have shown that when we read a very strong essay and then one not as good, the second one suffers by comparison. Also, the 20th answer will probably seem less wonderful than the second, even though they are similar. Although it does take time to read essay exams, they promote learning and provide opportunities for students to express ideas in their own words, making them well worth the time.

It is important to remember that students write the exams in class, where time and test anxiety are factors, and students may not use correct punctuation or spelling. Therefore, it is inappropriate to take these skills into account when evaluating exams. We are looking for understanding of the literature, and that is all we need to pay attention to. When one is concentrating on thinking, one can misspell the most common word. There are occasions when mechanics are important, but not in a testing situation.

Evaluation can take many forms besides an exam. Teachers often require papers as a final project instead of an exam. Group projects are also valid ways of evaluating whether students understand the literature. It is wise to use a variety of evaluation methods to accommodate different learning styles and to add interest to class activities. We need to be as creative in evaluating as we are in writing assignments and planning activities.

DISCUSSION QUESTIONS

1. Think back to your junior and senior high school years. What literature do you remember? What were your favorite books? Were your favorites read in or out of school? What books did you talk about with friends?

2. What do you recall about literature study in junior and senior high school? What literature studied in school had the greatest impact on you? Try to think of what the connections were between you and this literature.

SUGGESTED ACTIVITIES

1. Choose a short story appropriate for a grade level you would like to teach. Develop and describe two or three activities to generate students' interest in the story.

2. Write responses for a novel you are reading, perhaps for another class. If possible, discuss the responses with others.

3. Choose an appropriate poem and write several questions designed to encourage responses from secondary students.

4. Using a novel for young adults, write a series of activities for middle school students.

5. Describe several activities a teacher could use for evaluating students' understanding of a particular text.

6. Choose a Shakespearean play other than *Romeo and Juliet* and design activities to help secondary students enjoy and understand the play.

REFERENCES

Farrell, Edmund J., and James R. Squire, eds. *Transactions with Literature: A Fifty-Year Perspective.* Urbana: National Council of Teachers of English, 1990.

Graves, Michael F., Rebecca J. Palmer, and David W. Furniss. *Structuring Reading Activities for English Classes.* ERIC, 1976.

Griffith Jr., Kelley. *Writing Essays About Literature.* 3rd ed. San Diego: Harcourt Brace Jovanovich, 1990.

Guerin, Wilfres L., et al. *A Handbook of Critical Approaches to Literature.* New York: Harper & Row, 1979.

Iser, Wolfgang. *The Act of Reading.* Baltimore: Johns Hopkins UP, 1978.

Kahn, Elizabeth A., Carolyn Calhoun Walter, Larry R. Johannessen. *Writing About Literature.* ERIC, 1984.

Lothe, Kurt. "Crime & Punishment, The Musical." *Wisconsin English Journal* Fall 1990: 76–77.

Maxwell, Rhoda J. "Exploring Characters in *All Together Now.*" *Notes Plus* Jan. 1989: 7–8.

Miller, Bruce E. *Teaching the Art of Literature.* Urbana: National Council of Teachers of English, 1980.

Nelms, Ben F., ed. *Literature in the Classroom: Readers, Texts, and Contexts.* Urbana: National Council of Teachers of English, 1988.

Olson, Vicki L. "Connecting with Literature: Activities for *The Cay* and *The Bedspread.*" *Literature—News That Stays News: Fresh Approaches to the Classics.* Ed. Candy Carter, Chair, and the Committee on Classroom Practices. Urbana: National Council of Teachers of English, 1985. 19–25.

Peck, David. *Novels of Initiation: A Guidebook for Teaching Literature to Adolescents.* New York: Columbia University Teachers College, 1989.

Phelan, Patricia, ed. *Literature and Life.* Urbana: National Council of Teachers of English, 1990.

Probst, Robert E. *Response Analysis: Teaching Literature in Junior and Senior High School.* Upper Montclair: Boynton/Cook, 1988.

Purves, Alan C., Theresa Rogers, Anno O. Soter. *How Porcupines Make Love: Teaching a Response-Centered Literature Curriculum.* White Plains: Longman, 1990.

_____. "Testing Literature: The Current State of Affairs." *Clearinghouse on Reading and Writing Communication Skills Digest.* ERIC, Aug. 1990.

Rosenblatt, Louise M. *Literature as Exploration.* 3d ed. New York: Noble and Noble, 1976.

_____. *The Reader, the Text, and the Poem.* Carbondale: Southern Illinois UP, 1977.

Simmons, John S., and H. Edward Deluzain. *Teaching Literature in Middle and Secondary Grades.* Boston: Allyn and Bacon, 1992.

Smagorinsky, Peter, Tom McCann, Stephen Kern. *Explorations: Introductory Activities for Literature and Composition, 7–12.* ERIC, 1987.

Smith, Frank. *Comprehension and Learning.* New York: Holt, Rinehart and Winston, 1975.

▼

CHAPTER 4

▼

▼

▼

Selecting Literature

CHAPTER HIGHLIGHTS
- Objectives for teaching literature.
- Canonical literature.
- Organizing literature study.
- Reading levels.
- Young adult literature.
- World literature.
- Literature by women.
- Minority literature.
- Media in the English classroom.
- Censorship.

> Every time we select a piece of literature to read, we are exposing ourselves to a vision: a vision of people and places and things; a vision of relationships and feelings and strivings. (201)
>
> —*G. Robert Carlsen*

▼

OBJECTIVES FOR TEACHING LITERATURE

Deciding what literature to teach seems a relatively easy matter at first glance. School districts may have decided who reads what when, and new teachers have their literature notes from college. A closer look at why we teach literature and what we want to achieve in teaching it reveals that literature choices may be difficult.

In general, teachers want students to read, to think about what they read, and to enjoy the experience. More specifically, a list of objectives could include the following:

1. Developing an enjoyment of reading so that lifelong reading is realistic.
2. Understanding the past by becoming more knowledgeable about not only what people did, but how they felt.
3. Understanding one's own experiences and how they may or may not fit with those of others.
4. Knowing and appreciating a wider view of life, both different cultures and different circumstances.
5. Learning how to make critical judgments about literature and to understand literary devices.

Only through a wide variety of literature can we hope to achieve these goals. One of our purposes in teaching literature is to help our students read well; because our students have different personalities, experiences, and abilities, we must provide as wide a range of literature as possible.

Many new teachers teach the literature they recently studied in college classes because they are most comfortable with it and know the most about it. Some of the selections may be suitable for high school seniors, but the way the literature was taught is never appropriate. The gap in maturity between high school seniors and upper division college students prohibits use of the same teaching material and approaches. The wealth of literature from which to choose leaves no excuse for not choosing selections appropriate for secondary students.

The literature we select for students to read has both social and political implications and far-reaching consequences. One may think it is not difficult to decide what to ask our students to read, but a serious problem is what we do *not* ask them to read. For years the literature of ethnic minorities has been ignored in the schools, and only recently have women authors been included in anthologies. In collections of American poetry, it is not uncommon for Emily Dickinson to be the only woman represented. By omission, the impression is created that great works are written only by white men. Northrup Frye calls literature an organization of human experience. The question is, whose experience? Because we can't teach everything, we make selections, and those selections determine whether we are providing opportunities for students to become truly literate.

Being literate means having the ability to use knowledge to better understand the world and ourselves. It is not decoding words. Frank Smith, who has written many books and articles on language and learning, in "Overselling Literacy" describes what literacy is and is not, and how our understanding of literacy affects the way we teach literature in the classroom. His main point is that the press makes too much of illiteracy and assumes too much for literacy. He writes that literacy "doesn't generate finer feelings or higher values. It doesn't even make anyone smarter." He goes on to explain that "people who don't read and write think just as well out of school as people who can, especially if they are members of a culture in which strong oral language traditions have prevailed" (254). The important point here for teaching is that literacy is not just a set of skills but an "attitude toward the world." "Individuals become literate not from formal instruction they receive, but from what they read and write about and who they read and write with" (355). Seeing their teachers read with pleasure goes far to convince students that they too can enjoy reading. Trying to talk students into believing that they will enjoy a piece of literature is usually not successful. Smith suggests the following:

> They [teachers] can promote interest by demonstrating their own interests. Nothing attracts young people more than activities, abilities, or secrets that absorb adults; they want to know the things that we find worth while. Demonstrating the imaginative possibilities of literacy and collaborating with students should be a classroom delight for teachers and students alike. (358)

Smith's statement emphasizes the responsibility teachers have to select literature that can interest the variety of students we find in our classrooms. Being literate does not mean that students have read a particular list of titles, but rather that interest and understanding were generated when students read literature they could relate to.

On what basis do we select literature? A strong influence is the society we live in. Frye writes that every society produces a social mythology or ideology, and he describes the two aspects of this mythology. One is a body of beliefs deeply held by a society. For Americans, those beliefs are probably self-reliance, independence, democratic process, and tolerance. All are important values for creating the kind of society we want to live in. The second is an adjustment mythology by which our ideology is learned by the society's citizens. One of the functions of education is to teach this adjustment mythology, and we do so, Frye explains, by keeping alive a nostalgic version of the American past, relying heavily on Washington's honesty, Lincoln's concern, and stories about pioneers, hunters, and cowboys (16). Such a design is not intrinsically wrong; we value certain ideals and we want future generations to value them as well.

When the adjustment myth becomes perverted, however, some groups of people in society become subordinated. For example, in Victorian times women were thought to be exceedingly delicate—a perverted myth. Protecting women was taught as a social value. As a result, women were actually deprived of equal participation in society (Frye 22). For a variety of reasons, some more vicious than others, minority groups have remained outside the mainstream of the adjustment myth education. When an act of bravery is studied in the classroom, the literature chosen is still, too often, a story of whites fighting off Native Americans or men defending helpless women. There are exceptions, of course, but the multitude of literature selections available leaves no excuse for promoting such stereotypes. Becoming aware of this situation and realizing that the literature we choose can do much to help our students develop an imaginative social vision make our society a better place to live—for everyone.

▼
CANONICAL LITERATURE

In the late 1980s a movement called cultural literacy gained popularity when William Bennett, then Secretary of Education, argued that students need to read particular authors and works that represent great Western literature. The movement affected the public's opinion about what students should know. Cultural literacy gained momentum when E. D. Hirsch, Jr., wrote *Cultural Literacy,* in which he listed the titles of texts that all students should read. One difficulty with Hirsch's list is that he sponsors only the cultural literacy of rich and educated white Anglo-Saxon Protestants of the 19th and 20th centuries. At a time when our country's population is nearly 40% minorities, Hirsch's cultural literacy is too narrow in scope and limited in perspective to adequately meet the needs of teachers and students.

A second difficulty with Hirsch's concept of cultural literacy is the simplistic view of learning. Peter Elbow in *What Is English?* describes Hirsch's list as ideal for learning chunks of information that have right or wrong answers, but it leaves no room for interpretative imagination or the ability to create meaning from reading texts (163). Hirsch has a specific plan to encourage the teaching of his list—a test of general knowledge for 12th grade. He is planning to write tests for 3rd, 6th, and 9th grades as well. For Hirsch, then, knowledge is a set of memorizable facts.

However, as Chris Anson explains, knowing about something is not the same as integrating content into prior knowledge, perceptions, and beliefs, or even more important, knowing how to know (17). We want to provide learning situations that encourage students to explore many varieties of discourse. This is a very different kind of learning from what Hirsch proposes. The best argument against such an approach to teaching literature is a well thought-out philosophy of one's own. Teachers need to take literature selection into our own hands and first establish goals and then choose literature that facilitates those goals. If we don't, we run the risk of someone else deciding for us.

Literature anthologies include more selections by women and minorities than they did 10 years ago, but many still contain a disproportionate number of white male middle-class authors. In a 12th-grade British literature text published in 1989, there are 15 women authors among a total of 102. Our literature curriculum should reflect the multicultural nature of our society. We need a variety of forms, a variety of perspectives. If the anthology does not provide the spectrum we want, then we must supplement it with paperback books and copies of stories and poems to give our students reading experiences that reflect the lives of all.

MAKING CHOICES

Teachers need to be in control of the literature program for their school. They know the abilities and interests of their students, as well as the units of study in which particular themes would be appropriate. We want to choose "good" books for our students to read, but what criteria do we use? In *Experiencing Children's Literature,* Alan Purves and Dianne Monson suggest that teachers use three questions to judge the quality of a book:

1. Did the book arouse my emotions? (Are the emotions trite or realistic? Is it interesting?)
2. Is the book well written? (Are characters believable and language appropriate to the theme?)
3. Is the book meaningful? (Is the audience respected? Is the theme treated seriously?)

For the book to appeal to student readers, it has to appeal to the teacher as well.

▼
ORGANIZING LITERATURE STUDY

We don't believe that particular types of literature should be taught at specific grade levels. Rather, teachers should select literature based on what they believe are important considerations for a unit or a theme designed specifically for their classes. In many curricula, tall tales are designated for only one grade level and fables for another. Rather than attach a grade level to a kind of literature, it is better for teachers to consider the developmental level of their students and the literature that best meets their purpose. For instance, it is appropriate to use Dr. Seuss books and Shel Silverstein's poetry at the senior high level when discussing how authors can integrate morals into literature or the creativity of language play. Tall tales, myths, and legends can be used at any grade level because readers bring different levels of sophistication to their responses.

Literature study is often organized by genre. Our university, for example, offers courses in short story, drama, novels, and poetry. Or the literature is organized by historical periods and geographical locations: British literature before the 18th century, American literature after WWII. We strongly believe that if we want to interest secondary students in literature we should not use these divisions. Students have little interest in literary periods, and this approach relies heavily on "teacher" knowledge, discussed in the preceding chapter. Literature tied to a unit in social studies or history is certainly appropriate, however, because historical facts become more "real" to students when they understand them through the feelings and thoughts of people who lived at that particular time. But teaching John Dryden because he wrote before Oliver Goldsmith and after John Donne does not turn students on to reading. Providing literature by genre is just as troublesome. Rarely in the real world do we read only poetry for several weeks. The same is true for any genre. We mix forms, styles, and periods, and we believe the same should be true in the classroom.

ORGANIZING AROUND A THEME

Organizing around a theme has many advantages. First, several types of literature can be included, providing for a variety of reading levels and interests. Second, the choice of themes can include current issues, developmental stages, and selections from an anthology. In choosing a theme, teachers can keep their students' interests and ages in mind, but they can also rely on their own enthusiasm for a topic. A teacher's special interest in travel or sports or mysteries can be the foundation for a successful unit.

The first unit a teacher designs is time-consuming and may be somewhat overwhelming, but once the unit planning gets underway, it becomes easier. A large file for each unit enables teachers to add material as they find it. For instance, when teaching a unit on heroes to middle school students, a teacher might want to convey the idea that many ordinary people are heroes, and therefore collects articles that describe heroic deeds over a period of several weeks prior to teaching the unit. Then, during the unit, several current nonfiction selections can be made available to students. After the unit is over, teachers continue to add new material and suggestions as they discover them, so that the development of units is continual.

Thematic units work well in classrooms for both middle and high school for several reasons.

1. *They promote student interest.* Students are more likely to be interested in learning about "what is a hero" or "high adventure" than in reading a single book title, even though that title may be included in the unit. Reading one book after another with no connection among them makes it more difficult to compare books or to develop serious discussions on, for example, relationships with parents. By using a variety of sources, students better understand the complexities of issues. Because units contain a wide variety of material, students are more likely to bring in suggestions and reading material for the class; in other words, they become more involved in their own learning.

2. *They integrate genre.* Choosing a variety of poems, stories, novels, plays, and nonfiction related by themes introduces forms of literature to students in a natural way. Students are not required to read a poem because it is the week to study poetry, but because the poem provides insights or other ways of looking at the theme. For example, in a unit titled "Who am I?" designed by an 8th-grade teacher, Liz Rehrauer, the following literature was included: a novel, *The Light in the Forest* by Conrad Richter; the short stories, "The Moustache" and "Guess What? I Almost Kissed my Father," both by Robert Cormier, and "Raymond's Run" by Toni Cade Bambera; and several poems—"Me Myself, and I" and "Sometimes" by Eve Mirriam, "The Ballad of Johnny" by May Sarton, "Speak to Me" by Calvin O'John, "Celebration" by Alonzo Lopez, "The Question" by Karla Kuskin, "Self-Pity" by D. H. Lawrence, and "Will I Remember?" by Richard J. Margolis. Rehrauer also included a list of novels for young adults that students could choose from for further reading.

Including many forms of reading materials helps broaden students' concept of "school learning." For example, a comic book may provide an excellent model of one type of hero to begin a discussion of the attributes of heroism. This could be the basis for comparing heroic character traits in other forms of literature. Students then can develop their own definition of heroism.

3. *They provide for different reading levels.* Some thematic units are more appropriate for one level than another. The "Who Am I?" mentioned above is an excellent choice for middle school; a unit on war might be more appropriate for high school. Many themes can be used at any level, and the literature selections reflect the level of the students. The following list provides a few suggestions for topics that might be used in grades 6 through 12:

- What is it like to grow old?
- Becoming an adult.
- Making choices.
- The American West.
- Journeys, real and imaginary.
- Values: Developing and changing.
- Love and friendship.
- Utopian communities.

Because students read a wide variety of literature in thematic units, the whole class does not have to read the same material, or they may all read the same material but not at the same time. If the unit includes three or four novels, a class period is devoted to introducing all of the novels by explaining a little about each. All of the novels are related by theme, although the reading levels are different. For example, a unit on family relations might include *Home Before*

Dark by Sue Ellen Bridgers, *Ordinary People* by Judith Guest, and *Tell Me a Riddle* by Tillie Olson, listed in order of difficulty. Students are free to read all three novels and many do, especially the better readers, but they are required to read only the one assigned to them. It is wise to tell students during the time the books are introduced that they can read as many as they want to but not to mention reading level. It is important to avoid any stigma attached to who reads which book first.

General class discussions based on issues related to the theme involve all students. Students also meet in small groups to discuss their assigned book. Group projects might be based on just one of the novels, or two, or all three. It isn't necessary for everyone in the group to have read all the novels because each can make contributions based on one book. In this way, students of varying abilities can work together.

▼
READING LEVELS

The literature we select for our students depends on many factors. The most obvious, of course, is the grade we teach, but we must also consider the age of our students, their interests, their developmental stage, and our own interests.

Reading levels are rarely considered in secondary schools. Students are handed *Hamlet;* if they can't read the text, they watch the film. We believe this practice is grossly unfair to students who have trouble reading difficult material, because if we do not give them material they can read, their reading ability does not improve. Secondary school teachers must be as concerned with reading levels as elementary school teachers.

Reading levels vary greatly across a grade level. A rule of thumb in determining the span of reading levels in an "average" class is to divide the grade number in half, subtract that number to establish the low end and add that number to predict the high level. For instance, in teaching 6th grade one can expect reading levels to range from 3rd grade to 9th grade. The higher the grade, the greater the differences; 12th grade levels range from 6th grade to well beyond college. We often think of reading problems as a concern of elementary grade teachers only, but difficulty in reading is a major cause of problems in school for older students. Secondary teachers also must be concerned and must make their classrooms places where more students can succeed. One way to achieve this is to choose literature that is interesting, but at a lower reading level. Young adult literature is a good choice.

▼
YOUNG ADULT LITERATURE

Young adult literature deserves a solid berth in the literature programs of secondary schools. A growing number of talented authors are writing for the adolescent audience. Writers such as Maya Angelou, Chris Crutcher, M. E. Kerr, Sue Ellen Bridgers, Cynthia Voigt, Ursula Le Guin, Robert Lipsyte, Emily Cheney Neville, Katherine Paterson, Gary Paulsen, Sandra Scoppettone, Ouida Sebestyn, and Brenda Wilkinson, to name just a few, hold their own with respected authors of adult fiction. As with literature for adult audiences, some pieces are trite and/or poorly written, but others receive critical acclaim. Intricate plot structure, multifaceted characterizations, interesting and varied settings, symbolic interpretations, and artistry of language can all be found in young adult literature. Writing for a teenage audience is a serious undertaking for many fine writers. The results are important contributions to the study of literature in secondary schools.

Young adult literature didn't come into its own as a genre until the 1950s. Since that time, novels for adolescents have become increasingly realistic. Young adult books cover a wide variety of topics: murder, theft, child abuse, mental illness, fatal illness, abortion, pregnancy, self-esteem, relationships, and responsibility. The protagonists are always teenagers and the stories are told from their point of view. Although the themes are as varied and universal as those found in adult fiction, the stories are about the adolescent experience; it is this characteristic that defines the genre rather than a particular plot.

The study of young adult literature enhances students' understanding and appreciation of more difficult works. By including young adult literature, we can ensure greater success in meeting the goals of teaching literature: to gain an understanding of themselves and others, to achieve a wider world view, and to become lifelong readers. Specifically, we believe teaching young adult literature achieves the following outcomes:

1. *Students learn to make critical judgments about what they read.* It is difficult for students to critically analyze more sophisticated works, yet the skill of analyzing literature—that is, critically thinking about what they read—is important. By using young adult literature, students can more easily understand the motivation behind characters' actions. Students not only can discuss how fictional teenagers react to a situation, but they also have a sense about the validity of the author's perception. These books deal with experiences they know something about. As students consider cause and effect—that is, the relation between plot and characterization—they gain understanding beyond the work itself. Once students gain skill in analyzing fiction, they are better able to look critically at more difficult works.

2. *Students learn to support and explain their critical judgments.* The simpler vocabulary and sentence structure in most young adult literature allow students to understand the text better. The National Assessment of Educational Progress (NAEP) 1979–80 test results showed that students have a difficult time using material from a text to document judgments they make from their reading. Even when they make appropriate judgments about the reading, they are at a loss to explain and defend their opinions. This lack of ability mandates that we look at the way we teach literature and the liter-

ature we choose to teach. In the preceding chapter, the discussion of response theory described ways to help students understand what they read. Using literature that has easier vocabulary and style helps students get beyond surface elements. Archaic language often has a beauty of its own but can interfere with comprehension. Because young adult literature uses vocabulary more easily understood, it is an excellent source for teaching the difficult skills of documenting judgments because the language does not interfere.

3. *Students gain an understanding of themselves and others.* Adolescence is a time when young people critically examine their own beliefs and values. As they grow away from dependence on their families, they are often confused by anxieties and uncertainties. The teenage fictional characters in young adult literature mirror the readers' experiences and provide helpful insights. The characters are realistically portrayed, so readers relate to the concerns of physical appearance, family relationships, and sexual experiences. It is reassuring for teenagers to discover through young adult literature that others have the same concerns they do, and in the process of understanding the fictional characters, they gain understanding of themselves. Maturity is enhanced as they learn more about themselves and others.

4. *Students gain a wider view of life.* Young adult literature covers every historical period and country in the world. Because the teenager's point of view is central to the novels, a personal response on the part of the reader is likely; therefore, a better understanding of historical concepts and different cultures is possible. The vicarious experiences broaden students' views. Young adult literature celebrates the uniqueness of individuals. The central character is often one, who for a variety of reasons, must overcome obstacles and prejudices. Accepting one's own handicap or relating to people with handicaps is a popular theme. Because ignorance fosters prejudice, the more knowledgeable students become, the more they understand and accept individual differences.

5. *Students' enjoyment of reading increases.* Because the protagonist is a teenager and the plot involves problems teenagers encounter, young adult literature provides high-interest reading. Every literature curriculum includes an objective for helping students to enjoy reading. Motivation occurs naturally when teenagers can read about situations they are knowledgeable about and interested in. Young adult literature does much to establish the habit of reading for pleasure.

▼
WORLD LITERATURE

Awareness of other cultures becomes increasingly important as the world shrinks via television. Yet secondary students know very little about cultures other than their own. Teachers need to become aware of the possibilities of selecting literature that helps students develop a wider world view. Prejudice and fear come from ignorance; literature can do much to overcome these by increasing awareness of other people—their hopes, their fears, their dreams. Studying world literature helps students see not only the differences among cultures but also the similarities. And by learning about other people, we learn about ourselves and the part our culture plays in shaping individuals' life experiences.

Including world literature in English language arts classes generally means selecting literature from Third World countries. Students and teachers know little about this body of literature, which is why we should include it. Teacher and students learning together creates a dynamic class. Contemporary Third World authors are concerned with the tension between the old values and way of life and the changes modern life brings to their country. The themes often involve struggles between the old and the new. Young adults understand the problems inherent in such a struggle and find that they have more in common with Third World people than they may have thought. Also, much of the literature is reminiscent of early American concerns as these countries work toward developing strong independent governments.

In the introduction of *Guide to World Literature*, editors Warren Carrier and Kenneth Oliver make the case for including world literature in English language arts classes.

> As we move into multi-national economic, ecological, and cultural enterprises and inter-dependencies, it becomes increasingly important for students to recognize national similarities and differences, but above all to recognize our common bond, our common lot. A study of world literature contributes much to an appreciation and understanding of the heritage we share. (3)

Teaching world literature brings a special set of concerns. We rely on the same practices as we do in teaching any literature: encouraging responses, valuing students' opinions, helping students to think beyond the obvious. But how do we select the literature and organize it for teaching? Teachers offer a variety of suggestions.

THEMATIC APPROACH

Carrier and Oliver believe that the thematic approach is the best way to teach world literature. The thematic approach works for all literature and is especially important when reading about other cultures. When studying one country's literature apart from other cultures, we might emphasize differences between them. Although great differences may exist, we want students to realize that they have more in common than may be apparent. Carrier and Oliver suggest themes of love, injustice, conflict, separation, and war, among others (3). They give as an example the theme of time. In *The Great Gatsby* by F. Scott Fitzgerald, Gatsby tries to recapture time. In a Japanese novel, *The Sound of the Mountain* by Yasunari Kawabata, the hero is very aware of the passing of time.

The transience of time is also a theme in *My Mother's House* by Colette (French), *The Tale of Genji* by Murasaki (Japanese), and *Lucy Gayheart* by Willa Cather (American) (4). Selections can come from a variety of countries and be grouped around a common theme.

STUDYING ONE CULTURE

A teacher may want to focus a unit on one particular culture if the area of study is largely unknown to students. An intense study of the literature is an excellent way to acquaint them with that culture. Alan Olds, a high school teacher in Colorado, explains in a recent article that he taught Chinese literature to his students to help them understand China's rich heritage. To understand our own culture, we need to understand ideas and traditions from other voices (21).

> I constantly remind my students (and myself) that we are visitors, not tourists, when we read literature from other cultures. We try to prepare for our visit, so that we do not stumble about in an unfamiliar setting. We are not reading these writers to check them off our list of books, the way a tourist checks off destinations without really tarrying to see beyond the surface attractions and rushes on to see the next stop. Instead, we intend to arrive informed and sensitive to a new culture, open to its wonders. We want to stay long enough to see beyond the clichés. If we are lucky, our visit will broaden our sense of what it means to be human. (21)

Olds wants his students to be able to read Chinese literature with an Eastern viewpoint, for example. The article contains a rich variety of sources and a description of how he teaches the unit.

In writing about teaching South African literature, Robert Mossman, a high school teacher in Arizona, warns of the danger of choosing only one representative novel from a culture.

> A study of South African literature in an American classroom, to be valid and legitimate, cannot consist of merely one work and be successful. By the very fact of the polarized nature of the apartheid system and the literary responses to it, students must encounter and examine works which represent viewpoints from different racial perspectives. Reading only one work may do a disservice because it inevitably provides only one perspective. The richness and complexity of South Africa's literature deserves better. (41)

Mossman explains the problems that occur when *Cry, the Beloved Country* is the only South African literature taught in English classes. Students read and learn only one perspective which, particularly in South Africa, creates a false impression. "If *Cry, the Beloved Country* must be taught in the curriculum, then it should be taught in conjunction with *Mine Boy* by Peter Abrahams" (42). Mossman suggests six other pairings of South African literature that offer different perspectives.

RESOURCES FOR WORLD LITERATURE

An excellent resource for selecting African literature is *Teaching African Literature* by Elizabeth Gunner. Her handbook contains teaching suggestions, information about the novels and authors, and an extensive annotated bibliography of books, films, and recorded sound. In the introduction, Gunner emphasizes the importance of including African literature in the curriculum. "Texts by African writers often provide an alternative view of history, or illuminate an aspect of history and individual experience previously not available to a particular pupil or group of pupils" (v). In addition to the teaching ideas for individual novels, Gunner describes thematic units that include novels, poetry, and film. For teachers not well acquainted with African literature for secondary students, this book is invaluable.

Another book in the same series is *Teaching Caribbean Literature* by David Dabydeen. The format is similar to Gunner's and the text provides information about the authors and literature as well as teaching ideas. Dabydeen describes 12 units, each dealing with a particular novel or a set of poems. He includes related readings and audiovisual resources.

▼ ───

LITERATURE BY WOMEN

Gender imbalance in the literature choices teachers make for student reading continues in spite of numerous articles, reports, and editorials arguing for a change. One reason for the reluctance to change is that the lists of required reading go unchallenged; teachers do not re-examine literature choices but simply teach what has always been taught. A second reason it that the literacy canon is perpetuated by agencies that carry a voice of authority. Patricia Lake, a high school teacher, reports that the Advanced Placement Course Description published by the Educational Testing Service includes few women authors. Lake found that "According to the guide book, only fourteen women (versus eighty men) have written prose of sufficient merit to warrant its study" (36). ETS is a powerful influence on literature selections for advanced placement English classes. Lake asks,

> Why then is there continued propagation of such severe gender imbalance in the reading lists provided by ETS? High-school literature courses should be broadening students' perspectives, not directing them into predetermined stereotypical channels which, by their exclusionary nature, actually prevent students from reading about life in other than traditional contexts. (36)

Often lists of books taught in secondary schools are interpreted as lists of what *should* be taught. Teachers need to look at such lists with a critical eye because not only are important authors ignored, but the lists give an erroneous message to young people. Lake explains,

If we do not work for a greater gender balance in teaching literature, we present a distorted picture of our literary heritage and the society which spawned it. We do a wonderful job of showing that indeed men did—and do—receive most of the recognition, but we also suggest that there were no women doing anything of scholarly or literary merit.

Another danger for the young women in our classes is that when they read male authors almost exclusively, they develop a male perspective on understanding the women characters. They really have no choice when both the authors and the critics are men. The readings need to be balanced to give young women a better sense of the value of their own experiences. Literature by women is as rich and varied as literature by men. We owe it to our students (and ourselves) to provide a gender-balanced literature curriculum.

▼ ───

MINORITY LITERATURE

The population of the United States is shifting from a predominantly white culture to one with an increasing number of people of color. Nearly one of every three Americans is from a non-English-speaking home. The Hispanic population is the fastest growing and will be around 17% of the total population by the year 2000. African-Americans will comprise 16%. Mary Sasse, a high school English teacher, stresses the importance of teachers gaining an understanding of the term *ethnic*. "With those understandings comes an acceptance of the universality of human experience, which teachers can use as a bridge between themselves and other ethnic peoples and as a recognition of the richness and diversity of American ethnic literature" (171). She provides three criteria for selecting minority literature:

1. Selections should be by minority authors, not just *about* minority people; otherwise stereotyping can be a problem.
2. Selections must represent the total dynamic nature of an ethnic group. Historical accounts should be balanced with contemporary ones. Both urban and rural experiences need to be represented.
3. Selections should represent a broad spectrum of experiences to avoid romanticizing or stereotyping (170–171).

Teaching minority literature is vital if we are serious about reaching all our students. Roseann Duenas Gonzalez, a teacher at the University of Arizona, explains that classrooms have changed dramatically in the past 10 years. Our students come from widely diverse backgrounds, both culturally and linguistically, and "are fast becoming a significant proportion of the school-age population" (16). We are not meeting the needs of these children. If these culturally and linguistically different children do not stay in school and receive an adequate education, "our society incrementally loses the productive capability of an entire generation" (16). Gonzalez discusses the problems that teachers have in teaching minority literature and presents recommendations. Minority literature should not be taught as "special" but should receive the same concern for style, honesty, and language as any other literature. To fail to do so sends a message to students that this literature is inferior and cannot stand up to critical analysis (19).

Selection is difficult for literature with which we are not familiar. Several resources listed at the end of the chapter contain annotated bibliographies. Searching for appropriate books does take time, but the time is well spent and the books are interesting. Not taking the time ensures that the same list of books that teachers have used for the last 25 years will continue with no changes. Arthur N. Applebee, Director of the Center for the Learning and Teaching of Literature, did a study in 1989 to determine what book-length works are most commonly taught at secondary schools. The lists of the top 10 books included few by women and minority authors. Classics dominate the lists, and while we should continue to teach classics, we need to make room in the curriculum for literature that all students can identify with and develop an appreciation for.

NATIVE AMERICAN LITERATURE

A study of Native Americans is an essential part of our American past and does much to enrich our curriculum. Because of the oral traditions, students learn a great deal about the nature of language; the songs and chants provide beauty and meaning, helping students to understand the importance of lyrical quality. The themes carried through Native American literature are of special interest and importance to adolescents: developing self-identity, establishing values, understanding one's relationship to nature, making decisions that are often at odds with the majority.

Not long ago, Native Americans were portrayed with a negative or outdated stereotype, and for many students those images still exist. As a way to discover what students think Native Americans are like, a teacher can ask them to write everything that comes to mind when they think of Native Americans. The results are usually shocking, from comments that are ludicrous—such as they live in tents and wear feathers all the time—to comments that are negative and cruel—such as they are lazy and drunkards. The contrast between such misinformation and actual Native American beliefs and behavior is startling. Students have much to learn from Native Americans: the spiritual nature of the universe, respect for the land, importance of ritual and ceremony, oneness with nature. If we include literature by Native Americans, we can dispel erroneous impressions with the understanding, knowledge, and empathy that comes from reading.

Excellent literature written by Native Americans is not difficult to find. A sampling that is particularly appropriate for middle and high school students might include *The Education of Little Tree* (nonfiction) by Forrest Carter, *Tracks* by Louise Erdrich, *The Indian Lawyer* by James Welch, all of Tony Hillerman's books, and *Night Flying Woman: An Ojibway Narrative* by Ignatia Broker.

HISPANIC LITERATURE

Hispanic literature is poorly represented in anthologies, even more than other minority literature. A 1989 anthology of American literature published by a major company contained over 1,000 entries but had no literature about the Hispanic experience in the United States. What message does this give to our Hispanic students? If a particular literature is not included in a new anthology, it must not be important. Two teachers, Patricia Ann Romero and Don Zancanella, explain why they include Hispanic literature in their program:

> We . . . believe that outside the traditional American canon lie works by less familiar names—classics of the future, we would argue—demonstrating to our students that the American story becomes much richer when we hear it told in all its voices. For example, alongside the traditional American anthology pieces, we place the works of contemporary Hispanic writers. (25)

Romero and Zancanella believe that it is important for students "to read literature that validates their own experience and know that authors and artists of substance and value have come from their culture" (29). Teachers who are fortunate enough to have cultures outside the mainstream represented in their classrooms can enrich the learning not only of these students but of all their students by including authors from the various cultures.

AFRICAN-AMERICAN LITERATURE

Many high school graduates are familiar with African-American male writers, in particular Richard Wright, Ralph Ellison, and Langston Hughes, as well as others. In recent years, African-American women writers have been included in college literature classes but are not likely to appear at the high school level. Exceptions exist, of course, but, on the whole, African-American women are not represented. We have wonderful selections to choose from, such as *Their Eyes Are Watching God* by Zora Neale Hurston. The story centers on a young woman who, in spite of immense difficulties, develops a strong sense of self, an ideal topic for adolescents. In addition to a good story, the book has an incredible lyrical quality. Hurston's use of figurative language stays with a reader long after the book is finished. Other outstanding African-American authors include Maya Angelou, Virginia Hamilton, Langston Hughes, Alice Walker, Mildred Taylor, Terry McMillan, J. California Cooper, Nikki Giovanni, and Toni Morrison. Teachers need to include both male and female writers from different literary genres and sources.

ASIAN-AMERICAN LITERATURE

The term *Asian-Americans* includes Chinese, Japanese, Filipino, and Korean-Americans, as well as immigrants from Laos, Cambodia, Vietnam, and Thailand. Ogle Duff and Helen Tongchinsub describe the thematic concerns of modern Asian-American writers as love, personal liberty, injustice, and inner struggles. However, when Asian-Americans were first published, their writing tended to be nonthreatening, nonassertive, and self-negating because otherwise it would not be accepted. An example of this type of writing is *Fifth Chinese Daughter* by Jade Snow Wong, published in 1950. Although the story denigrates certain Asian values, it was often included in secondary school literature anthologies. Contemporary Asian-American literary critics are critical of the story and others like it (222). In choosing literature, teachers need to look for accurate portrayals of other cultures. A representation of a balance of positive and negative characters struggling with contemporary issues is important in literature selection to ensure an honest view and to avoid stereotyping (238).

When selecting Asian-American literature, teachers have many choices. Ellen Greenblatt in *Many Voices* suggests combining the reading of *The Joy Luck Club* by Amy Tan with the more difficult *The Woman Warrior* by Maxine Hong Kingston. *The House of the Spirits* by Isabel Allende, a Chilean writer, could also be a companion reading with *The Joy Luck Club*. Another suitable book by Tan is *The Kitchen God's Wife*. *The Sound of the Waves* by Yukio Mishima, a book about forbidden love, could be paired with *Romeo and Juliet*. Greenblatt highly recommends *A Boat to Nowhere* by Maureen Crane Wartski, a novel of the boat people's desperate flight from Vietnam (7).

READERS AND LITERATURE

We are not suggesting that traditional literature from the white male Protestant perspective be excluded, but to accurately present the American experience the literary canon needs to be redefined and expanded to include American minority authors. At one time, the difficulty of finding literature by minorities, women, and Third World authors created a serious problem for teachers. That is no longer true because many readily available bibliographies and articles provide annotations of titles; a list of resources appears at the end of this chapter.

Should we teach literature from the cultures represented in our classrooms? Regardless of the cultural makeup of our class, should we teach literature from other cultures? The answer to both questions is yes. We live in a pluralistic society, and our literature selections need to help our students come to a deeper understanding and appreciation of the multiple cultures in America and in the world. Students may experience difficulty in understanding references and idioms from cultures other than their own. Even though the same can be said for Chaucer, teachers believe that the value of helping students understand *Canterbury Tales* far outweighs any difficulties encountered. That belief should transfer to teaching a wider spectrum of literature than the canon.

RECOMMENDED BOOKS BY OR ABOUT MINORITIES

What follows are personal choices or those recommended by other English teachers. (Special thanks to the Cooperative Children's Book Center, University of Wisconsin–Madison.) The list is in no way comprehensive but is perhaps a starting point for those not familiar with minority literature.

Native American Literature

- *When the Legends Die* by Hal Borland
- *Anpao: An American Odyssey* by Jamake Highwater
- *Ceremony* by Leslie Silko
- *The Man to Send Rain Clouds: Contemporary Stories by American Indians,* edited by Kenneth Rosen
- *House Made of Dawn* by Scott N. Momaday
- *I Heard the Owl Call my Name* by Margaret Craven
- *Brothers of the Heart: A Story of the Old Northwest, 1837–1838* by Joan W. Blos

African-American Literature

- *I Know Why the Caged Bird Sings* by Maya Angelou
- *The Women of Brewster Place* by Gloria Naylor
- *In Search of Our Mothers' Gardens* by Alice Walker
- *Blue Tights* by Rita Williams-Garcia
- *Trouble's Child* by Mildred Pitts Walter
- *Marked by Fire* by Joyce Carol Thomas
- *Let the Circle be Unbroken* by Mildred D. Taylor
- *Scorpions* by Walter Dean Myers
- *Out from This Place* by Joyce Hansen
- *Sweet Whispers, Brother Rush* by Virginia Hamilton
- *Rainbow Jordan* by Alice Childress
- *Cotton Candy on a Rainy Day* (poems) by Nikki Giovanni

Chicano Literature

- *Bless Me, Ultima* by Rudolfo Anaya
- *The Road to Tamazunchale* by Ron Arias
- *The Day the Cisco Kid Shot John Wayne* by Nash Candelaria
- *The Last of the Menu Girls* by Denise Chavez

- *The House on Mango Street* by Sandra Cisneros
- *Across the Great River* by Irene Beltran Hernandez
- *Schoolland* by Max Martinez
- *The Iguana Killer: Twelve Stories of the Heart* by Alberto Alvaro Rios
- *Kodachromes in Rhyme* by Ernest Galarza
- *The Crossing* by Gary Paulsen
- *Black Hair* (poetry) by Gary Soto
- *Nuyorican Poetry: An Anthology of Puerto Rican Words and Feelings,* edited by Miguel Algarin and Miguel Pinero
- *Chicano Voices,* edited by Carlota Cardenas de Dwyer

Asian-American*

- *Tule Lake* by Edward Miyakawa
- *Woman from Hiroshima* by Toshio Mori
- *Citizen 13660* by Mine Okubo
- *Nisei Daughter* by Monica Sone
- *Homebase* by Shawn Hsu Wong
- *Child of the Owl* and *Dragonwings* by Laurence Yep
- *Woman Warrior: Memoirs of a Girlhood among Ghosts* by Maxine Hong Kingston
- *The Joy Luck Club* by Amy Tan
- *Asian American Authors,* an anthology edited by Kai-Yu Hsu and Helen Palubinskas
- *Aiieeee!,* an anthology of Asian-American writers edited by Frank Chin, et al.

Other Selections

- *Waiting for the Rain: A Novel of South Africa* by Shelia Gordon
- *Somehow Tenderness Survives: Stories of Southern Africa,* selected by Hazel Rochman
- *A Thief in the Village, and Other Stories* by James Berry (Jamaican)
- *The Honorable Prison* by Lyll Becerra de Jenkins (South American)
- *The Return* by Sonia Levitin (Ethiopian)
- *Rebels of the Heavenly Kingdom* by Katherine Paterson (19th-century China)

* Many of these selections are recommended by Duff and Tongchinsub.

- *So Far from the Bamboo Grove* by Yoko Kawashima Watkins (Japanese)
- *The Third Women,* edited by Dexter Fisher includes selections of Native American, Chicano, and Asian-American literature
- *Invented Lives: Narratives of Black Women,* edited by Mary Helen Washington
- *Breaking Ice: An Anthology of Contemporary African-American Fiction,* edited by Terry McMillan

▼

PUTTING IT ALL TOGETHER

Literature selections might be appropriate in several thematic units, depending on what aspect or theme a teacher wants to emphasize in the unit. For instance, *Summer of My German Solider* could be used in a unit on family relationships, war, or the need for acceptance. The groupings of literature that follow are examples of how some teachers combine their selections. The groupings include novels at different reading levels. Minority authors are represented, as well as a balance of gender. The lists include many selections to highlight the variety of available literature. The final chapter in this text describes detailed units with lesson plans and specific teaching ideas relating listening, speaking, writing, reading, and creative dramatics for a comprehensive idea of how the units work.

FAMILY RELATIONSHIPS
Novels

- *Home Before Dark* by Sue Ellen Bridgers
- *Summer of My German Soldier* by Bette Greene
- *Everywhere* by Bruce Brooks
- *The Disappearance* by Rosa Guy
- *Ordinary People* by Judith Guest
- *Family Reunion* by Caroline Cooney
- *A Fine Time to Leave Me* by Terry Pringle
- *Unlived Affections* by George Shannon
- *Thief of Dreams* by John Yount
- *IOU'S* by Quida Sebestyen
- *Sarah, Plain and Tall* by Patricia MacLachlan
- *But in the Fall I'm Leaving* by Ann Rinaldi
- *Cold Sassy Tree* by Olive Ann Burns

Poetry

- "My Papa's Waltz" by Theodore Roethke
- "Those Winter Sundays" by Robert Hayden
- "Blaming Sons" by T'ao Ch'ien
- "Fifty-Fifty" by Carl Sandburg

COMING OF AGE OR DEVELOPING A SENSE OF SELF

Stories

- "Train Whistle Guitar" by Albert Murray
- "The Tree in the Meadow" by Philippa Pearce
- "Thank You, Ma'am" by Langston Hughes

Novels

- *Anywhere Else but Here* by Bruce Clement
- *The Catcher in the Rye* by J. D. Salinger
- *Come Sing, Jimmy Jo* by Katherine Paterson
- *Far from Shore* by Kevin Major
- *In Summer Light* by Zibby Oneal
- *The Moves Make the Man* by Bruce Brooks
- *Notes for Another Life* by Sue Ellen Bridgers
- *Long Time Between Kisses* by Sandra Scoppettone
- *I Will Call It Georgie's Blues* by Suzanne Newton
- *A Place to Come Back To* by Nancy Bond
- *A Day No Pigs Would Die* by Robert Newton Peck
- *Lily and the Lost Boy* by Paula Fox
- *Spanish Hoof* by Robert Newton Peck
- *The Crossing* by Gary Paulsen
- *To Myself* by Galila Ron-Fender
- *Permanent Connections* by Sue Ellen Bridgers
- *The Moonlight Man* by Paula Fox
- *A Solitary Blue* by Cynthia Voigt
- *The Birds of Summer* by Zilpha Keatley Snyder
- *My Antonia* by Willa Cather
- *A Portrait of the Artist as a Young Man* by James Joyce
- *Member of the Wedding* by Harper Lee

Poetry

- "Well Water" by Randall Jarrell
- "Curiosity" by Alastair Reid
- "Dreams" by Langston Hughes

HEROES OR COURAGE
Novels

- *Chernowitz!* by Fran Arrick
- *Eyes of Darkness* by Jamake Highwater
- *Ganesh* by Malcolm J. Bosse
- *The Autobiography of Miss Jane Pitman* by Ernest Gaines
- *If Beale Street Could Talk* by James Baldwin
- *M. C. Higgins, The Great* by Virginia Hamilton

Poetry

- "They Tell Me" by Yevgeny Yevyushenko
- "Wild Horses" by Elder Olson
- "Icarus" by Edward Field

▼

MEDIA IN THE ENGLISH CLASSROOM
MOVIES

Young adults like to go to the movies; movie studios make more money from teenagers than from any other segment of the population. Harold Foster, a high school English teacher, believes that ignoring movies in the English classroom prevents us from helping students to become aware of how movies influence them (86). Objectives for teaching about movies are similar to those involving advertising. We want students to become more objective and to understand how they are influenced. Not all advertising is bad, nor all movies poor, but we want to teach students to tell which are and which are not. Foster suggests the following goals:

1. Transforming students into discriminating viewers who can distinguish good from bad, communication from exploitation.
2. Sensitizing students to how films are designed to influence and manipulate them.

3. Educating students to understand films visually and thematically, so they can analyze and critique films they see.

4. Developing critical awareness so that students occasionally pass up the worst of these films and stay home and read a book (86).

To achieve these goals we need to talk about current films in the classroom and to use videos in the literature units. Visual literature can be powerful; we and our students benefit from this added dimension.

TELEVISION

Television is a major influence in our lives, yet rarely are TV shows discussed in English class unless we tape and show something like *The Nature of English*. Many of the same goals for movies apply to TV. We want students to become more objective observers and to make critical judgments. Television is a showcase of American life and an excellent vehicle for making students aware of stereotypes. Teachers can move students away from passive viewing and into critical analysis.

To accomplish this goal, students choose an area to focus on and then write questions to guide their viewing. For instance, begin a discussion in class of favorite or not-so-favorite TV shows. Start by asking why they like or don't like a show. Conversation will be lively, with strong opinions and much interruption of each other. Students then choose a series, type of show, or commercials shown during particular shows. Individually they write three or four questions that will guide their viewing: Are there consistent stereotypes? Are stereotypes more likely to be of minorities or women? What image is portrayed of children, parents, and their relationships? What audience is the show or commercial geared to? Do the commercials and shows complement each other? Are sports announcers biased, and if so, in what way? Students share questions in small groups, where they help each other refine the questions and think of others to add.

To be effective critics, students must keep track of what they view. The action on the screen goes by too quickly to monitor accurately. Taking notes while watching is almost impossible, but students can write notes at every commercial break. And when they get used to keeping a pen and paper handy, they become better at recording dialogue and action. Students see things they never saw before and become much more objective.

We owe it to our students to help them become more critical viewers, and by doing so they become better critical thinkers. Discussing whether violence is essential for the show, whether humor is appropriate, and whether people are portrayed honestly also helps students grow in confidence that they have something important to say. Sometimes the confidence transfers to discussing similar elements in literature, but even if that doesn't happen, they gain knowledge and objectivity.

VIDEOS

Because they are so easily obtainable and the visual aspect appeals to students, videos are an important addition to the study of literature. Videos make some literature selections accessible in ways that a book cannot. A common way to use a video is to have students read a novel or play and then see the video; however, teachers use videos in class in other ways as well.

1. Rather than showing the video of the book students read, the teacher selects a different title, but one on the same theme. Harold Foster, a high school English teacher, suggests that for a thematic unit on coming of age, *Sixteen Candles* is a good choice. Also, *The Alfred G. Graebner Memorial High School Handbook of Rules and Regulations* fits in very well, describing with humor what life as a high school freshman is like (87). Many videos on the popular theme of growing up are available and can be ordered from the school's catalogue. Teachers do need to plan ahead because it takes several weeks for the films to arrive, and popular ones are booked early. We found it best to order the films for the following year in the spring.

2. Show a video different from the novels read, but select one based on a novel that is too difficult for all or most of the students. Seeing the film first does not detract from their enjoyment in reading the novel later. In fact, students report that they liked and understood the novel better because they saw the film first. Our students do not always need to read the book. We can greatly broaden the literary experience for many students by showing the film only and discussing it in class.

3. The visual interpretation of literature is always different from the printed form, and helping students learn how to analyze these differences deepens their understanding of interpretations. "The Revolt of Mother," based on a short story of the same title by Mary E. Wilkins, is an appropriate choice for secondary students. Observing expression and action focuses on a different dimension.

   • Where do the two versions differ?
   • Is the film true to what students believe the author presented?
   • Why are changes made?
   • If you made a film based on this or another story, how would you film it?
   • How do music, shadows, and light affect the meaning?
   • In what ways does camera angle make a difference?

   An offshoot of this activity is to have students choose well-known TV or movie actors for the characters in a literature selection and explain why they made the particular choices. Characterizations often become clearer when they think about matching a fictional character with an actor.

4. Classic films like *Stagecoach, The African Queen, The Wizard of Oz,* and *Gone with the Wind* are excellent for analyzing the use of prototypes, directing techniques, and story line. A unit on films is very appropriate in an English class. Incidentally, comparing the novel and film versions of *The Wizard of Oz* is an interesting activity because the two are quite different, yet the intended audience for both is children.

▼
CENSORSHIP

One cannot think about literature selections without considering censorship. The basic premise in censorship cases is that reading certain material results in a change of values, beliefs, and behavior. For years, researchers have been trying to prove or disprove the connection between books (or television) and behavior. If children see or read about violent actions, will they then be more likely to perform violent acts? No clear conclusions either way emerged from the studies.

For parents, school boards, and teachers who believe books should be censored, it doesn't make any difference what studies show. If they believe a book is harmful, we teachers must deal with that belief. Although a few teachers around the country refuse to teach certain books or want them removed from library shelves, teachers on the whole are in favor of having students read the books that continue to be the most common targets in censorship cases. A look at the books most often censored explains why. Lee Burress, who has long been involved in censorship issues, lists the 30 most frequently attacked books since 1965, according to six surveys (180–181):

- *The Adventures of Huckleberry Finn*
- *The Diary of a Young Girl* (Anne Frank)
- *Black Like Me*
- *Brave New World*
- *The Catcher in the Rye*
- *Deliverance*
- *The Electric Kool-Aid Acid Test*
- *A Farewell to Arms*
- *Go Ask Alice*
- *The Good Earth*
- *The Grapes of Wrath*
- *A Hero Ain't Nothin' But a Sandwich*
- *If Beal Street Could Talk*
- *I Know Why the Caged Bird Sings*
- *Johnny Got His Gun*

- *The Learning Tree*
- *Lord of the Flies*
- *Love Story*
- *Manchild in the Promised Land*
- *My Darling, My Hamburger*
- *Nineteen Eighty-Four*
- *Of Mice and Men*
- *One Day in the Life of Ivan Denisovich*
- *One Flew Over the Cuckoo's Nest*
- *Ordinary People*
- *Our Bodies, Ourselves*
- *The Scarlet Letter*
- *A Separate Peace*
- *Slaughterhouse-Five*
- *To Kill a Mockingbird*

Burress compiled a list of the reasons people objected to each book. Sex and obscene language were the most common complaints, but people also objected to reference to God, comments they perceived as un-American or Communist propaganda, references to homosexuality, and depressing story lines. One important point to note is that 40% of the books most attacked were written by women and minorities. A hidden agenda is certainly a possibility.

The best defense against censorship is for teachers to know why they are teaching a particular book. Sometimes teachers think they can avoid trouble for themselves by not teaching a book someone might object to. But self-censorship is wrong because it is driven by fear and emotional response. Our reasons for teaching a book must come from our knowledge of literature, our desire to teach our students about America's culture through a multitude of voices, our ability to help our students learn about other ways of life, and a wider world view. Of course, teachers make choices on personal preferences as well; we can't teach everything. However, choices must not be based on fear but on meeting our objectives for teaching literature.

Several sources provide rationales written by teachers for books most likely to meet with objections. The Ohio Council of Teachers of English published (1984) a book of rationales for 10 books, describing the strengths of the books and how they meet teaching objectives. The Wisconsin Council of Teachers of English also published (1985) a book of rationales for 33 of the most commonly challenged books. The rationales are really discussions of the books, but from them teachers could write their own rationales. Both publications make the point that when teachers know why they are teaching a particular book and can back up their selections with well thought-out reasons, they are as prepared as possible for censorship questions.

Parents may question a literature choice and, after hearing the reasons for teaching it, may be satisfied. Teachers can always select an alternative book for a student as long as it is on the same theme. Teaching thematic units with two or three selections makes this an easy solution. An important principle in the censorship issue is that parents do have a right to influence what their children read, but they do not have the right to decide what other children read. Teachers must be prepared to provide options.

Susan B. Neuman, a teacher at Eastern Connecticut State University, explains:

> Censorship is negative because it eliminates choice and discourages reading. It does not encourage or create opportunities for positive reading experiences. Further education, rather than censorship, can lead to an informed citizenry. That is the goal educators must emphasize. (49)

Because censorship problems occur all over the United States in every size school district, all teachers are affected. We do not have to fight censorship problems alone, however. State departments of education, universities, the National Council of Teachers of English, and the Office for Intellectual Freedom of the American Library Association can provide assistance.

The National Council of Teachers of English passed a resolution in 1981 that reaffirms the students' right of access to a wide range of books and other learning materials under the guidance of qualified teachers and librarians. To assist teachers in resisting censorship, Geneva T. Van Horne wrote "Strategies for Action" for the NCTE publication *SLATE*.

STRATEGIES FOR ACTION

1. Develop and promote, on a regular basis, good public relations and communication with community groups and parents about the school's philosophy and goals, the English language arts educational objectives, the curricula, and classroom and library media programs.

2. Distribute the NCTE booklet, *The Students' Right to Read*, to all faculty, school board members, administrators, and community and parent groups.

3. Prepare, and have adopted by the school board, a written selection policy for all media, both print and audiovisual. Include a well-defined procedure for handling challenged materials. Coverage should include:
   A. Philosophy and goals of the school system
   B. Goals and objectives of the instructional program
   C. Responsibility for selection of instructional materials
   D. Criteria for selection of instructional materials
   E. Standard professional and current selection tools to be consulted (e.g., Elementary School Library Collection, W. H. Wilson Company Catalog Series, Book Finder, and NCTE booklists)
   F. Procedures for reconsideration of instructional materials

1. Statement of policy
2. Guiding principles
3. Specific procedures
   a) Informal resolution
   b) Formal resolution
4. Forms would include
   a) Instructional objectives rationale form
   b) Reconsideration of instructional materials form
   c) Reconsideration of nonfiction instructional materials form
   d) Reconsideration of fiction instructional materials form

4. Follow the procedure for handling challenged materials without deviation.
   A. Attempt to resolve the challenge informally, but if at the end of the meeting, the complainant still wishes to challenge the material, a form for reconsideration should be provided.
   B. Only when the written request for reconsideration has been filed should the formal review process commence, as outlined in the selection policy.
   C. Adhere to the policy established for reconsideration of instructional materials. There should be no restrictions or curtailment of use of the questioned material while it is being reconsidered.
   D. Follow the time line established in the policy. Complete the process with the written report.
   E. Consult your NCTE state president, local English supervisor, and English language arts state department consultant for further assistance and advice.

5. Acquaint the faculty, administrators, and parents with all aspects of the selection policy and the challenged materials procedure through in-service programs and workshops yearly so that there is no question of what is involved or what is to be done.

6. Keep on file a written faculty rationale, an explanation of the controlling principle, for any materials students read or study in common and for those most often censored.

7. Permit students to have an alternate assignment or allow students choices when developing course assignments and objectives.

8. Provide a variety of books and materials addressed to different levels of readability, maturation, and interest.

9. Honor a parent's right to exempt his or her child from content or assignments to which he or she objects.

10. Use standard and current professional bibliographies when selecting materials to support the instructional program.

11. Include a clause in the bargaining contract protecting academic freedom. Work for Board adoption of grievance procedures to protect teachers' due process rights.

12. Consult current references on censorship available from NCTE, ALA, and other professional organizations.

Censorship in your school system may well be prevented if you follow the foregoing guidelines and those in the NCTE *Students' Right to Read*.

SOURCES FOR LITERATURE SELECTIONS

- *Booklist,* an American Library Association publication
- *Bulletin of the Center for Children's Books*
- *The English Journal,* a National Council of Teachers of English publication for secondary school teachers
- *The Horn Book Magazine*
- *Interracial Books for Children Bulletin*
- *Journal of Reading*
- *Media and Methods*
- *School Library Journal*
- *Wilson Library Journal*

DISCUSSION QUESTIONS

1. What literature did you study in middle and high school? Did the selections reflect the cultures represented in your school?
2. Do you read more or less often than you did as a high school student? Why?
3. What books do you choose for recreational reading?
4. What literature selections are middle and high school students reading now? If you have an opportunity to visit local middle and high schools, look at the anthologies. Check out what paperbacks the students are carrying around. Discuss your findings in class.
5. Name five novels you have read that are written by white American men, by women, by African-Americans, and by Native Americans. Male authors in any culture are published and recognized before female authors. Why do you think this is true?

SUGGESTED ACTIVITIES

1. Select three novels on the same theme. Then find a short story that could be taught in the unit. Write summaries of all four.
2. Choose a theme you are interested in. Write summaries of three books at three different reading levels that fit in your unit.

3. Locate a poem and a play on the same theme for middle school students and then for high school students.

4. Check back on the selections you made for the first three activities. What cultures are represented? Is there a balance between genders? If necessary, select other literature to ensure a nonbiased list of readings.

REFERENCES

Anson, Chris M. "Book Lists, Cultural Literacy, and the Stagnation of Discourse." *English Journal* Feb. 1988: 14–18.

Applebee, Arthur N. *A Study of Book-Length Works Taught in High School English Courses.* Albany: National Research Center on Literature Teaching & Learning, 1989.

Burress, Lee. *Battle of the Books.* Metuchen: Scarecrow Press, 1989.

Carlsen, G. Robert. "What Beginning English Teachers Need to Know about Adolescent Literature." *English Education* 10 (1979): 195–202.

Carrier, Warren, and Kenneth Oliver, eds. *Guide to World Literature.* Urbana: National Council of Teachers of English, 1980.

Dabydeen, David. *A Handbook for teaching Caribbean Literature.* London: Heinemann, 1988.

Duff, Ogle B., and Helen J. Tongchinsub. "Expanding the Secondary Literature Curriculum: Annotated Bibliographies of American Indian, Asian American, and Hispanic American Literature." *English Education* 22 (1990): 220–240.

Elbow, Peter. *What is English?* New York: MLA, 1990.

Foster, Harold M. "Film in the Classroom: Coping with Teenpics." *English Journal* March 1987: 86–88.

Frye, Northrop. *On Teaching Literature.* New York: Harcourt Brace Jovanovich, 1972.

Gonzalez, Roseann Duenas. "When Minority Becomes Majority: The Changing Face of English Classrooms." *English Journal* Jan. 1990: 16–23.

Greenblatt, Ellen. *Many Voices: A Multicultural Bibliography for Secondary School.* Berkeley: Bay Area Writing Project, 1991.

Gunner, Elizabeth. *A Handbook for Teaching African Literature.* 2nd ed. London: Heinemann, 1987.

Lake, Patricia. "Sexual Stereotyping and the English Curriculum." *English Journal* Oct. 1988: 35–38.

Mossman, Robert. "South African Literature: A Global Lesson in One Country." *English Journal* Dec. 1990: 41–46.

Neuman, Susan B. "Rethinking the Censorship Issue." *English Journal* Sept. 1986: 46–49.

Olds, Alan. "Thinking Eastern: Preparing Students to Read Chinese Literature." *English Journal* Dec. 1990: 20–34.

Purves, Alan C., and Dianne L. Monson. *Experiencing Children's Literature* Glenview: Scott, Foresman and Co., 1984.

Reichman, Henry. *Censorship and Selection: Issues and Answers for Schools.* Chicago: American Library Association, 1988.

Romero, Patricia Ann, and Don Zancanella. "Expanding the Circle: Hispanic Voices in American Literature." *English Journal* Jan. 1990: 24–29.

Sasse, Mary Hawley. "Literature in a Multiethnic Culture." *Literature in the Classroom: Readers, Texts, and Contexts.* Ed. Ben F. Nelms. Urbana: National Council of Teachers of English, 1988. 167–178.

Smith, Frank. "Overselling Literacy." *Phi Delta Kappan* Jan. 1989: 353–359.

Stensland, Anna Lee. *Literature By and About the American Indian.* Urbana: National Council of Teachers of English, 1979.

Tatum, Charles. *Mexican American Literature.* Niles: Harcourt, 1989.

Van Horne, Geneva T. "Combatting Censorship of Instructional Materials." *SLATE Starter Sheet* Feb. 1983.

CHAPTER 5

Teaching Composition

CHAPTER HIGHLIGHTS

- Research on writing.
- The writing process.
- Types of writing.
- Stages in the writing process.
- Types of writing assignments.
- Journal writing.
- Writing short stories.
- Writing poetry.
- Writing reports.
- Collaborative writing.
- Research papers.
- Additional writing assignments.

What more important service can we perform for ourselves than to write; to write, that is, not to get a grade or pass a course, but to sound the depths, to explore, to discover; to save our floundering selves. (7)

—*James E. Miller, Jr.*

▼
BACKGROUND OF TEACHING COMPOSITION

Writing is a complex skill, and the teaching of writing is therefore multi-dimensional. We must help students discover their own knowledge and their own voice. We need to help young writers develop the techniques necessary to write their ideas coherently in a form comprehensible and appropriate for others. No one method is best for teaching writing, but the work of educators and researchers over the past 20 years has given us an understanding of how to improve the teaching of writing.

▼
RESEARCH ON WRITING

Concerns with how we teach composition are not new. From the first issue of the *English Journal* in 1912, teachers have struggled to find the most effective ways of helping students write well. Although the emphasis has changed over the years, many of the issues that teachers of the 1920s worried about are still with us, including writing in other subjects, lessening the burden of composition teachers, balancing the teaching of skills and content, and choosing topics of interest to students (Maxwell 2–4). During the 1930s, the emphasis was on motivating students to write and finding ways to make writing meaningful to them, although concern with correct punctuation also appeared in articles. Although we think of journal writing as a fairly new idea in teaching writing, Eleanor Brown introduced journal-keeping in 1934 as a way of breaking down the stiffness of formal writing (7).

Articles during the 1940s focused on the importance of students writing about subjects that matter to them. The 1950s re-emphasized the concern with errors and ways to help students learn the basics of writing, although many of the *English Journal* authors continued to examine ways of bringing real-life experiences into student writing (9–11).

A growing concern in the 1960s was that, although teaching composition was an established part of English programs and had been since the early 1900s, there was no comprehensive understanding of how to teach writing. Educators were moving from a concern with the written product to an emphasis on the process of writing, but not until a conference in 1966 at Dartmouth College did the process of writing become integrated into the teaching of writing in the schools. The Dartmouth Conference emphasized personal growth in both writing and literature, and the participants advocated moving from product to process in the teaching of writing.

John Dixon, one of the participants, described the thinking, discussion, and exchange of ideas that went on at Dartmouth in *Growth Through English*. He stressed the need for students to talk over their experiences before attempting to write. "Talking it over, thinking it over, and (as confidence is gained) writing, can be natural parts of taking account of new experiences (cognitively and affectively)" (28). The ideas of exploratory talk before writing and talking in groups as the writing progresses were quite different ways of viewing the teaching of writing.

Traditionally, when writing instruction focused on the product, teachers told students what they did wrong, hoping that they would then do it right. Such an approach has the wrong emphasis. Learning is much easier when we are praised for what we do right. If we concentrate on what we do wrong when we are learning to ski, golf, or roller skate, we tend to repeat our mistakes. If we are praised for what we do correctly, we learn more easily because we are concentrating on what we do right. We all find learning easier and more pleasant when we receive praise and encouragement.

Writing instruction took just the opposite approach. On Monday, teachers typically assigned a theme. They explained the assignment carefully and asked if there were any questions. The students handed in the themes on Friday, and dedicated teachers spent the weekend going over the papers, noting every error in the hope that if students saw what they were doing wrong, they wouldn't make the same mistakes again. The model was a negative one—what not to do. As a result, students did not write well. Nor did they like to write.

Writing instruction did not improve for the majority of students. An inverse proportion seemed to exist between the amount of time a teacher spent marking papers and the degree of improvement in student writing. The more red ink and negative comments, the less students paid attention to what teachers wrote on their papers. What a discouraging situation for teachers! Students looked at the grade and, without reading the comments, threw the paper away. The situation was just as discouraging for students, particularly for those who had difficulty with writing. They did not know what area or skill to begin working on. Part of the problem was that they were looking at a finished product, when their main difficulty may have been generating beginning ideas for their topic. Basic problems were buried in a morass of red-penned punctuation errors. If writing is taught as a process, teachers can help students when problems occur.

▼
THE WRITING PROCESS

Viewing writing as a process means that writers can and should receive guidance and instruction throughout the time they are composing—from the first thoughts about a topic or idea to the end product. The process is described as loosely fitting into stages of writing: prewriting or discovery, drafting, revising, and editing. However, the writing process is not made up of a series of discrete steps leading to a finished product but is recursive. That is, a writer goes back and forth from one stage to another as the writing progresses. For instance, a writer first considers what to write about and how best to get started. As the drafting, or first attempts at writing, proceed, the writer may return to the discovery stage to rethink what to write or to explore other ideas and feelings. At the revision stage, a writer may return to discovery activities when it becomes clear that the writing needs more than minor revision. Throughout the process, writers move in and out of stages as the writing demands.

The term *prewriting* was coined by D. Gordon Rohman in 1965 when he conducted a study of first-year writers at Michigan State University. He believed that students needed time for thinking to develop their ideas and plans for writing. He used journal writing as the prewriting activity and found that students improved their writing when given the time and method to discover what and how they would write. Janet Emig, in a 1971 study, found that prewriting was a much longer process in self-sponsored writing than in school-sponsored writing. This is true partly because teachers do not provide time for prewriting, but also because a student cannot explore thoughts for writing when the topic is unfamiliar or uninteresting. Allowing time for students to think and talk about writing is essential.

▼
TYPES OF WRITING

Personal involvement in writing affects not only the process, but also the types of writing the students are asked to do. Traditionally, school writing was used by students to show what they had learned. In literature, they wrote essays and exams explaining what literary critics thought. In research papers and report writing, they read library material and wrote other people's words and opinions. Students were not allowed to use the word *I* because their own voices and ideas were not appropriate.

A major figure in helping educators to rethink the types of writing assignments was James Britton of the University of London Institute of Education. Working with Tony Burgess, Nancy Martin, Alex McLeod, and Harold Rosen, Britton sought to describe stages in the development of writing abilities. To begin the task they examined ways to classify the writing done by school children according to the nature of the task and the demands made upon the writer (3). Out of that study came fundamental ideas about writing that shape our present-day thinking and teaching.

Writing has been classified traditionally into rhetorical categories of narrative, descriptive, expository, and argument. Britton explains that using these four categories causes difficulty in teaching writing. The modes are "derived from an examination of the finished products of professional writers" (4). The result is a prescription for how people *should* write, not *how* they write. The system of categories essentially leaves out the writer and the writing process. Evaluation of writing is concerned only with whether the writer used the collection of rules that rhetoricians in 1828 decided were the "best sorts of things to say in various argumentative situations" (I. A. Richards qtd. in Britton, et al. 4). Throughout the 1950s, traditional categories shaped writing in secondary schools. In the 1960s, a distinction between personal and objective writing was made. School writing was dominated by objective writing—in other words, writing that was abstract and generalized (8).

As their study of writing progressed, Britton and his colleagues developed a description of writing based on the function of writing and the sense of audience. Britton describes three categories of function for writing. The first he calls *expressive,* a term he borrowed from Edward Sapir's work on linguistics. Expressive writing uses language the writer is most familiar with and relies on the assumption that the reader is interested in what the writer is talking about. Such writing is informal and natural, the kind people like to do. The second category Britton defined is *transactional.* Humans learn from experience, and to do this we need to interpret, to shape, to represent experience (41). When writers use transactional writing, they write about events that have already happened. They write in the "role of spectator" as they view past events. The more the writing "meets the demands of participation in the world's affairs, the nearer will it approach the transactional . . ." (83). Transactional language gets things done in the world and is the kind of writing taught in schools, usually to the exclusion of expressive and poetic. *Poetic* is the third category, and Britton defines it as language in art. To write in the poetic form is to create a verbal object, an end in itself (83). Poetry is the most obvious example of the poetic form, but the categories are not exclusive, and poetic writing can occur in any form. Britton explains that the words themselves are selected by the writer to form an arrangement, a pattern (90). As the idea of teaching writing as process developed, more emphasis was placed on including expressive and poetic writing in the classroom.

James Moffett describes the spectrum of discourse as a hierarchy of levels of abstraction: recording, reporting, generalizing, and theorizing. As in Britton's classification, the levels or kinds of discourse overlap. Shifting from one kind of discourse to another, "say, from narrative discourse to that of explicit generalization necessarily entails shifts in language and rhetoric" and thus raises different composition issues (53). He makes a strong point about keeping these issues centered in the context of writing. The writing process underscores this belief by teaching skills in the context of a student's writing.

The basic premise of the writing process is that writing can and should be taught as writers write rather than after the paper is handed in to a teacher.

▼ ────────────────────────────────────

STAGES IN THE WRITING PROCESS
DISCOVERY STAGE

The discovery stage is the most important step in writing something interesting, honest, and lively. Several activities help writers discover what they know and what they want to say. Activities might be creative dramatics, films, discussion, and reading as well as many kinds of writing. Many people call this stage *prewriting,* but that term does not reflect the many writing activities that can occur at this stage.

To be successful writers, students must be interested in what they write about. This means giving students the freedom to select their own topics. A teacher can provide a general area or list of possible topics, but students need to have choices. Even with choices, some students can't think of what they want to write about. Teachers can sometimes suggest alternative topics, but other students are a better source of help. After students select their topics, they meet in groups and the teacher instructs them to talk about their choices—why they think they would like to write about a particular one or what they already know about it. Members of the group help anyone who is having difficulty in deciding on a topic. Discussing ideas and getting immediate feedback are a tremendous help. If the general topic is writing about how one of the characters in a novel changed over the course of the story and the reasons for the change, hearing how others perceive the character development can help someone decide what to write about. The same is true with other kinds of assignments. If students are writing persuasive letters, taking part in discussions about why a particular letter needs to be written and to whom helps others generate ideas. Sharing ideas about writing is probably the most effective way of helping writers get started.

A writing classroom is a talking classroom. In the traditional way of teaching writing, students wrote in isolation. Opportunities for an exchange of ideas didn't exist in the classroom. In the real world, however, we share our writing. When we write a line or paragraph that we believe is particularly good, our first impulse is to read it to someone. We have all turned to someone with the words, "Listen to this!" Sharing writing is normal behavior. Except for private journal writing (and even that sometimes), writing is meant to be shared.

Another source of ideas for writing is responses to reading or viewing. In the chapter on teaching literature, response writing is discussed in detail. Responding to literature or film is important for many reasons. Instead of remaining passive learners, students become more involved in the act of reading or viewing. Also, the comments and questions students write become rich resources in the discovery stage as students look for ideas in writing. They have developed their own private source of writing topics.

Discovery Activities

Depending on the writing task, many discovery activities help students to get started.

1. *Free writing.* At the top of a page students write the name of their topic or idea, such as a person they admire. Then for a specified amount of time, not more than 10 minutes, they write everything they can possibly think of in connection with that subject. The term *free* means that the writer is free to

put down anything that comes to mind and free from any concerns about mechanics or spelling. When the allotted time is up, students read over what they wrote and circle phrases and words that seem especially appropriate to them. At this point, if time permits, they can meet in groups and share their writing with others. The next step is to write again, elaborating on the circled phrases, although they are encouraged to develop the piece in any way they want. Free writing often brings thoughts to mind that more structured writing would not tap into. This activity works best when writers are working on topics they know a lot about.

2. *Drawing.* Like free writing, drawing taps hidden thoughts and new connections between thoughts. One does not have to be very good at drawing for this to be a useful activity. If the assignment is to describe an incident from childhood, drawing a location or scene helps fill in vivid details, not because the writer draws them but because the drawing spurs the memory into recalling details. When writing a description of my grandmother, I drew a sketch of the pantry in her house. Although I didn't include the pantry itself in the essay, the act of drawing it brought to mind several incidents I had not thought of. It is a shame that drawing is left behind in elementary school. We lose an important way of thinking.

3. *Mapping.* When the writing topic is not familiar to the writer, mapping helps to generate ideas and organization. Mapping is sometimes called webbing because the resulting diagram resembles a spiderweb. By either name, the intention is to generate and connect subtopics. The subject is placed in the center and topics are added on extending lines as the writer thinks of them. A map on the topic of changing the school calendar might look like this:

After the map is completed, an informal outline can be written which then serves as a beginning place for the piece.

A more formal outline with the traditional Roman numerals, capital letters, and so forth can also be used. Outlines can be very helpful as writers begin their organizing, but for some the structure gets in the way. People have different ways of organizing their thoughts, and teachers need to keep these differences in mind. When English teachers require a formal outline with the writing assignment, some students write the paper first and then the outline because they have trouble using structure as a prewriting activity. However, not everyone has that difficulty. As with all the discovery activities, some writers find particular devices helpful whereas others do not. For that reason it is best to suggest two or three activities and let students use those most helpful to them.

4. *Creative dramatics.* This discovery technique works for many kinds of writing. The definition of creative dramatics includes impromptu acting, role playing, and skits, all requiring little preparation time. The audience is the class. The objective is not to put on a performance, but to engage in an activity that promotes better writing. For example, if the assignment is to write a persuasive letter about a desired change in school policy, students could role-play for each other, taking the parts of parents, school administrators, school board members, and other community members. Even though the letters are on different topics, exchanging roles helps to clarify the issues and encourages students to see different sides of the arguments. As a result, the letters are more convincing.

Taking on the role of a character in a story helps students to understand the personality and motivation of a character better. The actors do not memorize lines but improvise dialogue that a character might say. Empathy for and realization of a character's behavior are reflected later in the student's writing. To be successful, creative dramatics should be introduced gradually and always presented as an informal activity.

A dramatic activity that always produces enthusiasm is a discovery technique designed to help students write dialogue. The students assemble in groups of four to six, and each group receives a bag of props that the teacher filled ahead of time with an odd assortment of items from home. There might be a hammer, a hair clip, a copy of Robert Frost's poems, an apple, a feather, a knife sharpener, and a pair of safety glasses in one of the bags. The students have about 25 minutes to think up a skit, and then each group performs the skit for the rest of the class. The only rule is that every prop must be used. During the following class period we discuss how the dialogue carried the skit along.

This discovery technique provides practice for future writing assignments but does not necessarily lead immediately into writing. A teacher might provide several activities to help students discover how dialogue can be used effectively before having students write a short story.

DRAFTING STAGE

For successful writing, students must realize the importance of multiple drafts. First drafts should be messy. After the discovery stage a writer has a great deal to say. Because the brain thinks more quickly than the hand can write, there is no time to worry about spelling or punctuation. Helping students to realize that putting down something worth reading is far more important than putting something down right is an important lesson at this stage. The need for correctness at this early stage gets in the way of successful writing. Writers attend to correctness later in the process. Several techniques help students become fluent writers.

1. Always refer to the writing as drafts. Asking if someone is on a second or third draft helps establish the notion of multiple drafts. The version students turn in is called a final draft rather than a final paper because no paper is every really "finished." That's not to discourage writers but to acknowledge that given more time, they could have polished it even more.

2. Drafting does not have to proceed from beginning to end; in fact, papers are usually better if one does not start at the beginning. At one time or another, we all stare at a blank sheet of paper not knowing where to start. Even with discovery techniques, writing that first line is difficult. By encouraging students not to start at the beginning, we can help them overcome that writing block. Middle school students can actually fold down the top third of the sheet to concretely show they are not writing the beginning sentence. It is amazing how freeing that can be. When students complain to a teacher they "don't know what to say," the best help is for a teacher to ask them what it is they "want to say." Writers can usually articulate what they want to say but can't figure out how to get started on paper. The teacher may respond, "Why not write what you just said?" Some seem to need permission to write what they want to write—to be told yes, that sounds good. Often beginnings are best written after the rest of the paper is done, especially in expository writing.

3. When drafts are first shared in writing groups, no one but the writer actually sees the paper. Authors read their own papers aloud to the other students in the group, so that no one is embarrassed about errors or poor handwriting. The emphasis is on what is being said, which is where it should be at this stage.

REVISING STAGE

A very important point here is that not all writing goes through every stage of the writing process. To get better at anything we must practice, and many practice activities are not revised. Revision is important, but it takes time, and time is in short supply. If all writing assignments go through the entire process,

Box 5.1 REVISION MEMO

Your name _____ Title of writing _____

Date you read this piece aloud and made revisions _____

Date your writing group heard your paper _____

Names of writing group members _____ _____

_____ _____

_____ _____

Date your partner read your piece _____

Signature of writing partner _____

we can't teach all the different kinds of assignments that provide the experiences in writing our students need.

Revision has several steps and purposes:

1. Revision always begins with the writer. We all need help from other readers to improve our writing, but students first need to read their own work with as critical an eye as possible. Reading the piece aloud helps the writer to hear redundancies, omissions, and incorrect word choices. Reading the piece oneself is an essential first step before getting help from others. When the revision process is first introduced to students, a memo to fill out is a useful tool (Box 5.1). Later, when they are experienced with the three steps, the memo is no longer required. Perhaps this seems more detailed than necessary, but as students are learning the process it serves as a silent reminder of each step.

2. The second step involves the writing group mentioned in the memo. The groups are fairly large—five or six members—so that each writer benefits from hearing several responses. Groups can be formed in several ways. The teacher may form the groups so that a variety of ability levels are in each group, may do a random selection, or may select students on the basis of their personalities, such as putting quiet students with more outgoing ones. Many teachers allow students to form their own groups. Perhaps the key to success is to use a variety of methods. Working in groups helps students get to know each other; if they always work with those they know best, they won't expand their circle of friends. On the other hand, students resent always being told with whom they can work. The groups stay together for one piece of writing. With a new assignment, new groups form. Even though students may want to remain in the groups they have worked with,

Box 5.2   RESPONSE SHEET

Writer's name _____

1. What is the paper about? Sum up in a sentence or two what points the author makes.
2. In what ways is the paper interesting?
3. Where could more detail or explanation be added? How would the additions help?
4. What words or phrases are especially effective?
5. What information is unnecessary?
6. What parts should be changed?
7. What other advice can you give to the writer to make this a better paper?

Your name(s) _____

_____

re-forming group membership helps develop social interaction and eliminates the problem of cliques.

When the students meet in their writing groups, each student reads his or her piece aloud to the others. The others respond in ways designed to make the writing better, which takes some guidance from the teacher. The first time a teacher tries response groups, they may not work. Often, the students are overly pleasant to each other. They tell each other how wonderful everyone's writing is, which is no help at all.

The solution to that problem is to provide structure for their responses because they really don't know what to say. Response sheets for students to fill in after the writer reads the piece are helpful. An example is given in Box 5.2.

Students respond to all of these questions without actually looking at the paper, so they must listen closely. Students often ask to have a sentence or a part repeated. Usually each student fills out a sheet, so that the writer has five different responses if there are six in a group. Students may also work with a partner and fill one out together. We don't recommend having them all work on just one sheet because it ends up being the response of only one or two. They discuss what they liked best and ask for clarifications so that the writer and responders are all talking together about the paper. The procedure continues for each member of the group. This process takes an entire class period, and a teacher may have to make the groups smaller to make sure everyone has a turn. Students make revisions, usually as homework, before the next step in the writing process.

Students need to realize that they do not have to take all the advice they receive. They should give it careful consideration, but the writer must decide if the suggestions are appropriate for his or her paper. We want students to be responsible for their own work, in this case writing; to accomplish that, they have the right to decide for themselves what they want in their papers. They won't agree with some of the suggestions they receive; that's not how they want their paper to sound. It is their decision. On the other hand, they need to take the suggestions seriously. Students who have trouble writing offer suggestions that are just as valid as those who write with little difficulty. They know as well as anyone whether a paper is interesting and makes sense.

Sometimes students complain that the response group did not help them. This is partly the writers' responsibility. When they know they have difficulty with a particular area, they need to ask the group for specific help. Someone might be marked down consistently for not using enough detailed description. That student needs to ask specifically for help with including details.

EDITING STAGE

Editing and proofreading are necessary only when the writing is published—that is, has a wider and perhaps unknown audience. If students are working with word processing, they bring a clean copy to the editing session. Otherwise, students do not have to copy the entire piece, but it should be revised and ready to be copied for the final draft. A paper may look messy with corrections written above a word, words crossed off, and other words inserted, but everything should be as correct as possible, including spelling and punctuation.

The editing stage is the first time students are required to read each other's papers. Students meet in the same groups as they did in the revising stage. The first procedure is the same as last time; each reads the revised paper to the others. This time, however, they do not fill out a revising sheet but rather talk about the changes, and the writer usually explains the thinking behind them. Often writers have made more revisions than the group suggested because once they started revising they saw the need for more changes. The writer may jot down notes as the others respond.

After everyone has read their papers, the members pair up and edit each other's papers. With the less experienced writers, many teachers use editing guides. These vary with assignments and with the age of the students. The guides are used to focus attention on various problem areas; they are not handed in. At this point in the writing process, students may write on each other's papers. An editing guide for an expository writing assignment for juniors or seniors might look like the one in Box 5.3.

The points on the editing sheet should reflect the assignment. Also, the developmental level of the students affects the direction of editing. An editing guide for middle school students writing a descriptive personal-experience paper might look like the one in Box 5.4.

Box 5.3   EDITING GUIDELINES FOR EXPOSITORY WRITING

1. The paper must support the thesis. Read the paper over and come back to the thesis, making sure it is appropriate.
2. Semicolons are causing problems for some. Check especially for proper use. A semicolon followed by an incomplete sentence is the most common mistake.
3. Transitions between paragraphs are another trouble spot.
4. Borrowed material needs to be introduced. Why is this source being used? Who is this person? Is the source outdated?
5. Any questions about spelling should be answered at this point. Remember that it is better to look up a word than to take a chance if you are unsure.
6. Do a final check on punctuation, subject-verb agreement, and pronoun reference.

Box 5.4   EDITING GUIDELINES FOR DESCRIPTIVE PERSONAL-EXPERIENCE WRITING

1. Together check over every adjective and verb, making sure the mind's eye sees what the writer does.
2. Look at the sentences. If they all begin with a subject followed by a verb, decide which ones to change.
3. Read for clichés and change to more appropriate comparisons.
4. Check for spelling. Remember to look up words you are not sure of.
5. In the last papers many students had trouble remembering to use commas. Together check each other's papers, reading sections aloud where you are not sure about comma placement.
6. Check over the paper carefully for any mechanical errors. Remember that this takes patience and is a responsibility of both the writer and the editor.

Student editors, at any grade level, are more effective if they receive guidance in what to look for. Telling students to check everything over is too unfocused, and they catch few mistakes that way. Also, giving them checklists is not helpful. It is easy to go down a list of yes or no questions and not engage in the task of looking for ways to improve the paper. Checklists are particularly useless when writers use them for their own work. The lists are meant to be reminders, but if a writer already believes the paper is in good shape, the questions are answered with a yes, with little thought. The more the editors are involved in the process, the better they do. Sometimes teachers ask students to copy the writer's best sentence and explain why it works so well. They are then asked to copy the sentence that most needs to be rewritten. Editing guides can focus on specific areas that the class as a whole is having trouble with.

TEACHER HELP

Teachers are part of the entire writing process, providing suggestions and help and listening to writers read their papers to them. But teachers also need to know when to stay out of a student's way. The writing belongs to the writer, and when teachers suggest specific ways to change the paper, they take away some of that ownership. A teacher's opinions carry far more weight than another student's. Teachers are the authority figure; they give the grades. Although we want to be supportive, we don't want to interfere with students finding their own voices. Student papers should never be collected until the final draft. Once the papers are in the teacher's hands, the students are no longer responsible for them. When teachers read and mark rough drafts, they are doing the work for the writer. The ones who are getting practice in editing are the teachers, when it is the students who should be practicing. When a teacher marks the papers with suggested changes, the students have only to make the corrections and not think about why they are making them. Some teachers feel so strongly about the ownership of the writing remaining with the students that they won't even hold a student's paper. If a student asks the teacher to read a work in progress, the teacher can ask the student to read it aloud or can read it over the student's shoulder. The more a teacher takes over, the more students write to please the teacher rather than themselves and their writing loses vitality and originality.

THE WRITING PROCESS IN ACTION

Although the writing process is described in stages and always begins with the discovery stage, the process is recursive. That is, writers move back and forth among the stages as they write. During drafting, writers may come to a standstill and be unable to think of what to say next. The best way to overcome the problem is to go back to discovery activities. They could brainstorm on what they are trying to say, or try mapping with the present topic in the middle, or free write all they know about the topic and then move on to drafting again. At the revision stage writers often return to drafting, rewriting sections or whole pages; here, too, they may use discovery activities again. Students need to be reminded repeatedly of the recursive nature of writing. The strength of the process is that writers are learning how to improve their writing as they write, not by trying to learn what they did wrong after the writing is finished. Two major points are important in teaching writing using the process method.

1.   The process is recursive. Writers move back and forth among stages as the need arises.

2. Not all writing tasks go through all of the stages—in particular, the stage of editing.

PUBLISHING STUDENT WRITING

In some cases, publishing is listed as the final step in the process. Although publishing is important in widening the audience for student writers and can be used successfully for many writing activities, to increase fluency students need to do many different kinds of writing and for many different purposes. Also, publishing almost always requires careful editing. At the elementary level, publishing has a different connotation. Putting work up in the halls or around the room is publishing, and because these are developing writers, editing plays a minor role. At secondary level, however, public expectation is different: Writing that is published should be error free. The emphasis for publishing, then, is always on a polished final draft. When students know their work is really going public, they are motivated to make the writing error free. The time taken up in editing cuts down on the variety of writing experiences, however. During the year a few assignments can be considered for publication, but not many, so that fluency remains a priority.

Places for publication are plentiful. We can use students' interest in issues to encourage them to write letters to newspapers and school publications. Organizations and businesses usually respond to a student letters asking for information. Many businesses publish student work in their own publications.

The classroom may want to set up its own literary magazine and publish works by student authors. Other outlets for young writers are available. A few examples include (*Notes Plus*, April 1988: 15):

- *Flip*, published four times a year for ages 13 to 19. Address: 265 E. Emmett, Battle Creek, MI 49017.
- *The McGuffey Writer*, published three times a year for ages preschool to 18. Address: 400 A McGuffey Hall, Miami University, Oxford, OH 45056.
- *Merlyn's Pen*, published four times a year for ages 12 to 15. Address: P.O. Box 1085, East Greenwich, RI 02818.
- *Prism*, published six times a year for ages 9 to 18. Address: P.O. Box 030464, Fort Lauderdale, FL 33303.
- *Stone Soup*, published five times a year for ages 6 to 13. Address: P.O. Box 83, Santa Cruz, CA 95063.

▼ _____

TYPES OF WRITING ASSIGNMENTS

The types of writing assignments students do in secondary school usually involve expository and creative writing; these might be divided into cause and effect, persuasion, argument, classification, analysis, summaries, poetry, and stories. In most cases, informative writing is more prevalent than personal. One characteristic consistent throughout curricula is that personal narrative becomes progressively less frequent at the higher grade levels. Writing for "the real world" takes over composition classes: reports rather than stories, analyses rather than opinions, formal rather than causal. Other serious consequences of the emphasis on expository assignments are the reliance on sources outside the students' experiences and the omission of *I* in this type of writing. Some teachers go so far as to tell students that they must never use *I* in expository writing. Yet, in major magazines like *The New Yorker*, first person is commonly used, as are personal experiences, in order to make a point. When the writing must not reflect the identity of the writer, the students' importance diminishes greatly. The message the students get is that they don't count and what they think doesn't matter.

Although students need to learn how to write a convincing persuasive paper, a strong thesis, major points supported by subtopics, and a well-organized argumentative essay, the lines of distinction among types of expository writing and so-called creative writing are blurred. Certain elements are unique to a particular type, but many occur in all writing. Descriptions occur in science writing, reports, letters (friendly and formal), and essays as well as in fiction. As writers we want readers to see and understand what we do. One of the best ways to achieve this goal is to describe in detail the physical appearance of a lake, a chemical reaction, a character, frog body parts, a graph, or a battlefield. Using figurative language as part of the descriptions helps, too, in providing a mind's-eye view for readers. Comparisons with similes and metaphors work in any type of writing. A letter to the editor or a board member is more effective with personal examples, and political speeches are full of them. As we teach specific ways to write reports, we also need to teach how and when to use descriptive language and personal experiences in report writing.

▼

JOURNAL WRITING

Journal writing has a place in every subject and is indispensable in English class. Because journals are never evaluated, students soon learn to rely on them for recording thoughts and ideas on a multitude of subjects. Teachers may read students' journals and write comments in a conversational tone, but the comments should never sound negative. The only criterion teachers can use to evaluate the work students do in their journals is effort, which is an elusive quality. Counting pages doesn't help, most obviously because some students write larger than others but also because a writer may put a great deal of thought into one page, whereas another could write pages of rambling prose. Reading the journals to see if the students did the work is all one has to do.

Journals can have many different purposes: recording thoughts and feelings, organizing plans, figuring things out, observing life. A variety of journals are useful in the classroom.

PERSONAL RESPONSE JOURNALS

The most common journal is one for personal response, in which students write about anything they want. If journal writing is frequently used in elementary school, this purpose is no longer as appropriate for secondary school. However, if students are not familiar with this type of journal, it is a good way to begin. The advantage to writing whatever comes to mind is that it helps to develop fluency; students get used to writing on a daily basis. The disadvantage is some students have a very difficult time thinking of anything to write. No matter how many suggestions a teacher gives, it remains an impossible task for some. Providing open-ended questions helps solve the problem. For example: What I remember best from last year is . . . , What I like least about school is. . . .

List making is a good place to start:

- My 10 favorite songs or the ones I dislike the most.
- Ten things that could never happen. Choose the one you most wish would happen and explain why.
- Name your three favorite people and describe them.
- Name three famous people. Why are they famous?
- Name three places you would like to visit and explain why.

One high school teacher writes a quotation on the board each day and students write a response to it. They have the option of writing about something else, but they all have to write.

Even though it takes time, reading student journals is important because they won't put effort into something we don't care about—which makes sense. The following points make the job a little easier:

1. Read them quickly. Responding every page or two seems to be enough. Students just want the sense that teachers are reading.
2. Stagger the date students hand the journals in so the teacher has journals from only one class at a time.
3. Students keep journals for three or four weeks, stop for two weeks, then start keeping them again.

PROJECT JOURNALS

When students are doing long projects, a journal helps them remember deadlines, organize tasks, and keep track of where they are. A project journal begins with notes from the teacher's description of the assignment and the dates each part is due. At the end of the project, the journal must be handed in, too. The teacher checks to see that each part is completed. Notes from outside readings can be kept in the journal. Outlines, mapping, and brainstorming are all part of the project journal. When students meet in response groups, the journal is a place to jot down notes to use when revising. Keeping a project journal is a great help in staying organized, something students have trouble with.

LANGUAGE JOURNALS

Paying attention to language in use is a way of appreciating its playfulness and diversity. Talking about language serves the purpose, too, of learning how new words come into our vocabulary, how punctuation patterns change, and how language belongs to the people who use it. A language journal might begin with an assignment to look for unusual signs, especially ones that use a play on words. Students note the signs in the language journal and share them in class. Even with a new focus each day, students continue looking for examples of all the suggestions for about a week. We take a few minutes at the beginning of the class period to share what they found. Other suggestions to use are unusual names, including connections between name and occupations. We had a dentist, Dr. Toothacker, and a doctor, Dr. Paine. Students come up with unbelievable examples. They have to be authentic, however. Names of businesses provide unusual examples, especially barber shops. Advertisements are a rich source, as are newspaper headlines. Overheard conversations provide examples of clichés. The language journal is a good starting place for discussions about language.

WRITER'S JOURNAL

The purpose of this journal is to provide ideas for stories and poems. Many students are shy about writing poetry; in their journal they can practice phrases, beginnings, and endings without having to write a complete poem. The same is true of stories. Perhaps they think of a description of a house; that might be all they write. Or they can write a plot outline. If they see an interesting-looking person, they should write a description in the journal; he or she might become a character in a story later. However, the connection between what one sees and later writes, may not always be concrete, as author Joan Didion explains. She keeps a notebook to record what she sees around her for the purpose of remembering her own sense of self at the time. Although a line or image may appear in her writing, the journal is a private recording of the world as she relates to it (136). Likewise, students can use their journals to recapture a mood or outlook or frame of mind.

An interesting source for writing is stories cut out of the newspaper. Sometimes all that is kept is a headline. Students tape the stories in the journal for reference later on. If students have difficulty getting started in noticing the world around them, teachers might provide specific leads, for instance, describing someone or something they noticed on the way home from school. Entries in the writing journal are a rich resource for sharing in the classroom.

WRITING SHORT STORIES

Discovery activities are especially important when students write stories, Plot, characterization, setting, descriptions, and dialogue all combine to create a well-written story. The writer's journal can provide help, as mentioned in preceding sections. In addition, a teacher can design many other activities.

ROUND ROBIN STORIES

Round robin stories are a way to get students interested in writing stories, and they work for a wide age span. Round robin stories foster creativity and the writing activity is one the students enjoy—an important result. Once a teacher uses it in class, students will probably ask to do it again. Because it doesn't take much time, about 15 minutes, it is handy to use when one can't begin something else—like the 15 minutes left in a class period after a fire drill. Students are divided into groups of four. Each student has a sheet of paper. At a signal from the teacher, each student begins a story. Sometimes teachers provide the kind of story it must be: mystery, science fiction, adventure. After 1½ minutes they stop writing. They finish a word if necessary, but not a sentence. They fold the part they've written down so that only the last line is visible; this might be one word or a whole line. Then they pass the paper to the right. This time they have 1 minute to write and follow the same procedure as before. It works well if the stories go around about three times, but the process can be adjusted to the time available. Just before the last pass, students know they have to write an ending, and when they hear the word *stop*, they finish the sentence rather than just the word. Students love to read the stories to their group.

DEVELOPING CHARACTERS

Students seem to have the most trouble with this area. Plots are the easiest. Most of the time, characters are there to carry the plot along and nothing more. An especially successful way to show students that characters should have personalities is an activity described by David Sudol, a high school teacher. Sudol began by telling his class that characters have to be developed and discussed different levels of character development. He places an empty chair in the center of the room and announces that Stanley Realbozo is sitting in it. He explains that the students have to bring him to life. He guides the discussion that follows with questions.

1.   What does Stanley look like? Can you describe him sitting there or doing something?

2. Where does Stanley live, work, and play?

3. What does Stanley think about? What is he thinking?

4. What is Stanley's conversation like? How does he speak?

5. How does Stanley react to people, places, and things?

6. How do other characters react to Stanley? What do they think and say about him?

7. What does the author think about Stanley? (The author is the class.)

When students have discussed all the questions, they put together a composite picture of Stanley. How real he is depends on the amount of detail in the class's answers. "But no matter what his level of development, he always comes alive. More than the responses to the questions, he is now an actual member of our class" (65).

At this point the students create a plot for Stanley using five questions as guides:

1. What is the situation of the story? What is happening at the beginning?

2. What is the main conflict of the story? What are the generating circumstances? What gets the action going?

3. What events in the story increase the conflict and push forward the action?

4. What is the climax or highest point of the story?

5. How are the conflicts resolved? (63–66)

Sudol uses the activity to help his students understand literature better; it can also be used as a discovery activity for short story writing. The first part— describing Stanley—is a whole-class activity; the plot questions then assist students in individually writing a story about Stanley. This activity, or any activity for that matter, can be adapted to meet the particular needs of a class.

STORY STRIPS

Most students are fairly good at writing plot but have trouble with characters and settings. This activity is designed to help them connect all three elements. Beforehand, cut strips of paper about 8½ inches long and 4 inches wide from three different colors. Begin with a discussion of what a setting could be. We use examples from stories they have read. In some cases, the setting meant a great deal and, in others, it made no difference at all. With help if necessary, they come up with a list of what settings could include. The teacher hands out strips of one color, and they each write a description of a setting.

Next, we discuss how characterization may be described in several ways: physical appearance, personality traits, behavior. Using the second colored strip, students write a character description.

The last strip is used for a single line of plot. At first, students tend to write too much for plot so it is better to limit it to one sentence. They might write, "She opened the door slowly."

When the students finish the three strips, the strips are placed in a container and students choose one strip of each color. Their assignment is to write a story incorporating the information on the strips. Some of the combinations bring out loud cries of "This is impossible!" "No way will this work out!" But the stories are always interesting and very creative. This activity is an excellent way to teach students how to use flashback in story writing. Sometimes flashback is the only way the writer can weave together dissimilar elements into a coherent story. When they say with despair, "I can't put a guy in a desert in 1834 in the same story as someone taking off in a rocket!", they might be encouraged to consider flashback as one solution (Maxwell 2–3).

PERSONAL NARRATIVES

Personal experience and fiction writing go hand in hand. Professional writers use their own experiences for stories, but we don't often ask students to do that. Students are not easily convinced that it is permissible to change facts when writing fiction. A student once said, "That's lying." But as Ben Logan explains in the dedication of *The Land Remembers*, one can ignore the facts and capture the truth. When people ask Logan how factual his book is, he explains that it is "feeling-level truth." That's what realistic stories are and we can help students create stories based on their own experiences.

When students begin a personal narrative, thinking about each sense, one at a time, helps bring back details they did not know they remembered. Logan explains, "The line between memory and invention is confused" (280). He made up some details to capture an image he knew to be true, only to discover later that they were indeed accurate. If writers want to convey an idea to a reader, say how cold the day was, they can make up a temperature that puts the feeling in the reader's mind. A former student wrote a wonderful story of helping out his 1st grade teacher, or so he thought, by painting leaves of the classroom plants with shellac. When Mark retells that story now, some of the facts change: the number of plants he shellacked, the grade he was in, and so forth. But what never changes is the image of a little boy trying so hard to please and failing because he didn't have an adult's knowledge of the world. Mark is using "feeling-level" truth.

▼ _____

WRITING POETRY

Before attempting to write poetry, students should be very familiar with reading and hearing poetry. Concentrating on poetry writing is often done as a unit for a week or more, but poetry itself should be integrated throughout the year. And once poetry writing is familiar to students, it, too, can be part of many units.

To begin the unit, we write a class poem based on Kenneth Koch's suggestion of the "I Wish" poem. Everyone in class completes the line that begins "I wish. . . ." It is much easier to organize the lines if students write them on 3 × 5 cards. All the cards are laid out on a table and arranged and rearranged to create a poem. If the same line or similar lines are written by more than one student, this becomes the refrain in the poem. It is important to put in everyone's lines; students look for their own. Even students who are antischool write a line and eagerly anticipate seeing their contribution in the completed poem. Type the poem that evening, run off copies for everyone, and hand them out the next day. Staggering the activity for multiple classes makes it easier on the teacher. The poem always comes out sounding like a "real poem" and impresses everyone. This activity works with students in elementary grades through the graduate students in the writing project. With that introduction we begin writing individual poems.

To bolster students' confidence, begin with formula poems. If students are familiar with these forms, a teacher might use only one or two as warm-up activities. A formula poem is one that follows a specific structure; although this method may seem simple, secondary students write interesting and insightful poems. Writing a poem can be very difficult for some people and this type of poetry gets them going.

1. *Five liners*

   • Write the name of someone or a noun on the first line.
   • Write two adjectives describing the person or noun.
   • Write three words describing what they do (end in *ing* or *s*).
   • Write a phrase about the person or noun.
   • Repeat the name or noun from line one or another name for the same person.

All of the following poetry examples are written by students.

Holden
Confused, introspective
Wandering, wondering, running
Looking for answers
Holden

Hester
Spirited, censored
Sins, sews, survives
Nobel brave victim
Hester
—*Gail Servoss*

Light
Reflect, shimmer
Shining, sparkling, glowing
Taking away the dark
Light
—*Becky Olien*

Summer
Hot, fun
Swimming, playing, traveling
Free from school
Summer
—*Jessa Olien*

2. *Diamond-shaped poems.* This is similar to the one above but has a twist in the middle. The first half refers to the noun on the first line; the second half to the noun on the last line.

- Begin with a noun.
- Write two adjectives describing the noun.
- Write three participles referring to the noun on the first line.
- Write four nouns: the first two refer to the name on the first line, the second two to the name on the last line.
- Write three participles referring to the noun on the last line.
- Write two adjectives describing the noun on the last line.
- Write the second noun on the last line.

Lady Macbeth
Greedy, ruthless
Scheming, controlling, cleaning
Blood, death—king, trouble
planning, killing, worrying
paranoid, pawn
Macbeth
—Laurie Anderson

3. *Concrete poems.* A concrete poem is one in which the words project not only an image but the actual shape of the subject of the poem. These can become trite unless writers use descriptive words, but with creativity they are enjoyable to eyes and ears.

a customized window
of plexi glass and bolts.
The windshield is graced with a
crack and a scratch from the stub that
was once a windshield wiper a hole in the
floor to complement the heater that works!— constantly. and a
back seat which folds down!— permanently the ashtray is lost, the
seatbelts won't click the radio is falling out, but who needs the extra

noise with	the spft pft t	spft
sputtering	pft rattling	pft
banging	clink clunk	t.

—Victoria Gillhouse

4. *Preposition poems.* The poem is seven lines long and each line begins with a preposition. Students write about themselves, about how they feel right now. Giving each student a list of prepositions is helpful.

Where I Am
In a place of wind and sun
As far as can be seen
Upon the mind a vision forms
Of grass and trees and green.
Throughout the swing I concentrate
About the ball so white
Against all odds I hit the thing and sent
it out of sight.
—*Cheryl Mortensen*

5. *Mood poems*. Students begin with a one-word description of their mood at the moment or one they felt recently. On the first line they write the mood. The next two lines begin with the word *not*, describing the mood by writing what it isn't. The fourth line is also a "not," but stated as a comparison. The fifth line is what the mood is, followed by three lines of description of the mood.

I'm happy
Not silly
Not falling off my chair happy
Not like the happiest I've ever been in my whole life
But quietly satisfactorily happy.
Happy that vacation is starting soon
Happy that my brother is coming home
Happy that I'm going skiing with my friends.

6. *Found poems*. Poetry defies definition: some rhyme, some do not; some are long, others short; some tell a story, or evoke a feeling, or describe a single image. The spacing of lines and arrangement of white space can create a sense of poetry. Found poems illustrate that point vividly. A found poem is "found" from any printed material: TV Guide, cereal boxes, student hand-books, textbooks, advertising, newspaper headlines, and so forth. Students have fun creating the layout of the words; some are silly, others more serious.

Why Brown Rice?
Brown rice is the most
nutritious
Rice of all.
It's also the least
Processed.
While most rice is
Polished

To remove the bran,
brown rice is
Whole
With only the outer hull
Removed.
—*Kellogg's Kenmei Rice Bran*

Experimenting and playing with words become the focus of poetry writing. Students, of course, can write haiku, limericks, sonnets, parodies, and other forms, but the goal is always to enjoy writing poetry and to increase confidence. Writing structured poems helps achieve these goals.

▼

WRITING REPORTS

Report writing is a way of getting students into the library to look for information, take notes on what they find, and organize the notes into a first draft. When students self-select the topic, they enjoy writing reports because they have the chance to pursue an interest, but problems may occur in locating information and organizing notes. Writing a report can overwhelm some students, but the following method helps them keep track of what they are doing. The first time we put it into action, the students who usually did not complete the longer assignments not only handed in reports on time, but wrote reports that were better organized than others. From then on, everyone used the same method involving concrete steps.

1. *Students choose a topic.* The discovery technique described earlier of meeting in groups to make a selection is used. The teacher may provide wide guidelines to help students think of a topic, but the students must be free to explore a topic of their own choosing.

2. *Using prior knowledge.* After choosing their topics, students write down everything they already know about them and they know a surprising amount. This is free writing; they are encouraged to write as quickly as possible, not worrying about spelling or punctuation. They read over what they have written and devise a list of questions they want to answer.

3. *The following day they bring the list of questions to class and share them in small groups.* Each student in turn explains the topic and reads the questions that will shape the report.

    Without the questions, students go into the library with only a vague idea of what they are doing there. They discover that finding answers (information) is very difficult if one doesn't know the questions—somewhat like going into a room to get something and then forgetting what one was looking for. Finding an unknown is almost impossible.

When each student shares the topic and questions, the others make suggestions and provide more questions. If the others aren't responding enough, I ask them to write one or two more questions for each person. As with other revising activities, students decide for themselves if they want to use the additional suggestions, but they have no lack of ideas. Talking over their plans for the reports is a help in itself because when they start explaining them to the others, their own ideas become clearer. By the next class period they have a list of four to six questions for which they need to find answers.

4. *Before starting the library work, they write each question on a separate sheet of paper.* If they have four questions, they have four sheets of paper. Then they take a final piece of paper and title it "References."

5. *Now they are ready for library work.* As they locate a reference, they begin finding answers to their questions. First they record the reference on the Reference sheet, numbering it 1. Then they jot down notes under the appropriate question and place a 1 by the notes to signify where the material came from. The first reference might provide notes for two or three questions. With the next reference they read, they go through the same procedure, numbering it 2. The question sheets soon look like this:

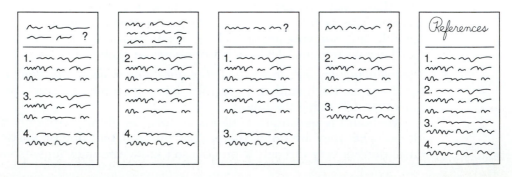

If they need help from a librarian, they can be very specific about what information they need. When the pages fill up with notes they staple more on. When the questions are answered, it is time to write the report. Before using this method, students who had trouble writing reports never knew whether or not they had enough information; with this method they can see when they've answered each question. If they cannot find the information needed to answer one of the questions, they may substitute another question if they clear it with the teacher.

With notes in hand, they return to the classroom and begin writing the report. All of the notes about one area are on one sheet; organizing is no problem at all. For many students, completing a report is a new experience. This method works for 4th through 12th grade. The more experienced writers do not need help with developing questions, although the idea of writing questions before looking at references may be new to them. All of the students report that keeping track of notes, seeing where more information is needed, and organizing the writing is easier using this method.

▼
COLLABORATIVE WRITING

Students working together to create a single work has many advantages. Writing alone never provides opportunities to see how others go about deciding what to say and how to say it. In a group, students see what discovery techniques others use: a mapping outline, free writing, listening, and so forth. Brainstorming in a group is more productive than doing it alone. One idea leads to another; what one person says makes another think of something else. And working together in a group helps with social interaction.

Many students loudly proclaim the disadvantages when a teacher brings up collaborative writing. Two areas cause the main difficulties: grades and work load. In collaborative writing everyone in the group receives the same grade. Students who usually receive high grades for their writing worry that their grade will drop. Some students worry that not all of the group members will do their share. Both are legitimate concerns, but there are ways around them, or at least ways to ease the problem.

Because cooperating with people is a skill we need throughout our life, learning to work with others is a major goal in collaborative writing, as important as writing a well-organized, interesting paper. To make collaborate writing work, teachers need to make sure the students work on both goals. By stressing the need to listen to others and respect what they say, teachers help students work through difficulties.

Receiving the same grade bothers some students, and they have to know from the beginning that there is no other way of weighing the grade. Knowing that they receive a common grade encourages students to work at cooperating with the others. When they hand in their final draft, ask them to evaluate individually how the process worked out—for instance, if they thought everyone did their fair share. Often, just having an opportunity to tell the teacher that they think they did more work than others is enough satisfaction.

Helen Dale, an English education instructor, describes in "Collaboration in the Writing Process" how she sets up the assignments in a way that provides a more even distribution of the work load. She puts as many students in a group as there are collaborative writing assignments. If she plans three collaborative assignments, she puts three people in a group. Each assignment has a primary writer, so the responsibility shifts from student to student. All of the group members contribute to each of the writing stages, but one person is responsible for collecting the others' work, doing the final polishing, writing transitions so that everyone's writing blends together, and whatever else needs to be done. For the next group writing assignment, a different member takes on that responsibility. Obviously, the groups have to remain the same throughout the semester or year.

Dale finds that the quality of the papers improves through collaboration. "There is peer pressure to think well and to write well. Students test ideas against each other, so you get their best and clearest thoughts." When she first started assigning group papers she thought students would write "patchwork prose," but she found that students "seem to integrate ideas, organization, and style" (15).

Collaborative groups provide first-hand experience in working together, an important ability in our life work. Dale believes that "Wonderful things happen when students are allowed to see other minds at work, puzzle things out, search for the right example or the right word, and arrive at a completed piece of work" (16). Although there are some negative aspects to collaborative writing, the positive outweighs the negative, and with planning teachers can make the experience worthwhile for students.

▼

RESEARCH PAPERS

Although research papers are a common assignment for high school students, many teachers are disappointed with the results. Unlike report writing, in which students select and record material from several sources into a coherent whole, the research paper requires, in addition, higher level thinking skills. Questions that students develop for the research paper cannot be answered simply by looking up material but require new insights that come from a study of the material, or, to put it another way, from doing research. It goes beyond answering questions with information already published and found in the library.

Many problems occur in research paper assignments. The description in the preceding paragraph indicates that research papers require a high level of cognitive ability. Developmentally, usually only students in 11th and 12th grades are able to successfully complete a research paper. Too often, younger students are assigned research projects. Teachers need to be mindful of the cognitive level of the task and the assignment.

Another serious problem is that teachers often do not use the writing process in research assignments. Students work too much in isolation with little guidance from their peers. The emphasis shifts from discovery activities to a stylized format. Only college-bound students could have any use for such a product. Many skills need to be taught and practiced when students undertake a research project. In preparing students for research projects, the skills of paraphrasing, taking notes, summarizing, and documenting all need to be included in class activities.

Many teachers unnecessarily structure the research assignment by limiting the types of sources or specifying a particular number of sources, rather than encouraging students to gather information. Robert Perrin of Indiana State University explains that students should be encouraged to

> look everywhere and explore every potential source of information. Why shouldn't students use interviews, both personal and telephone? Why shouldn't students conduct surveys when the results would be enlightening? Why shouldn't students use personal experience when it is appropriate? Why shouldn't students use films, pamphlets, lecture notes, records, or television programs when they supply helpful ideas, insights, and information? (51)

Tim Hirsch, a college educator, developed a research assignment for personal decision-making that uses many of the resources Perrin suggests. Hirsch believes research should center on a question students care about, one that has personal implications for them. High school students face important questions: Should they go to a post-secondary school? Should they work after school? Should they attempt to get on a team? Hirsch explains that:

> The first step, then, for student researchers is to begin with questions of critical importance to them. The answer to these questions should lead them to action. They should be questions which lead to choices rather than to simple accumulation of information and opinions about a topic. After the question is established, the student researchers need to define the "givens," and establish the criteria they are going to use to answer their questions. (11)

At first, students may think they can't find answers to questions like these in the library, but actually they can. Hirsch explains that students are better able to locate library resources when they have a "compelling need for information" (12). Other sources of information are important as well. We all discover information by talking to informed people, watching news broadcasts, or making direct personal observations. Evidence can come from a variety of sources, as long as it is verifiable. Students need to do their own calculations, comparisons, and evaluation (13). When students learn this type of research process, they can apply it to questions in other academic areas or other areas of their lives. They become lifelong researchers.

▼
ADDITIONAL WRITING ASSIGNMENTS

Assignments are related to purpose—the teacher's purpose. What do teachers want students to learn or practice from a particular activity? As teachers plan writing activities, they do so contextually—that is, in the context of a unit or goal. The assignments described in this section appear unconnected, but they are intended for use in different units depending on the teacher's purpose and provide illustrations of activities teachers find successful.

CHECKBOOK CHARACTERIZATIONS

Information about people can come from a wide range of sources; a checkbook register might be one source. In a whole-group discussion, introduce the idea of describing people through examining their checkbooks. In small groups, students write a register of about 10 lines. The groups exchange registers and write a character description based on the information. One group wrote the following example:

		100.50
4-10-91 Limited Express	60.30	40.20
4-11-91 Little Caesar's Pizza	8.15	32.05
4-12-91 Ron's Castle Food	12.05	20.00
4-12-91 Beauty Works Sal	50.00	-30.00
4-13-91 Deposit	100.00	70.00
4-13-91 Prange's	28.75	41.25
4-13-91 Waldenbooks	15.30	25.95
4-20-91 Wisconsin Bell	14.90	11.05
4-20-91 Everything $1.29	9.05	2.00

A student used the register to write this description of the character:

The owner of this checkbook is very organized. He or she balances the account after every check. Wow! He/she—probably a she because she spent over $100 on hair and clothes. She cares about her appearance, I guess. She's an English major—as determined by book purchase. She should have gone shopping at Ron's or 7-11 instead of ordering Little Caesar's. Perhaps she is a procrastinator. She's a sucker for low-price items because she bought approximately 7 items at that junk store. Despite her consistent balancing of money she still goes under or down to the last cent. Maybe she enjoys the good things in life but can't exactly afford them.

—Leslie Olmen

PERSONALS

Personal ads in the newspaper make interesting story lines. Tape each one on a 3 × 5 card and hand them out. Either in pairs or in small groups students combine the ads and create a story. Teachers prepare ahead of time for this activity by checking the ads on a regular basis for interesting personals.

Some recent discoveries include:

Phony Drivers Licenses
Fool people! For any age, state! Photo! Signature! (No rejection—No proof required.) Fast service with cash/money order. Guaranteed! Rush $20.

Become an ordained minister. Free ministerial credentials legalize your right to the title "Reverend." Write for information.

SECRET OF LIFE
Guaranteed. Send $2.00.

SUPER LOVE SPECIALIST
Prepared astrologer. Indian spiritual. Gifted! Complete satisfaction guaranteed. Send $3.00.

28-year-old man with several positive qualities seeks an adventurous lady for a sincere relationship. Must be attractive and slim.

One-woman Man non-drinker early 40s honest, sincere. Would like to meet one-man lady who is through having children.

Students write stories, either individually or in groups, based on an imagined story behind the ad.

MYSTERY PACKETS

Collect an assortment of items and place them in a large envelope. Matchbook covers, imprinted napkins, receipts, ticket stubs, notes, and torn bits of paper are good choices. Each group receives one packet. The contents of the packet represent material found at the scene of a crime. Together students write a story or police report about the crime based on the evidence.

The Writing Workshop, Vol. 2 by Alan Ziegler is a rich source of teaching ideas for writing. The following illustrate some activities he suggests.

1. *The most amazing things.* First ask students to write about the most amazing thing they've *never* seen. They can make up anything they like—the wilder the better. Then they write about the most amazing thing they've *ever* seen. The subject can't be anything they saw on TV or in a movie. It must be incredible, but true. The assignment could be on heroic acts, beautiful things, and so forth (27).

2. *The power of words.* Think of a time when someone used words that affected the way you felt about yourself or something that was going on, making you feel happy, sad, hungry, excited, nervous, relieved, etc. What was the context in which the words were spoken? Write about why the words meant so much to you (28).

3. *Word combining.* Write five or six words you have strong feelings about; you can like or dislike the sound or meaning of the words. Or they could be

words that for some reason happen to be sitting around in your head, like a word from a popular song that you find yourself humming. You don't even have to know the meaning of all the words. Now write a short, unrhymed poem (four to six lines) using all the words, not necessarily in the order you wrote them down, and not necessarily one preselected word per line (32).

Many sources for teaching ideas are available to teachers. One in particular that secondary teachers find useful is *Notes Plus,* a quarterly publication from the National Council of Teachers of English and written, for the most part, by teachers. A typical issue includes "Ideas from the Classroom," "Classic of the Month," "Writing Assignment of the Month," and "Literature Assignment of the Month." The next two writing ideas appeared in *Notes Plus.*

1. *Customized holidays.* Begin with a general discussion of holidays. Ask students why they think people create and celebrate holidays. Brainstorm about what holidays students think should be on the calendar but aren't. Then have students design or create a special day. They write a description of the special way in which this new holiday will be celebrated, and design a logo, slogan, or whatever trimmings it takes to make the new day a complete holiday. The final step is an illustrated poster or commercial announcing the new holiday. As a continuation, ask students to think of special experiences in their own lives that should be celebrated. A children's book, *I'm in Charge of Celebrations* by Byrd Baylor, is a great starting point for this discussion. Students deepen their awareness of the value of their observational experiences (Sally Hellman, Nov. 1990).

2. *The rewards of the wanted poster.* In order to help students focus on what they like about themselves, they design their own wanted poster. Using a form that looks roughly like the real thing, students write information about themselves: name, date of birth, a photo or caricature, physical description, caution, and reward. Students may choose which of their physical descriptions they feel comfortable sharing. Under the heading "caution" students list short phrases that describe problem areas—for example, sarcastic sense of humor, selfish, disorganized. The real focus of the activity is the reward section. Unlike real wanted posters, this is reserved for a list of positive personal characteristics—a list that highlights how others are rewarded by knowing this person. Many students have trouble with the reward section because they minimize their good attributes. The poster is not complete until their reward section is at least as long as the caution section. This activity can be a real eye-opener for students when they discover that their good qualities outweigh their less desirable traits (Mark Meisner, April 1991).

The writing ideas throughout this chapter illustrate the variety of activities teachers can use to include frequent writing assignments. Many of the assignments are for practice and not for polished drafts. Writing at all levels should be part of the ongoing activities of a classroom.

CLASSROOM CLIMATE

Students are not able to write well unless they feel comfortable in the classroom. Writing requires mutual respect and trust. To help students succeed at writing, the teacher must establish a rapport with them. The more the classroom is a place where students feel at home, the more willing they are to write. A classroom should never look bare but should be filled with colorful posters that have something on them besides punctuation rules. Part of a wall should be set aside for each class so that students have a place to display their work—not just the "best" work, but everyone's work. Small-group activities help to establish a friendly atmosphere. Arranging desks in a circle enhances discussion. Using a variety of activities helps maintain interest and involvement. Most of all, the sense that the teacher cares about them, listens to them, and respects them as individuals ensures that students become active learners.

DISCUSSION QUESTIONS

1. Do you consider yourself a writer? What kinds of writing do you do and how often?
2. What purposes does writing serve for you? In what ways might that be different for other people?
3. Should everyone know how to write well? Should everyone enjoy writing?
4. When you were in elementary school, what writing assignment was your favorite? Do you still have it? How about secondary school?
5. How do you think forms of writing differ—say a poem and an essay?
6. What English teacher helped you the most with your writing? Did other students in that class agree?
7. If you could spend time writing, what kinds of pieces would you write?
8. What problems do you think might occur when you are teaching writing to students?

SUGGESTED ACTIVITIES

1. Explain how you will help students who have "writer's block."
2. Write five poems using five different styles. Which ones are the easiest? The hardest?
3. Create an additional assignment for a discovery activity that helps students write detailed settings.

4. Create assignments for teaching students how to write dialogue.

5. Write a personal experience that happened to you before you were five. Rewrite the essay into fiction, keeping the style and the sense of the story the same.

REFERENCES

Britton, James, Tony Burgess, Nancy Martin, Alex McLeod, and Harold Rosen. *The Development of Writing Abilities (11–18)*. London: Macmillan Education Ltd., 1975.

Dale, Helen. "Collaboration in the Writing Process." *Wisconsin English Journal*, Spring, 1989.

Didion, Joan. *Slouching Towards Bethlehem*. New York: Dell Publishing Co., 1968.

Dixon, John. *Growth Through English*. Reading: National Association for Teaching English, 1967.

Emig, Janet. *The Composing Process of Twelfth Graders*. Urbana: National Council of Teachers of English, 1971.

Hirsch, Timothy J. "Student Research for Personal Decision Making." *Wisconsin English Journal* XXX.2 (1988): 9–14.

Jackson, Jackie. *Turn Not Pale, Beloved Snail*. Boston: Little, Brown & Co., 1974.

Koch, Kenneth. *Wishes, Lies, and Dreams: Teaching Children to Write Poetry*. New York: Vintage, 1970.

Logan, Ben. *The Land Remembers*. Minocqua: Heartland Press, 1975.

Maxwell, Rhoda J. "Story Strips." *Notes Plus*, April, 1987.

———. "So What's New?" Unpublished essay, 1982.

Miller, James E. Jr. *Word, Self, and Reality: The Rhetoric of Imagination*. New York: Dodd, Mead & Co., 1972.

Moffett, James. *Teaching the Universe of Discourse*. Boston: Houghton Mifflin, 1968.

Myers, Miles, and James Gray, eds. *Theory and Practice in the Teaching of Composition*. Urbana: National Council of Teachers of English, 1983.

Perrin, Robert. "Myths about Research." *English Journal* Nov. 1987: 50–53.

Rohman, D. Gordon. "Pre-Writing: The Stage of Discovery in the Writing Process." *College Composition and Communication* 16 (1965):106–12.

Smith, Frank. *Joining the Literacy Club: Further Essays into Education*. Portsmouth: Heinemann, 1988.

Sudol, David. "Creating and Killing Stanley Realbozo or Teaching Characterization and Plot in English 10." *English Journal* October, 1983.

Ziegler, Alan. *The Writing Workshop*. Vol 2. New York: Teachers & Writers Collaborative, 1984.

CHAPTER 6

Evaluating Composition

CHAPTER HIGHLIGHTS
- Evaluation by levels.
- Purposes of evaluation.
- Methods of evaluation.

> No matter how trustworthily we may evaluate any sample of a
> student's writing, we lose all the trustworthiness if we go on to infer
> from just that one sample the student's actual skill in writing. (221)
>
> —*Peter Elbow*

▼
PLANNING FOR EVALUATION

Evaluating compositions can be the most difficult task a teacher faces. Should one pay more attention to content or to mechanics? How do we give credit for creativity when standard conventions of writing are ignored? How does the evaluation of a research paper differ from that of a short story? The answers lie in the teacher's purpose for assigning the particular activity. To put it another way, what did the teacher want the student to learn? Evaluation means deciding if something worthwhile happened, not just measuring a skill. Consequently, teachers must be very clear and specific about what they expect to happen when they give students a particular assignment.

Teaching writing through a process approach means that the purposes for activities vary. For example, the purpose of a discovery activity designed for students to practice how to develop a character is different from assigning a library activity to acquaint students with Newsbank. The purpose of an assignment to practice dialogue is different from that of an assignment to write a story including dialogue. The differences in purpose of assignments shape the evaluations. What we want students to learn determines how we evaluate.

Creating the assignment and deciding how it is to be evaluated should happen at the same time. Evaluation can be troublesome if the connection is not clear in the teacher's mind and therefore not clear to the students. Students have the right to know how their work will be evaluated before they hand it in. Evaluation by levels means that students know the teacher's expectations and never have to ask if spelling or neatness counts.

▼
EVALUATION BY LEVELS

James Britton derived the functions of writing from research done on speech (13). The more informal function occurs when the speaker's focus is on himself or herself; Britton used Dell Hymes' term *expressive* to designate this function. When a speaker shifts focus to a listener or to a topic, it becomes *referential*. When the focus is on the message or on particular words, it is *poetic* (13). The levels of speech are the basis for levels of evaluation that correspond to the formality of the writing assignments. The levels of evaluation are determined by the teacher's purpose for the assignment. Level one compares to expressive in that the writer is writing mainly for himself or herself. The writing is shared only with people familiar to the writer and, in fact, is probably understood only by people close to the writer. The counterpart in speech is conversation with close friends in which often it is unnecessary to finish a thought or sentence in order to be understood. Level two is more formal or standard and can be read and understood by most people in the writer's social circle. It is comparable to speech used with acquaintances, teachers, and older friends.

Level three is formal writing or speech. It occurs in situations in which the form is as important as the message. All three levels are appropriate for school writing. Traditionally, level three was used almost exclusively. With the process approach to writing, however, all three levels are important for helping students to improve their writing.

Using levels of writing in the classroom cuts down on the paper load for teachers. Evaluation is clearly defined by levels; therefore, half of the writing required of students can be graded quickly and easily. Students, parents, and teachers are aware of which type of evaluation fits each particular assignment, and evaluation is never done for its own sake or because a teacher thinks it is expected. In addition, teachers know exactly what elements of writing to look for in the assignments that do call for a more formal evaluation. The time involved in evaluation is greatly reduced.

LEVEL ONE

A teacher's purpose for level one assignments is to provide a wealth of activities for ideas and practice. What teachers want from their students is a wide range of thinking as in brainstorming, connections between thoughts as in mapping, or practicing a variety of kinds of writing. If teachers add the layer of correctness to such activities, the purpose is lost. First drafts and journal writing are level one writing. Here students concentrate on getting ideas down; when they stop to look up a word or consider how a word is spelled, their train of thought is interrupted. A writer's mind should be free from distractions as much as possible when composing. The purpose is to get thoughts on paper and to try new forms of expression. Note-taking is also level one; the notes are jotted down to assist the writer in remembering, and that is their only purpose.

The audience for level one is, first and foremost, the writer. The writer may be the only one who hears or reads the writing, or peers may be part of the audience when the writing is shared in groups. An example of using peer groups for level one writing is the process of writing questions to use for a report or the sharing of ideas for a collaborative story.

To evaluate, a teacher may read the writing and make a comment or a checkmark to show that it has been read. Often, however, the teacher doesn't read writing at this level because it is not handed in. Students may keep it in a notebook or folder, but no evaluation is necessary. Level one writing is the foundation for all other writing and therefore is assigned most frequently. Assigning level one writing daily is not uncommon. Students practice writing, try out ideas, take notes, write in journals, and respond to reading or listening, all with level one writing. The major focus is on content; the main audience is themselves.

LEVEL TWO

A level two assignment is somewhat more formal, and its purpose is to explain, inform, or further develop a discovery writing activity. Teachers assign level two writing to see if students understand ideas and concepts. Examples of this level are homework assignments, essay tests, and multiple drafts students are working on.

The audience for level two writing is the writer, the teacher, and peers. The audience is always known, and the writing is often read by others, not only shared orally. Because others besides the author read the writing, a certain amount of formality is required. Writing conventions need to be adhered to so that others can understand the writing. On the other hand, level two writing is not intended as a final draft and is not evaluated as such. Correct spelling of common words and use of most punctuation marks are expected by a teacher evaluating a level two assignment. However, if a student uses an uncommon word and spells it incorrectly, the error is not noted. When teachers overemphasize spelling, students do not stretch their vocabulary but use a word they know how to spell rather than the one that captures the connotation they want. In an essay test, a teacher may circle a misspelled word, but spelling errors should not be included in the evaluation. The teacher's purpose is to see if students understand the material, not to check on their spelling ability. Level two assignments should reflect knowledge of common conventions of punctuation. What exactly the appropriate conventions are depends on the abilities and grade level of the students.

Organization is another area not evaluated highly at level two. Thinking is not a highly organized activity, and students often think of additional ideas and points too late to make coherent organization. In an essay exam, students may write in the margins or crowd words in between lines, which is evidence of thinking hard about the subject.

In homework assignments, the same intensity as in essay tests is not present; it is sufficient if students make an effort to organize their thoughts. Again, teachers want students to add new ideas even if they make the paper look messy. Level two assignments are rarely recopied. The emphasis is on content with a common level of correctness. Level two writing is assigned two or three times a week.

LEVEL THREE

Level three assignments are the most formal. The purposes for assigning level three are to give students an opportunity to write for audiences outside the classroom, to organize thoughts into a coherent form for readers outside the writers' circle of friends, and to learn the value of creating error-free writing when the occasion calls for it. Level three writing is always a polished draft that students carry through all stages of the writing process. Examples of assignments include research papers, reports, stories, letters, plays, poetry, and essays. Length is not a factor in determining levels. Level one might be the longest, such as journal writing; level three might be one page or less when writing a poem.

The intended audience is oneself, the teacher, peers, and unknown readers. Level three writing might be for a class or school anthology, the school or city newspaper, a gift for family or friends—any situation in which writing needs to be the best possible. The teacher's purpose is to help students learn how to carry a piece of writing through revising, editing, and proofreading in order to create a paper that is error free, well organized, and interesting to read.

Evaluating level three writing is similar to the traditional method of grading. Because the writer takes the paper through all of the stages, a teacher can expect it to be the writer's best work. However, the mechanical aspect of writing never outweighs the value of the content. Methods of evaluating are explained in the next section.

Students are more likely to value their creation of a polished piece of writing when the purpose is clear. If teachers require "perfect" papers every time a student writes, students lose interest in that objective. No one writes perfect papers all of the time because no one needs to. Writing done in the world outside the classroom is largely levels one and two, except for the occasional report. List making, notes to oneself, telephone messages, journal writing, and class notes are all level one writing. Letters we write to people we know are level two. College students write more level three papers than anyone else, far more than they will once they graduate. Secondary students learn how to produce a polished draft if teachers assign a level three piece no more often than once every four to six weeks. Going through the entire writing process takes a great deal of class time. That in itself is not a negative aspect, but running out of time to include a wide variety of writing forms and activities is. Teachers never have enough time to carry out all their ideas, and assigning level three writing more than once a month can crowd out creative dramatics, independent reading, discussions, and other activities.

By using the levels of evaluation, teachers know how to focus the grading, and students know how their writing is to be evaluated. Parents, too, need to know how students' papers are evaluated. With the process approach to writing, students have papers that contain mechanical errors, yet receive comments of praise and perhaps a high grade. When parents are informed of the three levels that are used for their children's writing, they are much less likely to criticize because they understand the evaluation procedures. Letters to parents at the beginning of the school year explaining the levels of writing and emphasizing expectations for each level are helpful. Also, at the beginning of the year, students write the level of the assignment on the paper. Then, when parents do read their child's work, they are more likely to understand the purpose of the assignment and consequently the evaluation as well.

▼
PURPOSES OF EVALUATION

Evaluation is not the same as measurement. We evaluate to see if something worthwhile was accomplished. We might evaluate our teaching methods or how our students are doing. In *The Evaluation of Composition Instruction*, Davis et al. describe two purposes for evaluation: formative and summative. Formative evaluation is used for discovering how writing can be improved; that is, what specific areas do students need to work on to become better writers. Summative evaluation is for reporting on the overall quality of the writing (3–4). Both are useful when used appropriately. When teachers want to know if their teaching methods are improving student writing, summative evaluation provides that information. When teachers and students want to know particular strengths and weaknesses of the writing, formative evaluation gives specific information about areas that need improvement. Holistic evaluation is summative and is commonly used to assess how successful a curriculum is. For example, a school district may collect writing samples from students in several grades and evaluate the writing holistically to check on the effectiveness of the writing curriculum. This type of summative evaluation does not supply information on individuals, only on the program as a whole. Analytical grading scales are examples of a formative evaluation that furnishes information on weaknesses and strengths of students' writing. Because of the amount of time needed for formative evaluation, it is more often used in individual classes than large-scale assessment.

ASSESSMENT

Most school districts have some method of assessing how well students do in reading, math, and writing. Assessment of writing can be either direct, which is a writing sample, or indirect, which is an objective test. Objective tests are editing tests in which students read test items to identify errors in punctuation, subject-verb agreement, pronoun-noun agreement, and other conventions of language depending on the grade level tested. Direct assessment more closely reflects what is taught in the classroom and provides a clearer idea of what needs to be improved. Our goal is to help students become better writers, and objective tests are not a good measure of that. A student may be able to pick out writing errors but not be capable of thoughtful, interesting writing, and the reverse may be true as well. Unless large-scale assessment and classroom grading reflect the teacher's purpose in teaching writing, the evaluations do not provide useful information, and, in fact, can be harmful to teachers and students because the information is misleading.

▼
METHODS OF EVALUATION

Depending on the purpose of the writing assignment, evaluation varies from formal to informal. Evaluation does not necessarily mean a grade is assigned. We evaluate to see if students are learning what we want them to learn. A variety of methods can supply that information. In fact, teaching writing by the process approach requires many different evaluation techniques, depending on the stage or level of the writing.

IMPRESSION GRADING

Discovery activities are always evaluated with impression grading. The teacher reads the material quickly to see if the student put effort into the writing. Teachers may write comments on students' papers, but not evaluative ones. When reading journals, teachers respond as an adult friend, someone who listens and nurtures, and responds in writing. Other discovery activities may require only a short comment: "good start, creative, interesting." Or the comment can be a way of encouraging students to expand their thinking and writing: "Tell me more about . . . ." "How did . . . happen?" "What did you think of the part where . . .?" If teachers ask specific questions, students have an easier time expanding on what they wrote. In some cases, a simple checkmark at the top is sufficient to let students know the teacher read their work and approved of what they did. Sometimes students ask if these discovery activities "count." Because discovery activities are essential to good writing, we want to make sure students value their work at this level, but we do not want to evaluate on a more formal basis. Informal grading and following up if a student does not turn in an assignment help students to realize that the teacher values their work, so that they, too, will come to value it.

HOLISTIC GRADING

Holistic grading gives an overall evaluation without identifying the particular weaknesses or strengths of the writing. Papers are evaluated on the overall success of the writing, not on specific elements. Papers are read as a "whole" piece, and the evaluator decides if the writing is competent or not. Because this type of evaluation is quite reliable and quickly done, it is useful for large-scale assessment such as evaluating writing in an entire school district. In the classroom, holistic grading may also be used as an assessment tool when a teacher wants to know, in general, how well the students write or if teaching methods are effective. At the beginning of the year, a teacher assigns a writing task and evaluates the writing holistically. Later in the year, the teacher gives a similar writing assignment and evaluates it in the same manner. By comparing the two pieces of writing, teachers monitor students' progress.

Writing used for holistic evaluation is usually done during one class period, or it can go through the stages of the writing process. In either case, when assignments are holistically evaluated, the final draft is not returned to the student because the teacher makes no comments and the grade is only a number. Such evaluation, although useful to the teacher, means nothing to students. Receiving a holistic grade does not help students improve their writing because they do not know what specifically they did right or wrong.

When evaluating holistically, evaluators spent about two minutes on each paper and use scoring guides to decide the category of competency for each paper. Using an even number of categories works best because the top two describe acceptable writing and the lower two, unacceptable. For instance:

$$4 \quad 3 \qquad 2 \quad 1$$
$$\text{acceptable} \qquad \text{unacceptable}$$

If an odd number of categories is used, the middle area becomes confusing.

$$5 \quad 4 \quad 3 \quad 2 \quad 1$$

Would papers that fall into the middle be considered competent or not? Evaluators have a tendency to score near the center of the scale. Providing a middle number increases the chances of that happening. Holistic grading requires that decisions on the quality of writing be made quickly and decisively.

Scoring guides describe what is expected in each category. Criteria include the amount of detail, the extent to which the writing reflects the writer's own experience, organization of the ideas, and control of the conventions of writing. Holistic evaluation determines overall fluency. Grammar, punctuation, spelling, organization, and expression of ideas together form a sense of fluency. When teachers evaluate students' papers using the holistic method, they read the papers very quickly to get an overall idea of the quality. Even the best papers contain errors; in fact, good writers tend to write longer papers and therefore may have more errors. Also, if the students had to produce the writing in a certain length of time, which is usually the case when collecting writing samples from a large number of students, the writing contains more errors. We can't expect the quality of writing we could if students wrote in a less stressful situation. Students may have time to read over what they wrote, but, at best, the writing looks more like level two than level three writing. The scoring guide needs to reflect the limitations of timed writing.

ANALYTICAL SCALES

Analytical scales evaluate the parts of a written piece. Because this method is slower than holistic, it is seldom used in large-scale evaluation but is a valuable tool in the classroom. Paul Diederich and associates at the Educational Testing Service (1974) developed a grading scale used for scoring SAT essays (Box 6.1). The scale puts the emphasis on content and organization, with mechanics counting only 20%. Analytical scales are useful evaluation tools. Teachers can adapt the scale to fit the assignment. Using such a grading scale ensures a fair weighting of all the elements that go toward creating the final grade for a paper.

The content of a paper should always be at least 50% of the total grade. If a student makes several errors in spelling, and spelling errors are designated as 10% of the grade, then regardless of how many words are misspelled, only 10% of the grade is affected.

Box 6.1   DIEDERICH SCALE

Quality and development of ideas	1	2	3	4	5	
Organization, relevance, movement	1	2	3	4	5	
						_____ × 5 = _____
Style, flavor, individuality	1	2	3	4	5	
Wording and phrasing	1	2	3	4	5	
						_____ × 3 = _____
Grammar, sentence structure	1	2	3	4	5	
Punctuation	1	2	3	4	5	
Spelling	1	2	3	4	5	
Manuscript form, legibility	1	2	3	4	5	
						_____ × 1 = _____

The scale represents a contract between student and teacher. Before students write their final draft, they have a copy of the scale and know exactly how the paper will be evaluated by the teacher. The scale is also used during peer response groups, particularly at the editing stage. The list of criteria on the grading sheet is the focus for the student editors.

We assign point values to each criterion rather than using the multiplication technique in Diederich's scale. The criteria and point values differ greatly from one assignment to another. The criteria reflect what the teacher wants the students to achieve in each assignment. For example, form might be important in one assignment but not in another. When the assignment is for seniors to practice writing a resume, the points might be divided up as shown in Box 6.2. The numbers in the parentheses represent the possible points for each criterion. The number of points actually received by the student is noted on the blank line. Students know exactly why they receive the grade they do.

For longer level three assignments, the analytical scale is more detailed to reflect the amount of time available for students to work on the writing and the effort they put into the assignment. Box 6.3 is a scale for a research project intended for juniors and seniors. The first five items relate to the content of the paper and are 50% of the total grade. The reason the conventions count for so

---

Box 6.2   POINT VALUES FOR DIFFERENT CRITERION IN
          RESUME WRITING (15 points)

Correct form (5)   _____

Sense of audience (2)   _____

Clear information (3)   _____

Mechanics (5)   _____

                    Total points   _____

---

much in this assignment is that a main purpose is for students to learn how to use documentation. Several smaller assignments at levels one and two gave students opportunities to learn these skills. The final draft went through a response group, an editing group, and a proofreading session.

Using scoring guides helps teachers to evaluate more accurately. We all have biases about certain errors. Someone may be really bothered by incomplete sentences, another by subject-pronoun errors. Mistakes should be noted for a paper that went through all of the revision steps, but every error should be counted in fair proportion to the rest of the paper. A scoring guide makes it easier for a teacher to grade in an unbiased way.

The scoring guide in Box 6.3 was used with students who were familiar with analytical scales. When students are not used to this type of grading, descriptions of the items are helpful. For example, students would not necessarily know what "Organization of subject clear" means. A description of organization might include the following:

Transitional words connect paragraphs. Paragraphs are in a logical order. Ideas in each paragraph are related. The paper as a whole has logical sequencing. Major points are supported by examples and facts.

Punctuation: Comma placed after introductory phrase. Semicolons between two independent clauses. (Or any particular convention you, as a teacher, have worked on with the students.)

When scoring guides are used, we do not need to mark on the students' papers. A checkmark in a margin calls attention to a particular place, but the comments go on the guide. When the papers are unmarred by teacher's comments, students can make revisions and hand the paper in for further evaluation. If teachers make all the needed corrections, students lose ownership of the paper. They just go through the motions when they make the revisions, not thinking about how and why to make changes.

Box 6.3   RESEARCH PROJECT (100 points possible)

Name _____

Thesis clearly stated	(5)	_____
Organization of subject clear	(10)	_____
Major points clear	(10)	_____
Supporting details and examples well developed	(15)	_____
Introduction and conclusion clear and concise	(10)	_____
Correct word choice	(10)	_____
Transitions clear	(5)	_____
Punctuation acceptable	(10)	_____
Spelling accurate	(10)	_____
Introduced borrowed material	(5)	_____
Correct documentation	(5)	_____
Accurate work-cited page	(5)	_____
	Total points	_____

Comments:

Some Final Points to Remember

- Scoring guides are a type of formative evaluation designed to help young writers improve their writing.

- The guides differ from one assignment to another and reflect the developmental age of the students.

- Students are familiar with the scoring guide before they turn in final drafts to the teacher.

CHECKPOINT SCALES

Checkpoint scales include specific criteria and an overall impression of the paper. Dan Kirby developed the idea for checkpoint guides. The one in Box 6.4 is designed to be used after two weeks of writing practice and is used on a student's revised draft (194–196).

Kirby's guide is for 7th graders. Teachers need to develop their own guides and tailor them to grade level and assignment. The advantage of checkpoint

Box 6.4   SCORING GUIDE: CHECKPOINT ONE
Your revised writing was rated as follows:

1. Honest writing.

1	2	3	4	5	× 4 = _____

Try again. Write fast. Use the words in your own head.

You're moving. Keep working.

Yes! Fresh, honest language. Good!

2. Vivid, concrete detail.

1	2	3	4	5	× 4 = _____

Try again. Your writing is bare. Add more specific detail.

Some good stuff in your writing. Add specifics. Stay away from generalizations.

Surprising words. Concrete word pictures. Good!

3. Strong verbs.

1	2	3	4	5	× 4 = _____

Try again. Use verbs that paint a picture.

I see you've been working at it.

Good. I like those words.

4. End punctuation and first word capitalization.

1	2	3	4	5	× 2 = _____

Many sentences do not begin with capitals. Many sentences do not end with appropriate punctuation. See me for help.

Several errors. Proofread carefully.

All sentences begin with capital letters and end with appropriate punctuation.

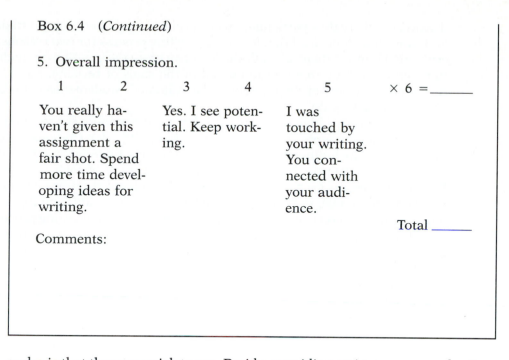

Box 6.4   *(Continued)*

5. Overall impression.

| 1 | 2 | 3 | 4 | 5 | × 6 = _____ |

You really ha-
ven't given this
assignment a
fair shot. Spend
more time devel-
oping ideas for
writing.

Yes. I see poten-
tial. Keep work-
ing.

I was
touched by
your writing.
You con-
nected with
your audi-
ence.

Total _____

Comments:

scales is that they are quick to use. Besides providing an in-progress evaluation, the guides suggest ways to improve the writing without actually doing the revision for the students.

PORTFOLIO EVALUATION

Portfolio evaluation is not a new way of evaluating student writing, but only recently have schools begun to use portfolios to determine improvement in writing. The major advantage to portfolios is that teachers can look at students' work over a period of time and at many different kinds of writing. This overall evaluation provides a much clearer picture of students' fluency and improvement in writing.

The portfolio is a collection of work assigned by the teacher, although students may include writing done on their own if they wish. All the writing done for class is put into a writing folder. After a period of time—two to three weeks is about right—students go through their folder and select pieces they want to place in the portfolio. Students know that the purpose of the portfolio is evaluation. In addition to the student-selected work, teachers may choose assignments to add to the portfolio. Usually teachers specify a minimum number of pieces students should select, and then add one or two teacher-selected pieces. The teachers select an assignment everyone has in common, perhaps a short story, a poem, or a report. Students are also encouraged to add assignments from other classes, perhaps a paper written for history or science. The student selections do not have to be final copies. They may wish to add a discovery activity they particularly like. Teachers need to encourage students to look at writing done at all the steps of the writing process for two reasons: (1) In evaluating improvement, early drafts may give more information on fluency and thinking than those that go through all of the steps of revising; and (2) when early drafts are part of the material to be evaluated, students learn to value all of the writing they do.

Margie Krest, a high school teacher, has used portfolios for several years to document her students' growth and risk-taking (29). Her students keep all of their writing, "including drafts, revisions, prewriting material, and final papers" (29). Students date the papers so they can keep track of their own progress. Because not every piece of writing is graded, students are more willing to experiment and to take risks. Krest devised a method for evaluating that rewards multiple drafting, revising, and practice, all elements of the writing process, and in addition, evaluates one final draft. She gives two grades on the portfolio; one for all of the writing and the other a paper grade on one final product. She weighs the two grades according to what she wants to emphasize. For instance, if fluency is more important than creating an error-free paper, the portfolio grade might be 75% and the paper grade 25%. The reverse situation might be appropriate for seniors. By adjusting the percentages, Krest finds portfolios adaptable to different grade levels and student abilities (31).

In *Portfolio News*, Martha Johnson, director of a cooperative writing program, lists several positive attitudes and behaviors that portfolios encourage in students (2, Spring 1991):

- To take more responsibility for their work
- To see themselves as apprentices
- To value daily work as a meaningful part of learning
- To see mistakes as opportunities for learning
- To see revision as an opportunity to succeed
- To spend more time thinking about their teacher's response
- To spend more time conferring with classmates
- To spend more time reconsidering and improving their work
- To be more creative, to feel more confident, to be more productive
- To take pride in their work, to perform, or to display what they know

Johnson's claims for portfolios might sound somewhat ambitious, but the involvement of students with the evaluation process does help students see themselves as part of assessment.

Some teachers have students meet in groups to help each other decide what pieces to select. Whether students receive help from peers or select papers on their own, they then write a rationale or explanation for the selections. Through this process of selecting and explaining their choices, students develop a sense of ownership in every step of the writing process.

High school teacher Roberta J. Herter uses portfolio evaluation because she wants a "fuller picture of a writer's growth over time" (90). She finds that portfolios help students assume responsibility for their writing.

Portfolios involve students in assessing the development of their writing skills by inviting self-reflection and encouraging students to assume control over their writing. Accumulating a body of work to return to, to reject, revise, or, simply revisit calls on students to become responsible for the content and quality of their portfolio, and ultimately to confront their personal writing inventories and investments in activities of the class. (90)

Selecting and evaluating portfolios takes time, but it is the most successful way of involving students in evaluation.

SELF-EVALUATION

First and foremost, writing must please the writer. No matter who finally evaluates it, if the writer isn't pleased with the piece, the writing lacks spirit and flair. The more involved students are with the whole process, the more they personally care about what they wrote. Too often, however, evaluation comes from a source outside the process. The portfolio evaluation involves students as part of the evaluation, but sometimes student or self-evaluation suffices as the only evaluation. With help, students learn to distinguish between good and not-so-good writing on their own. Criteria for judging writing are developed by the whole class. Students tend to be critical when they discuss writing in the abstract. They often describe criteria far too difficult to achieve. Through discussion, teachers can help them to understand what is important at each stage of the process and at each of the writing levels. The list of agreed-upon criteria then guides the self-evaluation.

The list is never a checklist or a series of yes or no questions. Checklists do not engage one's mind. It is too easy to just check off each item. Student textbooks commonly include checklists that are intended to help students with their own editing, but such lists do not require a thoughtful response. Students do a better job if teachers give them opportunities to slow down their reading and think about the writing. Items on a checklist can be turned into directions that help students locate errors or questions that require answers other than yes or no. For instance "Did I spell all the words correctly?" can be changed to a more helpful suggestion: "Read your paper slowly looking only for misspellings. Circle any word you are not sure of, and after reading through the paper, look up the words you questioned." Or, on the subject of description, "Where is your best descriptive phrase? Where else might you add descriptive details?"

Assignments selected for self-evaluation should not then be evaluated by the teacher. Self-evaluation means assigning a summation comment or grade to one's own paper. This is different from reading over one's own work before receiving help from a response group or turning a paper in for a grade. Self-evaluation is a way of helping students understand what it means to evaluate, and the experience improves their own writing. The self-evaluated papers may go into a writing folder, or the teacher may record the grade and return the papers to the students.

▼
SUMMARY

The most important point to remember in evaluating is to use a variety of methods. Evaluation should be as varied as the writing assignments. Because students bring different backgrounds, knowledge, and learning styles to the classroom, teachers must vary the methods of evaluation in order to best help students improve their writing. A variety of methods helps, too, in creating a fresh perspective every time a work is evaluated. Students need to share the responsibility for developing evaluation techniques and applying them to their own and other's writing.

DISCUSSION QUESTIONS

1. Discuss what learning goals a teacher might have for assigning a report. How would the goals differ for writing a poem?
2. What are the connections between the purpose of an assignment and the evaluation of the writing that comes from the assignment?
3. What level one writing do you do in your daily life? In school?
4. Discuss the importance of the levels in improving student writing.
5. What are the similarities and differences among assessment, evaluation, and testing?

SUGGESTED ACTIVITIES

1. Describe the purposes for assigning a poem to be written at each of the three levels. Write an evaluation plan for each of the three levels.
2. Write an analytical scale for a report written by 7th graders. The report is worth 100 points and is a level three assignment.
3. Write an analytical report as in Activity 2, but this time for 12th graders.
4. Describe how the purposes would be different for an assignment to write a short story at level two compared with one written at level three.
5. If possible, holistically grade papers written by high school students. As a class, first describe the four categories. Compare scores with each other and discuss any differences.

6. Using Kirby's checkpoint scale as a model, write one for 11th graders writing a report.

REFERENCES

Collom, Jack. *Moving Windows: Evaluating the Poetry Children Write.* New York: Teachers & Writers Collaborative, 1985.

Cooper, Charles R., and Lee Odell. *Evaluating Writing.* Urbana: National Council of Teachers of English, 1977.

Davis, Barbara Gross, Michael Scriven, and Susan Thomas. *The Evaluation of Composition Instruction.* New York: Teachers College Press, 1987.

Elbow, Peter. *Embracing Contraries.* New York: Oxford University Press, 1986.

Herter, Roberta J. "Writing Portfolios: Alternatives to Testing." *English Journal* Jan. 1991:90–92.

Johnson, Martha. "Wedding Process to Product and Assessment to Learning." *Portfolio News* Spring 1991:2.

Kirby, Dan, and Tom Liner. *Inside Out.* Upper Montclair: Boynton/Cook, 1981.

Krest, Margie. "Adapting the Portfolio to Meet Student Needs." *English Journal* Feb. 1990:29–34.

CHAPTER 7

Improving Writing Skills: Usage, Syntax, Mechanics

Chapter Highlights

- Working contextually.
- Activities to improve usage.
- Understanding syntax errors.
- Activities to improve sentence structure.
- Improving punctuation, capitalization, and spelling.

> I think we teach too many skills and not at the right time. We succumb to the temptation to cover English "content" because the surface features of written language are so obvious, teachable and testable. (144)
>
> —*Nancie Atwell*

▼
A FRAMEWORK FOR IMPROVING WRITING SKILLS

Writing skills generally improve when students care about their writing. As simplistic and laden with common sense as that idea sounds, it is nonetheless easily lost in a context of teaching and testing. Textbooks, curriculum guides, and standardized tests have consistently presented skills as a world unto themselves, separate from student writing. Writing skills—usage, syntax, mechanics—are part of the process of developing a written text, of making meaning, and part of revising and editing.

Writing is a complex process. Often we discover what we want to say in the very act of writing; thus, early concern about correctness may block discovery. At the point that we generate ideas and draft them in writing, we need to think of what it is we mean—the content—and save the urge to correct for later in the process, when editing and proofreading are appropriate. As Tom Romano reminds us:

> We [teachers] must strive to keep editing skills in perspective—a part of the writing process. Countless people have had their attitudes about the creative act of writing permanently darkened by a teacher who emphasized perfection in editing to the point that all other parts of the writing process did not matter. (74)

Dan Kirby and Tom Liner also support keeping skills in perspective, suggesting that we:

> Treat proofreading as something to be done quickly and efficiently, rather than as a climactic step in the process of composing. Only when proofreading is made a mysterious and complex part of the mastery of standard English does it become intimidating and therefore difficult for students. (235)

Writing skills need to be linked to the act of writing; further, they need to be kept "in their place." There is no argument over the need for the skills, for students learning standard usage, syntax, and mechanics as part of their versatility with language, as one of the dialects they command. However, a very useful perspective for both teacher and student comes from Emily Meyer and Louise Z. Smith: "Standard written English is a dialect nobody speaks" (219). Given this, it is even more important that students view writing skills as a critical part of their own written expression, not as lessons to get out of the way as quickly as possible.

▼
THE TEACHER'S ROLE

With movement to a more process-oriented approach to writing, the teacher's role had to be redefined. In the traditional model, a teacher was often the giver of information and the hunter of errors—the examiner. A more contemporary approach views the teacher as facilitator. Letting students write is the first step in gaining mastery over writing skills; allowing time for the entire writing process is the second. Teachers need to validate the importance of revising and editing, not through using red pens but through in-class time for these processes. Another aspect of teacher as facilitator involves modeling the processes of revising and editing, not the old marginal, more distant command of "Fix!"

MODELING

Modeling is best accomplished through student drafts on overhead transparencies or class copies for use with an entire class; it may take different formats, however.

TEACHER-LED DISCUSSION.   Ask students what changes need to be made, make the changes, and very briefly discuss the rationale or reason behind each change. Limit the focus to only a few errors, prioritizing them.

STUDENT/INDIVIDUAL.   Ask students to proofread a paper individually, prior to group work on the same piece. A collection of papers from previous or other classes, without names or other identifying features, provides experience with full-discourse proofreading or editing.

STUDENT/GROUP.   Ask a small group to pool their knowledge, decide on correction, and determine the reason for the correction; then follow with full-class discussion.

STUDENT/GROUP.   Ask a group to generate a checklist, perhaps assigning different groups different areas (e.g., usage, mechanics, sentences). Follow with full-class discussion, talking about errors that derail the reader and errors that are less serious but nonetheless irritating to many readers.

MINI-CONFERENCES.   Hold a brief focus on editing at a table or over the student's shoulder. The teacher's questions are the modeling part of the process, the types of questions we want students to internalize and apply themselves.

PEER CONFERENCES.   Give students guidelines for conferencing together; if students are unfamiliar with peer conferencing, provide models and/or questions and procedures. Establish rules: The author has first responsibility for proofreading, peers second; peers are not to make any corrections on paper without discussion with the author; when making corrections, peers initial them (in this way, we are able to see what students know). Peer conferences can be done in pairs or small groups.

MINI-LESSONS.   Limit the lesson to less than 10 minutes and use student draft material. Done throughout the year, mini-lessons offer some assurance of covering all the basic skills. These lessons can involve the whole class or a small group. Analyses of student error logs help determine which errors to focus on first and whether whole class or small group instruction is appropriate. The important thing is that students need to apply the lessons to their own work. They should not become a facsimile of the skills section of textbooks.

DAILY ORAL LANGUAGE. Developed by Neil Vail and Joe Papenfuss, two educators in the Racine (WI) school district, *Daily Oral Language* (DOL) provides students with two or three sentences with various errors in usage and mechanics. Vail and Papenfuss have prepared plenty of sentences for use at middle and senior high school levels, as well as a teacher's manual. Most teachers put the sentences on the board or a transparency and ask students to make corrections in their journals; full class discussion of corrections and the reasons for them follows. This process takes no more than 5 or 6 minutes. The value of DOL lies in its brevity, immediate correction, and oral discussion.

TEACHER'S MODEL. Using a short piece of their own, teachers talk students through revision and editing, pointing out why they make certain choices and what questions or problems they need to solve. This strategy is important not only for the modeling per se but also because teachers who share their own writing are generally perceived differently—they are writers, not merely critics of other people's writing.

SELF-EDITING

Students can self-edit with the help of individual checklists maintained as part of their writing folder. Although it is possible to be superficial and mechanical about this task, asking the students to both maintain and consult their individual skills list places the responsibility with the right person—the student. Students need familiarity with strategies that help them focus on proofreading:

- Reading one line at a time, ignoring meaning; students need to understand that we find it easy to read over errors because we carry the intended meaning in our heads.
- Pacing the writing, leaving the piece alone for at least 24 to 48 hours, and returning to it "cold"; again we need to provide them with an understanding of why this is important.
- If the draft is hand-written, we can ask them to move to type, where it is easier to spot errors; the professional sense of finishing a product also helps to reinforce the need for proofreading.
- Students write their most persistent error (or errors) at the top of each page and read through for that error(s) and that error(s) only.
- Students use a ruler or a blank sheet of paper, blocking out everything but one line, and read through with a focus on one line only.

- Students read their text backward to proofread for spelling errors, thus reducing any interference from content and meaning.

SELF-HELP

We can create a corner of the classroom where self-help is available: different types of dictionaries; one-page handouts to help with the most common mistakes; simple explanations and examples. Students can also create their own "handbook" for the corner. Many published handbooks are not only obtuse but difficult to access.

If the teacher is a facilitator rather than an error-hunter, students are given what they need most, the chance to internalize skills through guided experience. Too often, we have been neurotic about errors, focusing on them to the exclusion of everything else. This is not to suggest that we ignore errors; as we pointed out earlier, this simply leaves students more powerless. Establishing a classroom model that provides them with time, strategies, and experience goes far in developing self-reliant students.

▼

THE NORMALITY OF ERRORS

Although we have discussed student error at some length, the importance of the issue merits a final word. Writing skills take time to develop and become routine; in this way, they are no different than skills such as those in athletics or music. Teachers also need to keep in mind that "mastery" does not occur all at once. Students show varied competency or proficiency on a range of writing skills; further, regression is normal. The more complex the writing task, the more a student has to concentrate on making meaning; at such times, some skill may "drop out" momentarily. Similarly, the more complex the sentence structure, the more likely the mechanics within it will go awry. These are good errors, signs of development. Teachers who maintain this view and make their students aware of the nature of developing writing ability provide a good writing environment. If we learn through trial and error, we also depend upon tolerance for the motivation to make it through the process. We don't want to penalize students for taking risks, for trying out more complex structures and more sophisticated punctuation.

▼

SKILLS AS PURPOSEFUL

We need to maintain the relationship between skills and genuine communication: We write to convey meaning, and the use of appropriate conventions helps us do that. Teaching skills for their own sake, unrelated to creating a meaningful text, or worse, for taking standardized tests, is a waste of time. Students need good skills, and the only way that most will acquire them, internalize them, and apply them is in pursuit of communicating something *they* want to say.

▼
THE RESPONSIBLE STUDENT

Students, not teachers, should hold primary responsibility for correctness. This notion makes some teachers nervous: They mistrust student ability to self-correct, and they see themselves in the role of "the corrector." As noted earlier, students never learn to self-correct if they are not given, first, the understanding and strategies to do so and, second, the sustained requirement to do it. Kirby and Liner put it bluntly:

> Leave proofreading to the students. In every class there are some students who have mastered most of the proofreading skills. Often such students are simply "good spellers" or "intuitive punctuators." Acknowledge their skill by setting them up as proofreading consultants to the class. (234)

Most teachers admit that students learn well from their peers. Peers often have a facility for translating academic material into peer language, a facility which can be well used in our classrooms. We can train some of those "masters" to ask questions, to work inductively—and not simply to give the right answer. When students have had the benefit of teacher and peer explanation, they should take over proofreading and be held responsible.

In discussing error, we noted that little is gained by a teacher-marked or corrected paper. As much as teachers don't like this news, it remains true: Students don't pay much attention to teacher marks. If the paper is laden with them, students simply give up, having determined that they do nothing right. Students may not find every error on their own, but unless they try, little is gained.

To avoid worry about unedited papers making their way into hands of parents, other teachers, or administrators, some English language arts teachers invest in a rubber stamp which says something to the effect of "under construction." Before a draft leaves the classroom, it is stamped. Also, teachers who discuss their methods with parents or caretakers seldom run into trouble. If people understand why the emphasis on correctness shifts to the final stages of writing and that we do expect standard written English on final drafts, the chances of a problem are minimal.

ACTIVITIES TO IMPROVE USAGE

We have already discussed "bad grammar," which usually refers to deviations from standard usage: *he do* for *he does; me and her* for *she and I; them books* for *those books*. There is no question of misunderstanding the meaning here; thus, we are talking about conforming to a single form designated "standard" usage. The acquisition of standard usage, perhaps more than any other skill, is linked to motivation, to what benefit it provides for the student. For this reason, fault-finding doesn't work other than to strengthen student notions of us as 18th-century grammarians.

▼ _____

UNDERSTANDING USAGE

First, we need to establish a language environment through books, film, video, music, and other resources. We need to build student interest in language. One of the most valuable viewpoints the English language arts curriculum can provide is awareness of language diversity. American regional dialects are a good starting point; they function as a lens through which to view usage. Discussing usage in terms of dialect and versatility with language, in terms of the various subcultures through which people live their lives, makes sense to most middle school and senior high students.

USING LITERATURE

Young adult fiction is rich with language variation. Novels that portray the regional and cultural settings of American dialects offer a focus for discussing that variation. Black poets such as Langston Hughes, Paul Laurence Dunbar, and Gwendolyn Brooks demonstrate the versatility of voices that use both standard and nonstandard dialects; using comparative pieces of these poets can reinforce the concept of appropriate usage linked to audience and purpose.

USING VIDEO

Teachers today can access regional dialects easily through the many movies that use them. Boston, New Orleans, New York, Texas, Chicago, Los Angeles, Nashville, and Maine are but a few of the settings that provide different American voices. Taping portions of television shows, particularly call-in shows, also offers a rich diversity of American voices.

If the school district does not have access to commercial videos such as *The Story Of Language* or *American Tongues,* the public library may have them. A regional college or university is another resource for these excellent productions.

USING TELEVISION

SPORTS.   Students can collect data on usage, standard and non-standard, from listening to sports broadcasters and athletes from across the nation.

POLITICAL FIGURES.   Students can collect data from the nightly national news. Prominent African-Americans, Hispanics, Asians, and Caucasians from every region of the country provide a rich linguistic field. Students should speculate about the use of dialect: When do these people use their "home" dialect and when do they use their "public" dialect? What conclusions can be drawn about standard and non-standard usage?

CALL-IN SHOWS.   Popular call-in shows feature people from all regions of the country speaking naturally. Students would need to keep a journal of usage variation, noting their emotional response to the language itself.

ADVERTISEMENTS.   Students can work in groups to collect language data through ads for specific products. Ask them to identify the audience for the ads and the effect of audience on usage. Print media can also be used for this purpose.

USING MUSIC

Most students have access to many varieties of music. They might listen to the lyrics across several varieties (e.g., rap, country-western, rock, ballads) and identify differences in usage; they might also speculate on the reasons for the differences.

USING GRAFFITI

Graffiti on walls, desks, and other surfaces is a rich source of language variety and economy. Students can work in pairs or small groups to gather data, analyze it, and report back on what usage means to the authors of graffiti.

▼

MANIPULATIONS: LANGUAGE ACTIVITIES

For students who learn well through visualization and physical activities, activity cards are effective tools. Using different colors for different word classes (e.g., noun, verb), make stacks of subject and verb cards, both singular and plural. Be sure to include the types of usage problems most common to the grade level and to speakers of other dialects or languages. Students can work in pairs to match cards and solve usage problems.

A "spinner" card of subjects is another manipulation strategy. Students spin for their subject and then add an appropriate predicate, either oral or written. "Spinner" cards that include various usage problems provide good experience in a non-threatening way.

▼

INVESTIGATING BASIC LANGUAGE RELATIONSHIPS

Provide students with sufficient language samples through which to isolate problem areas associated with standard usage (subject-verb agreement, pronoun agreement, pronoun case, possession). Students work in pairs or small groups, analyzing the text and determining what constitutes standard written usage. Follow their investigation with a teacher-guided discussion on their findings.

▼
DAILY ORAL LANGUAGE

Use only two or three sentences per day, written on chalk board or transparency, and ask students to correct the sentences in their journals. Then, using only five minutes of class time, ask for their changes. The value of this activity lies in students hearing the standard forms and discussing them orally and briefly, but we need to remember that this exercise can become mindless and useless. Further, grading destroys its effectiveness. Many teachers use DOL as a "settling down" activity, students doing their journal sentences while the teacher takes roll. Vail and Papenfuss's preparation of sentences for correction and discussion covers every common usage problem.

▼
WORKING FROM STUDENT DRAFTS

Usage needs to be linked to student writing, so that students proofread as a matter of standard procedure. Using student drafts on transparencies, model the process. Teachers need to help students shift their perception from writer to reader through a systematic and detached line-by-line reading of the text. We can raise student awareness of where usage errors are likely to occur (e.g., separated subjects and verbs, pronoun case). Students need to learn to identify problems as well as to solve them.

▼
MINI-LESSONS

The mini-lesson, like DOL, is brief. Focus on a single problem, like the mix-up between lay and lie, and return immediately to writing activities. Because application is the point of the lesson, draw the usage problem from student writing as often as possible, using whole class or small group as appropriate.

EXAMPLE: PRONOUN CASE

Don't use terms like *case, nominative,* or *objective.* They're strange and scary and only convince students that their native language is arcane and unavailable to them. Show students how to test pronoun use through adding or eliminating words:

John threw the ball to Paul and I.
John threw the ball to——I?
John and me went to the game.
——me went to the game?
John is taller than me.
John is taller than me——is tall?

Most native speakers, those from standard-dialect backgrounds, recognize which form is correct when they hear and see it in this context. We can use this lesson to underscore that standard usage has nothing to do with understanding, with meaning per se. Otherwise, students are likely to remind us of that reality.

▼
KEEPING LOGS OR ANALYSIS CHARTS

As part of the writing folder, include a log or chart of the most common errors. The category names should be accessible and reasonable; the students are the ones to maintain the chart. Typical categories: word ending errors (e.g., omitting -ed); subject-verb agreement; pronoun agreement; pronoun case; wrong word (e.g., lie/lay). Using information from their error logs, students can work in small groups to assist and teach one another.

For speakers of other dialects or languages, prepare a more descriptive log:

Personal usage	Written usage	Reason for difference
Three boy went	Three boys	plural marker s
He done found him	He found	done is extra/emphasis

In introducing students to the chart, stress again that we have a variety of personal grammars and that we need to use them appropriately, depending upon purpose and audience. Similarly, stress the differences between oral and written English. If students consider written English another useful dialect, one that increases their versatility with language, they may be far more receptive to learning it.

▼
ERROR ANALYSIS

Teachers need to make judgments about their students' ability to analyze their errors, but eventually students need to take over this task. Teachers, nonetheless, must find the pattern and determine its origin: a lack of understanding or a performance error (e.g., overgeneralizing some rule, carelessness, native language interference, dialect).

▼

ATWELL'S SYSTEM

Atwell suggests a systematic approach to student editing and proofreading. Students are the first editors of their own work and are expected to do the best possible job. They then submit the draft to the teacher, who corrects whatever was missed. The teacher chooses one or two high-priority errors for an individual conference the next day, dealing with them in the piece of writing at hand. The writer adds the error(s) to the personal chart stapled in the writing folder. After teacher explanation, the student assumes responsibility for editing. In Atwell's system, three pen colors—original text, student editing pen, teacher blue editing pen—indicate who has done what work on the draft. Atwell also maintains a separate in/out basket for this editing procedure and a supply of tools of the trade—white-out and a supply of editing pens (106–107).

The editing procedure takes place only after content is set. Atwell notes: "Asking students to edit before the content is set reflects a misunderstanding of what writers do" (106). Keep in mind, therefore, that this process is for editing only. In a writing workshop environment, the teacher comments orally on the student's content.

▼

GRAMMAR GRAMS

Stephen Tollefson's *Grammar Grams,* as the name suggests, offer students a very brief explanation of a single point of usage (or punctuation). The brevity, the clarity, and the humor of a grammar gram allow senior high students to process the information easily. Teachers can also make their own grammar grams, adjusting for class level, or ask their most capable students to make some. Like DOL and minilessons, the grammar gram derives its power from a clear, single focus. Grammar grams or some other brief explanatory lessons could be part of a "Correction Corner," where materials are placed for student use at the editing and proofreading stage. Again, the student must learn to take responsibility for these stages of the writing process.

▼

SUMMARY

Usage is intimately connected with the communication situation at hand; appropriate usage is relative to audience and purpose. When students view usage in the context of flexibility with language, as empowering them across many communication situations, they are far more likely to adopt standard usage as one of their dialects. In working with student errors, we should be selective, focusing on only a couple at a time, those that most derail the reader or irritate the listener. Once we have explained the problem, the student can take over responsibility for corrections. With non-native speakers or speakers of other dialects, we do need to allow more time for assimilation and ask them questions (i.e., to apply it) to ensure that they have grasped the concept. In some cultures, students are not accustomed to asking questions of their teachers or elders. Moreover, some non-native speakers may be too shy or embarrassed to indicate that they don't understand. We can't expect one explanation or demonstration to suffice, especially if the student comes from a weak literacy background.

UNDERSTANDING AND IMPROVING SYNTAX

> Yet just as complete sentences do not necessarily reflect a wholly rational and coherent mind, so fragments do not necessarily reflect a fragmented and incoherent one. (87)
>
> *—Rei Noguchi*

Syntax can be defined as a system for indicating relationships among the words in the sentence. Syntax errors are usually considered serious, mainly because they keep a sentence from working or being understood clearly. Although native speakers have an intuitive understanding of sentences, the difference between the sentences we utter and those we write is considerable. Speech generally lacks the complexity and syntax of written language; speech also conforms to normal word order and carries a high level of redundancy. Writing, by contrast, demands consolidation through coordination and subordination and generally minimizes redundancy. It also requires certain conventions. All too often, students reduce their writing to short, simple sentences because they know that more complex sentences require punctuation and hold greater potential for making errors. Talking, on the other hand, holds fewer dangers and seldom needs "revision." Understandably, some students avoid writing as much as possible, especially if their confidence has been undermined by excessive marking and correction.

▼ ————————————————————————————

REVISING SENTENCES: HARDER THAN IT LOOKS

Revision of sentences is a fairly complex task, especially for the inexperienced writer. Mina Shaughnessy summarizes the processes:

> The ability to re-scan and re-work sentences . . . assumes several things: a memory for unheard sentences, an ability to store verbal patterns, visually from left to right, as in reading, and beyond this, an ability to suspend closure . . . until through addition, deletion, subtraction, rearrangement, the words fit the intended meaning. (80)

Scanning sentences and making judgments are cognitive acts that are more difficult than we assume when we write AWK or FRAG or SPLICE in the margin. Further, most students are simply not used to examining their sentences to understand how they work rather than what they mean. For this reason, sentences are best taught from the perspective of function—of how the parts work together to express meaning.

This perspective also provides a reason why textbook or worksheet exercises fail to help students gain control of sentence structure. First, students create sentences that are more complex and ambiguous than those found in exercises. Second, we make choices about sentences based on what we have already said and what we are planning to say, a point that most exercises fail to consider. Third, trying to untangle our own sentences, to express the meaning we ourselves intend, is at the heart of composing. When students have no investment in the sentences, the work appears to be nothing more than busy work. Sentence-combining exercises, although valuable, also suffer from this third important consideration. Also, giving students pages of exercises with sentence errors may actually reinforce errors. For example, students who had no trouble with fragments may start writing with them, and students who do have trouble with sentence boundaries may be even more confused. Further, students need to become readers of their own writing, habitual reviewers of their own sentences in their own essays.

From another perspective, reading experience is critical. Erika Lindemann points out the connection:

> Some students have trouble with sentences because they can't depend upon the eye or ear to help them identify prose rhythm. If they read poorly, have rarely been read to, infrequently converse with adults, or passively watch a great deal of television, they may have a limited repertoire of comfortable sentence options. (132)

Moreover, students who seldom engage in any language except that of peers, whose shared backgrounds allow almost elliptical expression, may lack knowledge of range of sentence types, especially those most used in academic writing. Even if they have knowledge of them, they may have had little practice in constructing them. Other sentence problems arise when students are trying to be "academic" and use lengthy constructions and unfamiliar vocabulary. The result is wordy, garbled and, at times, pompous prose.

Vocabulary itself is another area related to sentence problems. Students who lack an adequate vocabulary often end up composing lengthy, imprecise sentences. Moffett offers a striking example: a person who has not learned the word *dregs* must use "what is left in the cup after you finish drinking" (qtd. in Shaughnessy 73). Sentence problems may result from three different vocabulary problems: not knowing a word; not knowing the right grammatical form of the word; or not knowing appropriate context for a word. Unfortunately, vocabulary problems are difficult to solve. Our vocabularies grow slowly, and understanding the allowable contexts of words usually occurs through trial and error, not through word lists.

▼

IMPROVING SENTENCES

When we've asked secondary English teachers which sentence problems they see most often, their response is remarkably close to the problems we see in college composition. This isn't surprising, for learning to construct effective sentences takes time and experience. Consequently, the most obvious way to improve sentences is through guided experience, both in reading and in writing. Major problems of secondary students include the following:

- *Tangled, confused sentences.* They try to say too much in one structure and thus lose focus, meaning, and emphasis.
- *A series of short, choppy sentences.* The sentences are unconnected and often redundant.
- *More than one idea.* The relationship between ideas is unclear.
- *Non-sentences, fragments.*

As students mature and their cognitive abilities increase, their linguistic potential to express more complex ideas increases as well. For this reason, students need to know how to condense, simplify, join, and combine; they need to understand various ways to connect ideas using punctuation and connective words. Such instruction can and should be done through various means and, in all cases, with a minimum of grammatical terms. *Subject, verb, modifier,* and *connector* are probably all that are needed. Although *sentence* is often not technically correct, it serves just as well as *clause* and has been part of student vocabulary for many years. There's no reason not to use terms like *adjective* and *adverb* in the context of actual writing, but, for the most part, *modifier* works just as well. Teaching from a perspective of function, we ask these kinds of questions: How does this word or word group work in this sentence? What does it do? How does it help the reader? Students don't need to know *non-restrictive relative clause* in order to understand its function or accompanying punctuation, for example.

▼

MODELING

Teachers should respond to student sentences through questions, modeling the process that students need to internalize:

- How many ideas are in this sentence?
- List the ideas separately.
- What is the relationship between this idea and that one?
- How can you show this relationship? What word? What punctuation mark? What options do you have? Why?

- What's happening? To whom? How can you make this clearer?
- What's another way of saying this? What single word would mean the same thing?
- What punctuation mark is needed here? Why? How does it help the reader?
- What is the relationship between meaning and punctuation here?

Punctuation should be taught as part of syntax, not as a separate skill area, because very few marks are unrelated to syntax. Some students avoid complex constructions because they know a comma belongs in them somewhere, thus limiting their versatility considerably. We address this problem in more detail when we discuss sentence combining.

▼
MANIPULATING FOR MEANING

Students need to understand the concept of a sentence from a written, not an oral, perspective. Various activities provide some experience with and insights into what a sentence is. R. Baird Shuman suggested many of these (71):

A. Give students word groups to arrange into sentences. A variation on this activity: List the words alphabetically. After they have arranged them in one sentence, ask them to change the sentence without adding words— that is, to do variations. Then ask them to rank their creations and discuss which they like best. You can also ask students to bring in the word lists, limiting the list to 20 words.

B. Isolate typical sentences from a social studies text (or any content area textbook). Make a placard of each word or word group in the sentence and distribute them to students. Ask them to find a word they can "attach to" (e.g., adjective searching for a noun; auxiliary searching for a verb). Once the students have arranged their placards into an acceptable sentence, discuss it. Question them about the functions of the sentence parts, whether the part can be moved, if so where, and so forth.

C. Give students "jabberwocky" sentences in which they can demonstrate their knowledge of how English sentences function and carry meaning. This is a good way to reinforce the notion of noun and verb markers, tense, suffixes, and word position.

▼
SENTENCE COMBINING AND "DECOMBINING"

Sentence combining helps students build fluency. It is important to remember, however, that cognitive and linguistic maturity—development—are fundamental parts of syntactic maturation. William Strong, an early advocate of sentence combining, cautions that the ability to "tighten up" sentences is a later psycholinguistic development than expanding them; therefore, teachers need to delay this work until the upper levels of high school (18).

Sentence combining should always be done as a whole-class activity first, with the teacher modeling the process and asking questions. The value of the exercise lies in discovering the range of options in constructing the sentence. Usually it not a matter of right or wrong, but rather of more or less effective, more or less easy to understand. If some sentence parts are wrong, usually because a modifier is in the wrong place, we are able discuss modifiers from a sensible "what is happening here?" perspective. Following whole-class experience, sentence combining can be an individual, pair, or small-group activity as well. Asking groups to work on a "problem" is a good way for students to learn in a risk-free environment. For this reason, sentence-combining work should not be graded.

Although students need sustained work to ensure an effect, sentence combining exercises that are given too frequently can lead to boredom and a perception of busywork. Consequently, students must be guided to sentence combining/decombining potential in their own drafts. Strong reminds us:

> A basic aim of intelligent sentence combining is to make good sentences, not merely long ones. It follows that "decombining" may be at least as important as putting sentences together. (18)

Guided instruction in untangling and tightening sentences is important, then, at the upper levels of high school and with advanced students at any secondary level.

▼

COORDINATING AND SUBORDINATING SENTENCES

Some general activities for either coordinating or subordinating involve students in creating, analyzing, and discussing sentences.

A series of phrase, connector, and punctuation cards. Make cards containing noun and verb phrases, coordinators or subordinators, commas, semicolons, and periods. For older students, add the colon. Have students arrange the cards into sentences and then discuss the arrangement and punctuation. Focus on meaning, clarity, and effectiveness.

Models from literature. Choose poems or prose passages that illustrate effective coordinating or subordinating. Discuss how the author achieved a certain effect through manipulating sentences. Ask students to write their own poem or sentences, concentrating on patterns that will achieve an effect suitable to their subject.

Madcap or maddening sentences. Take sentences that drag on and on and write them on large sheets of paper. Ask students literally to cut the sentences apart, and come up with clearer, more effective sentences.

More models from literature. Use children's literature to demonstrate differences between sentences meant to be read orally (oral versus written tradition), to be recalled easily, and so forth and those that aren't. *Why Mosquitos Buzz in People's Ear, One Fine Day,* and *Where the Wild Things Are* are good texts for this purpose.

Gathering data. Ask students to compile a list of connectors for joining sentences by examining popular magazines, textbooks, and other sources. They will no doubt find all of the coordinators and most of the subordinators; those used for embedding—*that, who, whose, which, whom*—are less obvious.

▼ ─────────────────────────────────

USING STUDENT COMPETENCY

Because native speakers have a good intuitive sense of sentences, use inductive means of instruction. Give students a passage with a considerable number of coordinated or subordinated sentences of all types. Let them analyze and discuss the passage, working in pairs or small groups before whole-class discussion. You might also provide students with a passage that has been over-coordinated or subordinated and ask them to rewrite faulty sentences. Before doing this, however, model the process and suggest a certain word, phrase, or punctuation mark as the starting point for their revision. This practice helps students internalize syntax and draws upon their existing language competency.

Similarly, you might ask students to assemble a list of common sentence connectors, both coordinators and subordinators, and to determine the role these connectors play. Punctuation can be explored in the same way. Establish the role of the comma, for example, by means of student observation, not grammatical terms and rules. Then reinforce their understanding of how commas function and relate to meaning. When students see how often the comma sets off nonessential words and phrases, they also see that one rule, rather than what may seem like 100 rules in a textbook, is operating—and that it is actually a rather sensible rule.

As students work with sentences, especially subordinated ones, keep in mind that even their native, intuitive sense of how the English language works may be stretched at times. When we subordinate, we are adding to a base sentence, a cognitive act. This addition requires suspension of one part of the sentence, holding it in mind, while we complete the other part. As Shaughnessy reminds us, this juggling act requires a memory for unheard sentences, a memory that inexperienced writers may not have (80). That is, students may just plain forget what they have already written, thus unwittingly causing a problem in the second part of the sentence. Their native competency may also be thwarted, at least temporarily, by the differences between oral and written language. The boundaries of oral language are marked by intonation and pause, whereas in written language they are marked by capital letters and various punctuation marks. If students get into trouble writing, they may let the oral system take over. It is semantic, linked to meaning in their heads, and thus easier to manage (Noguchi 68, 73). Teachers can profit from this knowledge that native speakers group sequences of words based on meaning, not on syntax. Sharing such information with students ultimately assists them in analyzing their own sentence problems.

Unintentional sentence fragments, for example, reveal what students *do* know about their native language. Native speakers characteristically create fragments at predictable boundaries. Working with students orally, we can ask them to analyze the fragment: How is this information related to another sentence? Where does the fragment connect and why? If students have trouble identifying the structure as a fragment, it is probably because they are "thinking in oral." Our speech is peppered with fragments, mainly because the face-to-face context allows us to use them. Moreover, the pace of speech and conversational interactions makes fragments desirable. We simply cannot hang on to everything in long, complex oral sentences. Good discussion about the distinctive features of oral and written language enhances students' ability to sort out and apply native competency.

PUNCTUATION

> Punctuation marks, when used correctly, only sometimes have a noticeable effect; when used incorrectly, they almost always do. (46)
>
> *—Shafer*

▼
KEEPING PUNCTUATION IN PERSPECTIVE

As already indicated, punctuation is a response to sentence structure; punctuation should therefore be part of sentence work. The codes, once mastered, seem easy. However, we need to keep a perspective of just how long it takes for "mastery." We also need to keep motivation in mind. Students need to know why punctuation is useful: as a score for intonation, vocal nuance, pause; as a system of marks to help readers predict grammatical structures. It's tempting but incorrect to think that all punctuation errors are due to student carelessness. It is certainly true that some punctuation errors occur because the student doesn't think marks are important or doesn't take the time to proofread. But with inexperienced writers, errors are seldom a lack of care. Students master various aspects of writing over a very long time, achieving control gradually and unevenly. This means that they are juggling various skills when they write, and the skills are in different stages of development and competency.

Telling students to proofread doesn't help. We have to provide an explanation of the various marks and how they function. There are punctuation marks many students aren't even aware of, marks that bring voice to their writing, such as dashes and ellipses. There are also marks they are well aware of and often misuse: commas, periods, quotation marks, and apostrophes. Because of an overemphasis on rules, students half-know and half-apply those rules. They know, for example, that punctuation helps to connect and separate ideas, so it's not uncommon for them to ignore sentence endings altogether and run sentences together, either without punctuation or with commas. Or they may take the opposite approach, breaking sentences into fragments. As indicated earlier, fragments may occur because students are inexperienced with embedding (subordination) and find it hard to keep all the sentence elements in mind. We tend to work ahead, thinking of what's coming, and if we fail to review where we have just been, we may produce errors.

Punctuation needs to be aligned with work in sentence structure, so that students learn the roles of the punctuation marks rather than the definitions. Handbooks and textbooks often act as though fixing punctuation errors is a mechanical problem rather than what it most often is—a conceptual one. We also need to avoid punctuation as "rules for rules' sake," a perspective that handbooks and texts promote and students resent. When punctuation is viewed as critical to voice, style, and clarity, students find it to be an essential part of making meaning—their meaning.

▼ ───

WORKING WITH PUNCTUATION

Student drafts are the best resource for working with punctuation. Varied writing assignments provide students with an authentic need to learn and use the marks. For example, quotation marks are necessary when we write narratives with dialogue or scripts for informal drama. Fables are another form that calls for quotation marks, a form most students enjoy immensely. Commas are especially useful in descriptive writing or for qualifying information in expository writing. The more often students use punctuation marks in authentic writing, the more likely they are to recall just when and how the marks are used. Even middle school students use more "exotic" marks, such as the dash or ellipsis, when their own writing voice benefits from them. Having a reason to learn the marks makes a world of difference.

Similarly, varied and sustained reading provides students with a contextual view of the usefulness and visual effect of punctuation. Calling attention to effective punctuation during discussions of literature is a good strategy. Ask students to find passages that affected them and to determine the role punctuation played. The more student observational skills are invoked, the better. Using literature that relies on punctuation for effective oral reading, such as children's stories, may make the point quickly and easily.

Using student drafts and passages from reading materials on an overhead transparency, you can work inductively. Ask students to analyze the mark's use (or misuse) and to suggest options. Teachers are often surprised by the intuitive and very sensible responses. You might also ask some direct questions about the reasoning behind punctuation errors. Determining what assumptions have driven a student to use a certain mark is an important skill for teachers.

CAPITALIZATION

Again, one of the best ways to examine capitalization is through inductive teaching. Bring in materials that are "heavy duty" in terms of capitalization; let the students discover the rules governing when we capitalize. Linking capitalization to materials from history, literature, art, and music is another way to reinforce the skill. Similarly, linking it to commercial products that students like makes the point faster than any textbook can. Ask students to make directories of places where they "hang out," buy things, go for entertainment, and so forth. Have students compose "Capital Stories" that involve proper nouns, titles, dates, and similar elements. Older students could draw on Washington, D.C., and national politics as a source for plot lines; younger students could use their own town. Working with news stories is another way to provide students with experience in capitalization.

Most students have no problem with capitalization of names of people but a great deal of trouble with race, ethnicity, religion, and politics. Ensure that they receive ample exposure to readings that visually reinforce capitalization in these areas; lead them in a discussion of why capitals are used. School subjects are another area of trouble. Most students take a clue from English and generalize to other subjects, capitalizing everything from math to chemistry to art. You will no doubt need to explain why English and Algebra II are capitalized but algebra is not. Avoid giving them too many different rules at one time.

SPELLING

> Learning to spell is learning about words—their meanings, forms, and uses in communication. (15)
>
> —*Richard Hodges*

Spelling tends to be a publicly offensive error, the one most damaging to the writer in terms of what people think. A paper may have other errors far more serious, but spelling mistakes stand out as the most prominent feature of the paper—one that may mark the writer as "careless" or "dumb." Shaughnessy believes that the public views spelling as the hallmark of an educated person and failure to meet that standard may cause others to question both the quality of the education and the writer's native intelligence. Despite this, notes Shaughnessy, of all the writing skills, spelling is viewed by most teachers and students as the one most resistant to instruction and least related to intelligence: "It is the one area of writing where English teachers themselves will admit ineptness" (161–62). Nevertheless, secondary English teachers often experience frustration when faced with students who cannot spell, mainly because they didn't expect this problem and are not sure how to deal with it. Yet, as Richard Hodges points out, "Individuals make few, if any, random spelling errors. Each incorrect spelling has a cause, whether from carelessness or from insufficient or erroneous knowledge about the written language" (13). Moreover, says Hodges, some aspects of spelling are learned best at the secondary level, where students have both greater intellectual maturity and broader life experience (13).

▼ SPELLING WITHOUT PANIC AND DESPAIR

Students who are disabled spellers have most likely been told for years that they must "do something about spelling." Consequently, these students dislike writing and fear putting anything on paper, where each new word opens up more potential for making errors. However, it is critical that they write, for it is within the context of their own writing that spelling instruction must take place. Forget the textbooks and handbooks, forget the gimmicks offered by various commercial vendors, and stick to student drafts. In the first place, drafts have words that students want to use, in context and with a purpose in mind. Second, spelling can be put in its appropriate place, as the final concern for correctness. Students need to separate composing from editing and composing well from spelling well. For students who have been lost in a fog of errors, this is no small consideration.

The following list was adapted from Elizabeth Grubgeld and offers some useful suggestions for helping students emerge from the fog (48–50, 58–61):

1. Analyze the errors as they emerge in student drafts, "find clues to the hodge-podge of rules, visual memories, and systems of logic" by which students make spelling choices (59).

2. Once you have imposed order on the chaos of errors, provide the student with a limited number of words for proofreading, thus allowing the student ownership and control of the words.

3. Help the student see structures within their words that provide keys to words with similar structures.

4. Isolate words with similar structures and let the student work inductively to discover the patterns and principles.

5. Consider various ways for students to describe their own spelling rules: Write a series of conditions (questions) with which to examine the word in

question; conversationally write an answer to the question "what confuses me about this word?"

6. Forget the common practice of teaching confusing words together (e.g., *there* and *their*—put *there* with *here* and *where*).

7. Teach students the concepts of syllable, root word, and affixes so that they see words as divisible rather than as arbitrary groupings of letters.

8. Suggest that the student "read as slowly and with as much choppiness as someone who can barely read" in order to increase the ability to hear unstressed syllables.

9. Combine oral reading with practice in visual recognition of the grapheme-phoneme (i.e., written letters to sound) correspondence.

10. Establish ways to emphasize blurred pronunciations, such as associating *major* and *majority* to prevent spelling *majer*.

11. Develop spelling cards. Punch holes in the top of index cards and put rings through them (or buy a set that comes prepared that way for research writing). Have students list their spelling words alphabetically, using large handwriting or printing; they write only the correct version of the word, underlining the confusing part. If the confusion came from not hearing syllables, they leave spaces between the syllables. Next to the word, they write why this particular word gives them trouble. Finally, they record some means of remembering the correct spelling. Occasionally check the cards, noting error frequency, and provide extra work on problem words as warranted.

12. Encourage students to tape-record their words and then take dictation from the tape.

Grubgeld notes that this method is time-consuming and slow and that one semester or even one year may not dispatch the errors. However, she believes that students become critical readers in the process, recognizing spelling errors as they proofread (58–61).

▼ ───

SPELLING AND THE AVERAGE ERROR-MAKER

Although many of Grubgeld's suggestions work as well for the average student, you can expect more autonomy and responsibility from students who are not truly disabled in this area. Ask that students self-edit first. Have them edit in a color other than the one in which they wrote, circling any word that looks strange to them. They should then check a dictionary or other spelling aid. Students who use a computer may have the advantage of a spell-checker. However, they must understand that not every writing situation allows them such freedom and that they still need to have a good grasp of spelling. They also need to be aware of the limitations of a spell-checker.

▼

IMPROVING SPELLING

Richard Hodges' monograph *Improving Spelling and Vocabulary in the Secondary School* has a wealth of suggestions for increasing student awareness of and proficiency with language. Herbert Kohl's word books offer a similar resource for secondary teachers. The variety of word games, puzzles, and other devices keeps student interest high. Commercial games such as *Scrabble, Probe,* and *Wheel of Fortune* offer endless hours of experience with words. Vocabulary development is critical to all aspects of the English language arts. However, one should avoid giving students lists of words to memorize or match to definitions. This approach does little if anything to improve students' vocabulary, mainly because the words are divorced from context and the routine is rote and meaningless. As with any learning, we need context and motivation—a genuine purpose. Thus, reading and writing are central in the acquisition of new words.

The study of words (e.g., roots, commonalities, affixes) can be a fascinating and purposeful one if students apply this knowledge in their writing. Poetry is an excellent way to explore and exploit the power of vocabulary. Working with vocabulary from the students' other courses is also important. Content area teachers often fail to teach their students about discipline-specific vocabulary even though students need to understand the web of definitions found in texts and related materials. William E. Nagy's *Teaching Vocabulary to Improve Reading Comprehension* is an excellent resource for teachers who wish to learn about the importance of linking vocabulary study with students' prior knowledge. Nagy explains why traditional methods either fail or create problems and offers strategies for more effective instruction.

We need to remind ourselves of how students learn to spell. Hodges sums it up nicely:

> One learns to spell by having opportunities to generate useful "rules" about the written language, an outcome that becomes possible only through a rich interaction with written language in numerous and varied settings. Every instance of writing and reading is a potential moment for learning more about the properties of spelling. (13)

Spelling, then, is a contextual activity, not lists of words and a test on Friday. Hodges also makes an important point about spelling errors: "individuals make few, if any, random spelling errors" (13). It is up to us, through talking with students, to determine the causes.

▼

STAYING CALM AND ANSWERING QUESTIONS

Teaching English sometimes seems like risky business. Our "products" are visible in a way few other subject areas are: They are speaking and writing in the world at large. It's important, then, that we understand why some errors persist, why these errors continue to be in the public eye (and critical voice), and how we can respond. The more complete our understanding of how we acquire various language skills and of the time and environment we need to do so, the more easily we can quell parental fears or uneasiness about new methods in teaching writing skills.

DISCUSSION QUESTIONS

USAGE

1. Meyer and Smith make a useful observation: "Standard written English is a dialect nobody speaks" (219). What do they mean by this statement? How can this perspective help you as an English teacher? How can this perspective help your students?

2. According to Lucy Calkins, "English is a skill to be developed, not a content to be taught—and it is best learned through active and purposeful use" (204). Discuss the differences between English as a process skill and English as content. How might your role as a teacher be somewhat different from that of the mathematics or social studies teacher? Research and common sense tell us that students develop competency in English "through active and purposeful use." What are the implications for your classroom? Provide specific examples, not only of *what* you might do but *how*. How does this view of English affect even the physical arrangement of the classroom?

SYNTAX

3. Shaughnessy reminds us that the ability to rework sentences assumes a "memory for unheard sentences" and the "ability to suspend closure" (80). What does she mean? What is the relationship between these cognitive acts and the grade level you teach? How can your understanding of how we process language and form sentences help you maintain patience when working with students of various abilities and ages?

4. Students who are good readers are often good writers as well. Explain this relationship, especially the effects on sentence variety, clarity, and effectiveness. What would you tell a group of parents who are concerned about the amount of reading you expect from your 11th-grade English class?

PUNCTUATION, CAPITALIZATION, AND SPELLING

5. Lucy Calkins argues:

> It may not matter whether students can list the sixteen uses of the comma or define a prepositional phrase. What matters far more is that children get a feel for linking sentences and embedding phrases, for using symbols which encode the sounds of their voices. (204)

If the English teacher's goal is to produce students who can write both effectively and correctly (that is, apply the rules), how can Calkins, as an English language arts teacher, value rules and definitions so little?

SUGGESTED ACTIVITIES

USAGE

1. You have a 9th-grade English class with several students whose native dialect is non-standard. Prepare a model error analysis log to show these students how you would like them to keep track of the differences between their personal "usage" and school "usage." Be sure to use examples that would be typical for these students.

2. Using the model suggested by Vail and Papenfuss's *Daily Oral Language*, prepare four sentences for use with a 7th-grade class and four sentences for use with an 11th-grade class. Note how you would introduce and carry out the activity.

3. *Alice in Wonderland* makes a usage error:

   "Curiouser and curiouser!" cried Alice. (She was so much surprised, that for a moment she quite forgot how to speak good English).

   Prepare a mini-lesson in which you explain to Alice (and the rest of your class) standard usage in the comparative and superlative forms of both regular and irregular adjectives and adverbs.

4. In *Through the Looking Glass,* Alice has this interchange with the Frog:

   "I don't know what you mean," she said.
   "I speaks English, doesn't I" the Frog went on.

   Prepare a mini-lesson in which you help the Frog (and your 9th graders) understand subject-verb agreement. Keep in mind that underneath subject-verb agreement lie the concepts of singular and plural.

5. These student sentences contain common pronoun usage errors. How would you assist the student in finding and correcting the error?

   A. If one does not lose their license it will cost them in other ways.
   B. A friend is someone you can trust. You can tell them a secret.
   C. If parents expect certain performance standards out of him they will push you to do your best.

SYNTAX

6. "I quite agree with you," said the Duchess, "and the moral of that is—'Be what you would seem to be'—or, if you'd like to put it more simply—'Never imagine yourself not to be otherwise than what it might appear to others

that what you were or might have been was not otherwise than what you had been would have appeared to them to be otherwise.' "

—Lewis Carroll, *Alice in Wonderland*

Help the Duchess straighten out the syntax. How would you approach the problem presented in this very lengthy, complex utterance. List questions that you would use to assist her in finding her own central idea. Do not rewrite sentences for her. Think through options in punctuation at the same time you are considering the various ways in which she might restructure the sentences.

7. Each of these student sentences needs revision. Determine where the problem or problems occur; then decide how you would work with this student on revision. Approach the revision from a functional perspective: Where is the reader derailed and why? What idea or ideas are presented here? What, if anything, is missing? What can we do so that the reader understands the writer's intent? What options do we have in repairing the sentence? What punctuation do we need? Remember: help the student through your questions. Giving the student the answer to the revision problem is not teaching.

   a. For example in football I had a coach who wanted me to gain thirty pounds on the off season and when he found out that I wasn't even going to try he had a long meeting with me about the poor attitude in sports.

   b. But for more than eight days before this weekend the maintenance employees had not even touched the roads and sidewalks with any effort to clear the ice, except with a machine that has a brush type of roller which brushed the snow off the ice.

   c. Another point about athletics is it for all types of people.

   d. As you can see owning a car can be very expensive. Especially if you are going to school.

   e. A car can be a pain at school. For many different reasons like people borrowing it and different costs to the owner.

   f. An example of this is somewhat like a mutual relationship when you do things together and have fun.

   g. The frustration would consist of not having money, no transportation and no time.

   h. The solution to his problem was that he thought what he wanted the most and if his friends didn't want to share in what he wanted then they shouldn't have to.

   i. After careful consideration of these criteria my decision has been made.

   j. When eating them they break easily. (reference to potato chips)

   k. I can taste the grease that was left behind. Well not really that much grease unless you really think of it. (reference to potato chips)

l. The reason I remembered this is because of the way it looked. (reference to candy bar)

PUNCTUATION, CAPITALIZATION, AND SPELLING

8. The following sentences contain common student errors. Examine each sentence and decide how you could help the student choose an appropriate punctuation mark. Where more than one mark would be appropriate, think of questions and explanations that would help the student understand the options.

   a. The most common relationships are; parent relations, friendship relations, and boy-girl relations.
   b. There are many ways a student can make money, one is a summer job.
   c. Some people just do not show respect for others property.
   d. You experience more sour cream and onion taste as that fades so does the texture of the chip, it loses its crunchiness.
   e. The shape of the whole M&M seems to begin with the shape of the peanut since the chocolate and outer colored coating seems to have been built up around the peanut, so the M&M ends up being about the size of your thumb nail.

9. Using Vail and Papenfuss's model of *Daily Oral Language,* prepare sentences that contain common errors in mechanics. Prepare one set of two sentences for use with 8th graders; prepare a second set of two sentences for use with 12th graders, college preparatory level. Then write out the procedure you would use with the class.

10. The apostrophe continues to be the bane of students at all levels. Prepare a mini-lesson on this punctuation mark. Assume that you have several students who speak Black dialect and several others who speak Hispanic English and adjust your lesson accordingly.

11. Which punctuation marks must students control in order to link sentences and embed phrases? Which marks allow them to "encode the sounds of their voices?" How can you provide instruction in these critical areas without exercises? How can you evaluate without quizzes?

12. According to Tom Romano:

    Our profession has become synonymous with fastidiousness. And I don't like it. Spelling, usage, punctuation—editing skills—are part of a piece of writing, along with organization, diction, clarity, voice, style and the quality of information. Expert editing cannot make insipid writing vibrant nor does less-than-perfect editing negate powerful thought and language. (75)

    Is Romano suggesting that editing doesn't matter? Discuss his view of what's wrong with the profession. Have you ever experienced "fastidious English"? If so, how did you feel about it at the time? Now? What view of students does Romano hold? How do you know?

REFERENCES

Atwell, Nancie. *In the Middle: Writing, Reading, and Learning with Adolescents*. Portsmouth: Boynton/Cook Heinemann, 1987.

Calkins, Lucy McCormack. *The Art of Teaching Writing*. Portsmouth: Heinemann, 1986.

Fortier, John. Letter to the author. 15 October 1991.

Friedman, Thomas. "Teaching Error, Nurturing Confusion: Grammar Texts, Tests and Teachers in the Developmental English Class." *College English* Apr. 1983: 390–99.

Hodges, Richard E. *Improving Spelling and Vocabulary in the Secondary School*. Urbana: National Council of Teachers of English, 1982.

Grubgeld, Elizabeth. "Helping the Problem Speller Without Suppressing the Writer." *English Journal* Feb. 1986: 58–61.

Kirby, Dan, and Tom Liner. *Inside Out: Developmental Strategies for Teaching Writing*. 2nd ed. Portsmouth: Boynton/Cook Heinemann, 1988.

Lindemann, Erika. *A Rhetoric for Writing Teachers*. 2nd ed. New York: Oxford UP, 1987.

Madsen, Alan L. "Language Games and Usage." *English Journal* Oct. 1987: 81–83.

Meyer, Emily, and Louise Z. Smith. *The Practical Tutor*. New York: Oxford UP, 1987.

Mitchell, Arlene Harris, and Darwin L. Henderson. "Black Poetry: Versatility of Voice." *English Journal* Apr. 1990: 23–28.

Nagy, William E. *Teaching Vocabulary to Improve Reading Comprehension*. Urbana: National Council of Teachers of English, 1988.

Newkirk, Thomas, ed. *To Compose: Teaching Writing in the High School*. Portsmouth: Heinemann, 1986.

Noguchi, Rei. *Grammar and Teaching Writing*. Urbana: National Council of Teachers of English, 1991.

Romano, Tom. *Clearing the Way: Working with Teenage Writers*. Portsmouth: Heinemann, 1987.

Rosen, Lois Matz. "Developing Correctness in Student Writing: Alternatives to the Error Hunt." *English Journal* Mar. 1987: 62–69.

Sanborn, Jean. "Grammar: Good Wine Before Its Time." *English Journal* Mar. 1986: 72–80.

Schafer, John C. "Punctuation and Process: A Matter of Emphasis." *English Journal* Dec. 1988: 46–49.

Schuman, R. Baird. "Seeing and Feeling Sentence Structure." *English Journal* Jan. 1990: 71–73.

Shaughnessy, Mina. *Errors and Expectations*. New York: Oxford UP, 1977.

Tabbert, Russell. "Parsing the Question: 'Why Teach Grammar?'" *English Journal* Dec. 1984: 38–42.

Tollefson, Stephen. *Grammar Grams*. New York: Harper, 1990.

Strong, William. *Creative Approaches to Sentence Combining*. Urbana: National Council of Teachers of English, 1986.

Vail, Neil, and Joseph Papenfuss. *Daily Oral Language*. Evanston: MacDougal Littell, 1989.

Van DeWeghe, Richard. "Spelling and Grammar Logs." *Non-Native and Nonstandard Dialect Students*. Ed. Cindy Carter et al. Urbana: National Council of Teachers of English, 1982.

CHAPTER 8

Understanding Grammar

CHAPTER HIGHLIGHTS

- Defining grammar.
- What teachers need to know about grammar.
- Understanding student errors.

It appears that the teachers of English teach English so poorly largely because they teach grammar so well.

—Linda Enders, high school student

▼
WHY GRAMMAR IS AN ISSUE

Grammar is perhaps the most contested and the least understood area of the English language arts curriculum, even though it is the area most taught in American schools. Many people associate English classes with grammar: learning terminology and rules, diagramming sentences, filling in blanks and worksheets, and taking quizzes. Educators presume these activities enable students to speak and write acceptable English. That presumption, however, is false. Considerable research (Braddock, et al.; Haynes; Bamberg; and Hillocks), as well as classroom practice, has shown that these activities have little or no effect on student competency and performance.

Researchers continue to report what many classroom teachers already know: Practicing skills in textbooks or worksheets doesn't work. The skills fail to transfer to the messy business of composing a full essay. A student who has done 10 exercises and passed a quiz on a specific skill may make errors in that skill on the very next essay. There are several reasons for this. First, the isolated study of language skills has little or no effect on the permanent knowledge of language that we carry in our heads. Second, we make choices about language through the context in which we are using it; a drill sheet has no context, only unrelated sentences. Third, the "dummy runs" in texts and worksheets are usually far less complex than the students' own language. If students don't learn to untangle their own language, making judgments about effectiveness and correctness in an entire piece of writing, they gain little or no proficiency. Even more damaging is the time lost: Students who are doing exercises are not writing, nor are they learning about standard usage, appropriate mechanics, and correct spelling in the one context in which these skills are both meaningful and mandatory—real communication. Student drafts provide ample opportunities for teaching the various language skills as they relate to communication—to what students themselves want to express.

Because grammar evokes personal and even emotional responses, teachers need to understand the diverse meanings applied to the term *grammar*. When teachers say they are doing a "grammar unit," they usually mean they are concentrating on some aspect of standard American usage, conventions, or sentence patterns. For example, they block out two weeks to cover subject-verb agreement, or three weeks for comma use, or two weeks for sentences with a subject-verb-object pattern. Although the notion of a grammar unit is outdated, many teachers persist in it. School curricula and textbooks seem to resist change, despite research that refutes the value of teaching skills as isolated units.

▼
WHAT IS GRAMMAR?

As noted earlier, controversy and confusion arise when the word *grammar* is used. When people are asked why students must study grammar, the reasons usually reduce to these three: Students can't put a sentence together; students don't know a noun from a verb; and students can't speak or write without making mistakes. In exploring these reasons, we can find underlying definitions of the term *grammar*.

STUDENTS CAN'T PUT A SENTENCE TOGETHER

In the context of writing sentences, grammar refers to the set of rules native speakers know intuitively, the rules we acquired without lessons, as we acquired our native language between birth and age six. Grammar here is tacit, unconscious knowledge. As native speakers of English, we know how to form words and sentences, no matter how simple or complex, and we do so without making any conscious decisions about word order, word endings, and so forth. In brief, we know the grammar of our native language.

Assuming normal development (that is, no damage to the brain and capacity for language), all native speakers know the grammar of their language. They recognize non-grammatical English sentences immediately. For example,

*sees boy the ball red

would be rejected by every native speaker of English. Teachers and others may not like some students' sentences, which may be poorly constructed and thus awkward or unclear, may suffer from weak vocabulary, or may be punctuated incorrectly. These weaknesses are not a grammar problem, however, at least not to teachers who understand grammar as the system of language we learn as native speakers.

STUDENTS DON'T KNOW A NOUN FROM A VERB

In the context of knowing the functional names for words, the term *grammar* refers to the ability to talk about the language system, our conscious knowledge about our native language. In America, tradition has dictated that educated people do know some basic language terms: noun, verb, adjective, adverb, sentence. An understanding of these terms is not acquired naturally, the way the language itself is. We have to learn the terms through instruction—thus the heavy emphasis on them at every curricular level. In reality, however, few students learn all the terms. Their textbooks often define the terms poorly, probably because the concepts they represent are far more complex than people like to believe. For those who do learn the terms, the knowledge is fleeting, largely because students quickly come to realize that labeling nouns and defining verbs does not make any significant impact on their lives. As one 10th grader recently remarked, "Does anyone really believe that we have to know this stuff, that someday a person will jump out from behind a tree and say 'Tell me what a verb does.'?"

Students' aversion to learning terms for terms' sake is supported by research; understanding the function of language is more important than memorizing terms and definitions. However, English teachers have a persistent notion that "doses" of such directed study improve language skills, especially writing. As Rei Noguchi puts it, "Like the near mythical omnipotence of cod-liver oil, the study of grammar became imbued with medicinal power it simply did not possess, particularly with respect to writing ills" (15).

Thus labeling parts of speech, diagramming sentences, and other activities designed to "name" language rather than to use it continue. That same 10th grader who questioned the validity of studying terms also commented on their domination of the curriculum: "Different cover, same old stuff." We do expect an educated person to have literacy skills, that is, to be able to read and write competently, but these abilities are not the result of knowing the parts of speech. Moreover, forcing such information before students have a reason for knowing it or the cognitive maturation to understand it is an exercise in futility.

STUDENTS CAN'T SPEAK OR WRITE WITHOUT MAKING MISTAKES

Here *grammar* refers to rules of language etiquette or verbal manners: We adhere to a standard use of language in the academic or business world. This standard has nothing to do with communication because non-standard forms communicate meaning as well. For example, there is no confusion of understanding when we hear non-standard forms such as "she's taller than me" or "he can't hardly talk." There is no confusion of meaning when we read "them boys did pick a fight." What is involved is a continuum of verbal manners. Many people would fail to notice the error in "she's taller than me;" few would fail to notice the deviations in "them boys did pick a fight." "Mistakes," then, translate into a view of what constitutes standard American English, the dialect used in the world of formal communication and taught in schools, the dialect of social prestige.

Because standard American English is the dialect of schools, English language arts teachers want students to use it. Similarly, most parents want their children to know and use it appropriately. The key, however, is flexibility and appropriateness to the communication situation. Teachers sometimes assume that all "mistakes" are equally serious and all rules applicable in every communication situation, but this is simply not the case. Some mistakes derail the reader and force him or her to go back and sort out the meaning; these are serious in that they interfere with meaning. Others may irritate the purist but cause no confusion to the general reader. The issue of "mistake" is a serious one nonetheless. Teachers face a challenge in presenting students with a standard dialect and, at the same time, honoring other dialects used at home and in the community.

Patrick Hartwell offers a cogent explanation of the two grammars that get lumped together under the term *grammar:*

School Grammar. This grammar is the one of school textbooks. Although linguists cringe at fuzzy definitions (e.g., a sentence expresses a complete thought), school grammar makes no claims of scientific accuracy. School grammar presents the student with parts of speech, sentence patterns, standard usage forms, conventions of writing and spelling. Another name for school grammar is traditional grammar.

Grammar-as-etiquette. When speakers or writers deviate from certain forms or conventions (those taught in school grammar), they are accused of having "bad grammar." This grammar refers to standard American English, the dialect of school and business.

The basic controversy and debate over grammar are found in school grammar and grammar-as-etiquette. Does school grammar improve grammar etiquette? Research has attempted to determine whether or not instruction in traditional grammar improves student writing. That is, does it make any difference whether or not students engage in grammar exercises or drills? To date, the findings suggest that it does not, mainly because this approach has little effect on the internal language system.

What does affect it is the use of authentic language: communication, students listening, speaking, reading, and writing standard English; students manipulating their own language. English language arts teachers who recognize and teach standard usage and sentence clarity as products of revision enter into a process which, over time, affects the internalization of language. There is no debate over the basic issue—that students can and should become more effective and flexible users of their language—only over the method by which to achieve it. Few curricular areas are as visible as grammar or as open to criticism. Given these conditions, grammar will no doubt remain a force in the English language arts curriculum.

Grammar study as a means to improve students' language is a major reason for its place in the curriculum. Other reasons also exist, associated with everything from studying language for its own sake to preparing students for standardized tests. Teachers need to be aware of these reasons and prepared to discuss them with colleagues, administrators, and parents.

▼
STUDYING GRAMMAR FOR ITS OWN SAKE

Language is a uniquely human phenomenon; as such, it is worthy of study. However, studying English grammar at the expense of time for listening, speaking, reading, and writing costs most students dearly. To solve the dilemma, many high schools offer an elective course in English grammar at the junior and senior level. Such courses validate the study of language but reserve it for those students both motivated and capable of undertaking such a study, which demands advanced cognitive and analytical skills. In no way should a grammar course replace English courses that offer students a well-balanced experience in the language arts.

▼
WHY GRAMMAR UNITS PERSIST

Why does grammar dominate the English language arts curriculum? Cultural mythology is one reason. People tend to believe that studying grammar contributed to their ability to use language correctly and well. They either forget or ignore the fact that effective language skills arise out of a great many language activities and a supportive environment. People may also associate grammar study with "real" schooling, their own school days when the "3 R's curriculum" was the standard for literacy. This is, of course, a simplistic—indeed romantic—notion of schools. Those schools educated fewer students in a less complicated society and dealt with fewer social ills. Even then, literacy skills came from active listening, speaking, reading, and writing; literacy came from a motivation to become literate and an environment that supported it.

A second reason for the persistence of grammar study lies in English language arts teachers' convictions about themselves. They reason that their language skills came from studying grammar, diagramming sentences, and so forth. If we think for a moment who the English teachers were, we realize the falseness of their reasoning. Today's English teachers were students for whom reading and writing were constant companions, students who liked playing with language. They were highly motivated and probably reinforced continually. A secondary classroom often has at least one student with an aptitude for language in the same way someone else has an aptitude for and intense interest in math. In brief, English teachers forget that they were the exceptions in terms of language study throughout their own schooling.

A third and very pervasive force in maintaining traditional grammar lies in textbooks and workbooks, in which explanations, exercises, and drills come nicely packaged and easily tested. Publishers continue to give teachers what they expect; thus, it is fair to say that most textbooks are written for teachers, not students. It is no wonder, then, that language texts seem very straightforward and easy to teachers and so obtuse to their students. Many English teachers like teaching grammar and continue to choose texts and other materials that keep this model alive. It is not surprising that grammar still dominates the curriculum. The problem is that the study of grammar has not and cannot solve problems of literacy, nor does it enhance the skills of our best students, at least not as long as it is taught as a subject to be mastered. As Rei Noguchi points out, there is considerable difference between "teaching grammar as an academic subject and teaching grammar as a tool for writing improvement" (15). Unfortunately, many teachers are unaware of this difference. Thus the cycle continues.

WHAT TEACHERS NEED TO KNOW ABOUT GRAMMAR

Historically, the English language arts curriculum has shifted among different notions of teaching grammar. In the late 1960s, many educators turned away from traditional grammar as structural and transformational grammars became the new bases of instruction. It was not uncommon in the 1970s to find junior high school texts (e.g., Roberts; Laidlaw Series) worthy of a college English course in structural-transformational grammar. However, these new grammars worked no better than traditional grammar in producing more effective writers. With the perception of an impending literacy crisis, people determined that if the new linguistics had not worked, and perhaps added to the problem, then traditional grammar should be revived. Thus, the emphasis on formal grammar and correctness in the 1980s reflected a more conservative view of education after the turbulent 1970s.

It is not surprising that veteran teachers are skeptical of any claims related to grammar and language improvement. However, the 1980s also brought advances in our knowledge of just how people acquire, process, and improve their language abilities. Studies of students and classrooms, such as those done by Donald Graves, Lucy Calkins, and Nancie Atwell, demonstrated the difference between talking about grammar and applying grammar. The Bay Area Writing Project, under the direction of James Gray, also promoted the teaching of standard usage and conventions through student writing; as state after state initiated writing projects, more and more teachers became convinced of the value of teaching grammar contextually. At the same time, teacher-researchers such as William Strong and Donald Daiker applied principles of transformational grammar and developed sentence-combining as a means of improving syntactic fluency. Most textbooks today reflect to some degree the contribution of this new grammar. However, they also cling stubbornly to the old, causing dissonance for many teachers educated with a writing-process approach to grammar and mechanics.

English language arts teachers should be acquainted with all descriptions of grammar: traditional, structural, and transformational. We may be called upon to respond to concerns of parents, administrators, and other teachers: to explain what we are doing and why; to make informed decisions on materials and methods; and to evaluate our school curriculum. A good grammar background also enables us to help our students make effective language choices and to determine the source of their language difficulties.

▼ ──

TRADITIONAL GRAMMAR

The English grammar that we call "traditional" was modeled on the classical languages of Greek and Latin. Roman scholars took both the terms and descriptive methods of the Greeks and applied them to Latin. Because some similarities exist between the two languages, the application was fairly successful. This is not the case when these same terms and methods are applied to English; the result is a distortion of English.

For example, one of the rules of Latin grammar was never to split an infinitive; this rule is found in English handbooks today. A sentence such as "To fully appreciate this movie, you need some background in African history." would be judged flawed because the adverb *fully* is placed between parts of the infinitive *to appreciate*. Whereas not splitting an infinitive in Latin made sense because it meant splitting up a one-word verb, there is no reason not to split an infinitive in English. Sometimes, the rhythm of the sentence makes splitting an infinitive exactly what a writer *should* do. "To appreciate fully this movie . . ." strikes most English readers as strange, whereas splitting the infinitive makes sense. The admonition not to do so is the result of Latin grammar applied to English.

From models of classical Greek and Latin, English grammar moved into medieval times and acquired yet another emphasis that persists today: to "fix" the language, to stop its degeneration, and to eliminate error. This view of grammar matched the focus and instruction of the medieval church. Again, in the 18th century, the emphasis on correctness and rules was reinforced in an Age of Rationalism. Today, therefore, traditional grammar is Latin-based, rule-oriented, and prescriptive. Despite the fact that English is structured differently from Latin or Greek, the tradition of teaching the parts of speech is almost unchanged. Because Latin has more word endings than English, we have more categories than we need, along with rules that are equally inappropriate (Weaver 101).

The insistence on rules, based on the belief that learning rules helps students to write correctly, is another part of this heritage. Rules such as: "It is I" rather than "It is me" exist because Latin takes the nominative form "I" in a mathematical equation it = I. We are to utter "To whom do you wish to speak?" rather than "Who do you want to talk to?" because "To whom do you want to talk" is the base, and prepositions take the objective form "whom," not the nominative form "who." Following Latin dictates, definitions became singularly unhelpful and downright obtuse, as this passage from a 10th-grade textbook demonstrates (Laidlaw Language Series 1985):

> An adjective is a word that modifies a noun or pronoun. An adjective clause is a dependent clause that functions as an adjective. An adjective clause may be introduced by a relative pronoun or by a relative adverb.
>
>> When Nora arrived later, the old playground—empty and unkempt— shimmered in the heat of the Hawaiian afternoon. Crushed cans and paper cups littered the brown grass. The swings rocked slowly, creaking their rusty chains. The pond was dry.
>
> Adjectives are not the only words that can modify nouns. For example, the second sentence above begins with the phrase Crushed cans. Crushed would appear to be an adjective, modifying cans, but it is not. It is a verbal—

specifically a past participle—which functions in the same way that an adjective does.

It should be clear that students learn little of use to them from this type of textbook and the heritage of Latin grammar—other than a firmer conviction that such notions have nothing to do with them, their language, and their world. Learning to work with adjectives and verbals is important in the world of making meaning and of seeing options, but not as a study of arcane terms. When college composition instructors complain that freshmen don't know gerunds, they place pressure on secondary teachers to teach terms. When secondary English teachers express shock that students coming to their classes can't define adjectives, they place pressure on elementary teachers to focus on definition rather than function. Teachers themselves thus drive the English language arts curriculum back through the centuries and revive the long tradition of parsing sentences and hunting down errors.

The preoccupation with definition and classification of words and labeling and diagramming sentences also left us with some strange definitions:

A verb is a state of being.
An adverb modifies another adverb.
A noun is the name of a person, place, or thing.

Most of us memorized these and similar definitions, and, because we liked English, we had little trouble with them, nor did we offer any resistance to such tasks. However, they did little to improve our writing skills. Our being bookworms and closet writers did that. Many of our classmates—those less thrilled about English—not only had trouble with the definitions but also developed negative attitudes about English class in general. That seems a high price to pay for definitions that are so unhelpful as well as unnecessary for authentic language activities.

TRADITIONAL GRAMMAR IN THE CLASSROOM

Of what use is traditional grammar? For one thing, there is no reason to invent a new vocabulary for nouns, pronouns, verbs, adverbs, and adjectives. As Connie Weaver notes:

Traditional grammar is important, if only because its terminology is widely known and because its appeal to meaning is often vital in determining the precise function of a grammatical unit. (105)

There is nothing wrong in using traditional names when we speak to students about their own writing. Pointing out, for example, that a certain verb doesn't provide the reader with a good sense of the action, or that an adjective conveys just the right sense of description *within the context of the student's draft* provides a common vocabulary without drilling students about labels. But some terms, such as *gerund*, students really don't need to know.

Students do not have to learn every part of speech. The most common categories of noun, pronoun, verb, adjective, and adverb will do. Some teachers collapse adjective and adverb into *modifier* and have found that it works just fine. Rather than teaching prepositions, teachers can concentrate on the function of prepositional phrases—how useful they are in adding detail, for example. The same holds true for adjective and adverbial clauses, and again, the term *modifier* helps students to see function. However, native speakers can discern for themselves the function of these clauses; they need neither a label nor a lesson in underlining them. Students at all curricular levels benefit from sentence analysis in terms of function: Just how does that word or word group contribute? Is it in the right place? Is it in the most effective place?

Some teachers wonder if they should use the more accurate term *clause* rather than *sentence*. Because *sentence* is the common term, the traditional descriptor, we believe it's fine for student use. Teachers themselves do need to understand the concept of a clause and the difference between a grammatical sentence and a rhetorical one. Weaver provides us with workable definitions:

> Grammatically, a sentence consists of an independent clause plus whatever dependent clauses may be attached to it or embedded within it. Rhetorically, a sentence may be defined as whatever occurs between the initial capital letter and the final period, or between the onset of speech and the utterance-final pause. Hence a rhetorical sentence may be as short as a single word, or as long as several hundred words. (118)

Sometimes, teachers need to explain to students just why their "sentence" is not a sentence. The definitions, as just given, would be unsuitable, but the idea of "rhetorically correct," as well as some discussion of the differences between oral and written language, would be very helpful. As noted earlier, a great deal about traditional grammar is unhelpful, if not downright confounding, but English language arts teachers can view it as part of their professional background and draw upon it for common-sense applications.

▼ STRUCTURAL GRAMMAR

Whereas traditional grammar is prescriptive, telling us what we should or shouldn't do, structural grammar attempts to describe language as it exists. Thus, structural linguists divide language into three levels: (1) individual sounds (phonology), (2) groups of sounds with meaning (morphology), and (3) arrangement of words and relationships among parts (syntax). They also classify words differently. For example, *gangster* is a noun not because it is the name of a person, place, or thing but because its inflection *-s* marks it as a noun. This suffix belongs to nouns, marking a plural in English. *Gangster* is a noun because of another suffix that marks nouns, *-ster* (cf. youngster). Finally, the placement of *gangster* in English sentences marks it as a noun: "The gangsters were put in jail." "I saw the gangsters." Nouns lead off most English sentences; nouns often have *the* or *a* in front of them; nouns are in predictable places in English sentences.

We can see how this system works by examining what native speakers do:

1. The + kitten + s + jump + ed + play + ful + ly.
*2. The + kit + tens + jum + ped + pl + ayfully.

No native speaker of English would divide the sentence as in 2 because the system of affixes carries meaning to a native speaker: *-s* = plural on noun; *-ed* = past tense on verb; *-ful* + *-ly* = adverb. This knowledge is part of the internal grammar, the tacit knowledge, of a native speaker. A few irregular forms aside, we automatically add an *-s* when we want to make nouns plural and *-ed* when we want to make verbs show past tense. Structural linguists use this knowledge as the basis of their description of the language.

In English, the flexibility of affixes is characteristic:

green greener greenest   earn unearned
soft softer soften   visual vision visible

These are derivational affixes—changes in the form of the word that may change its function in the sentence. For example,

She will sweeten her coffee with sugar.
Do you have a sweetener here?
I find the sweetness sickening, but I will sweetly comply and bring the sugar.

There are also inflectional affixes:

for plurals: boy boys   church churches
for tense: work worked

These characteristics, then, became part of structural linguists' attempts to describe English as native speakers know and use it. Structural linguists also look at sentence patterns. These are the most common in English:

Subject	verb	direct object	
The boy	hit	his neighbor.	

Subject	verb		
The boy	lies.		

Subject	linking verb	complement	
The boy	is	angry.	

Subject	verb	indirect object	direct object
The boy	gave	his neighbor	a black eye.

Sentence features such as noun and verb markers are also identified: *a, an,* and *the* are common noun markers; *can, should, would, will,* and *might* are common verb markers. A native speaker can recognize the role of a nonsense word because of these features, the affixes, and the word order common to English sentences. For example:

The wibbels ruped lifly on the jip.

Any native speaker would indicate that *wibbels* is the subject, a noun. *Wibbels* is placed between the noun marker *the* and a word recognizable as a verb (*-ed* marking its tense). The *-s* on *wibbels* indicates plural form, a sign of a noun. The verb *ruped* is marked by the *-ed*. *Lifely* has an *-ly* to indicate how the wibbels ruped. And the phrase *on the* marks *jip* as place, another noun. Even in nonsense, a native speaker of English can identify how the parts fit together.

The flaw in this description of English, as other linguists have noted, is its inability to account for the creative use of language. As native speakers, we produce thousands and thousands of sentences never before uttered or written, yet understood perfectly by other members of the language community. When linguists asked how we can do this, transformational grammar took its place among the English grammars.

STRUCTURAL GRAMMAR IN THE CLASSROOM

Structural grammar is important, says Weaver, because "it lends precision to definitions and to procedures for identifying grammatical units and their functions" (105). Whereas traditional grammar defines a noun in somewhat vague "name of person, place, or thing" terms, which can get teachers into all kinds of trouble, structural grammar identifies a noun by certain endings, such as a plural or a derivational affix. Verbs, traditionally defined as words that "express an action or a state of being," are defined structurally by their endings or a distinctive verb form (Weaver 111). Trying to explain the concept of "state of being" to a 12 year old is something most teachers never want to do; in fact, we're not even sure what it really means. On the other hand, verbs can be identified by the inflectional endings we use to show tense. The verb also functions as the beginning word, or headword, of a predicate; it's essential to meaning. Structuralists identify adjectives and adverbs similarly, both by characteristic endings and by function. Youngsters can relate to concrete endings and functions more easily than to definitions that may fail them in complex sentences.

By the time students enter middle school, they have become very successful communicators, using nouns, verbs, adjectives, and adverbs at will, stringing them together in very acceptable sentences. The problems occur as students enlarge their vocabulary and their capability for more sophisticated syntax and increasingly have to deal with written rather than oral language. Recognizing endings, understanding the flexibility of English words, and recognizing the function of words or word groups can help them make this transition. They don't need to practice sentence patterns because they already know them. However, teachers usually have to bring this tacit knowledge into consciousness. Through questions that make students analyze their own words and sentences, teachers encourage independence and at the same time empower students. They soon realize how much they already know about their language. Structural grammar, then, has a place in the classroom.

▼
TRANSFORMATIONAL GRAMMAR

Transformational grammar attempts to explain the production of sentences through a number of basic (kernal) sentences that transform or expand into various patterns. Whereas the base of structural grammar is empirical—what native speakers actually say, the base of transformational grammar is theoretical. No one actually knows if these language structures exist or work in the way presented by linguists. Transformational grammar assumes the existence of deep structures that lead to surface structures—what is actually said or written. According to transformational grammar, we have two basic sentence types: kernal and transformed.

A kernal sentence: John is my friend.

A transformed sentence could be:

    A negative: John is not my friend.
    A question: Is John my friend?
    A passive: The ball was hit by John.
    Embedded: John, who is my friend, hit the ball.

According to linguists, we access these patterns in the production of sentences, automatically and effortlessly in the case of speech. With this ability, we are able to create endless numbers of sentences, all without instruction.

Transformational linguists devised a set of rules, called phrase structure rules, intended to describe how we form and transform sentences. They represented sentences in symbol strings:

    NP + pres + Be + NP
    John   is   my friend.

What transformational grammar shows are the patterns of English at work, how native speakers construct novel sentences out of basic patterns. For the student of language, this is a useful view of the creativity of language, of process rather than product.

TRANSFORMATIONAL GRAMMAR IN THE CLASSROOM

For many English language arts teachers, transformational grammar is a revelation, a means of viewing English from a very different perspective. When viewed as product, the language appears static, and teachers are often hard pressed to explain how certain sentences got that way or how the language was working. With an understanding of embedded sentences and transformations from one sentence form to another (e.g., to negative, to question), teachers found a useful classroom tool. Sentence combining became the most visible and applied means of transformational grammar. Indeed, this instructional strategy remains one of the best ways to improve student awareness of syntax, rhetorical effectiveness, and the function of punctuation.

▼ ───

WHY THE DIRECT TEACHING OF GRAMMAR FAILS
THE NATURE OF KIDS

Teaching grammar directly fails not only because of flawed methods but because of the inherent nature of language and of our students. The study of any grammar involves the study of an abstract system, a set of abstract rules about the nature of language as described by various linguists. This calls for both well-developed analytical skills and high motivation. Our students, almost without exception, lack both. As pointed out, students already know grammar—intimately and thoroughly, possessing nearly total competence to express meanings they themselves understand. Consequently, they see little reason to take sentences apart, label parts of speech, fill in blanks, and diagram sentences.

Student attention, if focused at all, is usually on the wrong thing. As one 16 year old remarked upon leaving her high school English classroom: "I *know* I got it straight; I used a ruler." So much for the importance of diagramming. Students also fail to see why a teacher or parent is upset with a statement such as "He ain't there." It communicates meaning, which is, after all, the point. And students lack enthusiasm for a course that tells them that "It is I" is any more useful than "It's me." As teachers, we can provide needed lessons on the varieties of American English, about audience and purpose, about choices in language. Only then might we change a student's mind about the suitability of "He ain't there." Lectures on rules, dozens of exercises, or weekly mastery quizzes merely reinforce the students' sense of "no concern to me, not my world."

IMPROVING STUDENT SKILLS

Teaching students to break down sentences does nothing to improve their capability to create and improve sentences. Syntactic maturity—the ability to write more complex and varied sentences—comes with cognitive and linguistic development, not with learning rules or memorizing sentence patterns. What is important is providing sustained experience in all the language arts; students improve their language through using language. This notion appears so simplistic that people sometimes resist it, yet it is the basis for competency. Rather than breaking down and labeling sentences, students need experience in building them. Through creating, changing, and manipulating sentences, students gain fluency and flexibility, much as a musician does through finger exercises. Once students come to understand that syntactic control is linked to making meaning, to what they themselves wish to convey, sentences take on a new significance—one certainly not appreciated with isolated exercises.

MAKING USEFUL DISTINCTIONS

As teachers, we need to keep the distinction between grammar and usage very clear. We have a native ability to create and comprehend sentences; this is our internal grammar. Usage, on the other hand, is linguistic etiquette, a set of socially acceptable styles of language. Problems arise when we insist on one standard usage as an absolute, the only way to say or write something. English permits many forms of language, a range of choices dependent upon situation and audience. Approaching usage from this perspective allows students to maintain their own voices. Often usage is extended to mean mechanics as well—punctuation, capitalization, and so forth. Again, the notion of an absolute standard causes student difficulty and apathy. For example, students partially learn a comma rule for *and;* then they add a comma every time *and* pops up on their paper, incorrectly breaking apart phrases most of the time. If, instead, students learned a more useful approach, how commas function to help us read more easily and comprehend more quickly, the world would be blessed with fewer commas and less red ink.

We also need to help students see the distinction between speaking and writing, that writing is *not* speech written down. Again, the more useful lessons about varieties of English come into play. Students do know their native language grammar orally but may be inexperienced with manipulating it, or even seeing it, on paper. If their vocabulary is impoverished, they struggle even more. If we work from a perspective of native language competence, from what students do know, we have the opportunity to influence their use of language in everyday life. Teachers who substitute grammar drills for experience in oral or written language, on the other hand, seldom have that pleasure. Grammar is alive, something we use—not a subject to be taught.

▼ ───────────────────────────────

DEMYSTIFYING GRAMMAR

We need to demystify language. No matter which grammar one is talking about, grammar is arcane knowledge, part of a teacher's repertoire. It is no wonder that students perceive it as a mystery, as something they aren't very good at, and perhaps as a rite of passage. Too many adults' only remembrance of English classes is grammar. Because students usually don't understand the abstract grammar system, they survive by learning some rules, memorizing others, and doing the exercises as assigned. With minimal motivation, most students can get by. The problem is that they are not internalizing anything; the activity has no real effect on their language patterns and behavior. Thus, it should not surprise a teacher when students make mistakes in composition, when the very skills drilled and tested turn up as errors in full discourse.

If teachers stopped to think about it, one mystery might be solved. Students who have had a steady immersion in grammar arrive every fall with little or no knowledge; every teacher more or less starts from scratch in teaching grammar. Why? Because for most of their academic lives, students lack the cognitive skills to take on analytical grammar. Most lack the motivation as well. Studying grammar in the context of their own writing is valuable and necessary, and when students see grammar linked to making meaning, their motivation increases. But when English language arts teachers turn grammar into another bit of content knowledge to be memorized and tested, grammar becomes disconnected and disliked.

UNDERSTANDING STUDENT ERRORS

NOVICE WRITERS

In her masterful exploration of unskilled writers, Mina Shaughnessy offers some of the most cogent explanations of student error. She first reminds us that "errors count, but not as much as English teachers think" (120). Teachers, she notes, are trained to evaluate students by absolute rather than developmental standards. Teachers forget that their students, for the most part, *are* novice writers. Thus, serious grammatical errors may be the result of a lack of experience in academic writing rather than a problem with the language itself.

Shaughnessy also argues that if we view novice writers in the same way we view foreign students learning English, whose errors are accepted as part of normal development—and not as evidence of their incapability of learning, their inability to be educated—we, and the students, would be better off (90). This view does not suggest that teachers ignore errors. Allowing students to write in a fashion in which we merely "catch the meaning" is irresponsible. However, as Shaughnessy suggests, many teachers embark on an error-hunt that fails to distinguish between the important errors, those that seriously impair our ability to comprehend, and the merely irritating, those that bother only the English language arts teacher.

EXPECTING TOO MUCH

Shaughnessy raises another issue in asking whether it is realistic to expect unskilled writers to learn what we set out for them in the time available. The acquisition of writing skills is highly individual to begin with, and for students lacking a good background in reading and writing, the process takes time. Moreover, students from homes where literacy is lacking and poverty is commonplace are disadvantaged to begin with. We cannot expect them to meet timetables based on some mythical average student or laid out by publishers unconcerned with adolescent growth and development or societal problems.

Inexperienced teachers often have unrealistic expectations of student learning, which may bring frustration to both teacher and student.

Textbooks can reinforce these expectations, especially if they present chapters of separate grammar skills, a nice linear plan that runs contrary to how we actually acquire and process language. Further, cognitive and linguistic maturity limit us: What we do, when we do it, and with what degree of competency or proficiency are related to growth and development. Another human reality lies in the gap between cognition and production, between the time when we comprehend something and when we can produce it ourselves. A parallel exists with the way we acquired oral language. We could understand far more than we could produce, a problem that time and sustained language experience solved. Thus student failure to correct grammar errors immediately is not necessarily a reason for repeating the lesson; rather, students may just need more opportunities to apply the lessons in original writing (Shaughnessy 120).

SMART ERRORS

Another view of error, but one seldom discussed anywhere, is a positive one: Many errors are errors of competency, a demonstration of student progress toward more complex language use. This phenomenon is perhaps recognized more often with second-language students, but it occurs among native speakers as well. In middle school, for example, students begin to use more complex syntax, thus increasing their potential for error. The errors are the result of progress, not regression; they're really "smart" errors. Kids need to know that.

▼ ──────────────────────────────────

TRIAL AND ERROR

In order to learn to write, one has to write—and to make mistakes. Errors are a normal part of the process, or as James Moffett puts it, "trial and error":

> Now, trial and error sounds to many people like a haphazard, time-consuming business, a random behavior of children, animals, and others who don't know any better . . . Trial and error is by definition never aimless, but without help the individual alone may not always see how to learn the most from his errors. (198–99)

In Moffett's opinion, teachers should present students with meaningful trials (assignments) in meaningful order and provide "feedback that insures the maximum exploitation of error" (199). Even more important in Moffett's view of student error is his contention that the "teacher does not try to prevent the learner from making errors" through preteaching (199). If, according to Moffett, a teacher does preteach, the student approaches the writing task with the notions of "good" and "bad," trying to keep them separate. In this way, errors are viewed as "bad" rather than what they are—part of trial and error, part of growth. Responding to those who might ask if this is not a discouraging way to learn, Moffett says:

> For one thing, trial-and-error makes for more success in the long run because it is accurate, specific, individual, and timely. For another, if the teacher in some way sequences the trials so that learning is transferred from one to the next, the student writer accumulates a more effective guiding experience than if one tried to guide him by preteaching. (200)

Moffett stresses the importance of feedback that is both plentiful and informed, given during the writing process and not after the fact. Within this context, error carries no stigma. If students view errors as normal and themselves capable of correcting them, motivation to do so should remain high.

Unfortunately, this view is uncommon in many secondary classrooms, especially in school systems where less able English students are routinely assigned to remedial classes. These classes are often designed on the deficit model, which assumes that students are incapable of recognizing and self-correcting language errors. This model also elevates the status of error; entire courses are built around stamping out various errors of syntax, usage, and mechanics, usually through rote drill and exercise formats. We are not suggesting that students in remedial English courses have no deficiencies, for they do. However, these deficiencies lie in written language only and relate to inexperience in reading and writing—not to native language competency. Thus, many remedial courses fail to build on what students *do* know, continuing a cycle of discouragement and frustration for all involved.

In *Errors And Expectations*, Shaughnessy speaks of student capabilities:

> Students themselves are the best sources of information about grammar. Despite difficulties with common errors, their intuitions about English are the intuitions of the native speaker. Most of what they need to know has already been learned. What they have not learned and are not used to is looking long and carefully at sentences in order to understand the way in which they work. This involves a shift in perception which is ultimately more important than the mastery of any individual rule of grammar. (129)

In this view, remedial courses should be built around a great deal of oral and written language experience; error takes its place as a normal part of learning to write academic English. Texts and exercises focused on error and those that proceed deductively would vanish. In their place would be time and an environment that allows for inductive learning, for Moffett's trial and error.

▼ _____

SOURCES OF ERRORS

When teachers are confronted with student errors, they must make certain assumptions about the source and then consider the implications for teaching.

Three basic assumptions are common: (1) that the learner doesn't know the grammatical concept; (2) that the error is due to a lack of information and habit; (3) that errors are developmental.

We would be wise to limit the first assumption, that the learner doesn't know the grammatical concept, to students for whom English is a second language. For these students, a particular concept may not exist simply because their native language lacks this feature (e.g., tense, articles). To assume this situation with speakers of American dialects, however, is wrong. A student whose first dialect is Black English Vernacular understands grammar and has a grammar very similar to that of the standard dialect. Some of the surface features do differ from standard dialect, including pronunciation. Therefore, we need to know these features to avoid judgments of error when the student is merely "translating" the standard printed dialect into his or her spoken dialect. For example: in reading, a student may turn "John's hat" into the oral "John hat," indicating she does understand the concept. In her dialect, 's is not needed.

There may be times when our least experienced readers and writers do not understand a grammatical concept, but these are infrequent with native speakers of English. If students don't understand the concept, we have to break it down, analyze its parts, and present it to them in a way that allows them to see the function. Subject-verb agreement, for example, relies on an understanding of singular and plural. We need to start there, not with agreement itself.

If lack of a grammatical concept is seldom a source of error, then what is? Some errors may be due to a lack of information or a language habit. In this view, language equals behavior, and "bad" behavior can be fixed. This notion often leads to intense correction of oral and written language, the fate of students labeled "remedial." The first problem with this approach is its lack of discernment about which errors count most. Some teachers attack errors as though all were equally important in derailing meaning. This shotgun approach to error usually overwhelms the student and contributes to further confusion, indifference, and, in some cases, hostility. Moreover, the approach takes on a life of its own if worksheets and workbooks are available. Such practice doesn't transfer when students undertake their own writing, where they are not told what to pick out, label, or underline. Shaughnessy puts it this way:

> It may well be that traditional grammar-teaching has failed to improve writing not because the rules and concepts do not connect with the act of writing but because grammar lessons have traditionally ended up with experiences in workbooks, which by highlighting the feature being studied rob the student of practice in seeing that feature in more natural places. (155)

"In more natural places" refers to genuine discourse—people involved in communication and making meaning. Because habits of any type involve a will to change, we need to link language habits to genuine discourse. Students need a reason to edit and proofread.

▼

ERROR ANALYSIS

Error analysis, a more developmentally based approach, asks us to discover the pattern and frequency of errors in student writing; because it asks for an explanation of what is happening, the approach is more aligned with language acquisition than with behavior. We discover that some errors are performance errors, which students should be able to correct. An oral check quickly sorts these out, for they are the type of error most associated with editing and proof-reading. These errors often form the basis of minilessons linked to student writing; the errors mar the final product but don't interfere with meaning. A grammar-based error, one for which the student lacks the information to self-correct, is best handled in a one-on-one teaching situation. In any event, error analysis assumes that one keeps a record of errors: types, where most pervasive (i.e., in which types of discourse), and frequency.

Another view of error, but one seldom discussed, is that of avoidance. We can't assume that the absence of grammatical or mechanical error means mastery. Some learners simply avoid certain words and constructions because they have had trouble with them in the past. For example, students who have had trouble punctuating descriptive clauses of some sort may decide not to try them anymore. College freshmen often admit to this "play it safe" approach to writing when confronted with questions about their "look alike" sentences. Thus, the absence of error does not necessarily mean competency or proficiency, especially among some of our best students. They may be afraid to take risks and need to learn about "good errors" and growth through errors.

▼

TAKING ON ERROR

Shaughnessy warns us against ignoring errors for fear of inhibiting students, a non-helpful approach with students who already feel helpless (127–28). Students are very aware that they make errors and that there is much they don't know about academic writing. Thus, ignoring errors, either from a sense of "kindness" or from a sense of "not that important," does nothing to help students. We need to convince them that they can take on errors, and, most importantly, we need to provide them with the strategies to do so.

ERRORS: FOR EDITING ONLY

Shaughnessy reminds us that "correcting errors is an editorial rather than a composing skill and requires the writer to notice features of a sentence he would ordinarily have to ignore during composing" (128). Given this perspective, students have to learn to look at their own sentences analytically. If students engage in a great deal of original writing, taking the writing process through editing and proofreading, they get this experience. However, they need strategies to guide them. We discuss these strategies in Chapter 7.

Errors cause so much trouble with novice writers because, as Shaughnessy notes, they "seem to demand more concentration than they're worth" (123). Students have been communicating successfully for years, something they learned to do without direct instruction. Writing correctly is a learned behavior, requiring them to shift vision and analyze, something they don't normally do in informal speaking.

ERRORS AND THE WORLD AT LARGE

For some adolescents, the situation is more complex than a shift in vision. Some speakers of various American dialects may find identification with standard dialect, the majority dialect and its culture, a somewhat troubling situation. Error thus takes on an emotional dimension not shared by mainstream students. Similarly, students accustomed to academic accolades and conditioned by expectations of "perfection" may also respond to error very differently. It is not uncommon for excellent students to be motivated negatively by error. For them, the emotional stakes are high: social status, grade point averages, scholarships, and expectations of a prestigious collegiate experience. Error, therefore, is something to be avoided at all costs, even the cost of continued growth in written language skills.

For many other students, errors bring ambivalence at best, apathy at worst. Young people carry a false notion that writing is not all that important; after all, the world seems linked by cellular telephones, television satellites, and other wonders of modern communication. Given this view, we must make a convincing case for the mastery of standard written English: It is the language of public communication, public transactions, school, and business. "Getting on in the world" and having choices are linked to language. Against a background of pragmatism, of respect for various American dialects, and of linguistic versatility, we can make a strong case for acquiring standard written English.

DISCUSSION QUESTIONS

1. Nancie Atwell's honesty about learning to teach comes through again and again in *In the Middle: Writing, Reading, and Learning with Adolescents.* She tells of a turning point, "When I stopped focusing on me and my methods and started observing students and their learning, I saw a gap yawning between us—between what I did as a language teacher and what they did as language learners" (4). What does Atwell mean? What are the implications for your classroom?

2. Mina Shaughnessy argues that "errors count, but not as much as English teachers think" (120). Because Shaughnessy was an English teacher herself, working mainly with "remedial" writers, how could she make such a com-

ment? Discuss Shaughnessy's perspective on error. How can her framework for working with "remedial" writers help you?

3. In an address to English language arts teachers attending the national convention of the National Council of Teachers of English, Robert MacNeil said: "Our language is not the private property of the language police, of grammarians, or teachers, or even of great writers" (18). As a respected television journalist, MacNeil certainly must adhere to current standards of English language. But what is he suggesting here? Why would he make such a strong statement to a group of English teachers?

SUGGESTED ACTIVITIES

1. You have been assigned to the committee that is to recommend an English language (composition and grammar) textbook for district adoption. Your task is to examine an English language textbook series for three consecutive grade levels (either middle school/junior high school or senior high school). First, your committee has to determine the criteria for selection. On what will you base your recommendation and why? Make a list of the criteria. Then apply the criteria to the texts themselves. For example, if one of your criteria is that students should work inductively, drawing their own conclusions about the way their language works, then you will evaluate student activities to see if they are based on inductive learning. When you complete your evaluation, write a brief, informal memo telling the rest of your committee whether or not you would recommend this text series.

2. During parent-teacher conferences, a number of parents ask why you aren't teaching grammar (meaning traditional grammar). How do you respond? After the conferences, you decide that parents might benefit from a more complete explanation. Draft a letter to the parents of your students, providing an explanation of how you approach grammar and why.

3. As the most recently hired English teacher in your school, you have been asked to update your colleagues. With sinking heart, you agree. You know some teachers are using methods and materials that run counter to how students learn language, and you risk alienating them, regardless of how carefully you frame your presentation. Your dilemma is terrible: You need to be accepted as a colleague; you also need to be honest about the state of the field as well as promote the best possible learning situation for students in your school. What will you say? Prepare an outline of your remarks.

REFERENCES

Atwell, Nancie. *In the Middle: Reading, Writing, and Learning with Adolescents.* Portsmouth: Boynton/Cook Heinemann, 1987.

Bamberg, Betty. "Composition in the Secondary English Curriculum." *Research in the Teaching of English* Oct. 1981: 257–266.

Braddock, Richard, et al. *Research in Written Composition.* Urbana: National Council of Teachers of English, 1963.

Hartwell, Patrick. "Grammar, Grammars, and the Teaching of Writing." *College English* Feb. 1985: 105–127.

Haynes, Elizabeth. "Using Research in Preparing to Teach Writing." *English Journal* Jan. 1978: 82–88.

Hillocks, George. *Research on Written Composition.* Urbana: National Council of Teachers of English, ERIC, 1986.

Lindemann, Erika. *A Rhetoric for Writing Teachers.* 2nd ed. New York: Oxford UP, 1987.

MacNeil, Robert. "Listening to Our Language." *English Journal* Feb. 1990: 36–40.

Meiser, Mary Jordan. "A Cognitive-Process Approach to Composition: A Comparison of Unskilled College Writers," diss., Harvard U, 1984.

_____."Borrowing from the Cognitivists: New Models of the Composing Process," qualifying paper, Harvard U, 1983.

_____. "Back to the Basics: The Wrong Direction." *Forward: Wisconsin Journal for Supervision and Curriculum Development.* Spring 1988.

Moffett, James. *Teaching the Universe of Discourse.* Boston: Houghton Mifflin, 1968.

Noguchi, Rei. *Grammar and the Teaching of Writing.* Urbana: National Council of Teachers of English, 1991.

Sanborn, Jean. "Grammar: Good Wine Before Its Time." *English Journal* Mar. 1986: 72–80.

Shaughnessy, Mina. *Errors and Expectations.* New York: Oxford UP, 1977.

Weaver, Constance. *Grammar for Teachers: Perspectives and Definitions.* Urbana: National Council of Teachers of English, 1979.

CHAPTER 9

The Nature
of Language

CHAPTER HIGHLIGHTS
- Language characteristics.
- Oral and written language acquisition.
- Activities for learning about language.

> Language is not only the principal medium that human beings use
> to communicate with each other but also the bond that links people
> together and binds them to their culture. To understand our
> humanity, therefore, we must understand the language that makes
> us human. (1)
>
> —*Clark et al.*

▼
THE IMPORTANCE OF LANGUAGE STUDY

Although most teacher education programs include the study of language, we don't always grasp the significance of language principles on first exposure. Nor do we necessarily make the cognitive leap from principle to practice, that is, to teaching adolescents, when we are not yet involved in designing and implementing lessons in listening, speaking, reading, and writing. Similarly, our understanding of language diversity may remain academic until we must consider diversity in our own classroom. For this reason, we address basic language principles before we discuss language activities for middle and secondary level students.

▼
LANGUAGE CHARACTERISTICS

Wherever you find humans, you find language. It binds us into communities of shared meanings, where our thoughts reach across time and space to connect us to those who have been and those who will be. In some cultures, oral language is the sole means of communication; in others, both oral and written language are used. Regardless, no language is any less complex than any other. It is a mistake to believe that the language of an African tribe, for example, is "primitive," simply because the culture is less technologically advanced than our own. Every language is equally complex and complete as a system of communication. That is, no language or dialect is inherently superior or more satisfactory as a means of communication, a fact that has implications for teaching students with dialects or limited English proficiency.

COMMONALITIES AMONG LANGUAGES AND LEARNING

All languages share certain characteristics. One of the most obvious is the arbitrary relationship between the sounds and the meanings of spoken language or, in the case of languages for the deaf, between the signs and the meanings. There is no intrinsic connection between an object and what a language group has chosen to call that object. People sometimes get confused by this notion, mainly because we attach so much importance to our own language. We tend to believe that it alone has the "right" names for things in the world; of course, millions of other people all over the globe are equally certain that their language has got it "right" too. All languages use a finite set of discrete sounds (or gestures in sign language) that combine to form an infinite number of words and sentences.

What makes a language different from others is the discrete set of sounds chosen. As we listen to French or Arabic or Russian, we are instantly aware of this phenomenon. Similarly, all languages have distinct rules for the formation of words and sentences. When we learned our native language, mainly between birth and age five, we learned these language patterns. No one taught us; we simply absorbed them from the language around us. Native speakers, then, come to school with considerable, although intuitive, knowledge about their language. We can use this knowledge when we work with students, especially in writing skills.

Any normal child is capable of learning any language to which he or she is exposed. Nationality or race has nothing to do with the acquisition of language per se; the sustained language environment is what provides the child with a native language. Children all over the world acquire their native languages in remarkably similar ways. Without instruction, they grasp the rules of the language: the basic sounds, how sounds are arranged to form words, and how words are arranged to form sentences. In the process, children also learn how to use their language appropriately in their cultural community. This knowledge does not always or easily transfer to the culture of the classroom. We have to help students make the adjustment from home language to school language, to ways of knowing and doing within the mainstream culture. At the same time, we need to value their home language, approaching the acquisition of standard American English as another variant needed for versatility and getting on in the world at large.

LANGUAGE VARIATION

It is important to remember that within a single language, variations exist in sounds, words, and, more rarely, grammar. In the United States, regional, social, and ethnic differences provide our language with a rich diversity known as American dialects. Generally, American dialects are mutually intelligible; that is, you can understand a speaker from any dialect region, despite differences in pronunciation, vocabulary, or grammar. Everyone speaks a dialect, although usually one dialect has risen to a position of prestige. This position has nothing to do with that dialect being superior, but rather with its speakers having achieved social prestige and power. Value judgments about dialects are common, however. When John F. Kennedy was President, people remarked on his Boston dialect as "aristocratic," mainly because it had traces of British English. Although some of our southern dialects also bear traces of British English, they are often dismissed as "hillbilly." Language judgments, then, are very much linked to social prestige.

Other variations in our language allow us to adjust to various social situations. With some people we speak very informally, with others very formally. We use certain vocabulary with one group but not with another. We know what is appropriate to the situation and the audience. We learned these language adjustments as part of our native language, which explains one of the most difficult aspects of learning a second language as an adult. We can get the sounds, words, and sentences down, but that is only half the knowledge. We also have to know the appropriate contexts for them. There is, then, an intimate connection between our culture and our native language. In the classroom, we have to be continually aware of both the social and cultural implications of language as we work with students from cultures different from our own. We also need to acknowledge the time involved in learning not only form but also function, especially in academic settings. Expecting too much too quickly only sets a stage for frustration and, ultimately, a high potential for failure.

▼ COMPETENCE AND PERFORMANCE

Students whose native language is English come to the classroom with considerable, although largely unconscious, knowledge of how the language works. Textbooks often fail to take advantage of this fact and approach students as though they had to learn English as a second language. Teachers can use many strategies to take advantage of native speaker knowledge or "competence."

There is, however, a difference between "competence"—what every native speaker carries as a linguistic system—and "performance"—how we use that knowledge in actual behavior. Every normal child is competent in his or her native language, but children differ in performance. Unfortunately, judgments about performance are linked to deviation from what is termed "standard American English." This is a social issue rather than a linguistic one. There is no such thing as linguistic superiority; every grammar is equally complex, equally capable of expressing whatever thoughts the speaker intends.

The rules of our grammar may differ from those of another language, but neither set of rules is better—only different. Thus grammar as we mean it here includes everything speakers know about their native language: the sound system, the system of meanings, the rules of word order, the rules of sentence formation, and a dictionary of words. The amazing thing is that we know, unconsciously and intuitively, this complex system, and that we learned most of it between birth and the time we started school.

▼ WHAT NATIVE SPEAKERS CAN DO

> "And how are you?" said Winnie-the-Pooh. Eeyore shook his head from side to side. "Not very how," he said. "I don't seem to have felt at all how for a long time."
>
> —A. A. Milne

The delight we experience at Eeyore's answer comes from our awareness of our native language and its social context. There are days when we would *all* like to respond "not very how," and go on to explain just "unhow" we are. Turning the language on its ear now and then is part of the fun, at least for the native speaker. It is only one of the many capabilities we have.

RECOGNITION OF GRAMMATICAL SENTENCES

As native speakers of a language, we know which strings of words form an acceptable arrangement and which do not. That is, other speakers of the language agree with us about whether or not the words form an acceptable sentence; native speakers know the grammar of their language. "Grammar" in this instance refers to what we know intuitively about our language, specifically its structure.

Alex hit the red ball into the street.
It was a red ball that Alex hit into the street.
*That was it red ball hit into the street Alex.
*It was street that red ball hit Alex into the.

These sentences are extreme, either grammatical or ungrammatical. However, there is an in-between area where native speakers recognize deviance from their normal expectations of an English sentence. Eeyore's response to Winnie-the-Pooh, for example, violates our normal expectations but nonetheless carries meaning in a most interesting and captivating way. Authors and poets know that native speakers not only understand these "violations" but also appreciate them. As native speakers, our ability to judge sentences for both sense and nonsense comes from our knowledge of the possibilities of meaning. It does not come from studying formal grammar, from diagramming sentences, or from labeling parts of speech—a fact we need to remember when working with students who have syntax problems.

RECOGNIZING RELATIONS WITHIN SENTENCES

One of the key principles in language is that of the relationships among parts. We know that acceptable sentences are not randomly ordered groups of words. Lewis Carroll makes the point with a conversation among Alice, the March Hare, and the Hatter:

"Then you should say what you mean," the March Hare went on. "I do," Alice hastily replied; "at least—at least I mean what I say—that's the same thing, you know." "Not the same thing a bit," said the Hatter. "Why, you might just as well say that 'I see what I eat' is the same thing as 'I eat what I see'!"

In English, word order does make a difference in meaning:

The angry teacher scolded the naughty boy.
The naughty boy scolded the angry teacher.
The angry boy scolded the naughty teacher.
*Scolded the angry teacher the boy naughty.

Who does what to whom is altered considerably by the arrangement of words. Deciphering a sentence with nonsense words is another way to test the importance of word order in English:

The tirly lapets linged silsily on the waping pob.

Even without any meanings for basic words, we can answer a number of questions about who is doing what to whom. Word order helps us. We know that subjects normally come before verbs, that adjectives normally come before nouns, and that adverbs normally settle around verbs. We receive more help than word order, however. The word endings, suffixes, provide important clues: the plural -s as a noun marker, -ed as a verb marker, -ly as an adverb marker. The structure words (e.g., the, on) also help us identify the function of various words and word groups. If we ask who did what, a native speaker would give a quick response of "lapets linged." If we asked how the lapets linged, we would be told "silsily"; if we asked where, we would learn "on the waping pod." Word order and endings, then, are important clues for the native speaker of English. Conversely, they represent a body of knowledge to be acquired by the non-native speaker.

In a basic English sentence, we can also determine where major breaks would or would not occur:

> The angry teacher was chewing on her pen.

We would probably make a major break between *teacher* and *was* and between *chewing* and *on*. No native speaker would see *the angry* as a unit. It is also very unlikely that anyone would note *teacher was chewing* without also noting what was being chewed. An intuitive sense of incompleteness would take over. If we take a longer, more complex sentence, we are still able to break it into units:

The old man raised his voice when he saw the mayor coming onto the platform.

a. the old man raised his voice
b. when he saw the mayor
c. (the mayor was) coming onto the platform.

Even without analysis, native speakers know how the units form a larger unit. This ability has little or nothing to do with the exercises and drills so often associated with secondary English classes. If we recall drawing one line under the subject and two under the predicate or diagramming sentence parts, we may erroneously think that those exercises are the reason we can easily pick out the units. Rather, our unconscious knowledge of how words cluster together and function as units enables us to recognize units of meaning. Although sensitivity to our native language probably allowed us to do the labeling, it is unlikely that the act of labeling caused us to know the division between subjects and predicates. Again, we need to be aware of this linguistic reality when we ask students to revise sentences. They know a great deal about their own language.

RECOGNIZING RELATIONSHIPS AMONG SENTENCES

As native speakers, we are able to move beyond the parts of a single sentence. We also recognize when sentences are stylistic variants, saying the same thing in different ways:

Alice's mother fed the cat at midnight.
The female parent of Alice provided food for the feline at the bewitching hour.

We can also recognize when sentences are not variants but are nonetheless related to each other:

Alice's mother fed the cat at midnight.
Alice's mother dislikes the cat.
The cat knows Alice's mother dislikes him.
The cat refused to eat.
Alice's mother didn't care.

RECOGNIZING AMBIGUITIES

Another language ability of a native speaker is knowing when a sentence could be understood in more than one way. For example:

The shooting of the hunters was terrible.
They are eating apples.
Visiting relatives can be boring.

In each of these sentences, the reader could come to two different conclusions about meaning. As native speakers of English, we know the possibilities. That does not mean every student recognizes all of them; the ability to recognize and deal with ambiguity varies with individuals.

CREATING NOVEL SENTENCES

Perhaps the most remarkable ability of native speakers is the ability to create and to understand sentences never before uttered. If we keep track of our utterances for a few hours, we will no doubt be astonished at the number of novel sentences. Aside from some stock sentences or phrases (e.g., see you around, how are you doing, nice to see you), we are constantly creating and listening to new sentences. The human mind creates rather than stores. This ability has led some linguists, notably Noam Chomsky, to believe that we come "wired" for language, which is now one of the leading theories of language acquisition. English language arts teachers need to know something of the acquisition process, mainly because this knowledge bears on how we approach writing instruction.

ORAL AND WRITTEN LANGUAGE ACQUISITION: IMPLICATIONS FOR TEACHING

Despite considerable research, we do not have complete knowledge of the language acquisition process, but we do know some of the things humans do in acquiring their native language. Understanding this process is critical to teachers in the English language arts because it allows us to intervene in the learning process in ways that make sense. Additionally, this understanding can provide us with insight when we are frustrated by what appears to be a lack of progress. It can also help us tap into students' intuitive knowledge of their native language. Some of the most basic principles of acquisition are these:

- We need a language-rich environment, one in which comprehensible language provides the data from which we draw our knowledge of how the language works.
- We are active participants in the learning process, analyzing (although unconsciously) language in use.
- We test our hypotheses of how language works, trying out various forms on our listeners, making adjustments from feedback and continued self-analysis of language in use.
- We receive positive feedback when we use language, regardless of the errors.
- We enjoy a tolerance for error and the expectation that we will get things right eventually.
- We enjoy sufficient time for practice.
- We concentrate on meaning first, developing clarity and fluency before correctness.
- We are acknowledged to be individuals, with our own maturation schedule and variable rates of development and competency.
- We are presumed to be growing in competency and proficiency, although at times we appear to be uneven or even regressing in certain areas.
- We develop confidence from sustained experience and positive reinforcement for our linguistic efforts.
- We learn about audience, appropriate language forms, and context through our use of language.

We learned to speak in a language-rich environment. We were surrounded by people talking and were encouraged to take part. We were provided with positive feedback as we worked toward clarity and fluency; no one penalized us for errors. In learning to speak, we first concentrated on meaning, later on correctness. People assumed we could and would talk, all within good time, on our personal timeline of maturation. We were motivated to do so because we had things to say. The acquisition and development of writing skills depend upon similar experiences.

Although oral acquisition of our native language is a natural (unschooled) process, it suggests an environment and pedagogy that foster writing development. The writing-process approach to composition draws on very similar principles of language and human development. Similarly, teachers who involve students in meaningful oral language activities are necessarily structuring their classrooms and lessons upon these basic principles of language growth and development. Most young students find language fascinating, but by the time they traverse years of language as textbook exercises, they associate language with drudgery rather than discovery and pleasure, mine fields of potential error rather than treasure troves of meaning and expression. As English language arts teachers, we have the opportunity to bring students back to the joy of language.

LEARNING ABOUT LANGUAGE: ACTIVITIES FOR ADOLESCENTS

> As English teachers, we can never make our students care about a semicolon if they do not care about language. (17)

> —*G. Lynn Nelson*

Movement from elementary to middle or junior high school often signals the end of playfulness with language. In senior high school, curriculum and instruction seem to move even further from language play. As a result, students at all levels miss opportunities not only for play and pleasure but also for learning about the nature of language itself. Teachers who keep basic principles of language in mind as they create lessons and units find many opportunities for including language lessons throughout the English language arts curriculum. Literature and young adult fiction, nonfiction, print and electronic media, and oral language units are rich resources for teaching language concepts. Occasional lessons or units concentrating entirely on language concepts are also a good idea. What is important is including language study as an integral part of the curriculum at every level.

▼ ─────────────────────────────

ORIGINS AND RELATIONSHIPS

One of the most basic principles of language is its arbitrariness. People all over the world have chosen different sets of sounds and symbols to represent the very same object or phenomenon. Although the impulse to label our world is a universal one, the result is specific to our culture. Most Americans, for example, have no need to define and label eight varieties of rice or ten varieties of snow. But some people do, simply because such definition is needed within their culture. We can introduce students to the principle of language as both universal and culturally specific through activities in naming.

NAMING PEOPLE

Naming is a basic human impulse and a lesson easily introduced through an old friend of many American students, Dr. Seuss. The correlation between naming and physical description is easily seen in such characters as the Star-Bellied Sneetch and the bug named Von Fleck. Illustrations from various Seuss books allow students to make other connections very quickly. Once provided with a representative list of American surnames, students can work deductively to discover other basic characteristics of naming: derivation from physical characteristics, occupation, place of dwelling, character traits, or parent (e.g., -*son*, *mac*). With the vast influx of names from diverse cultures, students have a fertile field of inquiry. Once students have discovered the various ways in which we name, they might enjoy researching their own names. I recall 7th graders, even the "toughest" of them, diligently going through their baby books, asking parents and caretakers about the processes of naming in their family, and calling relatives to learn more about family history. They were surprised, as well as very interested, to learn that their given and surnames had meaning. Their personal quest and discovery, culminating in oral discussion, were appropriate research for middle level.

Although given names are fairly easy to research, surnames require teacher assistance. For this project, bringing public library books into the classroom is a good idea. Students from Asian or Native American cultures may have to rely on family information rather than texts for their research. For senior high school students, name research offers an easy introduction to formal research methods and requirements. It is also an excellent way to combine library and people sources, because most students talk with parents and relatives in the process of gathering data. Middle school students might enjoy developing a family coat of arms or a personal crest based on information they gather, or they might keep a discovery journal, an informal record of how they proceeded and what they learned. Because linguistic and cognitive maturation are factors in formal research writing, most young students should not be asked to produce it.

Elizabeth Radin Simons offers an intriguing unit on the folklore of naming in *Student Worlds, Student Words: Teaching Writing Through Folklore*. She includes learning log entries, interviewing, reading a chapter in Alex Haley's *Roots*, role playing, and expository writing as parts of this unit—in brief, all the language arts. She has used this unit with junior and senior high students, from inner city to suburbia, and has found that it works well, especially because it goes to the heart of cultural diversity, family, and society.

NAMING PLACES

Investigating place names is another worthwhile activity. Students can use any level (e.g., city, street) or geographic site (e.g., river, mountain) to explore how and why these places received their names, as well as whether there is any relationship between the name and the site. Many states have a rich cultural heritage in place names, so students of Hispanic or Native American cultures may become important informants. City malls also offer an interesting view of naming places, which in some cases is linked to Madison Avenue advertising rather than to regional logic. For example, in our city, one of the malls is called

"London Square," despite the fact that the city has a French name, no British ancestry or ties whatsoever, and a predominantly Scandinavian heritage. The mall also offers first-hand research into the naming of businesses and restaurants. A telephone book, of course, can also serve as a resource for such investigation. Library resources are available for searching out place names, many of them appropriate for middle level as well as senior high students.

THE NAMING GAME

Most students enjoy the naming process itself. Alastair Reid's delightful admonition that "it is most important to be a good namer, since it falls to all of us at some time or other to name anything from a canary to a castle," offers endless possibilities. Thinking about naming elephants and whales, for example, brings into play the notion of how we name. Reid also suggests creating new names for numbers out of words not ordinarily associated with them: ounce, dice, trice, quartz, quince, sago, serpent, oxygen, nitrogen, denium; instant, distant, tryst, catalyst, quest, sycamore, sophomore, oculist, novelist, dentist; acreage, brokerage, cribbage, carthage, care, sink, sentiment, ointment, nutmeg, doom (Littell and Littell I). The interplay with sound and syllable, the search for the "right" combination, offers a valuable lesson in what makes a language unique and distinct from others. Vocabulary may be enhanced as students search for unusual words. Middle level students might also work backwards in the naming process. Armed with maps, they could choose a real place name that appeals to them and then develop an oral or written history for that name.

NAMING AND CULTURE

A lesson on the arbitrariness of naming "things" within a culture naturally emerges. Projects that present language as both a universal and culturally derived phenomenon help students see that what is needed and thus named in one culture may be superfluous in another. Students can discover this principle through a bit of field research in a subculture. One way is to group students by activities in which they participate, such as music and sports. Together they develop a list of vocabulary words they need in order to participate in this group. A group of skiers, for example, would differentiate snow into "corn snow," "powder snow," and so forth, something of no interest or importance to people who merely shovel it or never see it. People outside of music would have no use for the term *pianissimo* or *allegro*. Students who are whiz kids with computer programming could easily exclude everyone else with a specialized vocabulary. Using the teen subculture, both middle level and senior high students could devise a list of vocabulary relatively unknown to most adults. This vocabulary could be used in a multitude of oral or written tasks to demonstrate the principle of language and cultural relativity.

Students from diverse cultures could draw upon their home languages to develop informative oral presentations, informal classroom drama, or miniature written dictionaries for their classmates. Considering naming and culture from another perspective, students could demonstrate how things in mainstream culture have very different names and connotations if one is African-American, Native American, Asian-American, or Hispanic. African-American students have a particularly rich vocabulary for everyday things and actions. "Rap" is another way for them to showcase language that is culturally based, a variant of English that has the power both to exclude and to include (witness the popularity of rap with white students) at the same time.

▼
SOUNDS, RHYTHMS, AND RHYMES

Students need to understand that although humans are physically capable of making many sounds, we have chosen and use a finite set for English. Again, this is a basic language concept that many students are surprised to learn. Unless they are bilingual or have studied a foreign language, they tend to assume that all people, regardless of their native language, hear and represent real-world sounds in the same way. Literature, of course, has wonderful examples of the onomatopoeic features of English, as well as its rhythms and rhymes.

Dr. Seuss again provides an easy and playful way of demonstrating how our native language works. From *Horton Hears a Who:*

On the fifteenth of May, in the Jungle of Nool,
In the heat of the day, in the cool of the pool,
He was splashing . . . enjoying the jungle's great joys . . .
When Horton the Elephant heard a small noise.

The sounds, rhymes, and rhythms are English and would not translate well because they would lose the very elements that delight English listeners. Similarly, the rhythm and alliteration of Maurice Sendak's *The Wild Things* are built on English sounds and syllables:

The wild things roared their terrible roars
    and gnashed their terrible teeth
and rolled their terrible eyes
    and showed their terrible claws . . .

. . . and he (Max) sailed off through night and day and in and out of weeks and
    almost over a year.

The onomatopoeic features of English are illustrated in many ways in children's literature. Verna Aardema tells the African folktale *Why Mosquitoes Buzz in People's Ears.* The representation of various animals is tied to the sounds of English, to how we interpret the sounds as English speakers and listeners:

King Lion called the python, who came slithering, wasawusu, wasawusu, past
    the other animals.

The iguana did not answer but lumbered on, bobbing his head, badamin, badamin.

When the rabbit saw the big snake coming into her burrow, she was terrified.

She scurried out through the back way and bounded, krik, krik, krik . . .

KPAO! (a hand slapping a pesky mosquito)

The presentation of sound imitative of animal or action has been formulated from English sounds. The original African sounds would be very different, as would those of any other language. Many libraries have an audio version of this folktale, which makes the language point even more effectively.

One of the easiest lessons in the arbitrariness of language lies in common animal sounds. Mario Pei's worldwide investigation can make the point very quickly. The rooster's crow, for example, retains the initial "k" sound but little else: *Cock-a-doodle-do* becomes *cocorico* in French, *quiquirque* in Spanish, *Ko-ko* or *qee-qee* in Arabic, and *kokokkoko* in Japanese. Similarly, our favorite pooch may say *bow wow* or *woof woof* to us, but *oua-oua* (wah wah) in French, *vas-vas* in Russian, and *wan wan* in Japanese (*What's* 23,25). Students can work in pairs or small groups to discover contrasts; at the same time, they learn how various language groups distinguish sounds. Foreign language dictionaries, pronunciation guides, foreign language textbooks at the appropriate level, as well as library resources, can assist the students. They might also enjoy talking with natives of other countries to learn first hand how we hear and interpret sounds and rearrange them according to our culture.

TRANSLATING

Not only sounds and rhythm are intimately tied to English, but concepts and shared meanings as well. For this reason, translating from one language to another is not an easy task; straight, literal translations are not always possible, especially in literary works. Students whose native language is not English could provide examples for the class. At the same time, native speakers can work with a piece of translated material. "Chant to the Fire-Fly," a song of the Chippewa Indians, demonstrates what happens:

Chippewa Original

Wau wau tay see!
Wau wau tay see!
E mow e shin
Tahe bwau ne baun-e-wee!
Beeghaun—beeghaun—ewee!
Wau wau tay see!
Wau wau tay see!
Was sa kon ain je gun.
Was sa koon ain je gun.

Literal Translation

Flitting-white-fire-insect! waving-white-fire-bug! give me light before I go to bed! give me light before I go to sleep. Come, little dancing white-fire-bug! Come, little flitting white-fire-beast! Light me with your bright white-flame-instrument—your little candle.

Literary Translation*

Fire-fly, fire-fly! bright little thing,
Light me to bed, and my song I will sing.
Give me your light, as you fly o'er my head,
That I may merrily go to my bed.
Give me your light o'er the grass as you creep,
That I may joyfully go to my sleep.
Come, little fire-fly, come, little beast—
Come! and I'll make you tomorrow a feast.
Come, little candle that flies as I sing.
Bright little fairy-bug—night's little king.
Come, and I'll dance as you guide me along,
Come, and I'll pay you, my bug, with a song.

IF WORDS IMITATED MEANING

Just as onomatopoeic words try to sound like they mean, some words try to look like they mean—when forced by people who like to play with language. For example:

hic ups / conceIted / Be e s / Alligator

Poetry uses this principle as well:

If students work with form and meaning in these enjoyable ways, they come up with remarkable examples of relationships. Sometimes teachers think that such "experimentation" is a waste of time, perhaps because it appears to be

*   Reprinted from *The Sky Clears*, by A. Grove Day, by permission of the University of Nebraska Press. Copyright 1951 by A. Grove Day.

frivolous. But students actually learn a great deal about words and meanings as they create their own forms. These language tasks also provide freedom for students with varied ability. Right or wrong is not an issue, only a perception and personal interest.

MORE THAN JUST FUN

Relationships among language, thought, and culture are important concepts in their own right. But there is another reason for their place in the English language arts curriculum: They lay the foundation for later considerations of dialect and latent prejudice. Discussion of the complexity and integrity of all languages, of their usefulness as communication systems, and of our tendency to make value judgments about those different from our own must have a place in the classroom.

▼ ───

DISCOVERING RELATIONSHIPS

Relationships among various languages is another area of study well within the reach of middle and senior level students. With foreign language dictionaries, students can examine words across language families. Teachers can designate a corner of the room for gathering and recording data and provide a supply of foreign language dictionaries—not just Germanic and Romance languages but also Oriental and Middle Eastern. If the class has students from various language groups, these students can act as informants as well. Students should look up words that are certain to be part of every language group (e.g., family members, numbers, geographical terms). They can record their findings on a large chart and later analyze the information to draw conclusions about language families.

WORD SEARCHING

We tend to take words for granted; they're simply there. Students can begin to develop awareness by first hypothesizing about the origins of common idioms and expressions, literal and figurative. Once they have made some educated guesses, they can search for origins. The library has resources for this inquiry.

Students can also trace the origin of various American English words; most are surprised at the extent of global borrowing present in our language. Students could work in small groups or pairs to search in particular categories such as food, holidays, music, crime, art, science, and mathematics. Students could also be assigned a particular category and asked to discover how many words come from a single foreign language. For example, many of our words for such diverse categories as art, crime, and the military come from Italian; place names from Spanish; and mathematics and science from Arabic. Aligning this work with social studies, mathematics, literature, and music makes sense. Again, Mario Pei's books are good resources or sources for middle school and senior high students.

"England and America," said George Bernard Shaw, "are two countries separated by a common language." Students can discover what Shaw meant. If British newspapers or magazines are available, students can research vocabulary and spelling differences. The advertisements alone offer possibilities. If British publications are unavailable, library resources will do. Mario Pei's *Talking Your Way Around the World* is a good one. Common foods are an area that students enjoy (e.g., American potato chips = British crisps; British chips = American French fries). Pronunciation differences are another enjoyable area (pronounce clerk as clark, schedule as shedule), as are spelling differences (writing a checque to purchase some petrol or to replace a tyre). Working with oral language, the many varieties of English, is a natural companion activity. Videos from any of the **PBS** series set in Great Britain, as well as series on language (e.g., *The Story of English*) or recordings of modern British English, could introduce the lesson.

▼ ————————————————————————————————————

SEARCHING FOR MEANING

Words can be real chameleons, changing right in front of our eyes. We need an understanding of context before we can use and respond to words appropriately. We also need to understand the difference between literal and figurative language. A humorous way of reminding students of this reality lies in the *Amelia Bedelia* books, tales of the loveable maid who takes directions and idioms literally. When told to change the towels, Amelia takes scissors to them. "Putting out the lights" finds her hanging all the bulbs on the clothesline, and when she dusts, the furniture is covered with bath powder (Parrish). At every level of the curriculum, literature provides us with the means to explore both literal and figurative language. Although we most often think of poetry as a source of figurative language, we also need to think of all genres of written and oral expression as sources.

Another way for students to discover shades of meaning in our language is through advertisements. *Body,* for example, has various meanings, depending upon whether shampoo or diets are being sold. Middle level students can gather and analyze the data themselves and can then formulate language principles from their own conclusions. Similarly, older students can examine the language of politics and discover just how many ways words can be turned around, blurred, and generally misused. NCTE's Doublespeak Awards are good sources of such language in action. Older students should also study euphemisms, which can be approached from two directions: words that soften realities ("passed on" for death; "putting the cat to sleep") or cover up, deceive, or hide harsh truths ("final solution" for killing Jews in World War II; "soft targets" for killing humans in the 1991 Gulf War).

Cultural values also come into play. NCTE's 1991 Doublespeak Award went to the U.S. Department of Defense for its use of language during the Persian Gulf War. Because Saudi Arabia has significantly different views of women, our female military personnel became "males with female features." Aligning this aspect of language study with civics, social problems, or history is an excellent way to help students see how "meaning" permeates and directs our lives.

▼
WORD MAGIC

As Lawana Trout points out:

> For primitive people, words were alive before all else. Words were here before the sun, the earth, the dawn, and even man. Words had special power. If you lived in a tribal society, words could make things happen for you. You could sing songs to cure the sick, to scare enemies, to fight danger and fear, or to make someone love you. (46)

Modern people may be more sophisticated, but the power of words nonetheless affects them. Unfortunately, students often fail to see how language influences and shapes how we think about ourselves and others.

For this reason, they may not understand our concern over sexist language in their essays, why it makes any difference whether we use *he* or *she*. We can address the power of language through a discussion of labels. Senior high students can quite easily come up with lists of labels applied to males and females throughout their school years; with some nudging, they might classify labels by reference to animals, plants, and other objects (e.g., old hen, bat, fox, pansy, peach). Although we have to caution them about language that is too offensive for class, that in itself is another lesson in language as a social phenomenon. Also, we must make clear our point: We are influenced by labels. Referring to women as "girls," "chicks," or "broads" demeans them, just as references to a black male as a "boy" is, and was intended to be, demeaning. Writings by Alleen Pace Nilson, Robin Lakoff, Casey Miller, and Kate Swift are good sources of information for both teachers and upper division senior high students.

Younger students could work with "sticks and stones may break my bones but words will never hurt me," a modern incantation. Most students could supply personal examples to disprove the old taunt, but it might be more challenging to work through appropriate literature, with the characters rather than the students themselves as the focus of discussion. Young adult fiction offers powerful material for exploring the effect of language in everyday life. The important thing is to get students to recognize just how language does influence us.

CHANTS OLD AND NEW

Middle and junior high school students might enjoy learning about word magic through songs of the North American Indians and African tribes. Trout suggests the following activity:

heya heya heya-a-yo-ho-yaha hahe-ya-an
ha-yahe-ha-wena
yo-ho-yo-ho yaha hahe-ya-an
ha-yahe-ha-wena
he-yo-wena hahe-yahan
he he he he-yo
he-you-wena hahe-yahan
he he he he-yo
he-yo-howo-heyo
wana heya heya

—Navaho

Students would need to experiment with this song, first dealing with the repetition that creates such a strong rhythm and feeling. By varying the tempo and beat, students can place different moods in the chant (angry, warlike; lonely, mournful; happy). Students could create their own song, first delineating the mood and the audience for whom it is to be sung (46–47). Students might also search out modern examples, such as those found at sporting events throughout the world. For example, the New Zealand Haka, a chant performed before every rugby match, has a definite rhythm, a feeling of power and triumph.

Another creative activity, also from Trout, focuses on words as weapons. Trout notes that "songs always had a purpose for people living uncertain lives. They grew out of the important forces to be dealt with: fear, food, love, sickness, or war" (48). Students can easily relate to chants needed for support, for courage. They can experiment with writing their own chants, perhaps presenting them orally through masks, puppets, or shadow puppets if they appear a bit hesitant about performing them publicly.

This work can be aligned with social studies and cultural geography, in which students have the opportunity to see just how necessary and powerful language is, no matter how primitive or sophisticated the society. They also see how people of different cultures and different times used language for similar needs. One teacher we know related powerful auditory memories of a 16th-century ritual "calcio" match (soccer) in Florence, Italy. Each team had a haunting, beautiful chant reflecting 400 years of tradition. Even with no idea of what the words meant, she was deeply affected by the rhythm and the emotion transmitted through the chant.

Although most students have daily auditory experiences, they seldom talk about their effects. Nor do they often travel beyond their immediate culture unless we structure a means for them to do so, such as audio tapes. Students might discern what the chants or songs tell us about ancient peoples, of what was important in their society. They could also investigate what modern songs might tell people in the year 2500 about us.

Students of all ages can examine modern "chants" found in advertisements. Coke and Pepsi have both developed several, each with a distinctive tag line (e.g., "It's the real thing"). Using both print and voice media, students can classify the various ads by intended audience. Then, using only electronic media, they can analyze the words and music. They'll need to note differences between television and radio ads: What happens when vision is added to sound? Which "chants" stay with them? Why?

Another easy source of modern chants is the athletic field or court. Yet another is the playground, especially if children are skipping rope. Asking an older generation about chants associated with outdoor games is another way to create awareness and at the same time involve students in oral language activities such as interviewing. Most students like working with media and popular culture, welcoming the oral language activities they so easily promote. Writing activities are also easily included, everything from notetaking in a learning log or journal to development of ads in print.

A wonderful example of the power of words is found in Martin Luther King's "I Have a Dream" speech. The rhythm and repetition provide strength to the ideas Dr. King presented. The text of this speech is easily obtained, but a tape recording would be more effective. Students have to hear the cadence and feel the rhythm to understand their effects. Similarly, older students who have studied World War II might profit from seeing a film of Hitler at Nuremburg.

▼ ──────────────────────────────────────

THE SYMBOLIC NATURE OF LANGUAGE

A good way to introduce students to the symbolic nature of language is through logos. Students can easily collect logos by examining the yellow pages of phone books. Once they have a good sample, they can analyze the logos for the relationship to the reality the logo represents. Younger students might like to design a personal logo, a symbolic representation of themselves.

Ancient writing systems are another good way of introducing symbols. American Indian pictographs and Egyptian hieroglyphics are two interesting places to start. From the "Interpretation of Red Horse Owner's Winter Count" (Wagner):

1783–1784 "Soldier froze to death." A man with his knees drawn up and his arms clasped around him is shown. A Dakota warrior (soldier here means "warrior") froze to death in the winter; the drawing indicates his futile attempt to keep warm.

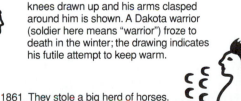

1861 They stole a big herd of horses.

1789 First time they rode horseback against the enemy.

From the Delaware Indians' creation story (Trout 6-7):

At first, forever, lost in space, everywhere, the great Manito was.

He made the extended land and the sky.

He made the sun, the moon, the stars.

He made them all to move evenly.

After students have read and discussed pictographs, they might read a creation story and draw pictographs in the margins. Or they might create both the story and the pictographs. Students would need a good sense of myth, of how ancient peoples wanted to explain the universe and its creatures, before doing this task.

Egyptian hieroglyphics are no doubt familiar to students from their cultural geography classes or movies. However, they may not have studied them from the viewpoint of a symbolic language system. With limited examples, they could figure out passages, as well as create some.

bull

beer jug

cobra

knife

leg

legs walking

hoe

house

Less familiar are Aztec symbols. Children's literature provides wonderful access to the world of symbols and their connections with culture. Deborah Nourse Lattimore's *The Flame of Peace* contains authentic illustrations, vibrantly presented. Students can examine the endpapers, where Lattimore has provided an additional key to the illustrations, and then explore the symbols in the text itself. The mythic tale echoes those of many cultures, so students might pursue comparisons of cultures and symbols.

jaguar

feathered serpent

blanket

eagle

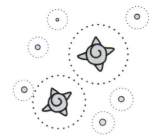

stars

coyote

reed boat

rattlesnake

bee

chicken

potted cedar trees

sun

Viking runes are another example of an early writing system. Whereas our writing system represents sounds we make, the runes are symbols for both things and ideas. The Vikings came to believe in the magic of the runes. An X, for example, offered protection against a poisoned cup; an arrow pointing upward ensured victory in battle; a figure somewhat like our letter "p" was a safeguard against giants (Born 2, 9). The runes, left on thousands of stones, are part of Norse mythology as well as an authentic writing system. Students could link history and mythology and try writing with runes.

With all writing activity, students should have a clear purpose in mind, associating that purpose with their imaginary audience and setting. The fact that ancient peoples developed various writing systems should make clear to students the power of words and the basic human need to communicate across time and distance.

f u þ a r k g w

▼

ADOLESCENTS AND LANGUAGE ACTIVITIES

Adolescents, whether they are 12 or 17, are inherently interested in language. Jokes, the Magic Ring Decoder in the cereal box, board games, music lyrics, cryptic notes, love notes, cheers and jeers, and even taunts are all elements of their experience with language. However, language is often transparent, something they see right through, to be used but seldom examined. We can make language opaque. We can bring it into focus for them through varied activities that ask them to discover for themselves the power of language.

Developing units that focus primarily on language is one way to do it. Another is to examine every unit for its potential to focus on language itself. With an integrated English language arts curriculum, that potential is virtually unlimited. The activities presented here are only a small sample, a suggestion. Observing students and asking them questions about language and their related language interests provide many ideas for working with language at any curricular level.

DISCUSSION QUESTIONS
ORAL AND WRITTEN LANGUAGE ACQUISITION

1. What are the teaching implications of the fact that students are creative, rather than imitative, language users?

2. If students have intuitive knowledge of how their native language functions, why do so many textbooks act as though they have none?

3. Review "What Native Speakers Can Do." What difference does it make that English language arts teachers understand these principles of native language abilities? What are some of the implications for the language arts classroom?

4. Based on your present knowledge of language learning, how would you respond to a building administrator or colleague who criticizes you for running a "noisy" class?

LEARNING ABOUT LANGUAGE

5. Robert MacNeil, a noted journalist and developer of the television series *The Story of Language,* made this statement about those who can't believe any-one would be interested in the English language, those who called it "essentially dreary and certainly a foolhardy exercise for television":

> It quickly became evident that people do not know they are lovers of the lan-guage, or that others are, or that finding joy in language is even an option. Why is that? Is it because they associate English only with the pain of the classroom, wrestling with exercises in composition, reading dead and long-winded au-thors? Or is it that so much about language today is a put-down: exhortations to improve one's language, stern denunciations of usage that may be nonstand-ard but common? Is it that English has become a nag, not a pleasure; a dread discipline, not a delight? (16)

Explore MacNeil's comments. Ask people not majoring in English to tell you their memories and associations with grade school or high school English. Be sure to ask them why, to get specific details and examples from them. What conclusions can you draw? What are the implications for you as a beginning English teacher?

SUGGESTED ACTIVITIES
ORAL AND WRITTEN LANGUAGE ACQUISITION

1. Examine at least one composition/language textbook for a middle school and one for senior high school. Do they take advantage of what we know intuitively about our native language, or do they treat English as though students were learning it in a foreign country? Give specific examples to support your opinion.

2. Devise several nonsense sentences, retaining English word order, structure words (e.g., *the, a, on*), and suffixes. Exchange them with a classmate and "translate" into acceptable English sentences. Discuss how you knew what to substitute for the nonsense part. What are the implications for working with students?

3. Written language acquisition has some parallels to oral language acquisi-tion. Make a physical sketch of an "ideal" classroom setting for writing instruction. Then make a list of some activities appropriate to your setting and knowledge of those parallels. Be prepared to defend your ideas.

LEARNING ABOUT LANGUAGE

Focusing on Language Concepts Through Literature

4. Select a piece of children's literature that illustrates one of the basic language concepts. If you are uncertain which books would be best, ask a children's librarian for assistance. Concepts to consider are meaning and context; symbolism; figurative and literal language; English sounds and rhythms.

    a. Note your rationale for selecting this piece of literature: What does it offer as an instructional tool? What thinking, reading, and writing skills might it enhance? How might it contribute to a sense of language appreciation? What curricular level are you using it with? Why?

    b. In an integrated language arts classroom, you may be emphasizing one language arts area or skill at a particular time, but you need to include all the language arts (listening, speaking, reading, and writing) in your planning. Similarly, you need to consider how to make the best use of both independent and group work (i.e., teacher-led discussion, student-to-student discussion, pair or small-group work). Determine which oral and written activities will be part of this lesson.

    c. Take yourself through the process you would use with your students. Consider where you need to model the process (if students are asked to write, for example, you should go through the process, producing a piece that exemplifies what you want them to do). As you work through this process, you will find some benefits: (1) You will find the rough spots, places where you need greater clarity, more examples, and so forth. (2) You will develop more ideas for presenting the material. As you indicate each procedure, also indicate why you include it as part of the lesson.

    d. Reflect on your development of this activity. What have you learned in the process? Your ability to analyze and to reflect on what you did and why you did it in a certain way is critical to your development as a teacher.

    e. Prepare to go through this process with students. This preparation will have several benefits: (1) You will find the problem spots. (2) You will be struck with more ideas, more ways in which to use the literature. (3) You may produce an example for the class.

5. Using young adult fiction or classical literature, select a piece or passage that illustrates a language concept. Poetry, of course, abounds with possibilities; for this assignment, however, concentrate on prose. Go through the process outlined in 4.

Word Games

6. Go to a book store and a toy store, or several if you have access to them, and examine materials useful for developing language skills and knowledge. In addition to preparing a list of these materials, annotate their use and value.

7. Prepare one collection of riddles, puzzles, and other "nonsense" word games appropriate for middle school students and another appropriate for senior high students. Some overlap will occur, especially as you consider the range of interests and abilities across those levels. Your library and book stores can provide you with many resources. How would you incorporate these into your classroom? Would they be used as part of larger units? As "fillers" on days when regular lessons would be suspended because of school programs, testing, or other activities? Of what value are these various activities and games? How would you defend their use to a colleague or parent who believes you are just wasting time?

REFERENCES

ORAL AND WRITTEN LANGUAGE ACQUISITION

Allen, Harold, and Michael Linn. *Readings in Applied Linguistics*. 3rd ed. New York: Knopf, 1982.

Berko Gleason, Jean, ed. *The Development of Language*. 2nd ed. Columbus: Merrill, 1989.

Cazden, Courtney B. *Child Language and Education*. New York: Holt, 1972.

Clark, Virginia, et al. *Language: Introductory Readings*. New York: St. Martin's, 1981.

Dale, Philip S. *Language Development: Structure and Function*. New York: Holt, 1976.

Falk, Julia. *Linguistics and Education: A Survey of Basic Concepts and Applications*. 2nd ed. New York: Wiley, 1978.

Fromkin, Victoria, and Robert Redmond. *An Introduction to Language.* 4th ed. New York: Holt, 1988.

Lindfors, Judith W. *Children's Language and Learning*. Englewood Cliffs: Prentice-Hall, 1987.

Slobin, Dan I. *Psycholinguistics*. Glenview: Scott, Foresman, 1981.

LEARNING ABOUT LANGUAGE

Aardema, Verna. *Why Mosquitoes Buzz in People's Ears*. New York: Dial, 1975.

Born, Thomas. *Understanding Language 1: The Magic of Words*. Columbus: American Education Publications, 1969.

_____. *Understanding Language 2: How Words Use You*. Columbus: American Education Publications, 1969.

_____. *Understanding Language 3: The Impact of Words*. Columbus: American Education Publications, 1969.

_____. *Understanding Language 4: The Levels of Meaning*. Columbus: American Education Publications, 1969.

Dunning, Stephen, Andrew Carrigan, and Ruth Clay. *Poetry: Voices, Language, Forms*. New York: Scholastic, 1970.

Kohl, Herbert. *A Book of Puzzlement: Play and Invention with Language*. New York: Schocken, 1981.

Lattimore, Deborah Nourse. *The Flame of Peace*. New York: Harper, 1987.

Littell, Joy, and Joseph Fletcher Littell, eds. *The Language of Man 1*. Evanston: MacDougal Littell, 1972.

Littell, Joseph Fetcher, ed. *The Language of Man 2.* Evanston: MacDougal Littell, 1972.

_____, ed. *The Language of Man 3.* Evanston: MacDougal Littell, 1972.

_____, ed. *Gaining Sensitivity to Words.* Evanston: MacDougal Littell, 1973.

MacNeil, Robert. "Listening to Our Language." *English Journal* Oct. 1988: 16–21.

Meiser, Mary. "Teaching Language Concepts in the Secondary School: Seuss, Sendak and Other Friends." *Wisconsin English Journal* Apr. 1989: 23–27.

Parrish, Peggy. *Amelia Bedelia.* New York: Harper, 1963.

_____. *Thank you, Amelia Bedelia.* New York: Harper, 1964.

Pei, Mario. *Talking Your Way Around the World.* 2nd ed. New York: Harper, 1967.

_____. *What's in a Word?* New York: Hawthorn, 1968.

Sendak, Maurice. *Where the Wild Things Are.* New York: Harper, 1967.

Seuss, Dr. (pseud.). *Dr. Seuss's Sleep Book.* New York: Random House, 1962.

_____. *Horton Hears a Who.* New York: Random House, 1954.

Simon, Elizabeth Radin. "My Name is Carlos." *Student Worlds, Student Words: Teaching Writing Through Folklore.* Portsmouth: Boynton/Cook Heinemann, 1990.

Tollefson, Stephen K., and Kimberly S. Davis. *Reading and Writing About Language.* Belmont: Wadsworth, 1980.

Trout, Lawana. *Myth: Student Log.* New York: Scholastic, 1975.

Wagner, Betty Jane. *Chronicle 1.* Boston: Houghton, 1973.

CHAPTER 10

Varieties of American English

CHAPTER HIGHLIGHTS

- Linguistic diversity.
- Students with limited English proficiency.
- Strategies for teaching writing.

[It took me] years to understand that my words weren't bad—they were just the words of the working class. For too long, I felt inferior when I spoke. I knew the voice of my childhood didn't belong to the group who made the rules. I was the outsider, a foreigner in this world. (40)

—*Linda Christensen, High School English Teacher*

▼

UNDERSTANDING LINGUISTIC DIVERSITY

Diversity is the foremost characteristic of oral language in America. Everyone in America speaks a dialect, which marks each of us as belonging to a certain race, gender, social class, and geographic region. With the exception of speech related to age or profession, most people retain their original dialect throughout their lives. Only when speakers change their status or role do they find it necessary to acquire another dialect; many speakers, therefore, have little need to learn a second American dialect. There is, however, a dialect called "standard American English," which is the form taught in American schools and to non-native speakers. This dialect is useful in that it facilitates communication across a multiplicity of situations. At the same time, we must also be aware of its dangers.

Because teachers value so highly the role of language and the forms we accept as standard, we may easily fall into linguistic chauvinism: We assume that our own dialect, standard American English, is the most appropriate way of speaking. Further, we may assume, as Jean Berko Gleason points out, that "differing dialects are . . . degenerate, illogical, or 'simpler' versions of our own" (334–35). Nothing could be further from the truth. And nothing could be more damaging in the classroom than an assumption that students with nonstandard dialects are less than competent—linguistically or cognitively. Standard American English may be the dialect of status, but it is not intrinsically better or more complete as a vehicle of communication than any other English dialect. Further, actual differences between the standard dialect and its variants are few. Understanding that variance is just variance, part of the rich linguistic life of America, should be the foundation for teaching and learning the standard dialect (Meiser 6).

▼

DIVERSITY IN THE SCHOOLS

Linguistic diversity is a fact of life in American schools. Students bring a wide range of backgrounds to school, and that diversity is reflected in their language. Marcia Farr and Harvey Daniel point out that although "all students have a highly developed linguistic competency, a set of underlying rules, which enables them to use their language, they do not share exactly the *same set* of rules." They further note that most language rules are shared by all English-speaking students; nonetheless, systematic differences in the rules result in English dialects, a variety of language that usually differs in vocabulary and pronunciation (13). In American English, with rare exception, speakers of one dialect can comprehend speakers of another, although perhaps imperfectly at first. American English dialects also borrow words from one another, just as we use words from hundreds of other languages.

Even within a dialect, speakers do not share exactly the same set of rules. That is, even within a single dialect, such as Black English Vernacular, considerable variation exists in use of the dialect by its speakers. This variation may be related to gender, age, social class, or the context in which the speaker is communicating. Speakers of standard American English demonstrate the same variations, but they are not usually subjected to being perceived as linguistically undeveloped or inadequate. Educators have consistently put a higher value on "standard dialect" than on American English dialects such as Black, Appalachian, and Puerto Rican (Farr and Daniel 24). The low prestige attached to these dialects is a serious matter because dialect differences do act as social class barriers (Schwartz 49).

Some educators cannot understand why students entering school with non-standard dialects leave school 12 years later with the same non-standard dialect. What these educators forget is a basic principle of language: Our ways of using and understanding language are deeply ingrained in our internal language system and thus are not easily changed through direct teaching (Farr and Daniels 24). This means that the failure to learn may be the result of cultural differences in American society and the subculture of our classrooms, where we reflect mainstream (usually white, middle class) culture. Shirley Brice Heath's *Ways With Words*, a study of home and school cultures, illustrates this phenomenon. Children, she found, are socialized into ways of using language, both oral and written, and are thus bound up in the patterns of their own culture. When they enter school, they generally enter the mainstream culture. It is no wonder, then, that complex differences between a student's home culture and the school culture contribute to frustration and failure. Farr and Daniel argue that "cultural differences in language practices that are part of very different ways of viewing and operating in the world must be taken seriously"(32).

▼ ──

WRITING AND DIALECTS

Teaching writing to students with different dialects can be a challenge, mainly because it is difficult to use conscious strategies to change a largely unconscious process. This also explains why the direct teaching of grammar fails, no matter which dialect students speak. Many educators believe that patterns of standard dialect are learned through meaningful and sustained interactions with speakers of standard dialect—not by exposure to school or television (Farr and Daniels 35). Mina Shaughnessy's powerful study of writing, *Errors and Expectations*, adds another view and a warning. Teachers should not be misled by errors in writing. The problem has less to do with dialect than with lack of exposure to written English; it is a problem of making sense on paper in an academic setting. The home dialect per se is not the issue (5).

Because fundamental language processes work the same for all students, there is no reason to believe that learning to write is different in kind for non-standard dialect students. This is not to suggest that instruction is identical or that we need not make some adaptations for non-standard dialect speakers. We do, both through oral and written work, but on the whole, we will teach writing—not writing to various subgroups within our classrooms.

▼ THE SUPPORTIVE CLASSROOM

Speakers of non-standard American dialects need abundant opportunities for using language in the classroom. This means committing time to the development of listening skills, oral comprehension, and production through (1) natural interaction among peers, (2) oral language built into all content area experiences, and (3) teacher anticipation of error and a positive procedure for reinforcing standard usage and syntax. In such a classroom, teachers and students not only use a great deal of language, both oral and written, but they also talk about language itself. The lessons are natural ones: What is a dialect? What features do our dialects share? What features of pronunciation and syntax are different? Which vocabulary words are different? How does vocabulary reflect our culture? How does rhythm differ? These lessons can be taught by the students. We need only lead them into critical listening and thinking, into keen observation of themselves and others as users of language, and then into discussion. Such discussions provide not only awareness of language but also respect for the diverse cultures represented.

▼ DIALECT AND IDENTITY

Because dialects are so closely tied to culture, family, and identity, they are an integral part of self-concept. Educators know that self-concept is perhaps the most powerful factor in academic success; therefore, we must not only understand these basic principles of language but also apply them in curriculum, methodology, and classroom environment. To ignore them is to place students at risk of failure. The student who feels deficient and devalued because of language differences will most certainly fail, thus continuing a cycle of illiteracy and poverty. We also know that attitude is a critical factor in a student's acquisition of a second dialect or language; thus, teachers themselves may make the critical difference. Moreover, teachers whose classrooms focus on linguistic and cultural diversity enrich all students, not just those in the process of acquiring standard American English.

Research has demonstrated that there is no reason to believe that a non-standard dialect, in and of itself, is a barrier to learning. All dialects are highly structured, logical, and complete. Standard English is no more expressive or logical and no more capable of communication than non-standard dialects. Judgments about the superiority of one dialect are social, not linguistic. Teachers who understand this do not underestimate the language abilities of students with non-standard dialects, and they are able to foster the self-esteem critical to academic success. Our knowledge, our attitude, and our willingness to acquire specific dialect knowledge make a difference.

▼ LINGUISTIC DIVERSITY

Philip Dale notes that "typically, [variation] is not a black problem but prejudice arising from inability of larger society to accept linguistic diversity—the Chicano, the Puerto Rican, the Appalachian, the Native American" (282). To these we can add Southeast Asian, Haitian, and Cuban immigrants. It is important to remember that beneath the categories of Hispanic, Native American, and Asian reside distinct cultures and languages: *Hispanic* may mean Mexican, Cuban, Central American, or Puerto Rican. The values, the customs, and the ways of speaking are different, despite Spanish being the common native language. Similarly, *Native American* refers to hundreds of distinct languages and Indian nations with differing cultures. *Asian* covers distinct national and language groups with distinct cultures as well.

As students acquire standard dialect, it is critical for us to understand that bidialectism or bilingualism is a complex situation—a matter of degree rather than all or nothing. A student possesses different levels of fluency in speaking, reading, and writing, all at the same time. This same student may demonstrate variation in listening comprehension or the capacity to understand. We cannot expect a student to be equally capable in all areas or acquire communicative competency evenly. Native speakers are similarly uneven, a fact often overlooked in the English language arts curriculum.

Language "problems" arising out of dialect or second language are not problems of intelligence or educational ability, but rather the consequence of certain differences between the language of home, certain ways of knowing and doing, and the language of school.

BLACK ENGLISH

Black English is perhaps the most widely discussed dialect of English; it may also be the most misunderstood. Too often people believe that Black English is simply sloppy talk. Pronunciations such as *jus* for *just* cause some teachers to label black Americans careless or lazy, despite the fact that southern white speakers demonstrate similar pronunciations. There is no one correct way of speaking, only variations that are appropriate to the situation. Attempts to erase Black English dialect differences through correcting "errors" are ineffective as well as insulting. Our goal should be to increase communicative competence: the student's ability to use language effectively in a variety of settings for a multiplicity of purposes.

Our job, then, is not to change a student's language but to expand his or her potential. Accepting Black dialect, recognizing it as different, not defective, is the first step in the process. We also need to understand that the label itself, Black English, is misleading. It equates ethnic identification with a genetic characteristic, being black. But many African-Americans never speak Black English, whereas people of other ethnic groups do. Moreover, certain standard dialects share features of Black English. Black dialect is important; many students speak it. Both for establishing a respect for the culture it represents and as a base for teaching, we need to respond by learning something of this American dialect.

UNDERSTANDING BLACK ENGLISH

This dialect has the same number of sounds as standard dialect but a different pattern of distribution; the real distinction is in rhythm, inflection, and tone. Anyone who has listened to the public speech of Martin Luther King, Jr., or Jesse Jackson, who keep the cadence of Black dialect even when using standard dialect, has no doubt been struck by these elements.

As with any dialect, notable variations in pronunciation (e.g., substitutions and deletions of certain sounds) are standardized and predictable. Teachers familiar with Black dialect are thus able to recognize the difference between an error and a mere substitution of sounds. For example, a student who reads *with* as *wif* is not making an error; in Black dialect, the final /th/ is pronounced /f/.

After an initial period of adjustment, most people readily understand the pronunciation differences. Some southern dialects have similar characteristics, and few people have real difficulty understanding a speaker from Georgia or Texas—if they want to. As Geneva Smitherman, a noted African-American scholar, reminds us: "Southern Black speech sounds pretty much the same as Southern White speech . . . when you talk about pronunciation, there is no national standard even among white speakers" ("It Bees . . ." 522).

Grammar is the most rigid part of our language system, the part least likely to change over time. Therefore, differences in grammar are fewer than those in pronunciation, but at the same time they carry a greater stigma. Most people, regardless of the dialect, find grammar differences irritating and unacceptable. Teachers are no exception. Despite their knowledge of the integrity of every dialect, many English language arts teachers respond negatively not only to Black dialect but to any variance in grammar. For some reason, knowing that certain verbs (e.g., *be*) pattern themselves in well-defined ways or that plural and possessive markers are absent often does little or nothing to alleviate a negative response. English language arts teachers who work with speakers of Black dialects must learn to overcome this response. Without respect for the home language, teachers cannot reach or affect any student's learning. Without knowledge of its distinctive features and thus the ability to tell when students understand a grammatical concept, teachers are unable to help their students when they most need help.

Although Black English has the concepts of plural and possession, it does not use markers: "that Tom hat"; "two boy left." Again, the context and other words make clear the intent. Repeating the subject ("my son he fix that") is an optional feature. Double negatives ("don't nobody know that") are common and often more complicated than this example. These are only a few examples of elements of Black dialect. English language arts teachers who work with speakers of this dialect find it beneficial to learn more about it.

As teachers, we also need to remember that not all African-Americans speak this dialect, and that many features of Black English are present in other southern dialects. Differences between Black English and standard English are not great. Many non–African-Americans react to the rhythm and rhetorical style and respond emotionally, thereby exaggerating the differences. The attitude of school personnel toward the dialect, rather than the dialect itself, often contributes to poor scholastic performance. No one assumes that a speaker of Boston dialect who says "idear" cannot learn to write "idea." Yet, many African-American students are victims of the assumption that their dialect is a barrier to learning.

NATIVE AMERICAN LANGUAGES

There is no such thing as an "Indian culture" or talking "Indian." There are about 300 different tribal groups in the United States, each to some degree divided by language, culture, and tradition (Knop 24). It is not surprising that linguists believe there are approximately 14 language groups and, within each, many dialects. Within the state of Wisconsin, for example, six tribes and three language groups are represented. Within one of these language groups, the Algonquian family, Chippewa, Menominee, and Potowatomi are all dialects.

Contrary to popular belief, the vast majority of Native American languages are still spoken today. Many Indian children grow up in families hearing the native language spoken around them but not to them. Unfortunately, the adults have been led to believe that speaking the native language to the children is detrimental to their growth. One of the consequences of this way of thinking is that the children do not have an adequate grasp of either one of the languages, English or native (Knop 25).

If we keep in mind that cultural and language patterns are set in childhood, we recognize that through school, some American Indian children are learning a new language that may be of no use at home and in very serious ways unrelated to the world and environment in which these students live. Further, the organization of classroom talk—interactions between student and teacher, interactions between students, regulation of getting and holding the floor, and so forth—is designed to fit the white, middle class student. This means that language in school neither fits with nor builds on interactional skills held by American Indian students. Dialect differences no doubt cause misunderstanding, not only because rules of discourse are different but also because little world knowledge is shared.

Susan Philips' study of the Warm Springs Indian Reservation, *The Invisible Culture*, illustrates how Indian children's verbal and non-verbal communication patterns conflict with those of the mainstream school. Philips argues that the conflict means that speaking is less easily integrated into the normal sequences and structure of classroom talk. This, in turn, leads to more instances in which American Indian students suffer the consequences of teacher judgments of inappropriate listening and speaking behaviors. Philips also points out that even well-intentioned teachers often find minority students' efforts to communicate incomprehensible. Unfortunately, because many American classrooms are built around the teacher as authority, the students are held responsible for breakdowns in communication (128).

BRIDGING THE DIFFERENCE

Teachers aware of language as a cultural phenomenon will want to learn something of language and interaction patterns in the native culture. With Native American students, we must take care neither to praise nor to scold publicly. Praise may be embarrassing for the student, in that doing the "right" thing is expected. Private consultation is more appropriate for correction. Our questions may also pose a danger because in many Indian cultures, questions are a form of trial. Native American youngsters more often observe, try things out on their own privately, and perform when ready. Privacy is important; therefore, we cannot expect native students to talk or write freely about themselves. We also need to be aware of non-verbal language patterns. Eye contact, for example, is viewed differently. Lowered eyes and head show respect for a teacher, not disinterest. One-on-one dialogue between teacher and student often does not work, nor does placing a Native American student in front of the class, which runs counter to cultural training in cooperation, a sharing of leadership and responsibilities among the group.

The attributes of Native American pedagogy are good for all students. Discovery and activity are basic to learning. Cooperative learning groups are becoming part of the mainstream classroom. According to Johnson et al., in cooperative learning groups, all students share leadership action and responsibility for learning in all members; students are expected to help and encourage their group members. Further, students are taught the social skills necessary for collaborative work; they are not assumed to have them (n.p.). The fundamental difference between competitive and individual learning, which is basic to American Indian philosophy, is addressed in cooperative learning groups. As with all students, opportunities to use language, rather than to hear about language, are critical to development of oral and written language skills.

HISPANIC ENGLISH

Hispanic English is a dialect spoken by students whose native language is Spanish. Although Spanish is the native language of students of Mexican, Cuban, Puerto Rican, and Central American descent, each of these cultures has its own ways of "knowing and doing." The dialect is found mostly among bilingual speakers; in areas of the United States that border Mexico, the Spanish influence continues to reinforce and maintain Hispanic English. As with all dialects, there are systematic differences in pronunciation, stress, and syntax (Fromkin and Rodman 270). Hispanic English, nonetheless, is comprehensible to speakers of other American dialects. Ricardo Garcia tells us that "while speaking his *colo*, or dialect of English, the Chicano thinks little of borrowing or mixing of Spanish and English," whether it be sound, vocabulary, or grammar (540). We can therefore expect Hispanic students to substitute Spanish sounds for English ones, as well as to make literal translations.

Roseann Duenas Gonzales notes that Chicano English (a dialect spoken by Mexican Americans) serves an oral communication purpose. In written form, however, it is "distinguished by characteristics such as incorrect or incomplete verb formations (no *ed*, no *s*, no *ed* on past participle), inappropriate prepositions (such as *in* for *on*), inappropriately used vocabulary and syntactic patterns that differ from those acceptable in edited American English" (21). She adds that the lexicon of this dialect is limited both in breadth and precision. Consequently, these students need to understand not only the differences between oral and written English but also to acquire an expanded and enriched vocabulary (21). Because Mexican American students generally come from highly structured families, Gonzales believes writing instruction that is structured (e.g., formal invention strategies, organizational patterns, sentence combining) will be more successful (20). Similarly, these students' orientation to communal family and neighborhood lives produces a learning style that thrives in small group and cooperative activities; they are also less competitively oriented. Furthermore, in observing Mexican American students, Gonzales concluded that the majority were interested in how to improve their writing rather than in grades (22). If mainstream teachers are to unlock the academic potential of these students, they must first understand and then capitalize on different cultural characteristics.

Because Hispanic English derives from Spanish, these students may be placed in programs or classes for non-native speakers. However, appropriate placement or instruction is complicated. According to Gonzales, "Understanding Mexican American students demands familiarity with their complex, yet simply perceived, linguistic situation" (20). She explains that too often people assume all Chicanos to be bilingual, whereas "their linguistic situation reflects a complex spectrum of bilingualism" (21). In reality, students may be Spanish dominant with limited oral and written English skills or English dominant with limited Spanish language ability or somewhere along a language continuum.

STUDENTS WITH LIMITED ENGLISH PROFICIENCY

▼

THE IMPORTANCE OF BILINGUALISM

Given the continuing numbers of immigrants to America today, most English language arts teachers can expect to have some ESL students, that is, those for whom English is a second language. Districts with significant numbers of ESL speakers may have a bilingual program. Because bilingual programs often come under criticism, it is important that English language arts teachers understand the role and significance of such programs. Although appearing to be counterintuitive, programs that provide limited English students with significant content instruction in their native language generally result in more English acquisition than do programs that spend all of their time instructing in English. The student's native language develops expressive skills and conceptual understanding that then provide a strong conceptual base for the acquisition of English.

Thus, students in a bilingual program not only acquire English more quickly and thoroughly but also become truly bilingual. Loss of the native language also means loss in English competency as well. Research also suggests that the level of proficiency in English depends partly upon the degree of native language proficiency at the time when intensive exposure to English occurs. For many students with limited English proficiency, this exposure coincides with their entry into American schools. Development of the native language and English are then interdependent to a certain degree, their interaction influencing the success of the student with limited English proficiency (bilingual).

The loss of native language is detrimental from two perspectives: the relationship to the development of the second language, in this case English, and the psychological limbo of the student. The native language has been the linguistic system associated with the development of basic concepts. If students are forced to drop it altogether, the loss affects conceptual development and identity. In extreme cases, students can end up with neither the native language nor English as a useful tool. The ideal program for the limited English student provides comprehensible and meaningful "input" in English, with, at the same time, content area instruction in both languages. Content instruction is critical to cognitive development as well as to helping students make sense out of learning activities conducted in English.

▼

LEARNING ACADEMIC ENGLISH

The difficulty of the limited English student in a mainstream classroom often relates to differences between conversational and academic English. When non-native speakers become reasonably fluent in English, it is easy to forget the level of difficulty they must confront in academic language, both spoken and written. Research reminds us that immigrant students may reach proficiency in basic oral communication in two to three years, but the level of proficiency needed in a school setting requires five to seven years (Chamot and O'Malley 109). The language of school is both unique and complex, although as teachers we don't often stop to consider this fact. The higher the curricular level, the more abstract we become, moving ever farther away from experiential and contextual learning. For the ESL student, this situation can be a formula for failure.

At greatest risk are students arriving in American schools at age 12 or older. The heavy cognitive demands and level of academic language used in secondary schools make it very difficult to catch up. Consequently, students need content area instruction in their native language rather than only intensive English language instruction (Chamot and O'Malley 110). Moreover, secondary students can't afford the loss of two to three years of academic instruction while mastering English if they expect to go on to post-secondary institutions (Collier 520). English language arts teachers can help by including materials and concepts from various content areas in their classrooms.

We must remember that academic language skills may or may not be developed in the native language, thus affecting whether the student must learn to transfer these skills to English or must learn them for the first time. Teachers need to make English comprehensible, fully contextual, and rich in nonverbal cues. The higher the grade level, the more decontextualized the language and instruction. Language no longer refers to the concrete, the here and now, but to ideas and events far removed from the student. Immigrant students also lack a historical and cultural context for some of these ideas and events, which compounds the level of difficulty.

A student's progress through the stages of language acquisition is both personal and uneven. The amount of time each learner spends in each of the stages and the consistency of performance at any given time depend upon several variables. One is the individual development of the student, another is his or her willingness to learn the second language, and yet another is the quality of instructional planning and language environment in the classroom. Self-esteem, the ability to take risks, and good learning strategies are critical to the process. Age may also be a factor (Raimes "Working"). However, assumptions that young children are faster and more efficient in acquiring a second language have been disputed by research (Collier 510). At the same time, research has not provided information about an optimal age. What is not disputed is that age cannot be separated from other key variables in language acquisition, mainly cognitive development and proficiency in native language.

With reference to students acquiring a second language, Raimes ("Working") notes some agreement among researchers on the following points:

- Acquisition is complex, gradual, non-linear, and dynamic.
- Acquisition of certain structures follows a definite order.

- Competency is acquired gradually; some learners remain stuck at one stage of competency.
- Learners develop an interlanguage midway between native and target language, a system of approximation to the target language that is neither the native nor the target language.
- Learners transfer cognitive strategies, which may be positive or negative for learning a second language. Learners rely on native language when target language is not adequate for their communicative needs.
- Fewer errors can be attributed to the native language, to interference, than previously thought.

Because of the nature of language processes themselves, some obvious parallels exist between native and second language acquisition. As with native language, a sustained and comprehensible second language environment fosters students' progress in both listening comprehension and oral production. And in both native and second language learning, grammatical and pronunciation errors are normal, indicating important developments in learning. Purposeful language, that is, authentic communication, is also central to both native and second language learning.

Despite some striking similarities, there are also profound differences between native and second language learning. One of these is time. Students learning a second language cannot return to infancy and enjoy a similar time frame for growth and the unconditional tolerance for error it provided. A necessary variable for the second language learner is as much comprehensible language (i.e., that they can understand) as possible in whatever time is available. A great deal of talking, reading, and writing is basic to acquisition; looking at language, analyzing it, and writing things down all assist the student. One inventive second language learner discovered toll-free telephone numbers and used them extensively to hear English and to learn new vocabulary; the same student also listened to an all-news radio station by day and watched eight hours of television at night (Raimes "Working"). Suggesting ways for students to access spoken and written English, however strange-sounding to the native speaker, provides them with options.

Unfortunately, many ESL students must hurry into literacy, attempting to gain reading and writing skills while the oral language base is still being formed. Another problem with acquiring literacy is the effect of the native language because rhetorical patterns are culturally based. For example, in Japanese text, the reader is responsible for "filling in the gaps." Japanese writers do not provide full explication, relying more on nuance, hints, and other devices. In most American texts, the writer is responsible for clarity, delineating everything for the reader. The concept of the topic sentence, for example, is very American. How students link sentences is also culturally based. In Arabic, the written language is linked to the Koran, resulting in rhythmic coordination and balance. Arabic students writing in English thus rely heavily on *and* and *so* rather than on subordination. An ESL learner, then, must learn an entirely new rhetorical system (Raimes "Working").

With our native language, we also acquire, gradually and naturally, its social uses and applications. Because expectations of speakers and writers vary from culture to culture, students cannot simply transfer this knowledge to English. Similarly, academic expectations vary considerably from culture to culture. Some students may be from a culture that venerates the written word and thus may have great difficulty with American expectations that students challenge it. Others may be from a culture in which rote learning is the accepted method of instruction; self-discovery would be very alien to them. Cultural differences also affect motivation for learning the second language. If students have negative feelings about American culture, they may resist its language. In any case, students acquiring English as a second language are finding and processing a new identity, an American one (Raimes "Working"). The emotional and social complexity of this undertaking should not be underestimated by mainstream teachers.

▼ ───

THE SCHOOL ENVIRONMENT
BUILDING THE ORAL BASE

When we learned our native language, we had substantial time in which to develop oral language—to easily absorb the sounds of our language with no contrasting influences and to build strong receptive skills. We had many language models and many varied opportunities to use the language, interacting constantly in various ways. ESL students must, therefore, have a good program in oral language, not only for its own sake but also as a base for literacy.

Because new sounds are being substituted for sounds and structures of the native language, students may experience some difficulty. Teachers need to learn major differences between the sounds and structures of the native language and English and teach *as needed* those that contrast with the native language. It's important to note, however, that language acquired in informal school activities is likely to be more important than any direct instruction (Holdzkom et al. 1).

Teachers also need to maintain a reasonable perspective on pronunciation. Flawless English is not the goal; comprehensible English is. The older the student, the more difficult it is for him or her to position tongue, teeth, and facial muscles for the new language. Because teenagers find it very difficult to master sounds, they are easily intimidated by the process. Teachers have to assure them that no one expects them to sound like native speakers. And in any event, syntactic control, the ability to control structure, is more important than pronunciation (Holdzkom et al. 4–5).

Listening skills are key to acquiring a second language and often are very limited. In some families, English is spoken little or not at all. Immigrant students may also cluster in national groups for out-of-school activities. Students thus have limited exposure to English, resulting in limited practice with listening skills. The classroom therefore needs a structure to promote listening, conversation, and interaction. Interaction is vital; learners need meaningful language practice, not exercises and drills. Teachers cannot assume that, because students are in an English-speaking environment, they will develop competency. As second-language learners, they need organized, directed, and purposeful communication. They also need varied contexts for this communication. Teacher planning, then, is critical in developing the oral base.

CONCEPTS AND CONTEXT

In learning our native language, we develop an understanding of a concept and then associate a word with that concept. A student learning English has to do one of two things: either match concepts already learned in the native language to English words or learn both the concept and the word simultaneously in English. For this reason, teachers need to ensure that the student understands the concept before teaching the word that represents it. Acquisition of native language takes place in a natural setting, language exposure occurring every waking hour. For a second language, the number of hours of learning are limited, and the language activities are structured and contrived and the setting more formal. Classrooms that simulate everyday life and varied language use assist ESL learners.

CULTURE AND REINFORCEMENT

Language is an integral part of culture and vice versa. In learning our native language, we are part of the culture and understand it in important ways. With a second language, the learner often has little or no knowledge of the culture, making it far more difficult to relate things. In teaching language, then, we need to include activities that teach about culture at the same time. In the native language, the learner is given wide latitude for error, for producing imperfect language, because people recognize the process as one of development. When working with ESL students, we need to give the same latitude, to attend more to meaning-making and less to form. If we concentrate on the communication effort of the speaker and provide the correct model, without being too explicit about it, the student will probably respond well and continue efforts to communicate.

The native language develops linguistically, socially, and cognitively, whereas the second language is often overconcentrated linguistically, providing less time for content knowledge acquisition and social interaction. If no bilingual program is present to develop content knowledge, teachers can ask for native language tutors. As native speakers, we received tremendous support and reinforcement for learning our language; people were pleased with our efforts, rewarded us, and tolerated error. An ESL student may encounter negative attitudes and settings, and reinforcement may be given for errors but not for what has been accomplished. The classroom should be a place where cultural and linguistic acceptance and appreciation are commonplace.

ACQUIRING ORAL LANGUAGE

As we consider language development, it is important to remember that each student's rate of progress is personal. Designating "stage" boundaries, therefore, is merely a guide to general progress, not an absolute. The Bilingual Education Department in the San Francisco School District developed these categories to help its mainstream teachers.

• In the preverbal stage, the student has no comprehension of English; a response may be based on guessing, using either context or another student's response as the basis. We should continue to surround the student with meaningful English, answer our own questions as a natural model of response, and demonstrate with concrete items and experiential learning as often as possible.

• In the next stage, the student comprehends English but still is unable to respond in English; he or she may respond appropriately in the native language, however. Acceptance of student response in the native language is important. We should continue to provide opportunities for the student to imitate or speak but not force a response. Through learning experiences, we can draw the student into speaking.

• Next, the student may try out English through spontaneously imitating teachers and other students. We need to encourage the student, inviting him or her to imitate a response after we have given it and, if necessary, correct in a positive way. Providing natural models through regular classroom interactions is important. From here, the student moves into simple spontaneous verbalizations that may not be grammatically correct. Again we need to encourage speaking and play down the correction of grammar. The more peer interaction, the better.

• Finally, the student moves into intermediate fluency, controlling many basic English structures. The student may be quite fluent in conversation and social situations, but lack comprehension and production related to academic language. At this point, we monitor both meaning and form and keep track of persistent grammar errors. Although we may use more complex structures in clear contexts, we still need to check that the student really understands us.

ACQUIRING WRITTEN LANGUAGE

Often, mainstream teachers believe that they have no knowledge of how to work with ESL students. However, teachers who understand the underlying concepts of native language acquisition and its relevance for teaching composition do have a good base for working with ESL writers. Similarly, teachers who approach writing instruction holistically, emphasizing process skills before turning to product evaluation, are already using beneficial strategies. Teachers who have integrated the language arts—weaving reading, writing, speaking, and listening into all instructional activities—also have a sound basis for working with ESL learners. Nonetheless, it is important that mainstream teachers treat ESL writers neither exactly the same as nor completely different from native speakers (Chan 85).

▼

STRATEGIES FOR TEACHING WRITING

One of the most important strategies is actually an attitude: Let students write, regardless of how limited their English vocabulary is. Based on her research and extensive experience with ESL writers, Ann Raimes ("What Unskilled . . .") believes, "The acquisition of adequate vocabulary does not necessarily have to precede writing. If ESL students are given enough time, shown ways to explore topics, and given enough feedback, they will discover and uncover the English words they need as they write" (248).

Raimes goes on to note that ESL writers need more of everything: talking, listening, reading, writing; instruction and practice in generating, organizing, and revising ideas; attention to rhetorical options; and an emphasis on editing for linguistic form and style (250).

A second strategy involves reading—lots of it. Because ESL writers do not have native intuitiveness to guide them in revision, they need to read a great deal of well-written English prose (Chan 84). Providing a wealth of reading resources, along with sustained time for reading, helps students see how the language functions. Asking students to keep a journal for reflection, both on what they read and on their own writing processes, is another useful strategy. A double-entry notebook is another strategy that asks students to reflect on their own learning. In it, they can record their errors and enter a corrected version and an explanation of what went wrong or why they made the language choice they did. Their responses provide an invaluable resource for understanding them and focusing instruction.

Group work and teacher conferences are needed strategies; students benefit most from response to work in progress. Further, as Raimes reminds us, we have to take into account the anxiety that accompanies writing in a new language; sharing with peer or teacher may alleviate some anxiety or frustration. Oral rehearsal, composing out loud, and other interactive activities work well for ESL writers ("Language . . ." 461). Providing written questions for revision and editing also helps, as do specific proofreading strategies.

▼

UNDERSTANDING STUDENTS' ERRORS

Traditionally, teachers focused almost entirely on anticipated interference from a student's native language. Although teachers must, of course, be aware of the major differences between English and the student's native language, recent studies have demonstrated that ESL learners often make errors that have less to do with interference from their native language and more to do with their developing competency in English. Another major consideration is the uniqueness of each student. The type of errors that occur in one student's work may be very different from that of another with the same native language. Errors generally fall into patterns, which makes it easier for teachers to analyze the source and devise instruction. Errors also provide evidence of systematic decision-making, providing a key to the student's language development and understanding of English.

ESL students make errors for some of the same reasons that native speakers do. One is simply performance—making a mistake despite underlying competency. Another is lack of exposure to the correct form or lack of correction, often in an oral pattern that the student simply transfers to paper. However, ESL writers also make mistakes because of transfer from native language or application of an idiosyncratic set of rules in an effort to approximate English.

▼ ——————————————————————————————————

TEACHERS' STRATEGIES
MONITORING CLASSROOM LANGUAGE

Teachers can begin by monitoring their own language for clarity, pacing, word choice; use of natural rhythms and pronunciation, normal tone, and gestures. Although we may slow down a bit, we shouldn't do so to the point that English becomes unnatural, an alien form that students may not be able to relate to outside of our class. We should use complete sentences and be continually aware of the importance of giving examples and paraphrasing. As we present information, we should provide as great a context as possible: concrete objects, pictures, manipulatives, demonstrations, and the like. Similarly, the chalkboard or overhead projector can serve as visual background, providing key words or other graphic representations.

Teachers need to be aware of the language in textbooks, which are generally dense with information and specialized vocabulary. Textbooks assume native language competency. At the same time, we should beware of workbooks that deprive students of the rich context of "real books." ESL learners should use trade books that support their language development. Vocabulary lists do not promote acquisition, simply because they have no context and the words are thus easily forgotten. Contextualized vocabulary, both oral and written, relates to meaning and is therefore more easily retained. The emphasis must be on meaning first. Because reading aloud has a significant effect not only on literacy acquisition but also on language development, we should provide many opportunities for this activity.

KEEPING LANGUAGE MEANINGFUL

The principles of authentic language (i.e., purposeful, not drills) that apply to native language acquisition and development are the same for a second language. Students without a rudimentary knowledge of natural spoken language should not be given formal training in grammar. Nor should they be doing exercises. Exercise sheets have a real weakness: The student asked to choose between correct and incorrect answers may end up confused and ultimately adopt the wrong usage. Fill-in-the-blank or forced-choice exercises do not demonstrate whether or not a student can speak or write a complete sentence correctly. We need to make good judgments, then, about when and why worksheet or text exercise is needed.

Teachers also need to be aware of nonverbal language in the native culture. How does the culture define space between speakers? Americans generally become somewhat uncomfortable when people stand too close to them; in other cultures, however, such distance is viewed as insulting. What are the rules for eye contact? In our schools, we expect students to look straight at us when they respond; such eye contact in other cultures indicates disrespect for the teacher. How does conversational turn-taking occur in the native culture? Americans tend to dislike "sound gaps" and fill them, allowing very little time for response. Other cultures use "sound gaps" as part of the conversation, signaling respect for what the speaker has just said. What gestures may have double meanings? Not finding out could have disastrous consequences. When students enter the classroom, they are entering a culture within a culture. We need to keep in mind that many "rules" are unknown to non-native speakers.

STRUCTURING A SUPPORTIVE CLASSROOM

Pat Riggs and Virginia Allen provide some general principles to support acquisition of English as a second language.

Grouping Students

Students with limited English proficiency (LEP) need to be with native speakers. Being in a language-rich environment with real interaction and students their own age is critical to language development. It is a mistake to view LEP students as though "speaking a language other than English were a terrible form of retardation that prevented communication and play" with native speakers (xi). The teacher should organize lessons so that small groups of LEP and native speakers work together on meaningful tasks. If a task involves particularly difficult information, the teacher may want to keep LEP students together and provide them with extra help. For the most part, however, groups should be a mix of LEP and native speakers.

Using "Real" Language

LEP students need many and varied opportunities to use language; the impetus for learning is tied to achieving communication with other speakers of the language. Thus, students should not be concentrating on the forms of language to use someday in some possible situation. Producing rows of correct forms is not the goal and certainly not the desired pedagogy.

Learning Holistically

A second language, like the native one, develops very gradually and not linearly. That is, "language is not learned as a jigsaw of tiny bits of mastered skills, each fitting into a pattern, but rather as an entire picture, that is at first blurred, only gradually coming into focus" (xi). The classroom implication is clear: Teachers should not waste students' time with worksheets, word lists, or pronunciation drills. Students need to be actively engaged in real activities, have a context for language, and hear and participate in conversations.

Achieving Literacy

Literacy is part of the LEP students' language development. "Writing, speaking, listening and reading all nourish one another; we don't wait for mastery of one before encouraging development of the other three" (xiii). Teachers should encourage reading and writing and not wait until the LEP student is a fluent speaker of English. Teachers must choose comprehensible reading materials and, as noted earlier, stay away from workbooks that fragment language. Writing should be authentic, not for purposes of answering text questions or evaluation. Dialogue journals provide an important place for student writing and teacher comment—not on form, but only on content.

A Nurturing Environment

Teachers also need continual awareness of the affective variables that influence learning English. Self-esteem and self-confidence are linked to acquisition, especially at the secondary school level. To achieve competence in English, LEP students need strong motivation to learn, to withstand the errors that are inevitable, and to take the risks critical to growth. A supportive classroom environment is key to this. ESL learners need to feel socially part of a group before they are willing to experiment with the new language.

Holdzkom et al. advocate the use of peer tutors as a means of helping students limited in English proficiency in the mainstream classroom. With peer tutors, LEP students are less likely to develop self-segregating behaviors that limit their linguistic and social development (3). At the same time, native speakers learn far more about language, as well as about another culture. Because peer groups and peer response are integral features of the integrated English language arts curriculum, such pairing is both natural and desirable.

DISCUSSION QUESTIONS

1. In *Alice in Wonderland*, the Mad Hatter tells Alice: "Your hair wants cutting." We smile because the verb *wants* is unnatural in this context. Do you think most people smile when a non-native speaker of English makes this type of error? Why not? How would you handle the errors of non-native speakers in your classroom?

2. Alice has many conversations that lead into questions of language:

> "Take some more tea," the March Hare said to Alice very earnestly.
> "I've had nothing yet," Alice replied in an offended tone, "so I can't take more."
> "You mean you can't take *less*," said the Hatter: "it's very easy to take *more* than nothing."

To a native speaker of English, this exchange makes a bit of sense (as well as nonsense). Why? What problems would a non-native speaker have with this text? List some basic concepts of English that a non-native speaker has to learn (e.g., words that show quantity, words that show time of action). What are the implications for your classroom?

3. In an article in *English Journal*, Betty Peterson tells us:

> I grew up in rural Kentucky, yet I had little understanding of why we spoke, believed, and lived as we did, and I'm sorry to say that I was ashamed of my heritage. The one thing that bothered me the most was the way people talked, because education had taught me that their use of language was incorrect, the result of their ignorance and illiteracy, and nothing more. (53)

Respond to the notion of language (dialect or native) being "incorrect," and discuss the impact of feelings of linguistic inferiority in the classroom.

4.
> It would be misleading to suggest people in our society will value my thoughts or my students' thoughts as readily in our home language as in the 'cash language' as Jesse Jackson calls it. Students need to know where to find help, and they need to know what changes [in their home language] might be necessary, but they need to learn it in a context that doesn't say 'The way you said this is wrong.' (Linda Christensen 37)

Discuss the issue of home language versus cash language. Can a teacher preserve home language while teaching cash language?

SUGGESTED ACTIVITIES

1. Find videos that feature English dialects (authentic, not stereotyped). For example, *Crocodile Dundee* features genuine Australian English through its main character, Paul Hogan, a genuine Aussie. Some PBS television presentations from Great Britain are good sources of diverse English accents. Keep track of differences in pronunciation and vocabulary, noting not only what they are but how you respond to them. Using video, prepare a lesson for either middle or senior high school students. Your goal is to get them thinking about the many varieties of English, why and how a language develops dialects, and why people have different attitudes about a dialect not their own.

2. *The Story of Language* is an excellent series on the development and migration of the English language. Choose a segment you believe would be of interest to senior high school students. As you preview it, develop "preview"

questions and "afterview" activities for the students. Remember, you want the students prepared to watch with their brains as well as their eyes.

3. Link the appropriate historical segment of *The Story of Language* with senior high school literature (e.g., Chaucer, Shakespeare). Devise a lesson in which the video supports an understanding of language as an historical phenomenon and of language change as normal.

4. Watch the video *American Tongues* for the representation of American dialects. How could this video be used as the center of a lesson on language variation in America? Plan a lesson for middle level students.

5. Check the media center for videos of Martin Luther King, Jr., and Jesse Jackson. View some of their speeches, analyzing the beauty and power of their language as you watch. How could you use these videos with middle or senior level students?

REFERENCES

Bilingual Education Department, San Francisco Unified School District. *Excellence in Leadership and Implementation: Programs for Limited English Proficient Students.* San Francisco: Unified School District, 1985.

Carroll, Lewis. *Alice in Wonderland and Through the Looking Glass.* San Rafael: Classic Publishing Company, 1970.

Carter, Cindy, and Committee on Classroom Practices. *Non-Native and Nonstandard Dialect Students.* Urbana: National Council of Teachers of English, 1982.

Chamot, Anna Uhl, and J. Michael O'Malley. "The Cognitive Academic Learning Approach." Ed. Pat Riggs and Virginia G. Allen. *When They Don't All Speak English: Integrating the ESL Student into the Regular Classroom.* Urbana: National Council of Teachers of English, 1989. 108–125.

Chan, Michele M. "What We Already Know About Teaching ESL Writers." *English Journal* Oct. 1988: 84–85.

Christensen, Linda. "Teaching Standard English: Whose Standard?" *English Journal* Feb. 1990: 36–40.

Clark, Virginia, et al. *Language: Introductory Readings.* New York: St. Martin's, 1981.

Collier, Virginia P. "How Long? A Synthesis of Research on Academic Achievement in a Second Language." *TESOL Quarterly* 23 (1989): 509–531.

Edelsky, Carole. "Putting Language Variation to Work for You." Ed. Pat Riggs and Virginia G. Allen. *When They Don't All Speak English: Integrating the ESL Student into the Regular Classroom.* Urbana: National Council of Teachers of English, 1989. 96–107.

Farr, Marcia, and Harvey Daniels. *Language Diversity and Writing Instruction.* Urbana: National Council of Teachers of English (ERIC), 1986.

Garcia, Ricardo L. "Linguistic Interference and the Chicano." Ed. Virginia P. Clark et al. *Language Introductory Readings.* New York: St. Martin's, 1981. 539–545.

Gonzales, Roseann Duenas. "Teaching Mexican American Students to Write: Capitalizing on the Culture." *English Journal* Nov. 1982: 20–24.

Gonzales, Roseann Duenas, et al. "The English Language Amendment: Examining the Myth." *English Journal* Mar. 1988: 24–29.

Heath, Shirley Brice. *Ways with Words.* Cambridge: Cambridge UP, 1983.

Holdzkom, David, et al. "What Teachers Can Do With Non-English Speaking Children in the Classroom." *Research Within Reach: Oral and Written Communication.* Washington: National Institute of Education, n.d.

Horning, Alice S. *Teaching Writing as a 2nd Language.* Carbondale: Southern Illinois UP, 1987.

Johnson, David, et al. "Circles of Learning." Association of Supervisors and Curriculum Directors, 1984.

Knop, Constance K. *Limited English Proficiency Students in Wisconsin: Cultural Background and Educational Needs.* Part III. Madison: Department of Public Instruction, 1982.

Meiser, Mary. "A Note on Diversity." *Classroom Activities in Speaking and Listening.* Madison, Wisconsin: Department of Public Instruction, 1991. 6.

Nelson, G. Lynn. "Bringing Language Back to Life: Responding to the New Literacy." *English Journal* Feb. 1991: 16–20.

Paul, Alice. "Cultural Aspects That Affect the Indian Student in Public Schools." *The Native American.* Santa Fe: New Mexico Department of Education, 1973. 10–12.

Peterson, Betty. "Why They Talk That Talk: Language in Appalachian Studies." *English Journal* Oct. 1982: 53–55.

Philips, Susan Urmstorm. *The Invisible Culture.* New York: Longman, 1983.

Raimes, Ann. "Working with International Students and Immigrants." CCCC Winter Workshop on Teaching Composition to Undergraduates. Clearwater Beach, 6 Jan.1992.

_____. "Language Proficiency, Writing Ability, and Composing Strategies: A Study of ESL College Student Writers." *Language Learning* Sept. 1987: 439–468.

_____. "What Unskilled ESL Students Do As They Write: A Classroom Study of Composing." *TESOL Quarterly* June 1985: 229–258.

Riggs, Pat, and Virginia G. Allen, eds. *When They All Don't Speak English: Integrating the ESL Student into the Regular Classroom.* Urbana: National Council of Teachers of English, 1989.

Rodriques, Raymond J., and Robert H. White. *Mainstreaming the Non-English Speaking Student.* Urbana: National Council of Teachers of English (ERIC), 1981.

Schwartz, Judith, ed. *Teaching the Linguistically Diverse.* New York: State English Council, 1980.

Seymour, Dorothy Z. "Black Children, Black Speech." Ed. Paul Eschholz et al. *Language Awareness.* New York: St. Martin's, 1986. 74–81.

Smitherman, Geneva. "White English in Blackface, or Who Do I Be." Ed. Gary Goshgarian. *Exploring Language.* 5th ed. Glenview: Scott, Foresman, 1989. 294–305.

_____. " 'It Bees Dat Way Sometimes:' Sounds and Structures of Present-Day Black English." Ed. Virginia Clark et al. *Language: Introductory Readings.* New York: St. Martin's, 1981. 521–538.

Urzua, Carole. "I Grow for a Living." Ed. Pat Riggs and Virginia G. Allen. *When They All Don't Speak English: Integrating the ESL Student into the Classroom.* Urbana: National Council of Teachers of English, 1989. 15–38.

"What's A Good Technique For Teaching English as a Second Language?" Our Readers Write. *English Journal* Nov. 1986: 76–78.

C H A P T E R   1 1

Understanding Curriculum and Instruction

CHAPTER HIGHLIGHTS

- Defining curriculum and instruction.
- Issues and controversies.
- Components of a curriculum guide.
- Selecting textbooks and software.

> I know that as a person who is planning lessons right at the moment [preparing for a teaching internship] how frightening it is. One worries about how to fill the time, which activities work best, and one's own competence with subject matter.
>
> —*Nik Lightfoot, Senior English Major, 1991*

▼
DEFINITIONS

Curriculum and *instruction* are common words in education, but their very familiarity may mask surprisingly diverse ideas about their meaning. As a result, some degree of confusion or controversy may arise during discussions about curriculum and instruction. Broadly defined, *curriculum* refers to "what" is taught, the content. A curriculum guide generally contains a set of topics, goals, objectives, and student outcomes; it may contain specific materials, methods stated or implied, and evaluation procedures. *Instruction* refers to "how," the methods and strategies by which the curriculum is delivered to students. These definitions are not as straightforward as they sound, largely because people have different notions of what a curriculum is and how it should be organized. For example, some teachers believe that the English language arts curriculum should be centered on basic skills, others believe it should be centered on literature, and still others believe it should be centered on the developing (i.e., maturing) student. Although these areas are not mutually exclusive, choosing to center the curriculum on one of them makes a definite statement about what students in that district will be doing.

▼
WHO DOES THE DEFINING?

In some schools, curriculum occurs by default: Whatever is in the textbook becomes the curriculum, both the content to be taught and the general order or sequence to be followed. In this case, textbook editors and authors, not the district, have determined the curriculum. This raises another question: Just who does determine the curriculum? In some districts, school boards are thought to have this right, determining "what" will be taught although not "how," a matter reserved for the professional teacher. In other districts, administrative positions are designated for "curriculum development and supervision," which means that either administrators alone or administrators working collaboratively with teachers determine the district's curriculum. In some states, curriculum is mandated by the state itself, which means that every district has a common curriculum—a common set of topics, goals, objectives, and outcomes. A state-mandated curriculum may also specify the textbook series, materials, and methods to be used in each of its districts, as well as which tests are to be administered state-wide. The logic here is apparent: If every district has the same curriculum, then every district can use the same test to check on how well students have negotiated that curriculum.

Ideally, assessment *is* linked to curriculum, but the subject of assessment opens up another set of curricular problems. If a state or district mandates certain tests, no matter how inappropriate the test, teachers feel pressured to teach to it. Quite understandably, they want to ensure that their students' test performances are adequate. However, the cost of that one-time performance is high: reducing the English language arts curriculum to an opscan sheet, little circles that fail to consider important aspects of reading, writing, speaking, and listening.

Assessment is important. Teachers need to know how their students are progressing, and districts need to know which areas or programs need more attention. Assessment can be very controversial, however, as evidenced by the fact that it is fiercely debated on every educational level and in state legislatures as well. Because appropriate assessment may be quite costly, especially in disciplines for which machine-scored tests tend to be inappropriate, the English language arts curriculum may not enjoy an assessment program congruent with its stated goals and desired learner outcomes. Findings from such assessment need to be clarified, placed in context, and not allowed to drive curriculum in ways antithetical to effective classroom practice.

▼ _____

CURRICULAR CONTROVERSY

Educators and the general public have personal definitions of curriculum—of just what should be taught in any given discipline and, equally important, just what a student should know or be able to do upon completion of that course of study. These definitions often arise out of a specific ethnic and cultural background, social class, religious view, educational achievement, and a host of other experiences. Moreover, school districts may define curriculum not only in terms of the various disciplines within it but also in terms of the beliefs and values of the community itself. A community whose members believe strongly in parental rights in matters of sex education would probably reflect this belief in its curriculum or, in this case, the lack of school curriculum in sex education. It can be even more complicated. For example, a letter to the editor in a local paper, entitled "Mandated Sex Ed" and signed by "A Mother," stated that "SB [Senate Bill] 324, the mandated sex ed bill, is a blatant attempt to keep parents and local schools from teaching what they want." The author praised a program called *Sex Respect*, took issue with Planned Parenthood of Wisconsin and the ACLU for challenging the program, and ended her letter with this: "I'm hearing much about dysfunctional families these days. How do I know my kids aren't being taught by teachers from dysfunctional homes?" This type of parental interest in curriculum is not unusual, especially when issues involving sex education, racial and ethnic diversity, and basic skills are involved.

A CURRICULAR CONTROVERSY: BACK TO THE BASICS

The Back to Basics movement, which emerged in the 1970s, provides an example of just how community interest and debate may enter into seemingly academic concerns. Back to Basics was (and is) an educational reform movement that addresses core curricular areas such as English and mathematics. Believing that language and writing skills have shown serious deterioration, proponents of Back to Basics advocate a return to curriculum centered in grammar (which means sentence structure, usage, mechanics, and spelling). Through drills and exercises and rote learning techniques, students should master the parts of speech and learn syntax through parsing and diagramming sentences. Students should then demonstrate their mastery through a series of competency tests. Why are people so insistent that this content and instructional method is the answer? They recall their own English classes from the 1950s and earlier, when this content and method were the accepted practice. They believe, therefore, that their own writing competency is the direct result of this practice.

In the mid-1970s, Watergate, Vietnam, and a faltering economy created a somewhat dismal world view and suspicion of just about every type of bureaucratic structure, including the schools. Stephen Judy [Tchudi], a noted English educator, suggests that rumors that teachers were ignoring grammar and correctness and were concerned only with creativity aroused public concern (26). Further, parents and others noted that the traditional courses in English appeared to have vanished altogether, replaced by units with strange names (e.g., Death, Man and His Car). English curricula had shifted to a loosely structured collection of topical units in many schools, although this did not necessarily mean traditional literature was abandoned. And students were rewarded for more individualism and creativity, reflecting a growing interest in curriculum focused on affective goals rather than solely on cognition or basic skills. However, Back to Basics advocates believed that English curriculum was chaotic and that competency had been thrown out or devalued. When SAT verbal scores declined, people were further convinced that students were graduating without literacy skills.

Back to Basics advocates held a somewhat simplistic, perhaps even romantic, notion of the past, schooling in general, and their own English classes. In so doing, they ignored variables that directly affect learning. Prior to the 1960s, young people generally read and wrote more often, watched far less television, and lived in a somewhat more stable society, one less prone to drug and alcohol abuse, shattered families, and devastating economic problems. These are important factors in student achievement and school effectiveness. Additionally, in the 1970s, post-secondary education opened its doors more widely, providing opportunities for students who lacked traditional college preparation. The increase in remedial English classes fed the public's perception that secondary schools were not doing their job. Similarly, young people entering the work force appeared to be less competent in communication skills. A great many people were alarmed. They saw a return to grammar and mastery learning as a solution, and Back to Basics became a national force. However, as Judy points out, Back to Basics advocates, believing they had discovered the "deplorable" state of literacy, were merely part of a legacy that has existed as long as English has been taught. Judy notes, "*Every* generation seems convinced that it is in the midst of a decline in literacy, that standards have fallen, that the schools have been allowed to abolish all concern for the English language" (35).

Addressing Back to Basics, James Moffett attacked the double misnomer of the movement's title, noting that English curriculum, no matter what else it was doing, never left the drills and rules approach to grammar and writing. He contends that if this method worked, it would have done so decades ago, and that a decline in literacy skills cannot be separated from societal changes. Moffett defined the *basics* in the English curriculum as speaking, listening, reading, and writing. These, not some mechanistic parts-to-whole approach to literacy, are the "real basics" (96).

In his new book, *The Unschooled Mind,* Harvard psychologist Howard Gardner argues that "by focusing on basic skills, schools risk suppressing the positive aspects of children's minds—adventurousness, flexibility, creativity—as well as their natural enthusiasm for learning" (cited in Gursky 41). Gardner is not unaware of the controversy in his argument:

> To declare oneself against the institution of the three Rs in the school is like being against motherhood or the flag . . . Beyond question, students ought to be literate and ought to revel in their literacy. Yet the essential emptiness of this goal is dramatized by the fact that young children in the United States are becoming literate in the literal sense; that is, they are mastering the rules of reading and writing, even as they are learning their addition and multiplication tables. What is missing are not the decoding skills, but two other facets: the capacity to read for understanding and the desire to read at all. (cited in Gursky 41)

Because Gardner's work usually attracts national attention, fueling conversations and debate among academics and the general public alike, his assertions about the gap between teaching and genuine understanding will undoubtedly contribute to the ongoing controversy over Back to Basics.

The National Council of Teachers of English (NCTE) argues:

> Public concern about basic knowledge and the basic skills in education is valid . . . [but] the basic elements of knowledge and skill are only part of the essentials of education. In an era dominated by cries for going "back to the basics," for "minimal competencies," and for "survival skills," society should reject simplistic solutions and declare a commitment to the essentials of education. (*Essentials,* n. pag.)

The Council warns against "three easy tendencies" in curriculum and instruction: limiting *essentials* to the three Rs in an increasingly complex society; defining *essentials* by what can be measured; and reducing *essentials* to a few skills "when it is obvious that people use a combination of skills, knowledge and feelings to come to terms with their world" (*Essentials,* n. pag.).

Although the NCTE, along with 24 other professional organizations, called for balanced education in 1978, the issue remains a critical one in the 1990s. Faced with curricular controversy and a movement as persistent as Back to

Basics, teachers need a strong response. For this reason, curriculum and instruction need to be coherent and related directly to how students learn.

▼

CURRICULUM: A JOINT ENDEAVOR

Few curricular areas are as visible as the English language arts. Parents and members of the community ask questions about topics or materials that have been added or dropped, about instructional methods, and about student achievement. They have a right to ask these questions, in terms of both their children's education and the considerable taxes they pay to provide that education. Districts that have a well-defined written curriculum, based on a consistent philosophy K–12, are no doubt better equipped to deal with the challenges.

A district's curriculum reflects not only the policies and standards of the community but also those of the state. Although some states mandate curriculum, most do not. Curriculum is generally developed at district level, with guidance, recommendations, and requirements from the state department of public instruction. John D. McNeil speaks to the importance of local curriculum development:

> Effective schools have a strong sense of community, commonly held goals, and high expectations for students and staff performance. Successful schools are characterized by staff interactions involving aspects of teaching, whereby administrators and teachers work together in planning, designing, creating and preparing materials. . . . (Forward)

In brief, curriculum and instruction that arise out of a collaborative effort stand the best chance of success. Whatever the origin of the curriculum, however, the primary responsibility for it ultimately rests with the teachers who deliver it.

▼

TWO CURRICULAR TERMS: SCOPE AND SEQUENCE

Scope and *sequence* refer to the range or amount of curricular content and its order of presentation. In brief, *scope* tells teachers what content to cover and *sequence* tells them when—the order of instruction. There is no argument about the necessity of understanding appropriate content and sequencing for each curricular level, but there are questions about just how scope and sequence are perceived in the English language arts.

For many experienced teachers, the terms *scope* and *sequence* have traditionally brought to mind a detailed chart of concepts or skills to be introduced, mastered, or reviewed at each level of the curriculum. For example, every use of the comma is labeled for distribution at a specific grade level. Students might be introduced to commas used to separate parts of dates in 3rd grade, review this use in 4th grade, and "master" it in 5th grade. In 10th grade, students would be introduced to commas used with adverbial conjunctions, in 11th grade review, and by graduation "master" this skill.

A colleague refers to this model as the "language arts auto parts catalogue." The analogy is apt for several reasons. First, language and literature are broken down into discrete parts and labeled, ready to be issued at the appropriate moment. Second, the appropriate moment is prescribed: When student X is here, insert concept or skill Y. Third, the underlying assumption is one of the machine not functioning as a whole, not needing all its parts for simultaneous operation. This may be true for cars, but it doesn't work for humans and language. Research in linguistics and psychology as well as in reading and composition shows us quite clearly that language is a matter of synthesis and simultaneous operations, not discrete parts in some linear order. We use language holistically; therefore, we should not teach language as discrete parts. Nor can we assume mastery at a particular grade level—or at all, for that matter.

Some textbook series offer an "auto parts catalogue" scope and sequence, a detailed chart showing the introduction, review, and mastery of every concept and skill in the English language arts curriculum. Districts that use such series as the basis of their curriculum thus subscribe to a "part to whole" theory of instruction. Well-informed teachers would take issue with this approach, understanding that it violates how students learn in the English language arts, although not necessarily in other subject areas more amenable to a "building block" or linear approach.

▼
A SPIRAL CURRICULUM

The language arts do not represent linear learning, or as James Moffett and Betty Jane Wagner put it, growth is not a ladder or stepping stones, metaphors implying that we leave old learning behind as we acquire new. "Most learning is never shed but, rather, becomes assimilated or transformed into more advanced skills and knowledge" (3). A spiral more closely reflects the learning process; it is an old concept, but one not generally applied to curriculum in the English language arts.

Jerome Bruner, one of the most influential cognitive psychologists of our time, argues that any concept can be taught in an intellectually honest way at any time. In the English language arts we can do exactly that with a spiral curriculum: At every level of the curriculum K–12, we can work with the same concept or skill, regardless of the level of student development. We do so with increasing sophistication based on advancing levels of development; we do not, as some textbooks suggest, repeat the same lesson.

Composition is a good example. The concept of audience is quite difficult for primary age students; they simply aren't mature enough to see much beyond themselves. We might refer to audience, asking the child to consider what someone who has never been to the ocean might want to know, for example. But we would not expect the child to handle audience very well. By early adolescence, however, students are much better able to conceive of audience and to entertain more than one point of view. In late adolescence, students can handle multiple points of view, understand the significance of audience in written communication, and more readily manipulate language to respond to audience, no matter how remote it might be. Our focus and emphasis would thus shift, as well as our expectations of what students can do relative to this important writing concept.

In parallel fashion, aspects of literature are understood developmentally and returned to repeatedly. We teach literary character at all levels of the curriculum, but the expected level of response and understanding changes markedly from primary level students to those in senior high. For example, middle schoolers, with their limited experience and maturation, tend to understand characters' actions and responses in rather absolute terms. Juniors and seniors, on the other hand, generally can understand and respond to complex characters, an emerging range of emotions and motivations, and consequences resulting from beliefs and behavior. We would choose material, then, based on this knowledge and on the need to return to increasingly sophisticated handling of character in literature. What we teach changes both in degree and range, and we choose literary materials to match both the concepts being taught and a maturing level of understanding and response.

Thus, in a spiral curriculum, we return to concepts and skills in developmentally appropriate ways, understanding that our students are in a process of maturation—physically, emotionally, and intellectually. We expect students to grow in independence and to achieve greater control over these concepts and skills, and we gear our materials and teaching appropriately. In evaluating students, we expect the majority to demonstrate greater understanding and to articulate it more clearly and thoroughly than younger students. We do not, however, expect uniform understanding and performance.

▼ ——————————————————————————————

ANOTHER CURRICULAR TERM: TRACKING

However much we might talk about "providing for individual differences," tracking at best exists for the benefit of teachers and the listening/busy work mode. At worst, tracking allows us to blame students for our failure to teach them well—all those low-tracked adolescents of whom we ask and expect less and less. (40)

—Nancie Atwell

THE DANGERS OF TRACKING

Tracking, sometimes referred to as ability grouping, is a serious curricular issue and one that has a powerful effect on students. There are polarized points of view about this effect, despite research that indicates tracking is largely negative (Oakes; Gamoran and Berends; Good and Brophy; Maerhoff; Berliner and Rosenshine; cited in George, n. pag.). John Goodlad's study of American schools also pointed to the negative effects of tracking:

> Findings revealed significant differences in curricular content, instructional practices, and elements of the student-teacher relationship. They suggest the probabilities of marked inequities among students in regard to access to knowledge and pedagogical practices. (152)

Goodlad goes on to address another issue within tracking—that the distribution of students shows a disproportionately high percentage of minority students, especially those who are also economically poor, in low-track classes. Goodlad concludes that these students' access to knowledge is thus considerably limited (159). Moffett and Wagner agree. In their view, segregating slower students or students whose language or dialect is different from the mainstream causes *all* students to suffer from a lack of variety in their classes; it also produces negativism in the lower track and elitism in the higher track (38). Ernest Boyer's report on secondary education in America concludes that:

> Putting students into boxes can no longer be defended. To call some students "academic" and others "nonacademic" has a powerful, and in some instances, devastating impact on how teachers think about students and how students think about themselves. (126)

These educators, and others, are not suggesting that students of like interest or ability should *never* be grouped—only that creating a tracking system in which students go for years labeled as "slow," "regular," and "advanced" is a bad idea.

WHY TRACKING PERSISTS

We can understand quite easily how this practice not only came into being but sustains itself. Paul George explains:

> Faced with a dizzying array of differences among the students they attempt to teach, educators have struggled with ways to reduce these differences and make teaching more effective. One very common, and "common sense," way of dealing with these differences has been to divide students into class-size groups based on a measure of the students' perceived ability or prior achievement, and then design or deliver differentiated learning experiences to each group. (n. pag.)

Despite, as George points out, the appeal and apparently sensible goals (e.g., teaching and learning would be more effective and less frustrating), ability grouping simply doesn't work out very well for most students, often because it is very difficult to place students accurately and fairly. Owing to their construction, as well as their bias of race, gender, and social class, tests are often poor indicators of actual ability. This is particularly true with reference to language skills.

THE POWER OF EXPECTATIONS

A second problem with tracking and ability grouping is the lack of expected achievement for students at all levels. Citing recent research studies on academic achievement, George notes that the "expected benefits . . . simply do not materialize . . . at the secondary level, when differences occur, the results are favorable only to students in the highest tracks" (n. pag.). Research findings indicated that bright students were not held back by being in heterogeneously mixed classes, nor were the deficiencies of less capable students more easily remediated in homogeneously grouped classes (Oakes 8, cited in George, n. pag.).

In addressing the third problem with tracking, George notes:

> If the academic gains from tracking are negligible, we could hope that the affective outcomes are positive enough to justify the practice. Unfortunately, this does not appear to be the case. The weight of the research evidence indicates that the effect of tracking on individuals and classroom groups, affectively, is often *powerfully negative,* especially for students in lower tracks. (n. pag.)

Ted Sizer, Director of Research for the Coalition of Essential Schools, believes that because kids are always changing, "tracking flies in the face of rudimentary common sense" and can be both "profoundly cruel and wasteful of talent" ("Restructuring"). His point is well taken when we consider how rapidly middle school students develop within a couple of years, as well as how acutely they respond to a sense of being "different." Self-esteem, once damaged, is difficult to rebuild. Senior high school students also show remarkable growth between their sophomore and senior years; placing them into a three-year curricular track based on performance at age 14 or 15 is questionable.

WHY TRACKING IS UNNECESSARY

Tracking seems particularly unnecessary in the English language arts. If the curriculum is learner-centered, process-oriented, and integrated, students *can* work at varying levels of achievement within a heterogeneous group. Cooperative learning groups provide less capable students the opportunity to learn from their more talented peers in a less competitive environment. Similarly, very capable students can learn important "people" skills within heterogeneous learning groups. All students have talent of some type, and it is more likely to flourish in groups were diversity is valued and cooperation is needed to accomplish the task. In an increasingly pluralistic society, students need exactly that perspective.

Smaller in-class groups created as needed can provide for individual differences. More capable students unquestionably need to be challenged and less capable ones given more time and more assistance. However, these are matters of diverse curricular resources and teaching strategies. Building diversity, flexibility, and reality into lessons is critically important. The expectation that each student can learn—from one another as well as from their teachers—is similarly critical.

▼ ──────────────────────────────────────

THE INTEGRATED CURRICULUM
SPEAKING, LISTENING, READING, AND WRITING

A curriculum built on current research and effective practice in English language arts reflects realities of adolescent growth and development, as well as assumes language arts to be active, interdependent processes linked to experience and purpose. Students gain competency and proficiency in language through use. Students who listen, speak, read, and write gain immeasurably over those who don't. Students who see the language arts as critical to their experience, to meaning that they themselves are creating, not only use but value them. It is imperative, then, that students use *all* the language arts in an integrated fashion.

Integration can be viewed in several ways. Integration of the language arts strands (listening, speaking, reading, and writing) in every lesson, not as separate units, is usually the primary definition of the term. As indicated many times in this text, such integration is essential for students to gain competency and confidence in their oral and written language skills. In planning lessons, then, teachers must consciously devise activities that ask students to read, write, speak, and listen, regardless of the primary emphasis in one of these areas. We will address this more fully when we talk about individual planning and thematic units.

THE LANGUAGE ARTS AND OTHER DISCIPLINES

When educators talk about integrating curriculum, they are sometimes referring to different subject areas being linked with language arts. Writing across the curriculum or language across the curriculum is a common application of this idea. However, despite majors and teacher preparation programs that mandate courses specifically aimed at integration and cross-disciplinary teaching in the middle and senior high school, few teachers have the opportunity to teach in an integrated program. Many secondary teachers report that they have no time for planning within the English language arts department, let alone with other disciplines. Consequently, although many teachers believe that integrating the language arts with other content areas makes sense, writing or language across the curriculum remains an ideal rather than a curricular reality. In elementary schools, teachers have an advantage in that they are often in control of all subject areas, making the integration process a bit less complicated. Many middle schools also plan integrated instruction. Teachers from the core areas (e.g., language arts, mathematics, social studies, and science) plan together, consciously blending knowledge and skills from one area with those from another. In math or science, for example, students may be required to keep a journal or to write out their problem-solving; in social studies, students may use informal classroom drama as a way of understanding the concept or point of view.

Because senior high school teachers most often view themselves as content specialists (i.e., the math teacher, the history teacher), they also tend to view reading and writing as the instructional responsibility of the English teacher. Consequently, integration among content areas in senior high is more often the work of individual teachers than a school-wide curricular design. Ted Sizer, a national leader in school reform, believes the lack of integration in secondary schools is a kind of "intellectual chaos." Students move from bell to bell, hitting the curriculum horizontally in 52 minute snippets. Sizer questions the potential of any authentic intellectual and imaginative work in such a fragmented environment. In most traditional schools, students experience neither the logical connections among various courses nor a time frame for exploration and reflection ("Restructuring").

Some secondary English teachers do an excellent job of bringing history, art, and music into their units, largely because these areas blend so well with literature. Working with science or mathematics, however, is far less common. The language arts offer a powerful means of discovering and applying knowledge, as well as a means of diversifying and individualizing instruction. A curricular goal of integration is worth pursuing.

STUDENT NEEDS AND INTERESTS

Another aspect of integration is placing student needs and interests into the curriculum. How do we know what our students need or what their interests are? How do we find out? Similar questions need to be asked about integration of school with home and community. Moffett and Wagner explain the significance:

> A human being is made to synthesize all forms of experience into one harmoniously functioning whole. If experience is too incoherent to integrate, we may mentally or physically negate what we can't assimilate, as when some students tune out or drop out of school because they cannot fit it into the rest of their life. (36)

This is an important concept. When we think about classes we tuned out and ask why, several reasons come to mind. Were we consistently bored? If so, the materials and instructional approaches probably weren't connecting with our needs and interests. Were we lost? If so, the materials and instructional approaches weren't connecting with our level of understanding or background knowledge. Then we need to consider how a marginal student would feel. Already disconnected from much of the educational process, this student can quite easily sever the tie altogether. "Marginal," incidentally, can refer to students academically gifted, as well as to those academically disadvantaged or disabled in some way.

Moffett and Wagner extend the idea of connecting:

> . . . schools must accept widely varying dialects, lifestyles, values, and ethnic heritages. A student takes both home and school seriously. If they are made to conflict, he is caught in the middle and has to reject one or disguise the conflict from himself. Either choice is terrible education. (36)

We put into a curriculum not only concepts, skills, and topics but also attitudes. If a district ignores multicultural literature, for example, it ignores a body of literature representing many of its students. It also fails to prepare students for a world in which diverse cultures must come together to solve common problems and achieve common goals. If a district, or an individual teacher for that matter, refuses to use adolescent fiction, student needs and interests are being ignored. Exclusions such as these tell us something about the district, as well as about individual teachers. Failure to integrate academic experience with adolescent experience most often translates into either students who skim through the curriculum simply because they are bright and can play the academic game or students who disconnect altogether. Either way, students lose.

▼ ———————————————————————————

A K–12 PERSPECTIVE

Because we teach specific grade levels, it is easy to forget the importance of viewing the curriculum from a K–12 perspective. For this reason, we have been noting how important it is for a consistent approach to the English language arts. Students who are accustomed to writing in a student-centered, integrated language arts approach, for example, would be jolted by a skill-and-drill approach to writing. A colleague recently told of his nephew's experience with inconsistency. All through junior high school, the student was accustomed to a writing workshop approach similar to that advocated by Donald Graves and Nancie Atwell. Global concerns with content took precedence over surface errors; evaluation involved all aspects of composing, not just editing skill. In 10th grade, this student suddenly faced error as the sole determination of his grade. His teacher ignored the development and organization of his work and graded him on his performance in avoiding certain types of syntactic and mechanical errors, usually three per essay. The student, understandably, was upset and questioned this approach. The response: "Oh, you'll get graded on other things next year."

In a district where teachers work together to develop, implement, and maintain the curriculum, this is less likely to happen; in such a district, dialogue among teachers K–12 would bring the various perspectives and knowledge base into focus. Teachers at all levels of the curriculum vary in depth and breadth of professional knowledge, in creativity, and in many other aspects of teaching, including personality and style. Given this variation, we value some colleagues more than others; we must be careful, however, not to dismiss any colleague because he or she teaches at a lower level of the curriculum. The 1st-grade teacher may provide us with the best teaching strategies in the district. Respecting every level of the English language arts curriculum and learning the challenges specific to each level can only enhance our own teaching.

NEEDED DIALOGUE

In a recent course in a suburban school district, elementary and middle school teachers discussed, debated, and challenged senior high teachers on some critical issues: teaching parts of speech, drills, and diagramming sentences. It was clear that middle school teachers were very well informed about research and current practice. It was also clear that the secondary teachers were in a state of dissonance, knowing that what they were doing wasn't good practice but not quite ready to give it up altogether. Because none of them had worked on curriculum together, this course was their first K–12 forum.

One of the middle school teachers, feeling particularly frustrated, told a high school teacher: "The *only* reason I even use or work with grammatical terms is because you [high school teachers] insist kids know them. Even though it doesn't make any difference in writing and takes up time." The high school teacher was startled at this candid declaration but not offended, and from that point on, meaningful dialogue over a critical curricular issue took place. The middle school teacher couldn't understand why high school teachers were insistent upon a practice that has been proven ineffective; the high school teachers had no idea that anyone was upset about it. Students deserve a consistent and coherent approach to instruction from teachers who have figured out what students need to learn and how they can best learn it.

▼ _____

COMPONENTS OF A CURRICULUM GUIDE

Any English language arts guide should show evidence of the assumptions upon which it is based. NCTE's English Coalition Conference noted these for English language arts curriculum at both elementary and secondary levels:

1. The language arts (reading, writing, speaking, and listening) are inextricably linked to thinking.

2. Reading, writing, speaking, and listening are social and interactive.

3. Learning is a process of actively constructing meaning from experience, including encounters with many kinds of print and nonprint texts.

4. Others—parents, teachers, and peers—help learners construct meanings through serving as supportive models, providing frames and materials for inquiry, helping create and modify hypotheses, and confirming the worth of the venture.

5. All students possess a rich fund of prior knowledge, based on unique linguistic, cultural, socioeconomic, and experiential backgrounds.

6. Acknowledging and appreciating diversity is necessary to a democratic society.

In addition to a set of basic assumptions, a curriculum guide should reflect the district's aims or purpose relative to the English language arts. The English Coalition Conference centered its aims on empowerment:

- as lifelong learners with a command of language and a sense of fulfillment and pleasure from the language arts;

- as active inquirers, problem solvers who can use the language arts to gain insight into self and others, who can reflect on their own and others' lives;

- as productive citizens who can use language to communicate with others and take charge of their own lives;

- as theorizers about their own language and learning, who can read, write, and reflect on texts from multiple perspectives.

"Active inquirers" do not emerge from pages of exercises or from silent, non-collaborative classrooms; "theorizers" do not emerge from didactic methods and convergent thinking. Similarly, "lifelong learners" do not develop when ineffective and boring exercises replace actual language experience in reading, writing, speaking, and listening. These aims, then, guide teachers in choosing materials and methods in their classrooms.

Finally, the curriculum should reflect the best knowledge we have about how students grow and change from childhood to young adulthood, how they acquire and process language, and how they acquire and enhance literacy skills. The curriculum should also reflect the reality of individual differences in learning style and rate, as well as the impact of social, cultural, and gender differences.

CURRICULAR GOALS

At program level, goals are usually broadly stated. For example, Wisconsin's *Guide to Curriculum Planning in the English Language Arts* lists this one for composition:

The goals of the writing program are to promote and enhance student proficiency in writing through a commitment to

—a consistent K–12 philosophy for the teaching of writing.
—a realistic view of the developing student, of growth as cumulative.
—a regard for current research on writing and language learning.
—a view of writing as one of the related language arts skills, to be integrated with speaking, listening and reading experiences.
—a process that is holistic rather than an accumulation of skills. (123)

This admittedly broad goal clearly delineates the underlying theoretical and philosophical bases of the composition program. The teaching of writing is to be developmentally appropriate (i.e., congruent with linguistic, cognitive, and social abilities of students at a given age or level), process rather than product oriented (i.e., students understand and work through all phases of composing), holistic rather than mechanistic (i.e., skills are dealt with largely within student writing, not exercises), and consciously integrated with speaking, listening, and reading activities.

Inherent in the goal is a theory of instruction, which Jerome Bruner, an expert in cognition and language, defines as a consistent and coherent statement about what and how students need to learn (40–42). From this theory teachers would know the appropriate materials, methods, and environment needed to achieve the goal—to promote or enhance student proficiency in writing.

▼
CENTERING CURRICULUM ON LEARNERS AND LEARNING

Teachers sometimes tend to think in terms of "what can I teach?" rather than "how can my students best learn?". The English language arts curriculum should arise out of the latter perspective: How can we provide students with experiences that will help them to grow, not only intellectually but also imaginatively? Not only individually but socially? Not only cognitively but also emotionally? Young people are growing, regardless of what we do or don't do. How do we acknowledge the phenomenon of change? How do we prepare for it? How do we capitalize on it? Knowing that the capabilities and needs of a 12 year old are not identical with those of a 15 year old is useless information if we don't act on it. Intervening in the lives of students, however, should demand that we act on the best knowledge our profession has to offer. Once teachers and administrators focus on the learner, other questions flow:

• How might students become self-motivated learners?
• How might students become independent learners?
• How will students acquire competency in basic skills?
• How might students move from competency to proficiency?

- How will students learn to express themselves with confidence and authority in both oral and written language?

Questions guide not only development but also evaluation of the established curriculum:

- Is there a *consistent* theory of instruction?
- Where did it come from (e.g., research, observation)?
- Does the curriculum reflect current research?
- Are course goals, objectives, and materials congruent with current research and effective classroom practice?
- Does the curriculum reflect state standards?
- Does the curriculum reflect the expressed needs and concerns of the community?
- Does the curriculum connect with the "outside world," providing a link to everyday needs, problems, and interests?
- Does the curriculum indicate a concern for lifelong literacy?
- Does the curriculum address a multicultural, pluralistic society?
- Does the curriculum provide for development as students move through a K–12 sequence?
- How are students assessed?
- Are the language arts integrated and balanced?
- Does the curriculum provide for the rapid growth of adolescents? Does it acknowledge individual differences?

Some districts maintain a cycle of curriculum review and revision; others do not, undertaking it only when new state requirements and standards demand it. Whatever the situation, well-informed teachers should be at the center of curriculum development and revision. If a district has an English language arts curriculum that runs counter to well-established research and classroom practice, teachers need to initiate discussion with their administrators and follow through until curricular review and revision are under way. To ensure that students receive a consistent and coherent program in English language arts, a review should be district-wide, cover all grade levels, and involve teachers from each curricular level.

▼ ——————————————————————————————————

FROM GOALS TO OBJECTIVES

Objectives, also referred to as learner outcomes, are usually stated in terms of what students are expected to know or accomplish as a result of instruction. For example, a learner outcome in writing might state that the student will be able to formulate a clear controlling idea; one in literature might state that the student will demonstrate an understanding of figurative language. In most districts, teachers have considerable freedom in developing the ways in which their students achieve these outcomes. This is where individual creativity comes in, a necessary and wonderful part of teaching. At the same time, the district expects teachers to adhere to the theoretical and philosophical base either stated or implied in its curriculum. If, for example, grammar is to be taught contextually, within the writing process, teachers who teach mainly through textbook exercises violate district expectations.

Learner outcomes are the link between the curriculum and appropriate assessment instruments and procedures; therefore, clarity in stating them makes evaluation much easier. As with most aspects of curriculum, problems exist. Some language arts goals (e.g., literary appreciation) are difficult to assess, which can lead districts either to discard the goal or to use inappropriate assessment. Similarly, other language arts goals (e.g., basic writing skills) are more easily and cheaply assessed through machine-scored measures, which are at best an indirect and incomplete measure of student competency. For this reason, discussions of appropriate assessment should be part of curriculum development and revision.

DEVELOPING OBJECTIVES

To paraphrase Neil Postman and Charles Weingartner, authors of *Teaching as a Subversive Activity*, we need to ask ourselves three basic questions (cited in Burton 70):

- What are the students doing?
- What is it good for?
- How do we know?

These questions relate to both district and classroom level objectives. If a curricular goal were, for example, to understand and appreciate figurative language, the objective would be stated as the expected or desired student outcome. That outcome may be cognitive (knowledge), affective (attitude, personal values), skills (performance), or a combination. These are not mutually exclusive, but some district curricula or people may stress one over another. We will return to this idea shortly, for it is another area of curricular controversy. First, let us look at the example of figurative language and how the goal is implemented by an individual teacher.

A district curriculum guide might use language and formatting like this:

Goal: understanding and appreciation of figurative language
Objectives (learner outcomes):

1. Students will understand the distinguishing characteristics of metaphor and simile in both prose and poetry. [cognitive]

2. Students will be able to explain the effectiveness of these devices: how they help the author achieve his or her purpose; how they affect the reader's understanding; why and how they often delight the reader. [affective]

3. Students will demonstrate their understanding through writing tasks that use metaphor and simile. [skill]

Experienced teachers transform the district goal and objectives as they plan specific lessons to achieve the goal. They choose appropriate literature, determine methods for exploring the concepts, develop a variety of oral and written activities, and plan for evaluation. In an individual daily lesson plan book, these important implementation plans might look like the one in Box 11.1.

BOX 11.1   EXAMPLE OF A DAILY LESSON PLAN

5 October   Period 3   Eng. 7   Fig. Lang

Transp. from Lionni/metaphor

Small groups   indiv.   children's lit texts

Full class disc.

Assign   lit text pp. 10–12, 25–28, 31

reading journal response

By means of an overhead projector, the teacher would introduce one concept through children's literature, using direct or indirect teaching methods or both. In structured peer groups, students would then examine different pieces of children's literature, using a guide developed for this purpose. The teacher would circulate among the groups, offering assistance as needed. After 15 minutes, the teacher would call for a full-class discussion. Each group would present its text and ask for response from the entire class. The teacher would bring closure to the discussion and introduce the reading and response assignment for the following day. Good planning is essential to good teaching, and we will address this in more detail later in this chapter.

OBJECTIVES AND CONTROVERSY

In and of themselves, educational objectives in three different domains (cognitive, affective, skills) pose few problems. As students progress through the English language arts curriculum, they need to develop and enhance all three areas. Traditionally, however, cognitive objectives enjoyed the highest status in education; the student's intellectual development was of primary, if not sole, concern. In such a curriculum, teachers sought materials and means to develop the student's *knowledge* base. In literature, for example, teachers chose literary pieces intended to increase student awareness and understanding of specific literary periods or genres. Teachers then designed questions and activities intended to stimulate and enhance cognitive skills. The more students "knew," the better.

In the 1970s, however, some educators came to believe that this area had been overemphasized and advocated that the English language arts curriculum become more humanistic, addressing affective as well as cognitive objectives. Basic skills objectives in reading and writing also became more dominant in the 1970s.

Teachers should know what objectives or learner outcomes are and how to develop them for each of the language arts areas (i.e., listening, speaking, reading, writing, and viewing). Whether objectives are developed formally, perhaps for district-wide curriculum, or informally, for individual units and lessons, is not an issue. The important issue is that teachers think about what they are doing and why. Questioning the value of objectives with reference to students is part of the professional teacher's role.

Finally, English language arts teachers need to ensure that curricular objectives and student evaluation match. Students who have experienced a mismatch attest to the frustration and sense of injustice, feelings that affect their learning and motivation for the rest of the course.

Teachers do face a major question in developing objectives: Should they develop them for an entire class or for individual students? Most teachers develop one set for an entire class or preparation, perhaps acknowledging individual differences only for the most exceptional students. Given their limited preparation time, large classes, and various preparations, it is a reasonable thing to do. However, teachers may be challenged by parents who believe that the learner outcomes and subsequent evaluation fail to acknowledge that students do not all learn in the same way or at the same time. These are legitimate concerns. Providing alternative methods, materials, and means of assessment may be both a necessary and a sound way of approaching every unit. We'll address this in more detail when we talk about individual planning.

▼ ───────────────────────────────

RESOURCES

That English language arts textbooks are *the* curriculum is a reality in some districts. When the texts are congruent with how students learn, allow for diversity, and challenge the learner, the curriculum may be a good one. However, it is not unusual for a text series to be uneven (i.e., some grade levels or areas are excellent, others awful). For this reason, teachers may use the assigned text for some units and ignore it for others. If the text runs counter to current research and practice, some teachers may abandon it altogether. In the 1980s, for example, many teachers began to approach composition as a process rather than a product, addressing skill development as part of revision and editing. Many textbooks published in the 1980s, despite new cover designs, were essentially grammar texts. For these teachers, the text became a reference book, perhaps occasionally used when they wished to focus attention on a single skill. New teachers may feel pressured to use the texts supplied for their classrooms, but they need to question the texts' validity and usefulness.

Because textbooks represent a major investment, most districts use a replacement cycle for each curricular area. Therefore, new texts may be unavailable for a number of years, regardless of significant changes in the field. It is often up to individual teachers, then, to implement new methods and materials as warranted. At the same time, however, they need to maintain both horizontal (i.e., all English language arts teachers at one grade level) and vertical (i.e., K–12, 6–8, 9–12) communication with colleagues. If the school is large enough for a department head, teachers should probably direct their initial questions and concerns to that level. Lacking a department head, teachers can speak with whatever administrator is assigned responsibility for curriculum and instruction in their building.

A district may insist on a K–12, or at the least, 6/7–12 series adoption, largely because it believes such an adoption ensures consistency and continuity. However, if the series is uneven or its approach contrary to what a majority of teachers believe, there is no assurance that any consistency will result. Most districts ask teachers to be part of a textbook selection process, so it's important, despite the hours involved, for new teachers to apply their recent education to this critical work.

▼ ——————————————————————————

EVALUATING TEXTBOOKS
SELECTION CRITERIA

Selecting a textbook can be a challenging task. Because most of us are drawn to attractive packaging, we need to develop a list of criteria that helps us to compare texts on more than just their physical appeal. The criteria emerge from the curriculum itself, as well as from basic principles of language learning, adolescent growth and development, and the specific language arts area(s) addressed in the text. Criteria must also address a pluralistic society, taking account of racial, ethnic and gender concerns, issues, and contributions. The adoption of a social studies textbook series in California serves as a recent example of issues that can arise in adoption of a literature series.

California has a state-mandated curriculum; therefore, the adoption of any textbook is significant. Oakland, which has a predominantly African-American population, recently found itself in the midst of a fierce controversy over the text series that had been approved. Although social studies teachers found the series acceptable, balancing historical perspectives among the various races and ethnic groups in the United States, members of the community did not. At a local school board meeting, the argument was disruptive enough that people had to be removed; the final vote was a victory for members of the community—defeat of the series by one vote. Consequently, social studies teachers in the Oakland district are teaching without any texts, and one 7th-grade teacher noted he had spent more than $3000 of his own money on classroom materials for his students ("Cultural").

Although California, as a state with diverse racial and ethnic groups, addresses a pluralistic society in its curriculum and its textbooks, the question of "to what degree and with what accuracy" continues to arise. This is a serious question, one that certainly faces English language arts educators as well.

We need to point out here that some language arts areas really don't need textbooks. Composition, for example, can be taught without a "composition" text; student drafts become the primary text in a process-oriented curriculum, and only occasionally would students need reference to a text. For this reason, some teachers request class sets of various texts, using them selectively rather than as a primary learning tool. This is also a good way to individualize instruction, to meet the needs of both the most and least capable learners in a single class. Selecting appropriate textbooks and other classroom material is, then, a painstaking process, one that must be informed by research and effective classroom practice and the needs of a diverse student population.

SELECTING ENGLISH LANGUAGE ARTS TEXTBOOKS

NCTE provides teachers with assistance in the selection process through a publication by Timothy Shanahan and Lester Knight. They point out the controversy inherent in the decision to use textbooks: Some teachers view a text as a basic tool, as a way to organize and deliver a standard curriculum to all students, whereas others view a text as a prescriptive curriculum, limiting students and weakening teachers' responsibility and authority (1–2).

The issue of a standard curriculum is one administrators take very seriously. Craig Hitchens, a district-wide director of curriculum and instruction, defines curriculum as a "set of commonly held beliefs and expectations in the area," and from this perspective, he notes that "all students in the district have a right to a quality *common* curriculum." That is, district teachers have a responsibility to work toward the outcomes stated in the district's course of study for the English language arts.

Each student should be guaranteed, regardless of teacher, progress toward the stated goals and outcomes. Although Hitchens also believes that a centralized curriculum and standard textbooks may "lock in" some excellent teachers, he nonetheless argues that all students have a right to a minimum set of outcomes in the English language arts and that these outcomes cannot be left entirely to chance. From the perspective of district administration, then, the textbook may be one way to ensure that teachers pursue those outcomes.

Shanahan and Knight are quick to point out that their guidelines for textbook selection describe quality language arts instruction and not texts per se. They also caution that teachers involved in text selection need to do some research and to keep in mind that the text is only a tool, not a replacement for sound teaching methods. The following guidelines are adapted from Shanahan and Knight and applicable to text selection at any curricular level.

1. Students gain language skills through using language; therefore, the text should encourage language *use*. Activities should emphasize genuine communicative purposes and encourage students to think about their own language rather than about some artificial samples or exercises supplied by others. A violation of this criteria occurs when students are asked to revise and edit a sample essay or to do exercises.

2. The text should emphasize the social uses of language. The purposes for which we use language and literacy "shape the ways in which we use them." Therefore, students need varied experiences that are genuinely purposeful (e.g., to discover, to imagine, to persuade, to establish identity). Texts violating this criterion are those that ask students to fill in the blanks or give short answers or focus on skills unrelated to actual language use.

3. The language arts are integrated, interdependent processes, not separate subject matter. Shanahan and Knight note that "combined instruction has often been found to lead to the higher achievement. Despite this, language arts books have more commonly emphasized particular aspects of language learning while ignoring others" (17). Consistent with this guideline are texts that feature writing responses to quality literature or sharing writing orally. A violation occurs in texts that emphasize grammar, which has "little or no relationship to authentic composition."

4. Texts should recognize growth and development. Kids change, both in what they know and how they come to know. Although, as Shanahan and Knight point out, many subject areas are able to sequence the content of learning, "the process of reading, writing, speaking, and listening cannot be so easily or accurately divided up into types and sequences of information" (21). In the English language arts, "language processes are more alike than different across developmental levels" (21). That is, a 6th grader and a 12th grader both engage in the same processes when writing an essay; the level of sophistication in handling those processes is the difference, not the processes themselves.

   Similarly, Shanahan and Knight argue, their level of sophistication in language itself develops through the creation and use of language across a variety of settings, for diverse purposes—not by adding categories of information. In the English language arts, then, students refine language processes rather than accumulate information (22).

   Textbooks should reflect this process through activities that encourage students to participate in the language arts, not read about them. Texts should also provide teachers with information on adolescent growth and development and assist teachers in modeling various language processes appropriate to the curricular level.

5. Textbooks should assist teachers in assessing student learning. Shanahan and Knight note that good teachers are always observing and evaluating their students' performance; therefore, a text should help them collect data to evaluate growth (26). Traditionally, texts have supplied purely quantitative measures; however, the language arts are qualitative as well. Texts that

help teachers observe and evaluate language in use, implement portfolios, and respond to diversity are better than those using only traditional tests. The teacher's guide should also provide representative student samples, reducing the danger of applying adult standards to adolescents.

6. Textbooks should help kids think. Working with language has the advantage of making our thinking explicit; therefore, text activities should make students more aware of their own thought processes (31). We need and use various means of thinking, and texts should offer students a diverse experience: inventing and creating, drawing on previous knowledge, consolidating new information, solving problems, reformulating knowledge, analyzing critically, and evaluating. Activities that depend upon cooperative learning groups, for example, foster thinking skills.

7. Textbooks should respect our pluralistic society. We know that "different linguistic, cultural, ethnic, racial and gender groups use language in different ways" (36). A literature textbook should contain a balanced selection of representative pieces (not tokens). A text that ignores culture altogether or negatively portrays a minority group, through inference or illustration, should be rejected. A language text should address language differences, treating all dialects as variants of equal communicative value, with the goal of enhancing understanding and interpersonal communication. The relationship between our language and our culture should be clear.

8. The centrality of the language arts in all subject areas should be affirmed. Although reading, writing, speaking, and listening take place in every discipline, each requires or emphasizes slightly different reading or learning strategies. Ideally, teachers in other disciplines teach these; realistically, most schools expect English language arts teachers "to take care of" all areas of language teaching and learning. Given this, texts that provide experience with a variety of subject areas (e.g., non-fiction) or use thematic units drawing upon a wide selection of oral and written language activities are preferable. Activities that involve students in cooperative projects are also desirable. Literature texts that contain only fiction and poetry selections violate this guideline.

Teachers who would like to see these guidelines transformed into an evaluation chart should consult Shanahan and Knight.

BEING A GOOD SCAVENGER

Teachers can supplement textbooks with acquisitions from the school library, the public library, and used book stores. The school librarian is often a wonderful resource, not only in providing a constant flow of information about new works of fiction and non-fiction but also in assisting teachers as they develop thematic units. One junior high school English teacher in a rural district enlisted the help of the school librarian in selecting more than 20 adolescent novels to stash in her classroom for several weeks. Similarly, a children's librarian at the nearest public library, once drawn into the unit's theme and goals, prepared stacks of adolescent fiction and non-fiction for the classroom. With their help, the teacher was able to meet diverse student needs and interests, ranging from borderline mental retardation to intellectually gifted in one class.

The public library is also a good source of videos and cassettes, often matching or complementing literary selections. With the abundance of video stores, teachers now also have a low-cost alternative to ordering special films. Used book stores offer another low-cost source for alternative reading selections. Meeting the diverse needs of students is very challenging, but maintaining a classroom supply of paperbacks and periodicals can ease things somewhat. Even students who appear to dislike everything else about school and reading appear to like the *Guinness Book of Records,* books of trivia on sports, cars, music, or any aspect of popular culture, and word games or puzzles.

▼

EVALUATING SOFTWARE

With the impact of technology in the English language arts classroom, many teachers are called upon to evaluate software as well as textbooks. The NCTE's Committee on Instructional Technology, established in 1981, developed a set of criteria that could be used by educators at all curricular levels. The committee stipulated, however, that no single evaluation form could be applied to all software; thus, they tried to develop criteria "that embraced the most dynamic capabilities of the computer, and at the same time, to take into account the various instructional strategies which could be included in the design of a software program" (n. pag.).

The committee cautions that instructional software is still in an early stage of development, so that evaluation of it is an imprecise process. They recommend that teachers judge it against what publishers claim it can do and compare it with other products attempting to teach the same concepts or skills. The committee further recommends that teachers work through the software themselves, as well as allowing students to try it out. The committee believes that student response may be the ultimate evaluation of how well the software meets its claims.

The *Guidelines for Software Review and Evaluation* contains five major sections and an addendum for specific software purposes (e.g., word processing/text editing, simulation/problem-solving). Briefly, the major sections to evaluate single lessons are these: management features (e.g., record keeping system and options for teacher modification); content (e.g., accuracy, value, appropriateness, options for teacher modification); instructional strategy (e.g., practice, examples, logic of sequence, feedback, cognitive value, application); ease of operation (e.g., clarity of directions, student independence); supplementary materials (e.g., teacher's guide, student material, tests). The *Guidelines* offer specific criteria under each category, the most extensive in instructional strategy.

In the addendum, educators are asked to choose the category description that best matches the software under review. In "simulation/problem-solving," for example, the program would be geared to discovery learning and decision-making. Thus, teachers would evaluate the software on its realism and relevance to acquisition of English language arts skills, as well as the more procedural aspects of the program. Because word processing and text editing are among the most common types of software used in English language arts programs, the committee has provided its most extensive list in this section: management features, safeguards, editing, visual presentation, and printing. With these guidelines, teachers can easily add or delete criteria to complement the software under review. In addition to the guidelines published by the NCTE, teachers should check professional journals in the English language arts for current information on educational software.

DISCUSSION QUESTIONS

1. Ted Sizer, Professor of Education at Brown University, believes:

    > Obviously a low premium is placed on reflection and repose [in the American high school]. The student rushes from class to class to collect knowledge. Savoring it, it is implied, is not to be done much in school, nor is such meditation really much admired. The picture that these familiar patterns yield is that of an academic supermarket. The purpose of going to school is to pick things up, in an organized and predictable way, the faster the better. (*Horace* 80)

    Is this a fair assessment of today's secondary schools? Does this description fit middle school as well as senior high? What does this portrait have to do with curriculum and instruction in the English language arts?

2. Lucy Calkins, an English educator at Columbia University Teacher's College, similarly notes:

    > Like our society, our schools have adopted a one-draft-only mentality. Their motto appears to be "get it done" and "move along." It is a sign of the times that "silent sustained reading" lasts only twelve minutes. The entire school day is fragmented: ten minutes on spelling, six minutes on a ditto, fifteen minutes for a class discussion, three minutes to copy off the board. [Donald] Graves describes this as the cha-cha-cha curriculum. Many researchers emphasize that because the school day is so segmented, teachers spend an average of 40 percent of their time on choreography. We move the class from one thing to another: "open this book," "close that one," "get such and such out," "put it away." . . . (40)

    What do you think of Calkins' metaphor of the "one-draft-only" curricular mentality? Consider the language arts from this perspective. What examples in listening, speaking, reading, and writing can you draw from your own middle and senior high school experience? Now consider Graves' descriptor, the "cha-cha-cha curriculum." Is Graves overstating the case? How do you know? What are the implications here for your own curriculum planning and instructional methods?

3. In Charles Dickens' *Hard Times,* Master Thomas Gradgrind lays out a curricular plan (Signet ed. 11–12):

> Now what I want are facts. Teach these boys and girls nothing but Facts. Facts alone are wanted in life. Plant nothing else, and root out everything else . . . Stick to the Facts, Sir!

Is Master Gradgrind correct in his assessment that "Facts alone are wanted in life"? What would you consider examples of "facts" in English language arts? What would you consider "processes"? Has the English language arts curriculum been guilty of planting too many facts? Of being preoccupied with content? With testing content? Consider the world your students will live in: Would facts or processes be more critical to their well-being? How do you know? What do you envision as critical components of an English language arts curriculum of the 21st century? Justify your choices.

SUGGESTED ACTIVITIES

1. Examine a series of English language arts texts for three successive grade levels (middle school/junior high school or senior high school) in both a literature series and a grammar/composition series. What are the underlying assumptions of these texts?

   • Are the language arts integrated in the lessons and assignments?

   • Are the language arts treated as processes or as so much subject matter to be divided up?

   • Are language and learning approached holistically or as bits and pieces, as parts to be assembled?

   • How is the student viewed? As using language to communicate? As capable of discovering language principles? As a meaning maker?

   • Is the content of high interest to young people?

   • Does the content reflect the diversity of gender, race, ethnicity, and social class within our society?

2. Is the curriculum built in a linear (building block) or spiral fashion? Check the teacher's edition for a formal scope and sequence; check content in the text to see how it is approached in each successive year. Read the preface or author's introduction to the text(s). What do you learn? Review Shanahan and Lester's guidelines for selecting texts before making your decision about whether not to recommend these texts for district adoption.

REFERENCES

Assumptions, Aims, and Recommendations of the Secondary Strand. Comp. George B. Shea, Jr. English Coalition Conference. Urbana: National Council of Teachers of English, n.d.

Boyer, Ernest L. *High School: A Report On Secondary Education in America.* New York: Harper, 1983.

Bruner, Jerome S. *Toward a Theory of Instruction.* Cambridge: Harvard UP, 1966.

Committee on Instructional Technology. *Guidelines for Review and Evaluation of English Language Arts Software.* Urbana: National Council of Teachers of English, n.d.

"Cultural Kaleidoscope." *McNeil/Lehrer News Hour.* 28 Nov. 1991.

English Coalition Conference. *The Essentials of Education: A Call for Dialogue and Action.* Urbana: National Council of Teachers of English, n.d.

George, Paul S. *What's the Truth About Tracking and Ability Grouping, Really? An Explanation for Teachers and Parents.* Gainsville: Teacher Education Resources, 1986.

Goodlad, John I. *A Place Called School.* New York: McGraw-Hill, 1989.

Gursky, Daniel. "The Unschooled Mind." *Teacher Magazine* Nov.–Dec. 1991: 39–44.

Hitchens, Craig. Personal interview. 14 April 1991.

Judy [Tchudi], Stephen. *The ABC'S of Literacy: A Guide for Parents and Teachers.* New York: Oxford UP, 1980.

Lightfoot, Nik. Personal interview. 8 August 1991.

McNeil, John. Forward. *Curriculum Design: A Handbook for Educators.* By Kathleen M. Wulf and Barbara Schave. Glenview: Scott, Foresman, 1984.

Meiser, Mary. "A Perspective on the Guide: A Curricular Framework for the Language Arts." *Wisconsin English Journal* Oct. 1986: 10–13.

Moffett, James. *Coming on Center: English Education in Evolution.* Portsmouth: Boynton/Cook Heinemann, 1981.

Moffett, James, and Betty Jane Wagner. *Student-Centered Language Arts and Reading, K–13: A Handbook for Teachers.* 2nd ed. Boston: Houghton, 1976.

Mother. Letter, "Mandated Sex Education." *Leader-Telegram.* Eau Claire, WI: 8 Nov. 1991.

Shanahan, Timothy, and Lester Knight. "Guidelines for Judging and Selecting Language Arts Textbooks: A Modest Proposal." *NCTE Concepts Paper No. 1.* Urbana: National Council of Teachers of English, 1991.

Sizer, Theodore R. "School Restructuring." University Summer Forum: What Do We Want From Our Schools? Madison, WI, 18 June 1991.

———. *Horace's Compromise: The Dilemma of the American High Schools.* Boston: Houghton, 1984.

Wisconsin Department of Public Instruction. *Guide to Curriculum Planning in the English Language Arts.* Madison: Wisconsin Department of Public Instruction, 1986.

CHAPTER 12

Planning for Classroom Instruction

CHAPTER HIGHLIGHTS
- The challenges and realities of teaching: kids, chaos, and inequality.
- Principles of planning.

> Good teaching consists of the making and adjusting of day to day plans and depends upon a delicate balance between rational order and intuitive spontaneity. (27)
>
> —*Editorial Staff,* The English Journal

▼ ───

A REALISTIC VIEW OF PLANNING

Effective teachers plan well, laying out units and daily lessons designed to provide their students with a coherent course of study. Despite this, they face days when the reality of teaching—of dealing with students with diverse and complex needs—defies even the best planning. Teaching is more complex and unpredictable than we like to admit. As Joseph McDonald, a 17-year teaching veteran, succinctly summarizes it: "Teaching is a messy, uncertain business" (54). McDonald voices what many experienced teachers feel, that experience allows them to cope with uncertainty—not eliminate it. He depicts what he calls a "wild triangle of relations—among teacher, students and the subject—whose dimensions continually shift" at the core of teaching. Consequently, he believes that teachers rarely have "clean evidence" of what is happening both to themselves and to their students. "Technique," he notes, "however proved by research and practice, however skillful the application—is always hostage to so much else":

> the appearance of spring in the air or a bee in the room, the complicated chemistry of a roomful of humans constructing meaning together, the extent to which the conditions of their lives outside the room that day weigh on any of them that day. (54)

Like McDonald, because we have been there, we believe that "beginning teachers are astounded by these complexities and may try to pretend them away" (54). There is no magic answer to the complexity, other than expecting it.

No matter how well we plan, we simply cannot eliminate the variables involved in how and when people learn. If we need a rule of thumb for dealing with the inevitable clash between reality and our planning, it would be "go with the reality." Even with 18 year olds, the sight of a wasp swooping around the lights causes a lesson to cease. The loss of five minutes is hardly cause for alarm. Neither is a lesson that "bombs," for whatever reason. No matter how experienced we become, we will always be confronted with situations that are not what we planned and certainly not what we hoped for. Despite good planning, many aspects of teaching are trial and error. The saving grace of that is experience. The more we have, the more confidence we gain. Consequently, we are far less likely to be either totally surprised or totally devastated by events or people that sweep in and destroy our carefully designed plans. Sometimes we unwittingly sabotage our own lessons by not thinking through our expectations against the framework of student interest or ability.

One very experienced teacher we know provided a good example of this. Working with creation myths, she asked students to compare how various ancient cultures viewed the act of creation (i.e., a creator, creation of the world). Although she provided the students with a structure through which to examine the myths, the majority of them had a great deal of trouble, which showed up graphically in their essays. She had overestimated their ability to read and analyze the myths, as well as their ability to convey whatever understanding they had in written form. All her daily lesson plans went out the window, lost to reality. She simply had to start over, providing far more in-class assistance than had originally planned. However, the more reality teachers deal with, the more they tend to recall it when they rework or make new lessons or units. This teacher still uses creation myths but with far greater oral work and with students supported in collaborative working groups.

▼

SOME ACTIVITIES FOR CHAOTIC DAYS

In the course of any semester, we can expect days or even entire weeks that are chaotic. Groups of students are suddenly pulled out for testing, a sporting or musical event interrupts the normal schedule, or holiday expectations make students restless. Knowing this, many teachers keep a supply of materials or activities just for those days. Word games and puzzles, trivia books, special-interest magazines (e.g., cars, sports, "beauty," music) appeal to most students of any age. For some reason, the *Guinness Book of Records* never fails to hold student interest. Another fascinating book is David Macauley's *The Way Things Work*, explaining the workings of hundreds of things from levers to lasers. Few students, even the most physics-phobic, would resist playing with the idea that the principle of the zipper on their jeans is the same as that which built the pyramids. New forms of puzzles involve students in reading. *Murder Most Artful*, for example, requires reading a short whodunnit, and then, with the clues provided, building the puzzle to solve the murder involving struggling artists, forgery, and upscale galleries. *Sonata for a Spy*, as the title suggests, might appeal to the music contingent in a class.

A very different approach to literature can be found in *The Dictionary of Imaginary Places* by Alberto Manguel and Gianni Guadalupi, a guide to more than 1200 cities, countries, and continents invented by storytellers reaching back to Homer and including our own age. Students could easily become absorbed in this richly illustrated work. The list could go on. Teachers need only examine what's available at local book stores, toy stores, and—location permitting— museum shops. Most teachers we know are regular packrats, accumulating instructional materials the way other people collect knickknacks. It's a habit well worth developing, one that can save the day when chaos looms large.

Another habit worth cultivating is that of reading to students. No matter what else is going on, most students respond instantly and well to a good tale, especially when they need only listen. Teachers who keep a good supply of short stories or novels on hand, just for those days when students are restless, have less trouble maintaining control. At the same time, these activities do involve students in the language arts. Whether they are listening to a story or to a classmate recite weird facts from some book or magazine, they *are* listening. When they work through a word game, they are exercising thinking skills and often building vocabulary. In solving a puzzle, they are similarly engaged in higher-order thinking and, if working collaboratively, are putting speaking and listening skills to good use. With very young children, we tend to view play as purposeful and necessary; we should view occasional classroom play at middle and senior high levels in the same way. Planning for the occasional day or week of chaos makes good sense.

▼

OTHER REALITIES FOR THE BEGINNING TEACHER

Beginning teachers may find themselves running a more structured classroom than they imagined or would like, not only in their academic planning but also procedurally. Middle school and senior high students have had years in which to develop certain expectations of what teachers and school are all about. Teachers who depart radically from those expectations may be in for some shocks, simply because students, regardless of what they may say, like security and predictability. They also like to test their teachers. This is not perverse, just kid behavior.

And for some students, school is simply another "way station" in an unhappy world. They may come to school hungry, lacking sleep, lacking a nurturing and supportive environment; for these students, school holds little relevance. As the principal at a southern California middle school noted, "We can't fix the world" ("Good Morning, John Adams"). This perspective, however tragic, is reality. The principal also noted that in America, we try to educate everyone who comes through our doors, whether they are children of poverty or of traditional families or drug babies. Sometimes, teachers simply cannot reach students, no matter how often they try.

What can beginning teachers do? Above all, they can be consistent and fair with students. Few things rankle adolescents as much as the sense that they are being treated like yo-yos or unfairly or differently because of who they are. Middle school students in particular may react (or over-react) to a sense of inconsistency, largely because they themselves are in the midst of tremendous emotional and physical changes. When we tell students what we expect—in behavior, in work habits, in classroom procedures—we need to stick to it. If we need to make changes, we should tell students what we are doing and why, involving them in their own classroom. We are the adults, and there is no question that we need to set and maintain guidelines. However, the more we involve students in decision-making and the more we talk with them rather than at them, the better.

Following what they themselves have experienced, beginning teachers may talk too much and fail to listen to their students. Heather Berry, a 9th-grade student, said this in a letter to the editor of a local paper:

> Everyone says that in high school you are getting prepared for the rest of your life. Then maybe people should start treating us like adults instead of little kids. Even though I am 'only a freshman,' I feel very strongly in this matter and feel it shouldn't be taken lightly. Everyone has a right to be heard, even young people.

Berry was responding to being ignored, in favor of a parent speaking, at a local school board meeting. She and a number of friends were there to defend a teacher. Her point that young people deserve to be heard is a legitimate one, in the classroom and in the board room. In taking young people seriously, we build their self-esteem, teach them important communication skills, and learn important lessons for instructional planning.

Keeping one's sense of humor, especially in middle school, should be a priority. As noted earlier, things can and do go wrong, no matter how well we plan and prepare. We all tend to take ourselves a bit too seriously when we are new to the job, very conscious of our limited experience and caring that we do the best job we can with our students. A sense of humor goes a long way in helping us not only to get through an occasional bad day but also to enjoy the eccentricity of kids and teaching.

If students are truly disruptive, however, teachers need to have their own procedures, as well as know school procedures, for handling the situation. Berating a student in front of peers, for example, is the worst response possible. Ridicule is also an inappropriate response. Sometimes moving a student or talking to the student outside of the classroom works. Other times it doesn't. Talking to experienced teachers who seem to have good rapport and classroom control is one of the best ways of learning about what may or may not work in a particular school. Teachers also need to know what is considered serious enough to send a student out of the classroom and to whom that student should be sent.

▼ ────────────────────────────────────

THE ULTIMATE REALITY: ALIENATED STUDENTS

Recently, *The English Journal* addressed the question of alienated students through articles, letters, and rebuttals. Response varied to the question of just what teachers can do with students who "are as big as we are, who don't care about much of anything, who don't want to be in school and make that clear very loudly" (cited in Johannessen 72). Some teachers believe that the most one can do is "survive in a kind of holding pattern in which despair is a mere arm's length away" (Johannessen 72).

Others believe teachers can implement strategies to help themselves and these "unteachable" students. Johannessen is one of these teachers. He advocates actively seeking administrative assistance, rather than assuming that administrators don't care or won't help to whatever extent they can. Johannessen found that sometimes administrators are as frustrated as the teachers, and it is only through dialogue and cooperative planned action that problems are resolved. He suggests (73) four ideas to gain administrative help:

1. Initiate a meeting among the building administrator and teachers sharing the disruptive student; draw up a contract stating classroom expectations and the consequences for failure to meet them.
2. Document specific disruptive behaviors and make the administrator aware of them.
3. Invite the administrator to class for first hand observation.
4. Ask the administrator to set up a parent conference to discuss the problem and possible solutions.

Johannessen's next idea grew out of his observation that he was "struggling with a curriculum that seemed to be designed more for the teachers than for the students":

> We stumbled through a vocabulary book that was insulting busywork; we plodded through seemingly endless grammar exercises that taught nothing and increased student resentment of me and the school; and we tried to get through Aldous Huxley's *Brave New World,* a task which proved to be an exercise in futility. (73)

He and a colleague then determined what their students might be interested in reading and selected new materials. He believes subsequent success must be credited to materials that served the students' needs and activities that engaged the students in their own learning. Johannessen took issue with another English educator who believed that "any set of materials, any curriculum . . . if taught by a person passionately, truthfully convinced that it matters for teachers and students—will work" (cited in Johannessen 75). We tend to agree with Johannessen. For students who have difficulty reading, *Macbeth* or *Great Expectations* is a poor choice. *The Outsiders,* on the other hand, has a good chance of touching even the most alienated.

Similarly, students who are presented with exercises rather than opportunities for engaging in appropriate reading, writing, speaking, and listening activities are understandably turned off, even rebellious, in the face of language unconnected to their interests or their lives. In the course of implementing new materials and methods, Johannessen learned that "remedial students can and will learn if given a chance" (76). He admits that remedial or alienated students can be a trial, making teachers "downright angry," but he challenges those who believe these students are unteachable.

▼
THE LARGER PROBLEM

One thing these difficult students need is an environment conducive to learning, which may be hard to achieve given the current economics of both urban and rural education. Schools are *not* equal. School budgets set by tax bases result in disparity: Rich districts with large tax bases can and do spend more on schools. As Tamara Henry and William M. Welch point out ("Fundamentally Unfair" 3A), "The difference in education spending between poor neighborhoods and the more affluent ones is startling":

> The Coalition for Equity in Educational Funding, a group of 40 mostly rural districts in Virginia, says affluent districts in the state spend about $8000 per pupil, more than twice the amount in poorer counties. The group says it could cost the state $500 million a year to redress the imbalance. The gap is even larger in other states. In Illinois, the most impoverished school district spends less than $2100 per pupil while the wealthiest spends more than $12,000. The state average is $4500.

Students who are crammed into small rooms, forced to sit in beaten-up desks, and surrounded by peeling paint can hardly find comfort in learning. And teaching in such surroundings takes a great deal of "grit."

Poor neighborhoods also face violence and deprivation of even the basics of life: food, adequate shelter, and clothing. Teachers in such districts find their students' needs overwhelming, and "in neighborhoods seared by poverty, violence and neglect, just getting children to school is a victory" (Henry and Welch). Although many teachers are dedicated to the challenge, many more find it too much to deal with. The problem then continues to cycle. As Superintendent Howard Fuller of the Milwaukee Public Schools remarked: "If you have people standing in front of those kids who don't love them, care about them, respect them, learning is not going to take place" (1A).

▼
PERSONAL DILEMMAS

Regardless of where they teach, teachers may face the dilemma of whom must they please: themselves, the school, or the community. Teachers who abide by the standards, values, and beliefs of the school or community and ignore their own may find themselves frustrated and angry much of the time. Teachers who completely ignore the norms and mores of school or community may find themselves out of a job. Teachers often have strong ideas about freedom of speech and other rights guaranteed by our Constitution. No matter what they believe personally, however, they find themselves in trouble if they attempt to use a controversial, censored book as a class project. Similarly, teachers who convey their personal convictions about controversial subjects such as abortion within the structure of their class lessons may find themselves in trouble. For this reason, teachers who have exceptionally strong religious or social beliefs may choose to teach in schools that match their own beliefs and values and operate independently of state support.

Failing to follow the district's curriculum in individual planning and implementation is another area with serious consequences for teachers. If the district says traditional grammar is to be taught but a teacher refuses to do so, a violation of district expectations occurs. Being "right" is not much consolation when one is out of a job. What does a teacher do in this kind of situation, when the curriculum clearly is out of sync with learners and research? The solution is to work with the district and the community to educate people, despite the delicacy of the task. Craig Hitchens, a district supervisor of curriculum and instruction, believes that well-informed teachers need to assist in curricular change. John Fortier, another district coordinator of English language arts K–12, agrees, noting that unless teachers get involved, they are stuck with what they get. Incidentally, teachers have been known to teach only enough traditional grammar to ensure that students are not at risk when they move to the next curricular level, and for the most part, to teach grammar contextually, in ways congruent with the way language is learned. What is critical, whatever the situation, is that teachers do work on district issues of curriculum and instruction, despite the personal freedom enjoyed in individual lesson and unit planning.

INDIVIDUAL PLANNING

> Teaching is the art of blending a conscious agenda with the needs of the students. The best teachers, like jazz musicians, collect knowledge and resources, so they can move where meaning beckons. (47)
>
> —*Mark Vogel*

In their 1975 English education textbook, Dwight Burton and his colleagues offer a useful framework for planning units and lessons. They ask teachers to consider how they would plan if:

- They had no textbook.
- No one was required to be in their class.
- They had no school building, only the community.
- They had no set curriculum; they had to justify what they use and do by "what can I do to help kids survive, get on, in today's society?

- Their salary really depended upon how well they can help students solve problems in everyday life.
- Their salary depended upon how much they helped the average and below average kids. (37)

In responding to these provocative questions, teachers are forced to examine their assumptions about teaching and the English language arts. The questions are well worth serious thought and response. It's easy to get lost in the demands of day-to-day teaching, to forget some very basic beliefs about what we do and why, and to fail to examine our daily lessons against those beliefs.

Neil Postman and Charles Weingartner, in *Teaching as a Subversive Activity*, offer a few questions for daily consideration: "What am I going to have my students do today? What is it good for? How do I know?" (cited in Burton 70). These are not rhetorical questions. Rather, they are at the core of what teachers do day in and day out. They should be part of our planning.

New teachers sometimes overplan. This is normal. And they find some things out only by trial and error—how long things take, how well certain materials or methods work. In brief, planning and reality do not always match. This shouldn't be upsetting. One thing that teachers do need, however, is a certain predictability about what goes on in the classroom. Lucy Calkins, a teacher-researcher in English language arts, tells us why:

> I have finally realized that the most creative environments in our society are not the kaleidoscopic environments in which everything is always changing and complex. They are, instead, the predictable and consistent ones: the scholar's library, the researcher's laboratory, the artist's studio. Each of these environments is deliberately kept *predictable* and *simple* because the work at hand and the changing interactions around that work are so unpredictable and complex. (12)

▼ ───

CLASSROOM CLIMATE

Aligned with classroom predictability is classroom climate. Climate is just what it sounds like, the atmosphere or environment in which teaching and learning take place. Climate may refer to a physical, emotional, or intellectual environment, or more commonly, a blend of these. Climate has a major effect on what happens and on the success or failure of the plans. It is definitely something teachers create and control. The rapport that teachers establish with the students and the rapport that students develop and maintain with their teachers and with one another are critical. In composition class, for example, a collaborative writing task as a first assignment not only makes students externalize the writing process, negotiating it all the way, but also helps them get to know one another more quickly. They start to feel comfortable sharing their ideas and their writing, the basis for the entire semester's work in peer response groups. They need to feel that their class is a safe place. It *must* be a safe place because they will be asked to share their heartfelt thoughts and ideas on paper, where they are most visible and most vulnerable to criticism of both substance and form.

The environment is fashioned by the classroom's physical structure, as much as its emotional one, which may influence it to a certain degree. That degree may depend upon the relative wealth and well being of the district and its schools. As indicated earlier, some schools are poor physical environments for learning: dirty, peeling paint, broken-down desks, cramped and poorly ventilated classrooms. Teachers in these schools often add whatever they can to brighten up the area, but the environment still conveys a mood of neglect, reflecting the larger social problem. Nonetheless, we have seen extraordinary teaching and learning in schools that defy normal standards and expectations of a working environment. Teachers in such schools are often masterful in creating a classroom environment regardless of physical surroundings.

Within any classroom, teachers can make some important "people" changes relative to furniture and space. Row upon row of desks facing forward, for example, is not very conducive to discussion. Group work can take many configurations, from four desks pushed together to a circle arrangement. Some teachers keep a quiet spot in the back of the classroom for students to do independent editing, or keep a space for a table and a few chairs where they can meet with students who need individual help, conduct group minilessons, or have a student assist a peer. Nancie Atwell reminds us of another spatial relationship: "A curriculum puts limits on learning, kids' and teachers', spelling out what may be covered or orchestrated from behind a big desk" (21).

Atwell's point is well taken. "Orchestrated from behind a big desk" relates to whether teachers see themselves as the sole conductor or not, if they stay behind the desk. It sends an obvious message of authority and control. This is not to suggest that teachers don't need control; they do. But it is a matter of perception and degree. While doing a clinical supervision practicum in one of the nation's oldest independent schools, one teacher learned the difference.

In a 7th-grade classroom, student desks were arranged in various ways but never in rows. There was a single student desk off to the side, which the English teacher used. It was always overflowing with books and papers, and David could never quite keep things in place, including his own adult frame in a small adolescent space. After class one day, she asked David why he used this desk, which was obviously uncomfortable for him in many ways. He didn't respond right away, but then said, "I don't know. Or maybe I do. I guess I don't want the kids seeing me as *the* authority, the person behind the big desk." Verbalized or not, David's personal sense of authority and control had a profound effect on curriculum and instruction in his classroom.

David believed in and practiced cooperative learning, viewing himself as part of that learning circle, the ridiculously small desk a physical symbol. The rigidity of many classrooms was absent both physically and emotionally. These students were trusted with movement and with talk and were expected to work together productively. And they did, largely because David wasn't worried that they were wasting time, nor that he would be perceived as less of an "authority."

David knew 7th graders. He thus knew what environment would capture their restless bodies and minds, at least for an hour.

We need to keep in mind just how powerful classroom climate is. Students know when they are valued—by how often we use collaborative rather than isolating, competitive tasks; by how well we listen, rather than just hear; by how well we tolerate the errors and false starts that all of them make; by how we manage to include the most shy or the most rebellious among them; by how we respond to the diversity of background and capability. None of this is easy to do; much of it takes time, patience, and experience. The important thing is to teach with clear ideas about what to do, why to do it, and who benefits most from it.

▼

DO IT YOURSELF

If you don't know where you're going, then any path will take you there.

The Cheshire Cat,
Lewis Carroll, Alice in Wonderland

The Cheshire Cat's observation is an apt one when we consider curriculum from the perspective of individual classroom planning. New teachers often wonder just how to determine the amount of time to give to any particular unit of work or what should be included in a unit. Recent issues of *The English Journal* include advertisements to solve this problem. For $19.95, someone offers to "Cut your planning and preparation time from hours to minutes!" through literature unit plans "designed to be practical and easy to follow." These plans, available for a range of novels and plays from *Huck Finn* to *Animal Farm,* *Hamlet* to *The Glass Menagerie,* include: "unit outline, objectives, daily lesson plans (with objectives and activities), reading assignments, writing assignments, study guide questions (with answer key), group activities, extra activities, unit test, bulletin board ideas, ready-to-copy student materials." We are informed that "many units also include lecture and note-taking sessions, background information, vocabulary or grammar lessons, and miscellaneous helpful hints!"

We have no idea how good these units are; some may contain useful material. Even if they do, we shouldn't use them. Preparing to be an English language arts teacher means preparing to make decisions on what to teach and how to teach it. What's more, one of the most satisfying and pleasurable parts of teaching is developing units. We shouldn't let anyone, especially a commercial vendor, take away that responsibility and pleasure.

▼

PRINCIPLES OF PLANNING

When educators talk about principles of planning, they generally include value, appropriateness, flexibility, involvement, and feedback and evaluation

(Burton et al. 47–48). *Value* refers to the worth of the content—that what we plan to use and to do provides students with authentic learning. One 17 year old questioned this very principle in her world literature class. She viewed Greek drama as valued content, but not the corollary requirement to learn the Greek alphabet. With the drama in English translation, she and her classmates failed to see any real relevance. Had they been exploring various language systems, we suspect she would have not only accepted but also enjoyed the task. Her small rebellion had nothing to do with the Greek alphabet, which she could easily learn, but with purpose.

Appropriateness, as the word suggests, means that the content and activities are suitable for the curricular level; it also suggests consideration of community values and an understanding of what people find acceptable for teenagers. Although we need to guard against censorship, there is no point in needlessly angering parents and community members by using a novel or movie that flagrantly violates religious or moral beliefs.

Flexibility entails providing for differences in learning styles and learning rates, recognizing that not all students can or need to learn exactly the same thing at the same time or to do exactly the same tasks. It means planning for learners who are both more and less advanced than their peers.

Involvement refers to the type and number of activities students do, generally a combination of independent, collaborative, and whole-class activities.

Giving feedback and *evaluating* student progress is something we plan for, not something that just happens. In working out lessons, we also decide on ways to provide students with response, to let them know how they are doing, and similarly, to evaluate them more formally if necessary.

THE EARLIEST PLANNING

Most teachers learn what class or courses they will teach when they sign a contract. That is the point to begin planning. What textbooks are customarily used? What freedom is there to incorporate other books, films, videos, and other media? Is there a budget for supplemental materials? What resources are available, not just in the school library and media center but also in the community? What policies are district-wide regarding homework, grading, and response to parents or guardians? What district-wide testing is done? What cultures are represented in the school and to what degree? Are there any students with limited English proficiency? Are there developmentally disabled students? What are the curricular expectations for the grade level? What amount of freedom does the teacher have to change the content of the curriculum? These questions, of course, are also appropriate when teachers are considering a particular district, not only after they have decided upon one.

When their courses are identified, many teachers start collecting materials that may prove useful: magazines, newspapers, films, videos, art work, music. The most seemingly insignificant item sometimes yields a great class. For example, one teacher found a newspaper account about a group of Bulgarian diplomats touring Minneapolis who were thrown out of a neighborhood store.

The owner, believing they were a group of gypsies about to rob him, created quite an incident for our State Department. Without clear plans for using the article, the teacher clipped it out anyway. It proved its worth: After students in a composition class read it, they filled the boards with possible writing topics, delineating the difference between those suitable for exposition and for argumentation. The students did a wonderful job of generating ideas, and the goal that they understand how writing aims differ and how content influences purpose was met. Because the incident was so bizarre, they also had moments of both laughter and seriousness as they discussed prejudice and stereotyping. All of this grew out of a news item in a local paper.

To increase a personal repertoire of class activities and materials, new teachers can search back issues of *The English Journal* and journals from their state English language arts organization; these ideas from practicing teachers are a rich resource. When the opportunity presents itself, teachers should attend professional meetings and conferences, not just for the presentations but also for the chance to talk with other teachers informally and learn what they do and how they do it. Some ideas or methods won't work for us, but unless we hear them and try some out, we won't know that. The important thing is that we build a personal collection.

INSTRUCTIONAL UNITS

As teachers build tentative plans for classes, they need a calendar at their side. Some curriculum guides indicate roughly how much time to allot to a given topic; others do not. In either case, it is up to individual teachers to determine the days or weeks for particular units. A unit is simply an organized block of instruction (like the commercial literature units referred to earlier); it includes goals for the course of study, student outcomes (what we expect them to learn or be able to do as a result of the unit), the materials teacher and students will use, activities, the sequence of instruction, and ways student learning will be evaluated.

A unit varies in length from a few days to weeks, depending upon the content. Within a unit, the teacher focuses on an important concept or theme and selects the content to explore it; the material in the textbook does not constitute a unit, although it may be part of it. A unit is something teachers create; within it, they also develop daily lesson plans. These are not elaborate, merely a shorthand version of what they plan to do each class period. As noted earlier, many schools require teachers to turn in their daily lesson plans on a weekly basis, not just to check on what is happening but also as a guideline if a substitute teacher is needed.

PLANNING FOR REALITY

When veteran teachers consider their units for the semester, they look at a calendar and ask questions. When are school breaks or vacations? Teachers have to ensure that students are not in the middle of a unit when a break occurs.

Otherwise, they spend days reteaching, bringing students back to the point just prior to the break. Some breaks are not on the school calendar but are just as real. In one rural, northern district, most boys between the ages of 12 and 18 are absent for deer hunting season, roughly the week of Thanksgiving. Knowing this, the teacher can plan accordingly. Major school events (e.g., homecoming, prom, drama or music productions, athletic or music tournaments) that will undoubtedly draw energy and attention away from academics also figure into the calendar.

Teachers need to be realistic about these events and plan accordingly for less homework and more in-class activity. Other questions involve resources: how far in advance to get supplemental materials for a certain unit; to rent a video; to reserve the VCR. How far in advance should one arrange for a site visit in the community or secure a speaker on a special topic? Teachers who plan to take students off campus often need to work through their district administration office and secure parent/guardian permission as well. Any teacher who has sent forms home knows well that getting them back is a major ordeal; leaving enough time for this is critical. These are the practical elements of good planning.

Beginning teachers may not know how long a unit or individual lesson will take; even experienced teachers can't be sure. Different classes may need different planning, adjustments, and a degree of flexibility. Beginning teachers may feel overwhelmed at times, as every teacher does, but planning well ensures that the feeling is held at bay most of the time. None of us wants to end up with a scheme like the Mock Turtle in *Alice in Wonderland* (Carroll):

> "And how many hours a day did you do lessons?" said Alice, in a hurry to change the subject.
> "Ten hours the first day," said the Mock Turtle: "nine the next, and so on."
> "What a curious plan!" exclaimed Alice.
> "That's the reason they're called lessons," the Gryphon remarked: "because they lessen from day to day."

With foresight and a sense of adventure, many teachers enter into planning with enthusiasm. Many wonderful ideas come into our lives, and we urge beginning teachers to capture them in a special folder labeled "Flashes of Brilliance." Such a folder will certainly be needed and used. It's the very stuff good teaching is made of.

DISCUSSION QUESTIONS

1. Burton and his colleagues pose the following questions as a framework for planning:

   • How would you plan if there were no textbooks?

   • How would you plan if no one was required to be in class?

- How would you teach if you had to justify what you do and use by "what can I do to help kids survive, get on, in today's society?"?

Explore these questions with your classmates.

2. Using the above questions as a guide, ask middle or senior high school teachers their views on "what if?".

SUGGESTED ACTIVITIES

1. Visit book stores, toy departments, instructional media centers, and so forth and develop a list of resources appropriate for chaotic days or weeks. Annotate your list and share with classmates. Be sure to designate if each is appropriate for middle level, senior high level, or both.

2. Check collections of short stories that might be useful as one class period or partial class period "fillers." Find some that you believe would be appropriate for middle school students; find others that would be appropriate for senior high students.

REFERENCES

Atwell, Nancie. *In the Middle: Writing, Reading and Learning with Adolescents*. Portsmouth: Heinemann Boynton/Cook, 1987.

Berry, Heather M. Letter. *Leader-Telegram* (Eau Claire, WI) 10 Dec. 1991.

Burton, Dwight L., Kenneth Donelson, Bryant Fillmore, and Beverly Haley. *Teaching English Today*. Boston: Houghton, 1975.

Calkins, Lucy McCormack. *The Art of Teaching Writing*. Portsmouth: Heinemann, 1986.

Carroll, Lewis. *Alice in Wonderland and Through the Looking Glass*. San Rafael: Classic Publishing, 1970.

"Cultural Kaleidoscope." *MacNeil/Lehrer News Hour*. PBS. 28 Nov. 1991.

Editorial Staff. "English Journal Focus." *English Journal* Mar. 1981: 27.

Fortier, John. Personal interview. 10 October 1991.

Fuller, Howard L. "Into the Trenches with Teachers." *Milwaukee Journal* 19 Nov. 1991: 1.

Good Morning, John Adams. Narr. Anne McDermott. CNN, Atlanta. 29 Nov. 1991.

Henry, Tamara, and William M. Welch. "Fundamentally Unfair." *Leader-Telegram* (Eau Claire, WI) 17 Nov. 1991: 3A.

Johannessen, Larry R. "Three Offenses to End Despair: A Reply to Daniel Lindley. *English Journal* Sept. 1991: 72–77.

McDonald, Joseph. "A Messy Business." *Teacher Magazine* Nov.–Dec. 1991: 54–55.

Sizer, Theodore R. *Horace's Compromise: The Dilemma of the American High School*. Boston: Houghton, 1984.

———. "School Restructuring." University Summer Forum: What Do We Want from Our Schools? Madison, WI, 18 June 1991.

Vogel, Mark, with Janet Tilley. "The Dark Within Us All: Stephen Dobyn's 'Bleeder.' " *English Journal* Mar. 1991: 47--50.

CHAPTER 13

Developing Thematic Units

Chapter Highlights

- Organizing around a theme.
- Beginning to plan.
- Components of a unit.
- Comprehensive thematic units.
- Planning a unit.
- Units other than literature.
- Interdisciplinary units.
- Evaluation of units.

> The use of thematic units permits a broadening of pedagogical concerns in English studies beyond those of genres, periods, and particular authors and works. The thematic approach reflects a concern with the personal growth of the reader/writer versus an emphasis on specific literary works as objects worthy of study for their own sake. (72)
>
> —*Robert C. Goldbort*

▼

INTERACTIVE TEACHING

Throughout this text, the different aspects of teaching English are presented in individual chapters, but only as a way of discussing each one. Language, composition, literature, speaking, and listening are all part of what is called "English." The interaction among the parts is the foundation for planning the curriculum. For instance, a unit on listening is a poor way of teaching the skills of listening. When listening is incorporated throughout the curriculum, teachers have a better chance of achieving their goal of improving the students' listening habits.

The same is true for speaking. The most effective way to provide opportunities for both listening and speaking is to use small groups because the class shifts from a teacher-centered one to a student-centered one. Students listen to each other and contribute to the discussion. When groups become part of an instructional plan, the balance among reading, writing, listening, and speaking more closely approximates the world outside the classroom. In real life we speak and listen far more than we read and write. Creative dramatics also provide opportunities for interactions among the four components. One way to create a classroom situation in which a variety of activities provides for an ongoing interaction among all the components is through developing thematic units. The theme serves as an umbrella for a whole host of activities involving all strands of the language arts.

▼

ORGANIZING AROUND A THEME

Thematic units are designed with many different focuses: art, music, history, literature, and language, although literature is the most common focus. One reason, of course, is that literature is a major part of an English class; more importantly, using a thematic approach is a more effective way to teach literature than using a single author or a chronological organization.

In *Novels of Initiation*, David Peck agrees that the best way to teach literature is by theme. "Somehow our secondary literature curriculum has gotten locked into historical and genre approaches that have lost much of whatever usefulness they once had" (xxi). He explains that the ideas students find when reading related works bridge the ideas and characters to their own lives and to other works as well. As an example he writes, "Why is tolerance such an important idea in Harper Lee's *To Kill a Mockingbird?* How different is its treatment in Mildred D. Taylor's *Roll of Thunder, Hear My Cry?* What relevance does it have to our own lives? And what relationship does it have to the idea of self-respect that we find in both novels?" (xxi) To read with a focus, as in Peck's example of the theme of tolerance, helps students clarify their own ideas and values about things that matter in their lives.

When literature is taught chronologically, the teacher must play the major role of one who knows the answers. George Hillocks explains, "Since the knowledge gained about one writer is unlikely to be applicable to the next, students are almost necessarily forced into the role of passive recipient of knowledge about individual writers and works" (149). Chronological organization doesn't help students make connections from one text to another or connect the literature with their own life experiences.

A high school teacher, David T. Anderson, uses thematic units because a "problem with chronological sequencing is that it goes against a basic principle of education: Begin with simple experiences on which to base learning and move to complex understandings." He explained to his students that the next novel they would be reading was easier than the one they had just finished. "Upon saying this, one of my students raised her hand and asked, 'Then why didn't we read it first?' Even a junior in high school realized when this basic rule was compromised" (62). When novels for young adults are included in the units, students can read these easier works first and then be better able to understand the more difficult selections. Because the concepts are the same, the easier texts help students to comprehend the ideas in the more difficult reading.

▼
BEGINNING TO PLAN

Developing a unit in a way that encompasses many components might seem overwhelming to a new teacher. The best way to begin is to choose literature selections on a common theme. Every student in each class must be capable of reading at least one of the selections, and each unit must have at least three reading levels. Many other titles need to be available for those who want to read several books or for those who find the original choices too difficult. The key is that every choice, whether it is a poem, short story, drama, essay, or article, must be on the common theme.

Every unit does not have every genre of literature represented, but, as much as possible, a variety of readings need to be included. One type of text enhances another. For instance, Faulkner's "Rose for Emily," *To Kill a Mockingbird* by Harper Lee, poems by Dickinson, and current newspaper and magazine articles all contribute to a wider understanding on the theme of societal values. Organizing a unit around a theme provides opportunities to include poetry, non-fiction, short stories, drama, and novels. A unit ties all of the literature together in a unified approach to teaching.

TEACHING AND LEARNING IN GROUPS

Once the literature selections are made, the next step is to devise ways of discussing the literature and writing about it. The listening and speaking aspects are most naturally incorporated through small and large group discussion, although projects can be designed to include oral presentations as well. Traditionally, teachers talked and students listened. For students to improve their skills in listening and speaking, the focus must shift from the teacher to the students. Teachers do need on some occasions to give information and explanation through a lecture format, but students need the opportunities to talk among themselves. James Moffett describes discussion as "a process of amending, appending, diverging, converging, elaborating, summarizing, and many things" (46). He is referring to small-group discussion, not a whole-class discussion in which the teacher dominates the talk and only a few students join in. In a whole-class group, a teacher is often looking for specific answers to questions, but even if the questions are intended to draw out students' opinions, they succeed with only a few.

For an interchange of ideas, feelings, and opinions, four to six in a group works best, particularly if students are discussing literature or responding to each other's writing. Directions to the groups need to be clearly understood and have a well-defined purpose. To keep students on task, teachers may limit the amount of time for the group work to be accomplished and then have each group present the results of their discussion orally to the whole class. Middle school students may need further structure, and a teacher might require that written notes be handed in following the discussion. Also, if a teacher walks around the room listening to one group and then another, students are more likely to stay on task. Group work should be part of every unit and should be a planned activity, not left to chance or used as a fill-in for extra time.

INCLUDING WRITING ACTIVITIES

A unit offers many opportunities for writing. All three levels of writing, described in Chapter 6 on composition, are appropriate throughout the unit. A level three project is usually the final assignment, whereas level one activities occur almost daily and level two activities two or three times a week. Also, a unit provides many opportunities for different types and purposes of writing: poetry, factual, autobiographical, analytical, summaries, responses, and informational.

Developing a thematic unit that includes all of the elements mentioned takes a great deal of time, but a beginning teacher can start slowly and keep adding to the unit. Teaching units may never be "finished." Even if the unit is repeated for several years, it goes through revision each year. Because many include current news stories, a teacher needs to add magazine and newspaper articles and stories on a regular basis. Once teachers decide on the units and begin to develop them, material is not difficult to find. Files full of poems, articles, clippings, notes, and suggestions are continually added to. Longer units often grow into two files, providing an excess of material but also choices so that a unit isn't the same from one year to the next. All this takes time, but if new teachers enter the classroom with one well-thought-out thematic unit, they are way ahead in their planning and well prepared for the beginning of the year.

▼ _____

COMPONENTS OF A UNIT

Perhaps the easiest way to begin planning a unit is to choose a literature selection. The curriculum may specify that *Romeo and Juliet* is to be taught in 9th grade or *Great Expectations* in 10th grade. That is the place to start. Because many high school students are going to have difficulty with either one of these selections, the first task is to choose additional literature on the same theme that is easier to read. Literature as complex as either *Romeo and Juliet* or *Great Expectations* has several themes, and teachers decide what seems the most appropriate for their students. Young adult literature can be added fairly easily because many reference books are available with annotated bibliographies that are grouped thematically. Short stories are more difficult to find, but anthologies available in the schools help. Choosing poetry for a particular theme is more difficult and requires reading poetry from a variety of sources. Literature chosen for units must represent a variety of authors, including minorities and women. Once a few literature selections are made, the writing activities can be added. Group activities, language play, and creative dramatics are then included. Looking at the steps in planning a unit might be helpful, although the sequence varies. Sometimes a teacher selects a theme before deciding on any literature. Planning might follow these steps:

- Select a theme.
- Choose literature at two or three reading levels.
- Decide on writing activities for levels one and two.
- Add short stories, poetry, drama, and non-fiction appropriate to the theme.
- Look at the connections among the literature selections and between the literature and the students' lives. Include group activities that strengthen the connections, and allow listening and speaking to be major activities.
- Add creative activities—drama, drawing, music.
- Looking at the unit as a whole, create several choices for a level three writing assignment or some other type of final project or presentation.

DEVELOPING QUESTIONS FOR ONE NOVEL

To begin, a teacher inexperienced in planning might select one piece of literature and design only the writing activities. Dale Clark, an English education student, wrote this kind of unit for *The Catcher in the Rye* by J. D. Salinger (Box 13.1). Examples from students in the English methods class include a rationale for teaching the unit. Teachers are not required to do this, but we believe that knowing what one wants to accomplish in a unit and why the particular selections were made helps when talking to parents and administrators. We need to always know why we are teaching a particular topic or selection.

Box 13.1 LITERATURE UNIT: *THE CATCHER IN THE RYE*

CENTRAL PURPOSE OF THIS UNIT

The writing assignments in this unit are designed to give the students an opportunity to gain a better understanding of Holden Caulfield. The assignments center on Holden's progression in the story through his relationships and experiences, his reactions and feelings toward life. The basic question is "Why?" Why does Holden feel the way he does or do what he does? It is hoped that the students will gain a better understanding of the causes of depression.

The following assignments are designed for in-class work, where students meet in groups and discuss their responses. Much of the writing can be done collaboratively. When the teacher prefers individual writing, the group work remains a vital part of the writing process.

ASSIGNMENTS FOR STUDENTS

1. Write an initial reaction to the introduction of the story in chapter 1. Explain how you feel about Holden and what you think might happen to him. [level one]

2. Holden said, "I got the ax. They give guys the ax quite frequently at Pencey. It has a very good academic rating, Pencey." Compare Pencey to our school. In what ways do you think they are the same? Different? [level one]

3. Write a letter from Holden to his brother D. B. in Hollywood explaining why Pencey is a lousy school and why he flunked all of his classes except English. [level two]

4. The fencing team ostracized Holden for leaving equipment on the subway. Explain a similar situation that happened to you. How did you feel? Or explain how Holden felt. [level one]

5. Write a phone conversation between Holden and Jane Gallagher. [level two]

6. Have you ever had a special possession that someone else may not consider special, such as Alice's glove is to Holden? Write a description of that special item and explain why it is special to you. [level one]

7. "I'm not too tough. I'm a pacifist, if you want to know the truth," said Holden. Is Holden a pacifist because he isn't very tough or because he doesn't believe in violence? Explain what you believe to be true and why. [level one]

Box 13.1 *(continued)*

8. Write a plea from Holden to a TV audience asking them to not act phoney. Have Holden explain why they should not act phoney. [level two]

9. After Holden gets in the fight with Stadlater, he goes to talk with Ackley. Holden thinks to himself, "I felt so lonesome, all of a sudden. I almost wished I was dead."
   a. Write a letter from Holden to Ann Landers describing how he feels at this time and asking her for advice.

   OR

   b. Write a reply from Ann Landers explaining to Holden what he should do about his depression. [level two]

10. Rewrite part of chapter 8 when Holden is on the bus with Mrs. Morrow. Have Holden tell her the truth about Pencey and her son, Ernest. You may write it as a script. [level two]

11. Write a reaction from the prostitute's point of view explaining why she believes Holden won't sleep with her. [level one]

12. Holden accidently blows smoke in the two nuns' faces and is terribly embarrassed. Describe a situation in which you have done something that you didn't mean to do that was embarrassing and you regretted afterward. [level two]

13. Sally accepts Holden's proposal to go and live in the mountains. Rewrite the end of the story explaining what happens. [level two]

14. James Castle jumped out of the window instead of taking back what he said about Phil Stabile. From James' point of view, explain why he jumped. Describe his emotional state. [level one]

15. Phoebe asks Holden to name something he really likes, but he can't. Write a short paper, from Holden's point of view, about why he feels this way. [level two]

16. Mr. Antolini describes a "fall" he believes Holden is heading for. Explain what he means and describe what you think is going to happen to Holden. [level one]

17. Write a level three paper on one of the following two subjects, or you may select another subject, but discuss with me first.
    a. Explain Holden's emotional progression through the story and explain what you think his future will be.

    OR

    b. Write a comparison between Holden's depression and similar experiences you or someone you know have had. Explain how you feel Holden should deal with his depression.

Clark included a variety of purposes and modes for writing, as well as connecting the literature to students' lives. His next step would involve adding other reading selections on a common theme. Then he would add activities and opportunities for creative dramatics, art, music, and additional speaking and listening.

Both Maureen McManus, the teacher who wrote the following unit, and Dale Clark use writing activities to bridge the literature to students' lives. By making these connections, they help students to understand the characters in the novel. Consequentially, readers remember them better and gain a deeper knowledge of the literature. Maureen developed writing activities for *To Kill a Mockingbird* by Harper Lee (Box 13.2). She explains that the journal and in-class writing are assigned daily and used for class or group discussions. The activities labeled "writings" are all level two and are not daily activities but can also be the basis for class or group discussions. Although McManus wrote writing activities and discussion questions for every chapter, only a few are included here as examples of how a teacher might begin planning for a literature unit.

Box 13.2   WRITING ACTIVITIES: *TO KILL A MOCKINGBIRD*

CHAPTER 1

Journal Options

1. Describe a person, place, event, or TV show that frightened you when you were young, but now that you are older you realize you let your imagination get the best of you.
2. Discuss your family traditions or community customs. Are they important to you? Do they seem outdated?

Writings

Write a character sketch of Boo Radley. Describe his appearance, mannerisms, how he talks, and what he does.

CHAPTERS 2 AND 3

Journal Options

1. Reflect on how you felt about your experiences in kindergarten or 1st grade. How did you feel about school? Offer some examples.
2. What are some of Scout's innocent mistakes? How are ideas of good and bad, right versus wrong, manners, and politeness expressed so far in the story?

Box 13.2   *(continued)*

Writings

Write about a time when you didn't mean to be bad but did something because you didn't know better and people were angry with you.

CHAPTER 11

Journal Options

1. How are Scout and Jem changing their attitudes about Atticus? What are some reasons for this new outlook?
2. What are the various evidences of prejudice, not only racial, but ways in which Scout notices a great difference between other characters and herself? Do some of these prejudices exist today?

Writings

Prepare a dialogue between Boo and Mrs. Dubose concerning Jem and Scout.

CHAPTERS 13 AND 14

Journal Options

1. What are the differences between the town's acceptance of Aunt Alexandra and of Jem and Scout?
2. What are some evidences of Jem's growing maturity? How does this change his friendship with Dill? How does it affect the relationship between Scout and Dill?

Writings

Write a character sketch of Dill including his personality and physical attributes. Describe his family life and how it has affected him.

CHAPTER 16

Journal Options

1. What are the ways that Aunt Alexandra's views are even narrower than those of the children?
2. How are Scout and Jem finally beginning to realize the differences and similarities between blacks and whites? What are some questions they discuss about this?

Box 13.2   *(continued)*
Writings

Describe the atmosphere of the courthouse lawn and the moods of the various groups scattered about.

CHAPTERS 18 AND 19

Journal Options

1. Throughout the story what are the various ways Scout describes blacks? Name both physical and personality attributes. Is her particular association with the person a factor in her opinion?
2. Atticus once told Scout that she can never really understand a person unless she "wears his shoes." How is Scout's understanding of this statement becoming more apparent throughout the novel?

Writings

Write an account of the trial as it might appear in the Maycomb newspaper from Mr. Underwood's point of view.

CHAPTERS 22 AND 23

Journal Options

1. Jem gives serious thought to the trial and its outcome. What are various aspects about the trial that he questions? What people help Jem draw his conclusions?
2. What were the various reactions of different people when Bob Ewell spit in Atticus' face? How does this reflect their character?

Writings

Show how Scout's thought process changes, especially about prejudice, after the trial. Compare her to other characters in how they changed or failed to change. In what ways has Scout learned to question what others say rather than simply accept it? Who does she question now and in what ways? Create dialogue or cite actual passages in the book.

CHAPTERS 29 AND 30

Journal Options

1. In what ways are both Boo and Tom Robinson like mockingbirds? How is the way they are treated like killing a mockingbird?

Box 13.2 *(continued)*

2. How are the lives of Tom Robinson and Boo similar or different? How do Scout and Jem change their attitudes about both Boo and Tom as the story progresses? What brings about this change?

Writings

Scout tells this story in retrospect. Describe her as she writes this book. How old is she? What is her occupation and education? Where does she live? What are her contributions to society?

Writings

Level three writing options [to be completed after the students finish reading the novel].

1. Choose one character from the book and describe one wish the character would choose and explain why. Who else is affected by the wish? What does this say about the character? How would the wish change certain aspects of the story?

2. If Atticus was the guest speaker at a high school graduation, what kind of messages, warnings, and encouragements would he offer the graduates? How would he prepare them for the real world? Write his speech or take the standpoint of a graduate listening to him.

3. Write a series of letters between Scout and Dill. What would they share in a letter?

4. Choose a character from the book who keeps a journal or is a closet poet. Make a series of journal entries or prepare a collection of poetry by this character.

5. Write a collection of Letters to the Editor or journal entries from several different characters, showing their various opinions of the trial.

6. Compile a list of guidelines for raising children. How might parents and teachers promote open-mindedness or instill values/morals in children?

The discussion and writing questions described for both of the novels, *Catcher in the Rye* and *To Kill a Mockingbird,* are only the beginning of a unit. The next step is to find other novels, poetry, drama, and non-fiction on the same theme.

DEVELOPING WRITING ACTIVITIES FOR MORE THAN ONE NOVEL

A four-week unit written by teacher Gail Servoss for 9th grade illustrates how a teacher begins planning activities for a unit using more than one novel (Box 13.3).

Box 13.3   FOUR WEEK LITERATURE UNIT

Four novels are used in this unit. Students are required to read two of them but can read all four if they wish. The novels are paired, so that students have a choice during the first two weeks of reading *A Day No Pigs Would Die* by Robert Newton Peck or *The Bloodroot Flower* by Kathy Callaway. For the next two weeks, they choose between *Where the Red Fern Grows* by Wilson Rawls or *A Killing Season* by Barbara Brenner.

STUDENT GUIDE
First Week

Read the first two chapters in the novel you chose. Write reading responses in your journal (level one). Meet in groups to discuss your responses and to compile a list of adjectives that describe the main character in the novel you are reading (level one).

Read the next two chapters and write responses (level one). The first four chapters in both novels give us information about the parents. In class, begin to write a short paper on what you think Peck's father and Carrie's father are like as fathers. What does the story say about each of them? Give examples from the story that support your own view. For example, look at their personalities: Are they strict, lenient, happy, sullen, friendly, mean, or understanding? The paper is due the next day. Before handing them in, meet in groups to read aloud and discuss (level two).

Read the next three chapters and write responses (level one).

Second Week

Share responses in groups from the last chapters read. Hand in the response journals for teacher's comments. Working in small groups, discuss the values the characters have. Find phrases or paragraphs that represent the values.

Continue reading and responding. In small groups, discuss the feeling the text evokes by word choice and details about the weather,

Box 13.3 *(continued)*

actions, and character behavior. Choose one scene and write descriptive words about it. Write a poem using the descriptive words (level two). Work on the poems in class, sharing in small groups. Finish up reading by the next week.

Third Week

Read first two chapters in the novel you chose and write responses in your journal (level one). In small groups discuss what the setting says about the characters. Collaboratively, write a description of what would change in the book if the setting were urban (level one). Continue reading and writing responses.

Choose one of the characters from a novel and write a dialogue that person might have with someone else in any situation. Be sure to keep the character true to his or her personality. Do not tell anyone which character you chose. Other students will try to guess your character through listening to the dialogue you write. Be prepared to tell each other why you chose the words you did for the character. Base your reasons on examples in the novel (level one).

The following day share your dialogues in small groups. Discuss the influences of dialogue on developing characterization and moving plot along. Each group then reports to the whole group. Working in pairs, draw a map on a large sheet of paper of all the places described in the novel. Trace the action with short descriptions from the book and uses X's to denote important areas (level two).

Fourth Week

Continue writing responses. When you are through reading the novel, review the responses in your journal. In groups of four or five made up of people who read the same book, discuss your feelings and thoughts about the book. Answer the following questions in writing:

- How did this book make me feel?
- Was the book believable?
- What do I think about the characters?
- What other places or situations does the book make me think of?
- What are the major differences or similarities between the main character and me?

Discuss all the answers in the small group.

The final activity is to write a level three paper using one of the novels. Possible topic choices you might want to use:

Box 13.3   *(continued)*

1. The connection between nature or setting in the plot or/and characterization.
2. The relationship between a character and an animal.
3. The trials some people have to go through in their lives and how these trials change them.
4. Describe what a character might be like in 10 years from the conclusion of the story.

You are free to choose any topic you wish. You will meet in groups to talk over possible choices. With any topic you develop, be sure to include examples from the book to back up what you write. You may use, in addition, personal examples to help develop your ideas.

THE SCORING GUIDE FOR THE LEVEL THREE PAPER

	Possible points (30)	Your points
Introduction explaining what paper is about	3	_____
Main points clear and related to each other	4	_____
Examples from the book used to support your ideas	7	_____
Conclusion states what you discovered	2	_____
Word choice: descriptive, appropriate, correct forms	4	_____
Mechanics: spelling, punctuation, capitalization	5	_____
Original, creative, interesting	5	_____
	Total points	_____

Comments

A LITERATURE UNIT WITH A VARIETY OF LITERATURE

Literature units need to include a variety of genres as well as literature with different reading levels. This example of a literature unit is based on the theme "Families in Literature" written for 9th graders by Barbara Dressler, a high school teacher. Barbara's unit begins with a rationale explaining why she chose this particular theme (Box 13.4).

Box 13.4   FAMILIES IN LITERATURE

This literature unit for 9th graders centers on families in different eras and different cultures. The unit will last approximately four weeks. Selections were chosen to show the wide variety of combinations of people held together by a bond that we call family. Male and female characters and authors from minority groups including African-Americans, Asian-Americans, Shakers, and Native Americans are included. Special emphasis is given to relationships between teenagers and other family members because these relationships trouble most teens. I hope reading and thinking about characters in situations similar to their own helps students discover that they can achieve their individual identities and still appreciate and enjoy their families.

The problems encountered by today's teenagers in understanding and communicating with other members of their families are certainly not new. Through the years, young adults in literature experienced difficulty getting along with adults, especially parents. The rejection of "old ways and ideas," and even alienation from the rest of the family, is a common conflict. A goal of this unit is to allow students to experience vicariously the problems and resolutions that characters find. They will realize that they are not unique in having problems in their families and may find ideas for solving or living with the problems through reading the literature.

INTRODUCTION

The introductory activity for the unit starts with a short brainstorming period for students to write words and ideas they associate with the word *family*. After sharing the lists, commenting, and questioning, students write a paragraph defining family (level one).

PART 1

- "Blues Ain't No Mockin' Bird," short story by Toni Cade Bambara

Box 13.4 *(continued)*

- "Brother Carlyle," short story by William Melville Kelley
- "To My Father," poem by Wing Tek Lum
- "The Funeral," poem by Gordon Parks
- "Believing It Will Rain Soon," poem by Simon J. Ortiz

The first reading assignment is "Brother Carlyle." This short story centers on the behavior of one of two black brothers, and the disagreement between their parents on whether the boy's treatment of his younger brother is appropriate or not. Students write a response to the story when they finish reading. Responses are shared in a group, and a discussion follows based on the responses. Probably the issue of parents giving different treatment to children based on birth order will be part of the discussion. I chose this short story to begin the unit because students often feel they are treated differently from their siblings by their parents. Students enjoy talking about the advantages and disadvantages of being the first born, a middle child, or the youngest.

The second reading is "Blues Ain't No Mockin' Bird." I chose this story because it shows a loosely structured, non-traditional family with grandparents and distant cousins living together. The theme concerns the need for pride and dignity regardless of family income. After the reading, students respond in writing, and then choose specific details used for the development of one of the characters. Students write, with emphasis on significant details, a character description of someone they know well (level two).

PART 2

The poems are read aloud during class. The first, "The Funeral," tells of the great admiration and respect a young man feels for his father. Many things in the poet's childhood seemed enormous to him, but as an adult only his father remains larger than life. Students select lines that show how the poet's perspective changed as he matured. Many examples of hyperbole are used. As a group activity, students write their own descriptive sentences using hyperbole (level one).

"To My Father" tells of the rebellion of the Chinese against the emperor. The speaker, whose grandfather was involved in the rebellion, knows his way of life changed because of the revolt. In a group, students discuss ways their lives are affected by actions of their grandparents or other ancestors.

"Believing It Will Rain Soon" expresses a faith that is passed from one generation to another as shown through the description of the promise of rain over the mountains. Students discuss how their beliefs and values, including prejudices, are learned through the family. Stu-

Box 13.4   *(continued)*

dents write a letter to a future son or daughter expressing an important belief about the world (level two).

PART 3: INDIVIDUAL NOVEL READING

Students choose one novel from the list. Different reading levels are represented. All feature different types of families.

- *To Kill a Mockingbird* by Harper Lee
- *Growing Season* by Alden R. Carter
- *Permanent Connections* by Sue Ellen Bridgers
- *A Day No Pigs Would Die* by Robert Newton Peck
- *What About Grandma?* by Hadley Irwin
- *A Figure of Speech* by Norma Fox Mazer
- *Kim, Kimi* by Hadley Irwin

Students keep a response journal while reading the novel. After writing responses, students meet in small groups according to the book they read. They choose a character from the book that they would like to interview and answer interview questions as they believe their character would. Possible interview questions include the following:

1. Did the author describe you accurately? What would you like to change in the description?
2. How did you feel about your family early in the story?
3. How did your feelings change before the end?
4. What was the happiest time for you in the book?
5. What would you like to say to a member of your family that you didn't get a chance to say in the book?
6. If you could change anything in the story, what would it be? (level one)

When the time for the novel reading is about half over, students write a want ad in search of a good mother, father, teenage son, or teenage daughter. Ads are shared in groups (level one).

After reading and discussing the novels, students choose from the following level three writing assignments:

1. Write an obituary for the family member who dies during the time of the book.
2. As a friend of the main character, write a letter of condolence after the death of the family member.

> Box 13.4   *(continued)*
>
> 3. Imagine you are a good friend of the main character. How would you have tried to help at any point in the story?
>
> 4. As one character, write a letter to another explaining your actions during the book.
>
> 5. Write a campaign speech that the main character could use to run for student council president at your school.
>
> 6. Write a summary of the events of the story the way the main character would after 10 years have passed.
>
> 7. Write your description of a good parent. Include your evaluations of the parents in the book.

By including novels of different reading levels, Barbara allowed students to find the one they were comfortable with without embarrassing them. Some students choose books that are too difficult but later ask to switch to another book. Or they may find they don't care for the book they started. Students need the flexibility to change their minds about a self-selected book. A person may check four books out from the library but read only two because the others didn't hold his or her interest. We must make sure we apply the same common sense rules to our students that we use in our own lives.

Students who read well may decide to read all four books. Having a selection solves the problem of what to do when students come to the teacher two days after the unit begins and say they have finished the assigned book. The readings provided for these students are on the same general theme as the current unit. What they read then is part of what is going on in class, and they can share their reading with others.

Students with special learning problems are now usually mainstreamed, that is, included in the regular classroom rather than taught in a separate class. For these students to feel a part of the class, their work, however adapted for their needs, must be a part of the same thematic unit that the rest of the class is involved in. That's why including texts on a variety of reading levels is critical.

The same is true for gifted students. Too often, these students are sent to the library to work on their own. Perhaps more than the average student, the gifted ones need to interact with peers and feel part of a group. Social skills are vitally important and need to be part of the learning environment. Every student in a class is responsible for getting along with the other students and respecting their rights. Working in groups and all working on the same theme enhance a sense of community effort.

Selecting a variety of reading texts is a beginning in providing for all the students in a class. In addition, optional activities create diversity. One way to incorporate the activities into the current thematic unit is to tape the suggestions on the inside of file folders. The folders can then be placed in an open box available to students when they want additional projects. To accommodate all of the students in a class, the ideas need to vary greatly in difficulty: puzzles, reports, interviews, word searches, articles, essays, and poems. Also, they should cover a wide range of interests: reading non-fiction, writing movie reviews, writing based on art or music, drawing, creating music, reading and performing drama. Each unit has an accompanying box of activities, such as one on courage, growing up, choosing careers, or environmental issues. Finding additional materials is a difficult task for inexperienced teachers, but one starts with only a few ideas and gradually adds to the number and variety of the activities.

All of the activities include a way of bringing the work back to the class as a whole. Art work is displayed on the walls, reports are available for others to read or are orally presented to the class, skits are acted out, videos are shown, music is played, and puzzles are distributed. Students may work in the library on their own or do the work outside of school, but the end result enriches the learning for everyone in the class.

▼
COMPREHENSIVE THEMATIC UNITS

Units need to include a list of other readings on the same theme. Cathy Steffen, a former English education student, wrote a unit on heroes. An abbreviated version of Cathy's unit shows how she includes listening, speaking, reading, and writing (Box 13.5).

Box 13.5 **UNIT ON HEROES**

My primary objective in teaching a unit on heroes is to introduce students to alternatives to the traditional hero and to offer new perspectives on the idea of heroes. The activities in this unit include music, all levels of composition, language study, listening, and speaking. Both fiction and non-fiction are included.

PART ONE: INTRODUCTION TO THE UNIT

Propose the following questions to the class and write responses on the board. Explain, first, that the term *heroes* refers to both genders.

1. What are some examples of heroes?
2. What qualities are found in heroes?

Box 13.5 *(continued)*

3. What does someone have to do to be considered a hero?

4. Which of these people do you consider heroes? (Suggest people whom students know through the media.)

5. Do you know any "quiet heroes?" Read a recent newspaper or magazine article to the students about a quiet hero.

6. Who do you know who fits the description of a quiet hero?

Students search for articles on people (or animals) who acted heroically. They write a short paragraph describing some action they consider heroic (level one).

PART TWO: READING

Students read *A Hero Ain't Nothing but a Sandwich* by Alice Childress, *Roll of Thunder, Hear My Cry* by Mildred Taylor, or *The Chocolate War* by Robert Cormier. Students must read one of the novels but may read all three if they wish. Students keep response notebooks as they read (level one).

In class students write a description of one of the main characters based on the questions: What is she or he like? What do you like or dislike the most about the character? Students meet in small groups to share what they wrote. The group members then discuss how the character would react to this situation:

Your character is in charge of a public place where students and adults can come to read books and listen to music. He or she tries hard to give quality materials to the people who come in, but some have started to complain that the books and music are trashy. Your character is told to get rid of the books and records or else lose the job. What will your character do?

Then in one large group, the smaller groups report, and discussion follows of the possible consequences of the characters' actions.

PART THREE: LANGUAGE

Give the class examples of different ways that a sentence can be spoken. Point out that an author can establish the emotional tone of the speaker by using certain words. Such clues help a reader understand how a character feels.

Students work in pairs for this activity. Give each pair a slip of paper with an expressive word written on it. Explain that all the words come from the novels they are reading. Students look up the meaning of the word in a dictionary and then discuss when the word might be

Box 13.5   *(continued)*

used. Each pair writes the word on the board, pronounces it for the class, and gives an example of a sentence containing the word. A few examples of the words used: consolingly, taunting, tentatively, abstractedly, resignedly.

PART FOUR: MUSIC

Provide the classroom with headphones and players. Have several tapes available. All of the songs should suggest something about heroes. Some suggestions:

- ELO, "Wild West Hero"
- Dan Folgelberg, "Along the Road," "Face the Fire"
- Elton John, "Roy Roger," "The Ballad of Danny Bailey"
- Bonnie Tyler, "Holding Out for a Hero"
- Moving Pictures, "Never"

After listening to several songs, students discuss the themes and descriptions of the heroes. Each student writes a paragraph about one of the songs, exploring the sense of the hero.

PART FIVE: A FINAL WRITING ASSIGNMENT (LEVEL THREE)

Students write a two- or three-page paper on some aspect of a hero. Suggestions could include:

- Describe a hero from your own family history.
- Compare any two of the heros we talked about in class—from music, newspaper, novels, etc.
- Create a fictional story about a hero.
- Write a poem about a hero—real or fictional.

Also, students are free to select any topic as long as it deals with heroes.

ANOTHER UNIT ON HEROES

The concept of hero can be the basis for many thematic units. Teachers design units representing their own interests and try to capture their students' interests and imaginations through literature choices and selected activities. To provide an idea of the wealth of material available to teachers, this next unit is also on heroes. Connie Flug, an undergraduate student, wrote it for an English methods class. Only a small part of the total unit is presented here. Connie begins with her rationale for choosing the theme of heroism (Box 13.6).

Box 13.6   HEROISM

The theme of heroism has been present from time immemorial. Mom and Dad are probably the earliest heroes in most youngsters' lives; however, other figures, both real and fictional, through media, soon become an integral part of a child's life and development.

This unit is intended for students in 9th or 10th grades and looks at heroes through literature, art, film, music, and, most importantly, the students' own lives. The unit is planned for seven to eight weeks because of the amount of material available. Tall tales, western folklore, and many other stories and poems would have much to offer but are not included in the unit. Two novels for young adults, taught simultaneously, ancient and modern poetry, a 30-year-old film, and a modern version of *Cyrano de Bergerac* are the "meat" of this unit. Bridges from past to present are important, and the idea that heroism was "then" and is "now."

Connie begins the unit by sharing a quote with students.

> Heroes have within themselves the resonance that comes from imagination supplanting despair. These heroes can recognize the possibilities inherent in living a human life: to win and lose, perhaps, but also to discover and use our own voices yet in a common tongue; to use and be used by our passion and intellect; to deal with complexity and ambivalence; to be proud, to err, to be humbled, to grieve, and to grow. To live in such a manner is noble and heroic. (Sandra A. Engle, "Of Jocks and Heroes," *English Journal*, December, 1984:32–33)

The materials selected for the unit include the following:

Literature

- *Close Enough to Touch* by Richard Peck
- *Chartbreaker* by Gillian Cross
- *The Miracle Worker* by William Gibson
- *Class Dismissed* by Mel Glenn
- *Collected Poems* by Robert Hayden
- *Strings: A Gathering of Family Poems* by Janeczko
- "Negro Hero" by Gwendolyn Brooks

Box 13.6   *(continued)*

- "Ex-Basketball Player" by John Updike
- "To an Athlete Dying Young" by A. E. Housman
- "The Lady Pitcher" by Cynthia Macdonald
- "That Stranger on the Lawn" by Ray Bradbury
- "Fist Fight" by Doug Cockrell
- "Ulysses" by Alfred L. Tennyson
- "Flowers for Algernon" by Daniel Keyes

Films

- *Helen Keller*
- *Man as Hero: Tragic and Comic*
- *The Miracle Worker*
- *Roxanne*

Music

- "West Side Story"
- "Free to Be"
- "Great American Hero"
- "You Won't Believe in If Anymore"
- "Wind Beneath My Wings"
- "Big Dad John"
- "Oh, Mine Papa"

Although the entire unit is not included here, the beginning of the unit is explained because introducing units is an important part of creating student interest and sets the tone for the next several days.

DAY ONE

The bulletin board contains many pictures, poems, lyrics, and paintings. There is room for student additions during the next several weeks. The day begins with the following student responses to an opinionnaire on heroes.

OPINIONNAIRE: HEROES

Directions: Write agree or disagree beside each statement.

1. A hero does better than just about anyone else.
2. Heroes are forever.
3. The values of heroes are old-fashioned.
4. If you say something often enough it becomes true.

Box 13.6 *(continued)*

5. If you hear something often enough you come to believe it.
6. Heroes never have to say, "I'm sorry."
7. To become a hero one must be lucky.
8. TV has helped destroy today's heroes.
9. A real-life hero fills a need for all of us.
10. Anyone can be a hero.

Students agree or disagree to the items and discussion follows. Students brainstorm on the meaning of heroism. Responses are listed on the board. Questions leading into the session might include:

1. What do you think an heroic quality is?
2. What are some qualities in real-life heroes?
3. What makes a hero? Is it more deeds or personality?
4. Consider heroes of different ages, nationalities, centuries, and interests. Do they bring to mind any other characteristics?

The next day's assignment is to bring in examples of today's heroes using newspapers, magazines, TV, record jackets, and comics as resources. Every Monday for the rest of the unit, students are asked to bring in information on heroes of the week.

DAY TWO

Students share their examples of today's heroes. Discussion in small groups provides an opportunity for students to explore aspects of heroes. Then students watch the slide/tape presentation, *Man as Hero: Tragic and Comic.* Discussion follows. Students write in their journals, choosing from the following suggestions:

1. I was a hero once. . . .
2. My hero at school is. . . .
3. A local hero from this town is. . . .
4. If I were a hero I think I would feel like. . . .

DAY THREE

Students share their journal responses in small groups. The teacher writes a mystery formula poem on the board. For example:

Chunky, rumpful
Leaping, running, catching
Smiling, friendly, moon-faced, sincere
Hero

Box 13.6   *(continued)*

The students try to guess the name that goes on the first line, which in this case is Kirby Puckett, a major league baseball player. The class together writes a similar poem using one of the heroes from the bulletin board. The formula for the poem is to write the person's name on the first line. Then:

> Write two adjectives that describe the person.
> Write three verbs that tell what the person does.
> Write a thought or four words about the person.
> Write another noun for the person or repeat the name.

The assignment for the following day is for students to write their own poem, leaving off the name in line one.

DAY FOUR

Students share their poems and others try to guess who they are about.

Two other sections of Connie's unit are included here. One is her list of suggested end-of-the-unit activities for the students. The other is a partial list of additional readings Connie wrote for the students.

SUGGESTIONS FOR END-OF-THE-UNIT ACTIVITIES

1.   Write your own song about heroes.
2.   Create a comic strip featuring a hero.
3.   Write a folk tale about a hero.
4.   Interview a local hero and write a news article.
5.   Review the comic section of the Sunday paper and evaluate the images of heroes. Write a report of your findings.
6.   Write a modern fairy tale.
7.   Make a class scrapbook of all the heroes in the news over the duration of this unit.
8.   Put together a slide presentation on heroes.
9.   Write a poem about a personal hero.
10.   Invite a local hero to class for a presentation. Write a follow-up report.

What follows is a comprehensive list of readings students choose from as the unit progresses. The list demonstrates the wealth of readings available to teachers as they design units. Because Connie wrote annotations, the list is helpful to those looking at resources for units on heroes, survival, and self-esteem.

Box 13.6 *(continued)*

READING LIST

- Aldrich, Bess Streeter. *A Lantern in Her Hand:* Abbie MacKenzie, a talented singer and aspiring artist, is nineteen when she marries Will Deal in 1865. Homesteading in Nebraska, Abbie and Will face droughts, dust storms, blizzards, and locust infestations. Abbie's courage and her love for her husband and children lead her to sacrifice her dreams for theirs.

- Barrett, William E. *The Lilies of the Field:* Homer Smith, a young black man recently discharged from the army, comes upon a group of immigrant nuns who are trying to build a chapel in the desert. This is a delightful story about Smith's role in this undertaking.

- Brancato, Robin. *Uneasy Money:* Mike Bronti loses track of values after winning money in a lottery. Spending the money quickly, he finds himself losing family and friends.

- Chester, William L. *Kioga of the Wilderness:* This is the tale of Kioga, or Snow Hawk, who rises to war chieftain in the wild region north of Siberia.

- Ching, Lucy. *One of the Lucky Ones:* An autobiography of a blind Chinese girl's fight for education and a future. Her nanny helped Lucy find a productive life that resulted in her helping other blind Chinese.

- Collier, James L., and Christopher Collier. *The Winter Hero:* After the Revolutionary War, Justin is caught up in the Shay's Rebellion. Through his experiences, he learns the truth about heroism, cowardice, and war.

- Crutcher, Chris. *Running Loose:* For Louie Banks, living by what is right is more important than being popular. When instructed to "play dirty," Louie walks off the playing field. This turns out to be the most important decision of his life.

- Easwaran, Eknath. *Gandhi the Man:* Gandhi's own words and an array of photos accompany this biography. A string of failures led the young Gandhi to a job in South Africa, where he began his life of service to others.

- Froehlich, Margaret. *Reasons to Stay:* Babe's determination to piece together her past leads to hard discoveries, but she becomes a strong, memorable hero.

- George, Jean Craighead. *The Talking Earth:* Billie Wind, a young Seminole, survives on her own in the Florida Everglades. Her courage finds a link between an ancient and modern culture.

Box 13.6   *(continued)*

- Haskins, James. *Sugar Ray Leonard:* This biography follows Sugar Ray from the beginning of his boxing career at age 14 to his turning pro.

- Hughes, Monica. *Hunter in the Dark:* Mike Rankin, star basketball player, is dying of leukemia. He goes to the Canadian wilderness to escape overprotective parents. Through his experiences he comes to understand that death is not always the enemy.

- Magill, Kathleen. *Megan:* An independent woman struggles for freedom and a sense of self. She runs away to a boomtown where she discovers the truth about herself.

- Mazer, Harry. *The Island Keeper:* Cleo runs away from her family pressures and the death of her sister. She proves herself as she struggles to survive on a deserted island.

- McKinley, Robin. *The Hero and the Crown:* Aerin, with the help of a wizard and the blue sword, battles the Black Dragon. She wins her birthright as the daughter of the Damarian king and alters the history of Damar.

- Myers, Walter Dean. *Hoops:* Lonnie is at a key point in his life. If his team does well in a city-wide tournament, he may have a professional career. Integrity becomes as important as talent.

- Portis, Charles. *True Grit:* Mattie Ross, along with Rooster Cogburn, an old federal lawman, sets out on an incredible journey to avenge her father's death.

- Rosa, Joseph G. *They Called Him Wild Bill: The Life and Adventures of James Butler Hickok:* Hickok led an eventful life, working as a U.S. marshall, an army scout, and a wild west performer. This biography describes the man beyond the legend.

- Roth, Arthur. *The Castaway:* Based on a true story of a young man who is the lone survivor after a ship wreck. He survives alone for five years on a rocky reef.

- Savage, Deborah. *A Rumour of Otters:* This wilderness survival story takes place in New Zealand, where 14-year-old Alexa sets off on her own to prove she is as heroic as her brother.

- Townsend, Peter. *The Girl in the White Ship:* Tran Hue, a 13-year-old, and her family must flee Vietnam in 1978. She battles to survive and escape.

- Valens, E. G. *The Other Side of the Mountain:* A true story of Jill Kinmont, who became paralyzed while training for the

Box 13.6   *(continued)*

Olympic ski team. Jill's determination to lead a meaningful life is inspiring.

• Voigt, Cynthia. *The Runner:* A dedicated runner distances himself from other people. His experience coaching his teammates helps him to change.

• Wheeler, Robert W. *Jim Thorpe: World's Greatest Athlete:* Thorpe is probably best known for winning both the decathlon and pentathlon in the 1923 Olympics, only to be disqualified later. His early life on the reservation, Indian school, football triumphs, and Olympic feats are recounted.

▼
PLANNING A UNIT

To illustrate how one experienced teacher goes about planning a unit, Jackie Pickett shares a unit she is in the process of developing for her high school class (Box 13.7).

Box 13.7   FAMILY AND PEER CONFLICT

I decided to make a unit on family, peer, and relationship conflicts because these are the conflicts teens most commonly face. Therefore, I think kids will easily identify with characters facing some of the same conflicts. After some free writing about conflicts, the kids have a chance to share. Then I will introduce the first reading, "Through the Tunnel" by Doris Lessing. I'll mention that as they read they should note the relationship between Jerry and his mother and think about how that relationship affects his actions with peers. Students in my class are used to doing response writing, so I'll assign that for the next day. Then we share the responses in class.

Following the same basic format the students read and/or view the following stories, poems, movies, and a novel: "The Sleeper," a poem by Edward Field; the movie *Bernice Bobs Her Hair* from the story by the same name by F. Scott Fitzgerald; the short story "Sucker" by Carson McCullers; the short story "Sixteen" by Maureen Daly; the short story "A Visit to Grandmother" by William Melvin Kelley; the short story

Box 13.7 *(continued)*

"Forgiveness in Families" by Alice Munro; the poem "Lineage" by Margaret Walker; the poem "Mother" by Nagase Kiyoko; the movie *The Three Warriors;* and the novel *The Contender* by Robert Lipsyte. [*Note:* The movie *The Three Warriors* is about Native Americans and played by Native Americans—a fine film for junior and senior high.]

There will, of course, be breaks from the routine of reading and responding. Here are some of the ideas I'll use.

1. Choose a character from the story. Become this character for a short time, and write how you feel about "your" portrayal in the story. Were you presented accurately and fairly? Is there more to you than we saw?

2. Again, choose a character from a story. Become this character, and write a letter to Ann Landers or Dear Abby, describing a problem you have. Then exchange your letter with another person. This person is Ann or Abby and will answer your letter, giving advice, while you do the same for him or her.

3. (This is one of my own ideas) With rather dated stories such as "Sucker" and "Sixteen" and movies like *Bernice Bobs Her Hair,* re-write a portion. Bring it up to date, including modern slang and descriptions of what is stylish or attractive now.

4. (Another one of my ideas) As a post-script to *Bernice Bobs Her Hair,* write a story or play of what happened when Majorie woke up the next day to discover that her hair was bobbed. Or write what happened when Bernice returned to Eau Claire.

I usually have students write open-book essay tests after our units, and I expect I will do so with this unit, too. They work well and get the kids to write in a different format—gives some balance to the writing they do.

The novel—I'll do this last because I want to spend the most time on it. I think kids are more confident of themselves after successfully dealing with shorter writings, and are then ready to go on to novels. As a pre-reading activity, I'll have the kids do a variety of things: journal entries, personal experience questions, or conduct a survey. Another idea is to have them complete the Literary Characters' Values Profile (found in Kahn et al. *Writing About Literature*). I would like to incorporate some type of formal speaking activity in the unit, but at this time my mind is blank.

Jackie worked on this the year before she planned to implement it. She began with the literature choices and filled in activities she read about or developed on her own.

▼ UNITS OTHER THAN LITERATURE

Not all units are based on literature. A unit on an environmental issue might include some literature, but the major focus is current media information and perhaps community involvement. A unit on aging could also include community work, trips to nursing homes and interviews, as well as literature. Language provides the focus for many different units, such as politics, advertising, history, and cultures. In an advertising unit developed for middle school (Box 13.8), the theme is the power of language to persuade and the effect that has on middle schoolers becoming critical consumers of goods.

Box 13.8   ADVERTISING UNIT

The first purpose for teaching the unit is to help middle school students become better informed as consumers and more aware of the role of advertising in their lives. Because of the age of the students, literature isn't included, although there are many essays and articles appropriate for older students. The second purpose for teaching the unit is to give students opportunities to draw, sing, compose music, and act—in general, to be creative. This is a long unit—four to six weeks—and, because of the amount of independent and unstructured work, it is included in the curriculum later in the year. The teacher needs to know the students well enough to know who can work on their own and who needs supervision. The unit is divided into sections, not weeks, because the amount of time needed for each part depends on the interests of the students, and could be quite different from one year to the next.

SECTION ONE: ANALYZING ADVERTISEMENTS

The first activity is to ask students what their favorite advertisements are. They talk about TV ads exclusively. Actually, they do more than talk; they sing the songs, repeat dialogue, act out the scenes, interrupt and correct each other. After a time, the teacher asks what their least favorite ads are. Although less enthusiastic, they report several, with some saying that someone else's most disliked was their favorite. Then the conversation shifts to why they liked or disliked certain ads, which leads into a discussion of audience. Most of the ads they dislike are not meant for teenagers. From this point we move to the purposes of ads and how advertising companies conduct market

Box 13.8   *(continued)*

research. Next, we look more closely at the ads, examining the particular approach used to entice consumers. Together we put the responses into categories. The responses are not the same from one year to the next, but they fall roughly into the same categories: popularity with the opposite sex, you owe it to yourself, everyone has one, having fun, being healthy, staying young and beautiful, loving one's family, and owning the best. The assignment that follows is to collect printed ads that represent each of the categories, put them in booklet form, and label each one. Although the students consider the activity fun, they are improving a critical skill of classifying.

SECTION TWO: DESIGNING A PRODUCT

Next students design a new and unknown product that later will be advertised for sale. The design is on paper only, and they do not actually construct it. To help them get started, pose the following questions: What new product would make your life easier? Can you think of a product that might become a new fad? What item might be improved if you made major changes in the design? The assignment is to describe the product and draw it if they desire. They have to keep their product a secret because they do not own a patent on the design. Descriptive language is vital for an activity later in the unit, so we spend time choosing specific words and using comparisons. Because of the secret nature of the project, they cannot ask other students if the descriptions are clear, so the teacher acts as the editor. Students turn in the designs for the teacher's safe-keeping. The 6th-grade students thought of a variety of products: a watch-radio-telephone, edible dishes, a walkie-talkie am-fm radio pen, computerized pencil, convertible shoes, a shoe phone, and instant moat mix (in case you have a dry moat—it comes with creatures and muck).

SECTION THREE: ADVERTISING MEDIA

This is a short section in which we explore all the places ads might appear. We invite people who work in ad agencies to come and speak to the class. Also, people who design ads for newspapers or billboards talk to the class. The students write interview questions before the visitors speak to the class. Students need to prepare for a class visitor by planning ahead. Because asking appropriate questions is not easy, they meet in groups to brainstorm questions. Following the visits, students—again working in small groups—write letters thanking the presenters.

Box 13.8   *(continued)*

SECTION FOUR: MEDIA GROUPS

Students become part of a media group. The types of groups are newspapers, magazines, billboards, radio, and television. Students write their top two choices on a card and give it to the teacher, who then forms the groups. Each media group first selects a name for itself, then researches the cost of advertisements placed in their media. Next they design an ad for advertising space, trying to make their company the most attractive for people who want to advertise, but the rates have to be realistic. Each group makes one poster to try to entice customers.

At this point, each student receives five copies of the product description he or she wrote earlier. Individually they decide on where to place ads for the products. They all have a set amount of money to use on advertising, so it is impossible for anyone to buy the top five advertising spots. If they decide on a back page ad and a one-minute TV commercial, they will be out of money. However, if they use the money sparingly, they can afford five ads in a variety of media. To maintain secrecy, the teacher is the only one who knows who designed each product and serves as the broker. When students decide on the type of ad, they write the specific information on the back of each card, such as "1/2 page on an inside sheet of *Wonder Magazine.*" The teacher then delivers the card to the *Wonder Magazine* group. This procedure is repeated until all the students have selected the advertising they want for their product, and each group has received all the advertising jobs.

Before the ad production goes into full swing, we review techniques we discussed before: use of statistics, well-known personalities, humor, music, color, drawings, logos, animals, and children.

SECTION FIVE: PRODUCTION

Each media group designs the ads it received orders for. Except for the billboard group, the ads are placed in a larger context. The newspaper group produces a newspaper with local news, pictures, human interest stories, announcements, and sports. The television group produces a show: a situation comedy, soap opera, mystery, or talk show. The radio group usually uses music as the content. If the billboard company has extra time, it draws a public service ad.

At the conclusion of the unit the students display their work for other students, teachers, and parents. The last assignment is to write a one- to two-page paper explaining what they learned.

▼

INTERDISCIPLINARY UNITS

Units planned across disciplines are advantageous for a number of reasons. They provide a model for students who erroneously believe writing and reading fiction belong only in the English language arts classrooms. Also, breaking down the walls among disciplines creates more true-to-life experiences for students and consequently often heightens interest. Teachers of a variety of subjects can plan the objectives and activities together. Depending on the organization of the school, teachers may team-teach the units, but even if the classes have to remain separate, the students and teachers benefit from the shared planning. A word of caution is in order here. By working with other teachers we do not mean that the English teachers only grade a social studies paper for mechanical errors but rather that planning and carrying out the ideas is a joint effort.

A unit designed by teacher Becky Olien demonstrates how English, social studies, art, and music come together to create a rich tapestry of experiences for young people (Box 13.9). Becky is particularly fortunate because her classroom is multicultural. The unit can be used for a variety of age levels.

Box 13.9   TRACING ONE'S ROOTS

The unit begins with a discussion about the students' ancestors. What does it mean to say one has ancestors or an ethnic background? After students have an opportunity to talk about ancestors, ask questions, and listen to others, they get a survey on ethnic background to be filled out in class. The survey includes questions about where ancestors came from, how long ago they came, whether they were married, whether they had jobs, and whether they were with friends or traveled alone. By filling out the survey, students become aware of what they know and don't know about their family history. They take the survey home and ask parents and grandparents to help complete the information.

Once the surveys are completed as much as possible—and this may take a while—the discussion continues and students share their information with each other. Students then choose a person who is knowledgeable about their family to interview. Usually this is a relative, but not always. A Native American may interview a tribal leader; another student may talk to a family friend who knows a great deal about a particular immigrant group. Before the interview takes place, students develop the questions, meeting in groups for ideas and feedback. Once the interviews are completed—and again this may take a few days—each student writes a report based on the information from the

Box 13.9   *(continued)*

survey, interview, and additional sources as needed. Because many of the students are a mixture of ethnic backgrounds, they choose which one they want to work on.

Over the period of time the students are working on these activities, they also are reading historical fiction. The literature is discussed in class, and they consider what makes historical fiction interesting. When the reports are finished and the novels and short stories are read, the next activity is to write a fiction story based on their reports. Most of the stories are patterned after historical fiction, but students may wish to make the work more contempory. [This is especially true of the Hmong and Native American students in Becky's class.]

The culmination activity is a cultural week during which students work in groups to present their culture to the class. Students select the cultural group they want to work in; usually it is the one they wrote the report on. They may focus on any aspect they care to, but music, crafts, dance, and food are usually part of the presentations. Students bring maps, flags, or any artifact that helps explain the family background. Many teach the other students a few words of the language their ancestors spoke. Some dress in native costumes [particularly the Hmong girls]. Everyone learns from listening, talking, and sharing.

Units are a way to organize reading, writing, speaking, and listening so that continuity occurs among the activities. They give purpose to what goes on in the classroom and actually are a much easier way to teach than using disjoined lesson plans because they have a flow that carries students along. Often students themselves think of activities to do, and therefore can play a major role in planning curriculum. Once a theme is decided on, students can suggest stories, poems, music, films, and activities that complement the unit. The more students are involved, the more ownership and responsibility they accept, and that is the beginning of a learning/teaching partnership between student and teacher.

▼

EVALUATION OF UNITS

Evaluation occurs as students progress through the unit. Journal writings are evaluated only as a level one task and marked in a record-keeping book as a check for a student completing the work. The same method is used for much of the group work. Collecting the work and responding to it is important. Students need to know the work "counts," and when a teacher writes a response or comment on their work, they gain a sense that it was important. Level two writing such as homework and some group work deserves a grade or some type of numerical evaluation. Level three, the final project for the unit, requires evaluation based on a grading scale described in Chapter 6. Final projects are not necessarily writing assignments, and then a different type of evaluation is required, one for which students help develop the criteria and one with which they are well-acquainted before they perform or hand in the project.

Middle school students, in particular, need frequent evaluations as they progress through a long-term project. Individual conferences with students help keep them on track and aware of how they are doing. Students, for the most part, do not manage their time well, and teachers can't assume they are completing their work when the units extend over time. However, with help and encouragement, students can be taught to assume more responsibility for their own learning. Frequent checkpoints by a teacher and group work in which students are responsible to each other help students to complete their work.

DISCUSSION QUESTIONS

1. What are the benefits of including drama in classroom activities? What does drama provide that other activities probably do not?

2. Choose a novel appropriate for middle school and one for high school. What themes might be associated with each one? If you read these books as a class assignment, how were they taught?

3. What language topics could be the basis for a unit? How might language acquisition be incorporated into a unit for secondary students?

4. Discuss the activities you enjoyed the most in middle and high school. How might these activities become part of a larger unit?

5. Discuss what a teacher takes into account when planning units. What steps could you take now that would benefit you during your first year as a teacher?

SUGGESTED ACTIVITIES

These activities are designed to help you develop a unit on your own.

A. LITERATURE UNIT

1. In small groups, brainstorm ideas for unit themes. Decide on one that the group can work on. Now brainstorm ideas of literature that fit the theme. Share with the rest of the class.

2. Individually choose a theme you are personally interested in. Decide what grade level you would like to develop it for. Choose one or two pieces of literature that would be appropriate. In small groups, share your ideas and help each other think of additional literature.

3. Choose literature for young adults to include in your unit.

4. Select poems that are appropriate.

5. Look for films and music.

6. Plan activities that include listening and speaking.

7. Describe writing activities for the literature and other resources.

8. Share the units with the other class members, helping each other by critiquing and suggestions.

B. LANGUAGE UNIT

1. Devise a unit based on language. You might consider how new words are added to our vocabulary for middle school, or the power of political language for high school. Include activities for informational writing, creative dramatics, listening, and speaking.

REFERENCES

Anderson, David T. "An Apology for Teaching American Literature Thematically." *Wisconsin English Journal* Fall 1989: 58–66.

Goldbort, Robert C. "Science in Literature: Materials for a Thematic Teaching Approach." *English Journal* March 1991: 69–73.

Hillocks, George, Jr. "Literary Texts in Classrooms." *Socrates to Software: The Teacher as Text and The Text as Teacher.* Ed. Philip W. Jackson and Sophie Haroutunian-Gordan. Chicago: Chicago UP, 1989: 135–158.

Kahn, Elizabeth A., Carolyn Calhoun, and Larry R. Johannessen. *Writing About Literature.* Urbana: National Council of Teachers of English, 1984.

Moffett, James. *A Student-Centered Language Arts Curriculum.* Boston: Houghton 1973.

Peck, David. *Novels of Initiation: A Guidebook for Teaching Literature to Adolescents.* New York: Columbia University Teachers College, 1989.

Smagorinsky, Peter, Tom McCann, and Stephen Kern. *Explorations: Introductory Activities for Literature and Composition, 7–12.* Urbana: National Council of Teachers of English (ERIC), 1987.

Index